INSIGHT GUIDE

THE DOMINICAN REPUBLIC & HAITI

D0293722

Discovery
CHANNEL

APA PUBLICATIONS L
Part of the Langenscheidt Publishing Group

INSIGHT GUIDE
The Dominican Republic & Haiti

ABOUT THIS BOOK

Editorial

Editor
Lesley Gordon
Editorial Director
Brian Bell

Distribution

UK & Ireland
GeoCenter International Ltd
The Viables Centre , Harrow Way
Basingstoke, Hants RG22 4BJ
Fax: (44) 1256-817988

United States
Langenscheidt Publishers, Inc.
46–35 54th Road, Maspeth, NY 11378
Fax: (718) 784-0640

Canada
Prologue Inc.
1650 Lionel Bertrand Blvd., Boisbriand
Québec, Canada J7H 1N7
Tel: (450) 434-0306. Fax: (450) 434-2627

Worldwide
**Apa Publications GmbH & Co.
Verlag KG (Singapore branch)**
38 Joo Koon Road, Singapore 628990
Tel: (65) 865-1600. Fax: (65) 861-6438

Printing

Insight Print Services (Pte) Ltd
38 Joo Koon Road, Singapore 628990
Tel: (65) 865-1600. Fax: (65) 861-6438

©2000 Apa Publications GmbH & Co.
Verlag KG (Singapore branch)
All Rights Reserved

First Edition 2000

CONTACTING THE EDITORS
Although every effort is made to
provide accurate information, we
live in a fast-changing world and
would appreciate it if readers
would call our attention to any
errors or outdated information
that may occur by writing to:
**Insight Guides, P.O. Box 7910,
London SE1 1WE, England.
Fax: (44 20) 7403-0290.
e-mail:
insight@apaguide.demon.co.uk**

This guidebook combines the
interests and enthusiasms of
two of the world's best-known information providers: Insight Guides,
whose titles have set the standard
for visual travel guides since 1970,
and Discovery Channel, the world's
premier source of nonfiction television programming.

The editors of Insight Guides provide both practical advice and
general understanding about a destination's history, culture, institutions and people. Discovery Channel
and its website, www.discovery.com,
help millions of viewers explore their
world from the comfort of their
own home and also encour-
age them to explore it
first-hand.

This first edition
of *Insight Guide:
Dominican Republic*
& Haiti is carefully structured to con-
vey an understanding of the countries and their cultures as well as to
guide readers through the many
sights and activities.

◆ The **Features** section, indicated
by a yellow bar at the top of each
page, covers the history and culture
of the Dominican Republic & Haiti
in a series of informative essays.

◆ The main **Places** section, indicated by a blue bar, is a complete
guide to all the sights and areas
worth visiting. Places of special
interest are coordinated by number
with the maps.

◆ The **Travel Tips** listings section, which has an orange bar,
provides a handy point of reference for information on
travel, hotels, shops,
restaurants and
much more.

The contributors

For this edition of *Insight Guide: Dominican Republic & Haiti*, managing editor **Lesley Gordon** assembled an impressive team of experts. **James Ferguson**, the author of *A Traveller's History of the Caribbean*, plotted the island's turbulent history. He also wrote the Haiti introduction, *Island of Magic,* and provided extra editorial assistance.

Florida-based Haitian journalist **Yves Colon** worked at the Miami Herald when commissioned. He contributed *Modern Haiti, Haiti's Literary Art* and *Insight on... Architecture*. He also wrote the Haitian sections of the cuisine, language and people chapters.

Talented writer **David Howard** is a Caribbean and Latin America expert, who contributed *The Dominican Republic Today, Caribbean*

Metropolis about the Santo Domingo environs and the Dominican Republic section of the people chapter. **Maxine Schur**, a California-based writer produced *The Old Colonial City.* **Joann Biondi**, a regular Insight Guides contributor and a frequent visitor to Haiti, wrote *Haitian Art.* **Monika Latzel**, a talented German writer, contributed *Sporting Passions, The Samaná Peninsula* and *The Cibao Valley.* A second German contributor is New York-based **Ilona Weöres**, who wrote *From Caribe to Coco, West to Lago Enriquillo* and the box story on scaling Pico Duarte.

Simon Lee is an English travel writer, living in Trinidad. Lee contributed the authoritative essay on the *Origins of Vaudou, More than Merengue, Back to Nature* and a box story on Haiti's despotic emperors.

A Dominican brother and sister team, **José Velázquez** and **Beatriz Velázquez**, contributed *The Quiet Northwest, Cordillera Central,* the Dominican Republic section of the language chapter and *Travel Tips.*

Ellen Sarbone, a travel writer and a former editor at *Lifestyle Magazine* in San Francisco, wrote *The Amber Coast, Port-au-Prince, Excursions from Port-au-Prince* and *The South* after spending several weeks touring the island. She also painstakingly compiled the Haiti Travel Tips.

Photographer and journalist **Leah Gordon** wrote *Central Haiti, the West and the Artibonite Valley, The North Coast,* and provided additional text for the Haiti Travel Tips and photographs.

Principal photographers include **Yves Fonck** and **Catherine Karnow**. Thanks go to **Caroline Radula-Scott** for her invaluable editorial input and also to **Penny Phenix** for proofreading and indexing this book.

Map Legend

▬ ▪ ▪	International Boundary
▬ ▬ ▬	Province Boundary
⊖	Border Crossing
▬ ▪ ▬	National Park/Reserve
▬ ▬ ▬	Ferry Route
✈ ✈	Airport: International/Regional
🚍	Bus Station
❶	Tourist Information
✉	Post Office
✝ ✝	Church/Ruins
✝	Monastery
☾	Mosque
✡	Synagogue
🏰	Castle/Ruins
∴	Archaeological Site
∩	Cave
🗿	Statue/Monument
★	Place of Interest

The main places of interest in the Places section are coordinated by number with a full-colour map (e.g. ❶), and a symbol at the top of every right-hand page tells you where to find the map.

INSIGHT GUIDE
The Dominican Republic & Haiti

CONTENTS

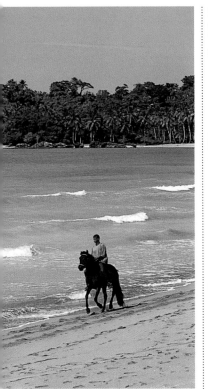

Riding on the beach at Playa Bonita, Las Terrenas, on the Samaná Peninsula

Insight on ...

Information panels

Places

Travel Tips

HISPANIOLA

This two-nation multilingual island has a colourful history,

beautiful beaches, distinctive rhythms, Vaudou and rich forests

One island, two very distinct nations – that sums up the complexity of the Dominican Republic and Haiti. History has taken its toll on the island and its peoples, ravaging them with the indignities of slavery, wars, foreign occupations and ruthless dictatorships. Through it all, the cultures have survived and developed, one heavily influenced by Spain and Latin America, the other by Africa and France.

The island was named by Christopher Columbus when he arrived in 1492 to claim the land for Spain. He called it La Isla Española – the Spanish Island – which eventually became corrupted as Hispaniola. Although it's a useful name because it refers to the entire island, Dominicans tend to avoid it in the same way as they avoid anything that associates them too closely with Haiti.

Standing at the back door of the United States, Hispaniola lies around 960 km (600 miles) southeast of Florida and has held a precarious position between stability and instability and the inevitable threat of US intervention – something neither part of the island has managed to avoid in the recent past. To the west is Cuba, southwest is Jamaica and east is Puerto Rico and the chain of the Antilles. The Dominican Republic covers about two-thirds of the island, totalling 48,734 sq. km (18,816 sq. miles), and Haiti has the remaining third, approximately 27,750 sq. km (10,714 sq. miles).

Volcanic origins

Eight spectacular mountain ranges extend across the length of Hispaniola. The main one within the Cordillera Central in the Dominican Republic has the highest point in the entire Caribbean, Pico Duarte, 3,087 metres (10,128 ft). The Central range is also home to the longest river, Río Yaque del Norte, and the vast Parque Nacional Armando Bermúdez and Parque Nacional José del Carmen national parks. To the west is the biggest lake, Lago Enriquillo.

The terrain betrays the island's volcanic origins but today no active volcanoes are known to exist. Hurricanes are much more of an issue, bringing with them dangerous tropical storms, high winds of up to 240 kph (150 mph) and flooding during the four-month hurricane season. Named by the National Hurricane Center in Miami, the hurricanes, which originate over the Atlantic, are measured using the Saffir Simpson Scale, rating winds on a scale from one to five. A rating of one means a wind speed of 119–153 kph (74–95 mph) and five, the highest category, means winds above

PRECEDING PAGES: carnival, Haiti; art on every street corner; Haitian musicians; cutting coconuts, Dominican Republic.
LEFT: Las Terrenas, Samaná Peninsula.

250 kph (155 mph). The storms can devastate people, property and crops. In 1979 Hurricane David hit the island hard, and in 1998 Hurricane Georges struck, resulting in thousands of deaths.

The tropical climate is warm and humid, with a rainy season in the summer and a dry winter season. January and February are the driest months and May and August are the wettest. However, the showers tend not to last too long and, as in all of the Caribbean, once the sun is shining things dry out and warm up again quickly. Daytime temperatures vary between 27°C (80°F) and 32°C (90°F) and at night remain in the region of 20°C (68°F). In the mountainous areas during the winter, temperatures have been known to drop to below freezing.

The island has a rich and colourful natural environment that is home to more than 5,000 plant species, almost half of which are endemic – from ferns and bamboo to frangipani and hibiscus. Protected parts of the coast in the Dominican Republic contain tangles of thick mangroves: red freshwater ones can exist in high water while black mangroves are more comfortable in shallow water and play host to flocks of pelicans, herons and other birdlife that feed off the shellfish, shrimps and small fish living there.

In contrast, Haiti's woodland has been devastated by deforestation caused by trees being felled for firewood, charcoal and building. Much of the land is now unable to sustain crops, as there are no trees to protect the earth from the elements. Although Haiti has not embraced environmental protection as enthusiastically as the Dominican Republic, there are reforestation programmes in place, but progress is slow.

Birds and beaches

There are almost 260 identifiable bird species, though birdlife is more diverse on neighbouring Caribbean islands. Look out for the Hispaniolan woodpecker and the Hispaniolan parrot.

There are some very beautiful beaches on Hispaniola, with clear sea water and fine golden sand. The coast and the coral reefs, although damaged by hurricanes, ships anchors and overfishing, still offer divers the chance to swim with a variety of marine life, including the manatee and turtles. If you travel to Hispaniola in the winter, you may witness one of the most amazing sights in the Antilles: thousands of Humpback whales migrate to the Atlantic waters around the Dominican Republic to mate from January to March and many can be seen off the Samaná Peninsula.

Hispaniola is truly a two-nation island; its peoples and landscapes are distinguishably different, yet they share land and history. The Dominican Republic and Haiti offer visitors an intriguing combination of Latin America and the Caribbean – a fascinating opportunity to explore two contrasting traditions. ❏

RIGHT: life in the Haitian countryside.

ISLE DE CUBA
aux Espagnols

Caya de Moua
Port de Baracoua
R. de Maravi
M. de Baracoua
Pointe de Mayosi
Baye de Tequiry
Porto Descondido

Cap St. Nicolas
Mole St. Nicolas
Cap aux Foux
la Plate forme

LES FRERES
BOU CANIER
DE LA T.

DE BARQUEMENT DE
CHRISTOPHE COLOMB
au Mole St. Nicolas

1492 1697

1697-1804

I. de Navaza

Pte. de la Seringu
Cap Dame Marie

Pointe des Irois

Cap Tiberon
B. du C. Tiberon
Pte. du vent
Pte. des aigrettes
les Basses
Tapion de la Caouane
les Anglois
Pte. des Chardoniers
Pte. a Piment
Roche a bateau
l'Ance a Juif
l'Ance a Dric
Port Salut
Pointe a Gravois

Cap Rose
Trou Bonbon
Trou Jeremie
Grande Ance
Petite Caymite
Caymites
Bte. de Marsoin
les Baraderes
R. de Nipe
Pointe

Pays desert
M. de la Hotte division de la partie du sud
Ligne de la partie du sud
QUARTIER
les Ances
Les 3 Rivieres
les Coteaux
le Fond
LES CAYES
R. de l'Acul
l'Etron de Porc
Isle a Vache
Pointe de l'Abacou
Cavaillon
R. de Cavaillon
Fonds
Aquin
R. serpente
Cabaye d'Aquin
Grosse Caye
Fort St. George
Fort St. Louis
Baye du Mesle
Caye et Cayemite
Cayecaican
la Folle
Port a Nonet

TOUSSAINT LOUVERTURE GOUVERNEUR GENERAL
1801

ABOLITION DE
L. ESCLAVAGE
1793

Decisive Dates

500 BC Arrival of the pre-Ceramic Ciboney people – fishers and foragers from Mexico and Florida.

AD 650–1200 Over several centuries, Taínos, after gradually migrating from what is now Venezuela, reach the Greater Antilles in dug-out canoes, escaping from Carib aggressors who follow them up the island chain.

THE SPANISH ISLAND 1492–1697

For nearly two centuries, Hispaniola (La Isla Española) was a Spanish possession, although

competing European nations were soon eager to challenge Spain's ownership.

1492 Christopher Columbus establishes the first European settlement in the Americas on the island he calls Hispaniola.

1493 Columbus's second expedition to Hispaniola brings colonists and gold hunters.

1494 Pope Alexander VI approves Treaty of Tordesillas, dividing up the New World between Spain and Portugal.

1496 Columbus's brother, Bartolomé, founds the south coast settlement of Nueva Isabela, later moved and renamed Santo Domingo.

1498 Columbus's third voyage; growing tension in Hispaniola ends in revolt.

1500 Columbus brothers are shipped back to Spain by commissioner, Francisco de Bobadilla.

1509–24 Diego Columbus presides as Governor of Hispaniola and Viceroy of the Indies.

1511 Fray Antón de Montesinos criticises the colonists' abuses of the Taínos' human rights.

1551 Publication of Bartolomé de Las Casas' *A Very Brief Account of the Destruction of the Indies*.

1586 Sir Francis Drake sacks Santo Domingo.

1650s French buccaneers settle in the northwest.

1655 English expedition captures Jamaica.

RISE AND FALL OF SAINT DOMINGUE 1697–1804

In the course of the 18th century, the French colony of Saint Domingue became the richest in the world, established on the fragile foundations of slavery.

1697 Treaty of Ryswick officially cedes western part of Hispaniola (Saint Domingue) to France.

1730 Slave population of Saint Domingue reaches 120,000.

1758 Planned uprising and mass poisoning, led by Mackandal, is foiled in Saint Domingue.

1789 News of French Revolution reaches the colony.

1791 Slave insurrection breaks out in the north.

1793 French republican Commissioner Sonthonax decrees the abolition of slavery.

1795 Treaty of Bâle cedes Spanish Santo Domingo on the eastern side of Hispaniola to France.

1798 British expeditionary force withdraws from Saint Domingue after failed five-year campaign.

1801 Napoleon Bonaparte removes Toussaint L'Ouverture from Saint Domingue and re-imposes slavery.

1803 Death of Toussaint L'Ouverture in France.

1804 Jean-Jacques Dessalines declares the independence of the new state of Haiti.

AN ISLAND DIVIDED 1804–1914

Haiti's independence ushered in a century of political turmoil and increased hostility with the Spanish-speaking east of the island.

1806 Death of Dessalines, murdered by mutinous officers; Henri Christophe takes power in the north of Haiti, Alexandre Pétion in the south.

1809 Eastern part of Hispaniola returns to Spanish control after 14-year French occupation.

1820 Death of Henri Christophe leads to reunification of Haiti under General Jean-Pierre Boyer.

1821 Independence of Spanish Santo Domingo, named "Spanish Haiti".

1822 Haiti occupies Santo Domingo under Boyer.

1823 US President James Monroe proclaims "Monroe Doctrine", underlining American domination of the Caribbean region.

1825 Boyer agrees to pay indemnity of 150 million francs to France in return for French recognition of Haitian sovereignty.
1838 Founding of underground La Trinitaria movement in Santo Domingo, which pledges to achieve independence from Haiti with the new name of *República Dominicana* (Dominican Republic).
1843 Boyer is overthrown.
1844 Independence of the Dominican Republic after Haitian troops are expelled.
1848 Haiti, under Faustin Soulouque, attempts invasion of Dominican Republic; a second invasion in 1859 also ends in failure.
1861 Spain re-occupies the Dominican Republic but withdraws in 1865 after "War of Restoration".
1882 Ulises Heureaux begins a 17-year dictatorship in the Dominican Republic.
1905 US takes control of Dominican customs to prevent further interference by European powers.
1914 Opening of Panama Canal increases strategic importance of the Caribbean.

OCCUPATION AND DICTATORSHIP 1915–86

US interventions in Haiti and the Dominican Republic were meant to impose stability on a troubled island; instead they provoked armed resistance and encouraged the rise of new dictators.
1915 US troops occupy Haiti after period of extreme political instability and a year later US forces take control of the Dominican Republic.
1918 Haitian guerrilla leader, Charlemagne Péralte, killed in anti-US campaign.
1925 The US withdraws from the Dominican Republic and leaves Haiti nine years later.
1930 Rafael Leonidas Trujillo takes power in the Dominican Republic, starting a 30-year dictatorship.
1935 Trujillo orders the massacre of some 15,000 Haitian migrants in the Dominican Republic.
1939 Founding of Dominican Revolutionary Party (PRD) by exiled anti-Trujillo social democrats.
1957 Election of François "Papa Doc" Duvalier as president of Haiti.
1961 Assassination of Trujillo.
1962 Reformist Juan Bosch of the PRD triumphs in Dominican elections but is overthrown by the military a year later, leading to civil unrest.
1965 US occupation of the Dominican Republic, intended to prevent "another Cuba".
1966 Joaquín Balaguer wins first of six controversial elections in the Dominican Republic.

1971 Death of Papa Doc and succession of his son Jean-Claude ("Baby Doc").
1978 PRD takes power in Dominican Republic after threatened military coup.
1986 After widespread unrest, Baby Doc flees Haiti as the military take over; Balaguer returns to power.

TOWARDS DEMOCRACY: FROM 1986

The end of the Duvalier dictatorship pitted the Haitian military against a people thirsty for political freedom, while in the Dominican Republic long-awaited change took place peacefully.
1987 Haitian elections end in bloodshed, as military and paramilitary forces attack voters.

1990 Jean-Bertrand Aristide wins a 70 percent majority in Haiti's first fair elections.
1991 Aristide overthrown in violent coup and exiled.
1994 US-led intervention restores Aristide to power after three years of intense repression in Haiti.
1996 Balaguer forced to stand down in Dominican Republic after disputed elections of 1994, and Leonel Fernández wins free and fair elections. Aristide steps down to elected successor, René Préval, the first constitutional succession in Haitian history.
1997 Historic meeting between Fernández and Préval raises hopes of better cross-border relations.
1998 PRD wins in congressional elections.
2000 PRD's Hipólito Mejiá wins the presidential elections in the first round of voting. ❑

LEFT: an engraving of Jean-Jacques Dessalines.
RIGHT: Jean-Bertrand Aristide returns to power.

THE EARLY SETTLERS

For several centuries the Amerindians led a Utopian existence. Then they welcomed Christopher Columbus and his Spanish fleet to their island

Viewing Haiti's bare, eroded mountains from an aircraft, it is hard to imagine that this was once one of the most beautiful and fertile places on earth. Where now barren hillsides reveal exposed rock and scar-like ravines, there were at one time tropical rainforests and vast expanses of pine. Around the coastal area – today stripped clean by charcoal-burners – mangrove swamps and wooded estuaries flourished, and there was a rich variety of wildlife and exuberant vegetation.

Some of this natural splendour continues to survive in the Dominican Republic across the border, but in Haiti there is little left to suggest what this island once looked like. Crossing the frontier itself makes clear the extent of the environmental catastrophe, for on the Dominican side there are still swathes of forest, pastures and streams. To enter Haiti, however, is to enter a parched and blighted landscape, where hillsides and valleys have been reduced to near-desert and streams have dried up for ever.

A promised land

It is poignant to read Christopher Columbus's breathless words of wonder as he looked at the island's spectacular scenery at the end of the 15th century. It was, he wrote, "fertile to an excessive degree… and filled with trees of a thousand kinds and tall, seeming to touch the sky." At first sight, it was nothing short of the promised land that Columbus had persuaded himself must exist across the Atlantic. Green, well-watered, seemingly full of natural riches, it also held out the prospect of infinite wealth. "In the interior," continued Columbus, "there are mines of metal, and the population is without number."

No records exist to tell us how many people actually lived on the island when Columbus's ships appeared on the horizon in December 1492, but the estimates of early European

LEFT: a portrait of a Taíno Amerindian.
RIGHT: Christopher Columbus and his crew set sail in search of riches in the Americas.

chroniclers range between 100,000 and a million. Modern historians tend to agree there was probably a population of around 500,000.

The arrival of the Taínos

These early inhabitants, who called their island Ayiti, meaning "high ground" were Taínos, the

descendants of a South American, Arawak-speaking people who had originally left the mainland of what is now Venezuela in about 500 BC. The Amerindians had been established on the banks of the Orinoco River for several hundred years before taking to the sea and moving up the Caribbean island chain.

The ensuing process of migration took centuries, as the discovery of one island followed that of another. Starting in Trinidad, the Taínos slowly progressed through the small islands of the Eastern Caribbean, or Lesser Antilles, sometimes sighting neighbouring territories in the distance or perhaps setting off in the hope of finding another island over the horizon. They had formidable canoes, measuring as much as 25 metres (82 ft) and capable of carrying 50 people, through treacherous seas. Using these vessels, they moved in successive waves up as far as Cuba, the Bahamas and Ayiti.

Carib enemies

The reasons for this great migration remain unclear, but it seems that the Taínos were pushed out of the Orinoco delta by another race of indigenous people, the Caribs, or Kalinagos as they called themselves. These less sophisticated Amerindians had also originated in the Amazon Basin and were highly aggressive in their dealings with the Taínos. Whether because of competition for natural resources or cultural conflict, the Caribs declared war on them, attacking villages, capturing women and killing men. The Taínos, although well organised, were no match for the war-like Caribs. Escape was the only option.

There is some dispute among historians as to whether the Caribs were really the bloodthirsty aggressors of legend. Certainly, the reports of early European observers should be treated with caution, as should the widespread belief that the Caribs were inveterate cannibals. While there is evidence that Carib warriors did eat

A LINGUISTIC LEGACY

The ancient Amerindian tongue still lives on in the English language forming the origin of several familiar words: hurricane / *huracan*; maize or corn / *maiz*; canoe / *canaua*; tobacco / *tobaco*; hammock / *hamaca*; savannah / *sabana*; barbecue / *barbacoa*.

Literally translated, other Caribbean Indian terms are jewels of creativity, for example: father of the fingers = thumb; soul of the hand = pulse; my heart = wife; he who makes me little children = son-in-law; God's plume of feathers = rainbow; the pot is boiling = earthquake.

A European was called a "misshapen enemy" because of his clothing and armour.

parts of their victims, it is probable that this was an occasional ritual rather than a regular habit. But what does appear clear is that they, in their turn, began moving into the Caribbean from the mainland in about AD 1000.

Again, the Taínos found themselves tormented by their ancestral enemies, as raiding parties arrived by canoe to kill, kidnap and pillage. This only drove the Taínos further west towards the larger islands of the Greater Antilles.

The earliest inhabitants

Here they encountered the earliest human inhabitants of the region, the Ciboneys, who had arrived in Ayiti and other islands around

500 BC. Originating from Florida or Mexico, they were much less culturally developed than the Taínos and established small settlements along the shore, living from fishing and hunting. They had no knowledge of pottery and used shells, stone or wood as basic tools. Their diet appears to have consisted of fish, reptiles and wild fruit, since they practised no settled agriculture.

These small primitive communities were soon absorbed or replaced by the Taínos, who came to dominate the whole of the Greater

CIGAR SMOKERS

The Taínos grew tobacco and used a pipe which was forked with two prongs that they inserted in to their nostrils; or they rolled the leaves up into cigars.

Amerindian lifestyle

The Taínos who welcomed Columbus ashore were by no means "savages". They lived in a structured social community, revolving around extended families and grouped into settlements of about a thousand people, normally situated by rivers or on the seashore. Each village had a chief or *cacique*, who doubled as a priest and local law-maker. It was a hereditary position, normally occupied by a man, but women could also be *caciques*. These chiefs were supported

Antilles, with the exception of western Cuba, by about 1200.

So it was that the Taínos had probably inhabited Ayiti for only two or three centuries before Columbus's expedition arrived. The Caribs, meanwhile, were not far behind, having reached what is now Puerto Rico. They were already launching raids across the 100-km (60-mile) passage separating the two islands and would almost certainly have overrun Ayiti in due course.

LEFT: an image of Taíno life, the Museo de l'Hombre Dominicano, Santo Domingo.
ABOVE LEFT: cabinet detail.
ABOVE RIGHT: Taíno petroglyphs.

and advised by a council of elders, who helped organise communal work according to age and sex. The villages were loosely structured into district chiefdoms, each one ruled by a prominent local *cacique*, which in turn were grouped into regional chiefdoms, headed by the most important district chief.

These tight-knit and ordered communities lived in permanent villages, consisting of large houses made of wood and thatch. Several related families might share such a dwelling, known as a *bohío*. Land was owned and worked communally, and the Taínos were accomplished farmers, raising sweet potatoes, peanuts and beans. Their staple was cassava or manioc which provided a flour for baking after the poisonous juices had been extracted. The surrounding sea and unpolluted rivers were full of fish and turtles, while birds and small animals were hunted and cooked on a *barbacoa* – one of the few Taíno words that still survive today *(see page 24)*.

These peaceful Amerindians were seemingly also religious, worshipping a trinity of gods: a male figure associated with cassava and volcanoes; a female fertility god related to the sea and the moon; and a dog-like deity whose role it was to look after the recently deceased. These divinities existed alongside a collective belief in

rival teams of 10 to 30 players propelling the ball to and fro without using feet or hands. These sports grounds were also used for dancing and rituals related to deaths and marriages.

Paradise lost

It is perhaps too easy to romanticise the existence of the pre-Columbian inhabitants of Ayiti and other Caribbean islands, but there is no doubt that their life before the Europeans' arrival was an idyll compared to what was to follow. Across the Americas the "encounter" between indigenous peoples and colonising cultures was to produce terrible dislocations and

the spiritual power of nature and dead ancestors. Such forces were worshipped in the form of *zemís*, fetishes made from the remains of the dead or from wood, stone and cotton. The *cacique* also played the role of shaman or priest, presiding over religious ceremonies with the help of a sort of hallucinogenic snuff.

Keen ball-players

Skilled potters and accomplished house- and boat-builders, the Taínos were also enthusiastic about games, especially a team sport played with a rubber ball on a court called a *batey*. Columbus and his followers were amazed at the sight of not only a bouncing ball, but of

human suffering, but nowhere was this process as devastating as on the island that Columbus claimed for Spain on 12 December 1492. The name he gave it was La Isla Española, "the Spanish island", or Hispaniola.

The motives behind Columbus's audacious transatlantic expedition are well known, but nonetheless complex in their ambiguity. The desire to find an alternative to the overland route to Asia, hence bypassing Turkish Muslim control of the eastern Mediterranean, was spurred by the knowledge that contemporary Europe craved the silk, spices and other luxury goods to be found in "the Indies". In this sense, Columbus's project was a simple business proposal, supported financially by powerful bankers from his native Genoa and given official sanction by King Ferdinand and Queen Isabela of Spain. The "Catholic monarchs" also backed the scheme because they were aware that the rival Iberian power, Portugal, was pulling ahead in the race to reach the Indies by sea.

There was also an ideological dimension to the Spanish involvement. The expulsion of the Moors from southern Spain in early 1492 ushered in a mood of militant Christianity, and Columbus's assurance that the wealth he found could finance a new crusade to re-conquer the Holy Land fell on receptive ears. He also pledged that his expedition would force the conversion of any "heathens" it encountered along the way.

> ### ENRICHING IDEAL...
>
> "Gold is most excellent; he who possesses it may do what he will in the world, and may so attain as to bring souls to Paradise."
> – CHRISTOPHER COLUMBUS

by his and subsequent expeditions and the title of "Admiral of the Ocean Sea".

Driven by a blend of political, pecuniary and personal goals, the tiny fleet of the *Santa María*, the *Pinta* and the *Niña* set sail from Palos in southern Spain on 4 August 1492, reached the Canary Islands a few days later and set off into the unknown on 6 September. Thirty-seven days later, after a period of unimaginable doubts and hopes, the expedition arrived at Guanahani in the Bahamas, an island that Columbus

Columbus sets sail

Among this mix of economic and spiritual considerations stood the explorer's own personal ambitions: 10 percent of all riches brought back

FAR LEFT: an anthropormophic inhalator made from manatee bone.
LEFT AND ABOVE: Taínos welcomed the Spanish ships.

promptly renamed San Salvador. There, the Europeans were greeted by hospitable Taínos, who informed them that the source of the gold jewellery they wore lay further to the south. "All the inhabitants could be taken away to Castile, or made slaves on the island," noted Columbus. "With fifty men we could subjugate them all and make them do whatever we want."

Believing himself to be in some remote outpost of Japan, Columbus was rather disappointed by the simplicity of Taíno culture and the conspicuous absence of wealth. The expedition pushed on around the coast of Cuba, where first impressions were no more promising, finally arriving off Ayiti two months after the first landfall in San Salvador. It was Ayiti's fortune – or misfortune – to provide the first permanent European settlement in the Americas, for on Christmas Eve 1492, the *Santa María* foundered on a reef off the north coast and Columbus decided to salvage its timbers and build a fort.

A warm welcome

The local Taínos, under their *cacique* Guacanagarí, willingly helped these strange newcomers with rescuing the ship's stores (Columbus was amazed that "not a lace

point" was stolen) and welcomed the construction of Puerto de La Navidad – Christmas Port – on their beach. Their generosity seemed boundless, and a garrison of 39 Europeans eagerly volunteered to stay on the island and collect what gold they could and search for potential mines, while Columbus returned to Spain to mount another expedition.

Leaving Diego de Araña, a trusted associate, in charge of La Navidad, Columbus set sail in early January. Before he left the island, however, he had a brief and violent encounter with another Taíno community at the eastern end of the island, at the Bay of Samaná. Here, attempts to trade European beads and trinkets for the

> ### HIGH PRICES
> The Taínos were made to collect a regular amount of gold dust for the Spanish colonists. If they failed, they were either executed or had their hands cut off.

Amerindians' powerful bows and arrows ended in a deadly battle, with the Taínos fleeing "surprised at our courage and the wounds made by our weapons".

Spanish steel and primitive artillery were infinitely more destructive than any weaponry owned by the Taínos, and it may be that this in part accounted for their initial docility. But Taíno patience, it seems, had its limits, for when Columbus eventually returned to La Navidad in November 1493 he found the fort burned down and the entire garrison dead or missing. Guacanagarí explained that his people had not been responsible for the attack, but that another, more powerful *cacique*, Caonabo, had ordered the massacre as a reprisal for the Europeans' violent demands for food, women and gold.

First Spanish settlement

In the meantime, Columbus had returned to Spain to a hero's welcome, telling exaggerated tales of the gold and other riches he had found in what he still took to be some part of Asia. With royal encouragement and a new coat of arms ("To Castile and León Columbus gave a New World"), he was quickly able to organise a second expedition. This fleet of 17 ships carried 1,200 men, animals, seeds and sugar cane shoots; it was an embryonic colonising force, lightly armed and including several priests. Some 200 *hidalgos* or Spanish gentlemen joined the voyage at their own expense, attracted by the prospect of easy wealth.

Finding La Navidad in ashes and relations with the Taínos uneasy, Columbus nonetheless proceeded with his plans for establishing a colony. Founding a settlement named La Isabela near the present-day Dominican town of Puerto Plata, he sent prospectors inland to look for gold nuggets in the Cibao area, where the trusting Taínos had directed him.

So began the first European gold rush in the Americas and with it the first genocide of the modern era. "In all the world no better people," Columbus had said of the Taínos. Within half a century, the indigenous inhabitants of Hispaniola were extinct. ❑

LEFT: gold was abundant in South America.
RIGHT: the Taínos were enslaved to mine for gold.

IN SPANISH HANDS

*In Spain's rush for gold and silver, Hispaniola's prosperity rose and fell,
destroying the Amerindians in the process. And then the buccaneers moved in...*

Hispaniola, so the tourist board slogan goes, was "the land Columbus loved best". But even if the explorer is remembered today as the individual responsible for the first European settlement in the Americas, his influence on the first Spanish colony was nothing short of disastrous. In the modern-day Dominican Republic, superstitious souls prefer not to mention the name of Columbus, for it is widely reputed to carry a *fukú* – a curse.

For the seven years since the second expedition of 1493, the European presence on the island had been dominated by Columbus and his two brothers, Diego and Bartolomé, and plagued by internal squabbling and violence. Much of this violence was directed against the increasingly hostile Taínos, who, after the destruction of the fort at La Navidad, were openly treated as enemies.

The Spaniards' futile quest for gold, when they discovered that the gold fields of Cibao had been a mirage, together with their cruel treatment of the Taínos, intensified the situation. In 1495 a Taíno uprising was easily put down by the Spanish, who shipped 500 captives to Seville as slaves. Most died en route or within weeks of arriving in Europe.

Unpopular Columbus brothers

In 1496 Bartolomé decided to abandon the pestilential settlement of Isabela in favour of a new location on the south coast, where he founded La Nueva Isabela, soon to be renamed Santo Domingo. But by now the settlers were restless, suspicious that Columbus's claims had been largely wishful thinking. Even the relocation of the main settlement was viewed as some sort of scheme, designed to reinforce the Columbus brothers' power. An open revolt broke out, led by the former mayor of Isabela, Francisco Roldán, who accused them of monopolising the island's wealth. Desperate to quell dissent, Columbus agreed to share out

land and Amerindian labourers among the colonists in a system known as the *repartimiento*, each being entitled to a number of Taíno villages according to his status.

But disappointment and frustration continued to fuel resentment against Columbus, and in 1500 the Spanish Crown, alarmed at reports

A 6

of unrest in its new possession, sent out a commissioner, Francisco de Bobadilla, to investigate. On his arrival, he was met with the scene of seven Spaniards hanging from the gallows. Pardoning any others accused of treachery by Columbus, he arrested the three brothers and sent them back in chains to Seville. Columbus would only see Hispaniola once more, in 1504, as his fourth and final voyage ended in debacle.

Growth of Santo Domingo

In the wake of Bobadilla's intervention, 2,500 more colonists arrived, as well as a new governor, Nicolás de Ovando. Under Ovando, the settlement of Santo Domingo took on the

---

LEFT: a memorial to Columbus, Santo Domingo.
RIGHT: the conquistador Hernán Cortés.

appearance of a town, with stone buildings and the beginnings of a grid system of streets spreading up from the Ozama River.

At the same time, the exploitation of the Taínos continued apace, but with some modifications. Dropping Columbus's *repartimiento* system, he introduced the *encomienda* model of forced labour, in which entire communities, under the leadership of their *cacique*, were allotted to settlers as feudal serfs or chattels. In return for working for six to eight months a year, the Taínos were supposedly protected by their master or *encomendero*, who was also in charge of their spiritual well-being.

deference to her status. By the time Ovando's governorship ended in 1509, there were fewer than 60,000 Taínos left.

Capital of the Indies

The Columbus connection did not disappear with Christopher's death, for Ovando's successor was Diego Columbus, the explorer's eldest son. He arrived in the colony, convinced that he was entitled to the share of wealth negotiated with the Spanish Crown by his late father. As Governor (1509–15) and then Viceroy of the Indies (1520–24), Diego regarded Hispaniola as a family business, to be exploited at will. He

Brutal repression

This system was perhaps marginally more benign than Columbus's wholesale enslavement policy, but it did little to reverse the Taíno genocide. Indeed, Ovando's repression of Taíno resistance was even more brutal than what had occurred before. In 1503, for example, Anacaona, the female *cacique* and widow of Caonabo (who had died in captivity in 1494), invited Ovando to a meeting of Taíno chiefs in the southwestern kingdom of Xaraguá. When the 80 or so *caciques* were assembled in Anacaona's longhouse, Ovando ordered his men to burn down the building with the Taínos inside. Anacaona was hanged, apparently in

liberally handed out *encomiendas* to himself and his friends and supporters and established one of the first sugar plantations on the island, on the outskirts of Santo Domingo.

The *nouveau-riche* Diego also had aristocratic pretensions, having married María de Toledo, a member of the Spanish nobility; he was determined to command appropriate respect. During his periods in power, he presided over the rapid development of the city of Santo Domingo, adding many fine and imposing buildings to those left behind by Ovando. His own Alcázar or palace, a beautiful two-storey residence on the river bank, was the centre of the Spanish New World empire, acting as administrative headquarters and focus for the colonial elite's social life. Nearby, work began on the first cathedral in the Americas, Diego having laid the foundation stone in 1514.

For a brief period, Santo Domingo was a place of power and prestige. It witnessed a series of architectural firsts: the first permanent hospital in the New World; the first university; the first overseas royal mint. It was the seat of a *Real Audiencia*, a court of appeal answerable directly to the Spanish

ENRIQUILLO'S REVOLT

In 1519, the chieftain Enriquillo led his *encomienda* in a successful revolt, fleeing into the mountains. They stayed there, giving shelter to other runaways and were eventually "pardoned" by the Spanish Crown.

the island, while the rapidly dwindling Taíno population was forced into makeshift villages, theoretically supervised by an *encomendero* but usually neglected. An attempt to bring this rudimentary system under some sort of control failed when priests from the Hieronymite order, dispatched from Spain to oversee a humane reform of the *encomiendas*, met with little cooperation from the colonists.

In any case, a devastating smallpox epidemic in 1519 put paid to any prospect of stemming the

Crown and it was soon the base for a growing cast of imperial bureaucrats – military, administrative and ecclesiastical. Religious orders arrived from Spain, establishing their own institutions and teaching centres. Here grew the embryo of Spain's future Latin American empire.

The Church intervenes

Yet outside this tiny enclave, Hispaniola was all but uninhabited. A handful of tiny villages and a few rough settlements connected by mule tracks were dotted around the eastern half of

LEFT: the capture of Amerindian *cacique* Caonabo.
ABOVE: an artist's impression of old Santo Domingo.

Taíno death toll; 3,000 at most survived, pushing them further to the brink of extinction.

By now, the Church was closely involved in the controversy surrounding the treatment of the Taínos and the resulting labour shortage. Mounting official disquiet over Diego Columbus's activities had led to his recall to Spain, but after a five-year period he was seemingly forgiven. In 1520, he returned to a colony where the primitive gold mines were yielding little wealth to their disillusioned owners, and where the economy revolved around little more than informal ranching. Vast areas of otherwise unoccupied land had been turned over to cattle, which often escaped into the wilderness.

Birth of the sugar industry

But one commodity did seem to promise a brighter future: sugar. The cane shoots that Christopher Columbus had transported from the Canary Islands in 1493 had prospered in Hispaniola's fertile soil, and some colonists saw that Europe's insatiable appetite for sugar, sharpened by a shortage of supplies from the Middle East, could be turned to their advantage.

One fundamental problem stood in their way, however: with the decline of the Taínos, there was no available labour to be deployed on the plantations. It was at this point that the colonists and the authorities in Spain began to take notice

of the Dominican friar, Bartolomé de Las Casas, and other advocates of indigenous rights, since he had perhaps inadvertently suggested the solution to their problem. Enslavement of the Spanish Crown's subjects, he had argued, was intolerable, but a Christian conscience could allow "heathens", particularly black Africans, to be used as slaves.

The religious rationalisation of black slavery was nothing new; Portuguese traders had been selling African slaves in Spain since the 1450s, but they were mainly employed as domestic servants and exotic status symbols. Black slave labour was also a feature of the sugar industry in the Canary Islands later in the century. The Catholic Church tolerated this system, as it considered that Africans could be converted to Christianity in the process, and so the Spanish Crown began to allot contracts, known as *asientos*, to those merchants who could guarantee a steady supply of slaves to the New World colonies.

A new slave labour force

In 1518 King Charles V contracted a Court favourite, Lorenzo de Gomenot, to ship 4,000 Africans across the Atlantic each year. According to Las Casas (a man sometimes given to exaggeration), some 30,000 black slaves had entered Hispaniola by 1540. The first slave revolt, meanwhile, was reported in 1522 – on the sugar plantation of Diego Columbus. The slaves, armed with sticks and stones, were massacred by the colony's militia in response.

The early sugar industry faced other difficulties. A lack of expertise, technology and capital created huge problems for the first planters,

---

PROTECTORS OF THE AMERINDIANS

At Christmas in 1511, Antón de Montesinos, a Dominican friar, delivered an unexpected and fiery rebuke to the assembled Spanish congregation in Santo Domingo. "By what authority," he asked, "have you made such detestable wars against these people who lived peacefully and gently on their own lands?" The outraged colonists demanded the plain-speaking priest's immediate return to Spain, where he pleaded directly at the Royal Court for better treatment of the Taínos.

Montesinos's sermon inspired another priest, Bartolomé de Las Casas (1474–1566), who had arrived in Hispaniola in 1502 and had witnessed the Taíno genocide. He

renounced his own *encomienda*, realising that the system was inhumane and spent the rest of his life championing the Amerindians' cause. He wrote the hugely influential *A Very Brief Account of the Destruction of the Indies* (1551), and caused deep embarrassment and concern in Spain, where few were aware of the extent of the indigenous disaster.

In theory, the Taínos were subjects of the Spanish Crown, and what had originally been presented as an exercise in evangelisation had in fact resulted in whole-sale slaughter. The reforms that followed were too few and came too late, but Las Casas is remembered as the "protector of the Indians" and defender of human rights.

who had to rely on man- or mule-powered mills to crush the cane. But gradually innovations such as the water-powered *ingenio* began to improve productivity, as did the arrival of skilled workers from the Canary Islands, encouraged by the Spanish authorities.

By 1523 there were 20 *ingenios* and in 1542 Hispaniola recorded exports of 1,200 tons of semi-refined sugar loaves to Spain. According to the contemporary historian and military man, Gonzalo Fernández de Oviedo, there was money to be made, for "there is no island or kingdom among Christians or pagans where there is anything like this industry of sugar."

expedition reached Mexico, from where rumours of vast silver and gold fortunes trickled back to the islands. As the Spanish Empire extended along the Central American isthmus and into South America, Hispaniola held few attractions for the would-be *conquistador*. Its population, never large, began to shrink from a peak of 14,000 to a mere 5,000 in the 1570s.

Spanish bureaucracy

If Mexico promised instant wealth, Hispaniola was increasingly stifled by Spanish bureaucracy. All trade had to be conducted through the port of Seville, where the state's percent-

Further conquests

However profitable sugar might have been, many Spanish colonists had bolder ambitions. From the outset, Hispaniola had served as a springboard for further conquests: Jamaica (1509); Cuba (1511); Puerto Rico (1512). But as the gold rush swiftly faded, the lure of new horizons became even more irresistible.

Hernán Cortés (1485–1547) was one such adventurer who was unprepared to settle for the humdrum life of a sugar planter. In 1519, his

LEFT: the sugar industry encouraged slavery.
ABOVE: Fray Bartolomé de Las Casas championed the Amerindian cause, Museo de las Casas Reales.

age of gold or sugar was deducted in a special warehouse. All imports into the island came from there, too, but with irritating irregularity. Spain was determined to prevent any other European nation from trading with her New World possessions, and her monopoly was jealously defended with a heavy naval presence, which accompanied the trading galleons across the Atlantic.

Heavily taxed, constantly regulated and yet subject to unreliable supplies, many of the colonists – particularly those who had been born on the island – began to resent the royal stranglehold on trade and the dominance of Spanish functionaries, the *peninsulares*.

Pirates and privateers

By the 1550s, Hispaniola had slipped into a gentle decline. The focus of Spanish activity had shifted to the mainland colonies and the former capital of the Indies was largely an irrelevance. As Santo Domingo languished, the Cuban port of Havana grew in importance as the place where the Spanish fleets, laden with bullion from Peru and Mexico, assembled before returning to Europe.

Spanish investment in fortifications poured into Cuba, while Santo Domingo was neglected. The city retained some administrative importance as the seat of the *Real Audiencia* but, in general, life was hard and unrewarding for most colonists. An earthquake in 1562 levelled the few settlements on the north coast, adding to the exodus of disillusioned settlers.

Meanwhile, an even greater threat to the colony was materialising in the shape of the pirates and privateers who began to infest the Caribbean from the 1530s onwards. Since Columbus's first discoveries and the ensuing Treaty of Tordesillas (1494), which had given papal backing to the division of the New World between Catholic Spain and Portugal, other European nations had been following developments closely. England, in particular, was

opposed to any Spanish monopoly of the Americas, while France was also determined to claim its own share of whatever wealth was to be found across the Atlantic. However, the first non-Spanish interlopers were not official navies, but pirates, more often than not operating with the blessing of their government and intent on seizing as much Spanish loot as they could.

Whether privateers (those at sea during times of war and carrying official commissions) or pirates (common criminals), this new breed of maritime terrorist spread panic throughout the Spanish colonies, plundering both ships and settlements on land. In the 1560s, English pirates ransacked what was left of Hispaniola's north coast, forcing the authorities to evacuate the area altogether. Sometimes, however, these sea-borne aggressors could offer a service of sorts, for many of them also worked as smugglers. The traumatised inhabitants of the north coast were relieved and delighted, for instance, to buy 300 African slaves from the English pirate John Hawkins in 1562.

Spain loses its grip

Once the Spanish New World monopoly was breached, Spain's European enemies began to give more serious thought to establishing their own Caribbean colonies. Spain, after all, was

weakness and the potential of her own sugar industry, England pushed harder against this half-open door. To the consternation of Madrid, an English expedition, dispatched by Cromwell as his "Western Design", took Jamaica with comparative ease in 1655. The English had previously attempted to attack Hispaniola, but had failed through their own conspicuous incompetence. With the capture of Jamaica, the balance of power in the Caribbean tilted further away from Spain.

Cromwell's force may have failed to capture Hispaniola, but Spain's grip on her first colony was becoming increasingly feeble and an English

over-stretched economically and militarily, often at war in Europe and unable to fend off the swarms of pirates who preyed on the bullion-heavy and vulnerable galleons.

At first, at the beginning of the 17th century, the newcomers settled in the smaller islands of the Lesser Antilles: the English taking St Kitts, Barbados and Antigua; the French claiming Martinique and Guadeloupe. Although, in theory, Spain owned these islands, it did little to prevent their loss. Encouraged by Spanish

LEFT: Francis Drake's fleet sails into Santo Domingo.
ABOVE: many battles were fought in the Caribbean.
RIGHT: buccaneers took over as Spanish control waned.

and French presence on the island's north coast had been growing steadily.

A base for buccaneers

The new settlers were mainly buccaneers, the successors to the pirates of the previous century, but different in that they were permanently based in the region. Taking their name from the indigenous word *boucan*, the wood-fuelled barbecue pit over which they cooked and smoked strips of wild cattle or pigs, these men were a tough and hard-living mix of deserters, runaway servants or shipwrecked sailors.

Making a living from piracy and smuggling, they first established a base on the offshore island of Tortuga (today La Tortue), from where they could attack Spanish shipping. Attempts to drive them away failed, and by the 1650s they had moved on to the no-man's land of northern Hispaniola, growing maize and tobacco, and ranching. Piracy was by now a risky business, and many buccaneers opted for a more settled life.

As the English buccaneers drifted off to the "pirate capital" of Port Royal, Jamaica, the north coast settlements became overwhelmingly French.

A BUCCANEERING LIFE

There were few female buccaneers and many men lived in pairs, adopting a sort of marriage arrangement known as *matelotage*, possibly as a quasi-legal way of dealing with property rights in the event of death.

The French move in

With the Spanish unable, or unwilling, to rid themselves of these unwelcome visitors, the northwest of the island became a *de facto* French colony called Saint Domingue. By 1664, it had been incorporated into the French charter.

A governor was duly sent from Paris, and the French settlement took more permanent shape, with the founding of several port towns such as Port-de-Paix and Léogâne. Eventually, the 1697 Treaty of Ryswick officially ceded the western part of the island to France, a paper transaction that merely formalised a *fait accompli* and confirmed Spain's increasingly tenuous presence in the region. The island was henceforth divided, albeit unequally, into what history would reveal as two ill-fitting pieces.

Pearl of the Antilles

The spectacular rise of Saint Domingue was unparalleled in 18th-century colonial history. Within a century, a lawless and backward outpost had been transformed into the most prosperous colony in the world.

Where the Spanish side of the island had stagnated for a century or more, the French territory boomed, spurred on by massive state and private investment.

Irrigation was brought to 40,000 hectares (100,000 acres) of land in the 1740s, sponsored by the French government; the latest technology was employed in milling and transporting the sugar cargoes that sailed back to Bordeaux or Nantes. Although sugar dominated, there were other lucrative export crops: indigo, cocoa, coffee and cotton.

Saint Domingue gradually became a place of grotesque social extremes. A small cast of white landowners, the *grands blancs*, lived lives of aristocratic luxury in their sumptuous estate houses or elegant town dwellings. Towns like the capital Cap Français, Port-au-Prince and Jacmel grew up around the coast, offering all the amenities of European cities. Theatres were founded, newspapers and books were printed, prostitutes, dance halls and gambling dens proliferated.

But this élite's decadent lifestyle depended on the forced labour of a huge majority of black slaves, who arrived at the average annual rate of about 8,000 throughout the 18th century. Brutalised and exploited by a middle stratum of *petit blanc* overseers, these slaves, torn from a number of different West African nations, were the motor of Saint Domingue's economy.

A rigidly hierarchical social structure, based on skin colour and, to a lesser extent, money, grew up: the wealthy planters on top, the poor whites and a minority of mixed-race people in the middle, and the black slaves, locally born or freshly imported, at the bottom. It was a recipe for spectacular profits and dramatic growth. It was also a recipe for disaster. ❏

LEFT: preparing indigo.
RIGHT: several religious men criticised Taíno abuse.

SANTO DOMINGO:
LLAVE, PUERTA Y ESCALA
DE TODAS LAS INDIAS.
FELIPE II

REVOLUTION AND NATIONHOOD

Inspired by the French Revolution, Saint Domingue exploded while Santo Domingo profited. The ensuing turmoil led to independence...

On the eve of the 1789–95 French Revolution, Saint Domingue stood as a monument to European imperialism. It was, wrote historian C.L.R. James, "the most prosperous colony the world had ever known; to the casual eye the most flourishing and prosperous possession on the face of the globe."

In 1787, the territory exported 87,000 tons of sugar, more than all British Caribbean colonies combined. Saint Domingue was also the world's leading producer of coffee. The vast sugar plantations that spread over the fertile northern plain produced fortunes for a few thousand white landowners; in the hilly south, coffee and indigo were grown on smaller holdings. A never-ending succession of ships called at the colony's ports, delivering luxury goods for the planters and salt fish for the slaves before returning to Europe loaded with "white gold".

Tensions in Saint Domingue

Other ships unloaded slaves: 27,000 in 1786, 40,000 the following year. In 1789, an estimated half million slaves worked in Saint Domingue, the death toll through exhaustion and ill treatment accounting for the annual import of fresh labour. The rest of the population numbered some 40,000 whites, most of them humble tradesmen, administrators or military personnel, and a further 30,000 free coloureds, the result of illicit, often forced, encounters between white men and slave women.

All sectors of society hated and feared each other; the whites disdained their coloured offspring, the mulattos envied the whites and despised the blacks. The blacks, meanwhile, awaited the day when they could take their revenge on their oppressors. Attempted slave revolts, escapes, the poisoning of animals and sometimes humans were commonplace.

In 1758, a slave named Mackandal planned to begin an uprising by poisoning the water

supply of hundreds of planters; he was betrayed and burned at the stake. The colony lived in constant fear of the slaves.

Santo Domingo recovers

In contrast, Spanish Santo Domingo was greatly poorer but altogether less explosive.

After the decline in the colony's fortunes, it had recovered somewhat in the second half of the 18th century, its population rising from a mere 6,000 in 1740 to 100,000 in 1780. Its modest prosperity was mainly due to the fortunes of neighbouring Saint Domingue, which imported beef and other foodstuffs.

But its social and ethnic composition was entirely different; immigrants from the Canary Islands arrived in large numbers, while black slaves accounted for at most 30 percent of the population. A colony of large ranches and scattered towns, it was a world apart from the industrial-scale plantation system across the mountainous border.

LEFT: Inigo Barlow depicts the revenge of the black army on the French oppressors.

RIGHT: the colonists lived in fear of slave revolts.

The storm breaks

When news of the French Revolution filtered back to Saint Domingue, each sector of society interpreted these distant events according to its own interests. The *grands blancs* were hardly in favour of social revolution, but they believed they could capitalise on disarray in Paris to obtain greater autonomy and a relaxation of the state's control over colonial trade. The blacks felt that the time had come to grab equal rights with the whites, while the slaves absorbed the message of liberty and equality, if not fraternity, entirely literally.

The mulattos were the first to act; an insur-

plantations of the north were reduced to ashes, and a thick pall of smoke covered Cap Français. The colonial militia fought back, and according to the Jamaican planter and witness Bryan Edwards, some 2,000 whites and 10,000 slaves were killed within two months. As the situation grew desperate in the north, a mulatto uprising broke out in the south, while in Port-au-Prince a mob of self-styled revolutionary poor whites went on the rampage.

Into this chaotic state of near civil war sailed an expeditionary force of 6,000 French troops in September 1792. Led by a triumvirate of revolutionary commissioners, its aim was to

rection broke out in mid-1790, led by the black Paris-educated Vincent Ogé, calling for immediate equality of political rights. The uprising was brutally crushed, and Ogé and his associates were tortured and executed, strengthening hostility between the white and mulatto minorities. Increasingly apprehensive, the planters and their political allies contemplated asking for protection from the British.

On 22 August 1791, the storm finally broke, when a secret meeting of slave leaders unleashed the long-awaited insurrection and an orgy of violence. According to legend, the meeting was presided over by Boukmann, a *houngan* or voodoo priest. Within days the

quell the anarchy by offering equal rights to the mulattos. For the slaves, however, there was nothing on offer. Both Spain and Britain, meanwhile, had been following events closely; the British had long coveted the fantastically profitable colony, and Spanish troops were assembled across the border, ready to reclaim the territory given away in 1697.

Toussaint – a cunning leader

It was at this critical stage that the slaves' main leader, Toussaint L'Ouverture (*circa* 1742–1803), displayed his instinctive genius for strategy. Unexpectedly allying his force of 4,000 men with the Spanish commander, he had no illusions that reactionary Spain would grant the slaves freedom, but realised that this move would place increasing pressure on the beleaguered French commissioners. His guess proved to be right, for in August 1793, the principal commissioner Sonthonax, hemmed in by white counter-revolutionaries and the threat of foreign invasion, unilaterally decreed the abolition of slavery.

Within weeks Toussaint had turned against the Spanish and joined forces with the republican French, aware now that the overwhelming threat to the black majority came from a British force that had landed in September at the southern port of Jérémie. For their part, the white planters welcomed General Thomas Maitland's expedition as their last hope of re-establishing slavery and ridding the colony of revolutionaries.

In 1795 Spain and France made peace at the Treaty of Bâle and Spain ceded control of Santo Domingo to the French. With the Spanish out of contention, Toussaint turned his attention to the British, who had made an effective start to their campaign, taking Port-au-Prince in June 1794. But this was to be the extent of their success as the British forces succumbed to yellow fever. In 1798, after the recall of Sonthonax, the French commissioner, to Paris and the departure of Maitland's surviving troops, Toussaint was finally able to crush the mulatto insurgence in the south.

By 1800 Toussaint was undisputed master of Saint Domingue, nominally governor-general of a French colony, but in reality ruler of what was really an independent country. He made trade agreements with the United States, encouraged investment in education based on new taxes and urged the ex-slaves to return to the plantations as free labourers. He even courted the remaining white planters (most had

LEFT: revolution on Saint Domingue cost many lives.
ABOVE: English ships sail into the harbour.

TOUSSAINT AND NAPOLEON

Toussaint L'Ouverture's authority was intolerable to Napoleon Bonaparte, who had emerged from France's revolutionary turmoil as First Consul. He was prepared neither to put up with the secession of the most valuable French colony nor a challenge from those he derided as "gilded Africans".

Perhaps spurred on by his wife, the Empress Joséphine, the daughter of a white, slave-owning Martinican family, he sent an imposing force of 22,000 troops to Saint Domingue in December 1801. Their objectives were to remove Toussaint, restore French rule and ultimately to re-impose slavery.

fled during the previous decade to Cuba, Trinidad or other islands), inviting them to help rebuild the shattered economy.

But his rule was also harsh; critics and opponents were not tolerated, and an army of 20,000 forced many back to work. For a short while, Saint Domingue resumed its exports of sugar and coffee, albeit at two-thirds the 1789 levels.

However, Napoleon Bonaparte was not happy with the situation and in 1801 set about restoring the pre-revolutionary

> ### WORDS OF WARNING
>
> "In overthrowing me, you have cut down only the trunk of the tree of liberty. It will spring up again by the roots for they are numerous and deep," Toussaint L'Ouverture is claimed to have said on leaving for exile and death in France.

and galvanised the ex-slaves once more. A fresh insurrection in the north gathered in strength, while yellow fever made its inevitable reappearance. Under the leadership of battle-hardened veterans such as Jean-Jacques Dessalines (1758–1806) and Henri Christophe (1767–1820), the black fighters began to pin the French down. "It is not enough to have taken away Toussaint", wrote Napoleon's brother-in-law, General Victor-Emmanuel Leclerc, before he died of yellow fever, "there

status quo. At first, the French appeared to face few serious obstacles. Lured by promises of promotion, some of Toussaint's officers defected, and guerrilla resistance to the massive French military presence soon fizzled out. In June 1802, Toussaint was captured and shipped back to France, warning that the people of Saint Domingue would rise up again.

Black retaliation

A strange stalemate followed. But in July news reached the island that French forces had restored slavery in Guadeloupe, having overthrown the mulatto-dominated government. The revelation confirmed Toussaint's warnings

are 2,000 leaders to be taken away." By this time, 24,000 French troops out of a total of 34,000 had died.

French hopes finally faded when hostilities with Britain resumed in May 1803 and the prospect of reinforcements evaporated. Fighting a savage and futile campaign, Leclerc's successor, General Rochambeau, set man-eating dogs on his enemies and turned on the mulattos. Such desperation merely strengthened the black army's resolve, and the fanatical, white-hating Dessalines led a scorched earth campaign that cut French supply lines and reduced the colony to ashes. *Koupe tèt, boule kay* ("cut off heads, burn down houses") was Dessalines' motto, and his troops wreaked vengeance on the few remaining whites and the tattered remains of the Napoleonic war machine. On 7 April 1803, coincidentally the date of Toussaint's death, Dessalines had ripped the white section from the French *tricolore*, creating the flag of a new nation, symbolically purged of the white oppressor. In November, Rochambeau's men could take no more and, like the British before them, evacuated the island.

Independent Haiti

The birth of Haiti was as sudden as the death of Saint Domingue was lingering. On 1 January 1804, General Dessalines declared the island's independence, restoring the Taíno-derived name meaning "land of high mountains".

"I have given the French cannibals blood for blood", said the country's first ruler, and his constitution expressly forbade *blancs* (foreigners) to own land or property in the new state. It was a nation born in ruins: after 13 years of conflict a huge army of ex-slaves, without land or work, roamed the devastated landscape.

The outside world was either thrilled or appalled by the creation of the world's first black republic. For liberals and abolitionists, it seemed to prove that the oppressed could triumph over tyranny, that slavery's days were numbered. But for the colonial powers and slave societies throughout the Americas, the world's only successful slave revolution offered a fearful example of what could happen elsewhere. As a result, independent Haiti was to be shunned by much of the international community and reviled as a place of unmitigated savagery, as proof that blacks could never be trusted to rule themselves.

The first decades of Haitian independence did not augur well for the country's future. Following Napoleon's example, the autocratic Dessalines declared himself emperor in October 1804. Within two years he was dead, shot by mutinous mulatto officers after a brief and bloodthirsty reign. Dessalines was succeeded by Henri Christophe, a former hotel waiter turned military commander, who, as King Henri I, became the first monarch in the Americas. An eccentric mix of reformer and megalomaniac, Christophe tried to introduce a

European-style education system, while imitating court life and surrounding himself with dukes and counts. His most lasting monument is the vast Citadelle Laferrière, a massive fortress built near what had been renamed Cap Haïtien to repel any future French invasion.

By now, the old enmities between north and south, between black and mulatto, had resurfaced. Under the leadership of Alexandre Pétion, the south of Haiti effectively broke away from Christophe's kingdom, forming a separate republic. This bizarre division lasted until 1820, when Pétion's successor, the mulatto General Jean-Pierre Boyer (1776–1850) reunited the

country after Christophe's suicide in the face of a popular uprising. Amid constant power struggles, Haiti remained a country at arms. Independence had been won by force, and the generals continued to wield overwhelming influence well into the 19th century.

In the meantime, the old colonial plantation system crumbled away and the estates were divided up into smallholdings, turning Haiti into a nation of small farmers. And as the rural landscape changed, two separate worlds evolved: that of the peasantry, black, Creole-speaking and mostly illiterate far removed from the towns; and that of the mulatto elite, urban, French-speaking and educated.

Left: Dessalines rides in, by Philomé Obin.
Above: Henri Christophe ends it all.

Birth of the Dominican Republic

When the French were driven out of Saint Domingue in 1803, they retained a presence in Santo Domingo until 1809 and the *partie de l'est* (eastern part) was returned to Spanish ownership. It was a state of affairs that seemingly neither Spain nor the colonists wanted, and a chaotic period, known as *España Boba* ("silly Spain") followed, in which ineffectual governors tried half-heartedly to impose colonial rule, including slavery, on an increasingly restless population.

In 1821, as anti-colonial movements took root in Spanish South America, a group of

notables proclaimed the territory's independence, choosing the name of Spanish Haiti and asking Simón Bolívar whether they could join his projected *Gran Colombia* federation. They never received a reply, and instead, in February 1822, Haiti's President Boyer led an army into Santo Domingo. It was to stay there for 22 years.

Haitian occupation

Even today, Dominicans are taught that the Haitian occupation was an extended nightmare of brutality. The truth, however, may be slightly different, for although Boyer ruled firmly, the Haitians introduced long-overdue reforms, not least the abolition of slavery. Those who com-

plained loudest were the powerful land-owners, notably the Church and absentee Spaniards, who saw their properties broken up and redistributed. The bureaucrats in Santo Domingo, mostly veterans of Spanish rule, were also resentful when Haitian administrators took their place. On the whole, though, the ranch owners and tobacco growers were left alone, as Boyer recognised their usefulness to the economy.

A more widespread grievance took root from 1825, when the Haitians imposed a number of taxes on the inhabitants of Santo Domingo, to fund an agreement with France, which guaranteed recognition of Haitian sovereignty in return for compensation of 150 million francs, to be paid to the dispossessed planters of former Saint Domingue. Understandably, the Spanish-speaking population was unhappy about contributing to this vast settlement through punitive taxation, and a nationalist movement took root.

Underground movement

But freedom from Haitian rule was a long time in coming. Slowly, a group of nationalists organised a secret network that in 1838 took the name of La Trinitaria. By 1843 the underground movement had extended its influence among Santo Domingo's disgruntled youth and its leaders had settled on what to call their dreamed-of new nation: the Dominican Republic.

The plotters' task was made easier by Boyer's growing weakness. A disastrous earthquake in 1842 had levelled most of the island's north coast towns as well as the east's second city of Santiago. The looting carried out by Haitian forces had deepened hostility, while in Haiti various factions were conspiring against an increasingly corrupt Boyer.

When the veteran president was eventually shipped off to exile in Jamaica in late 1843, La Trinitaria judged the moment ripe for revolt and on the morning of 28 February 1844, the inhabitants of Santo Domingo awoke to find themselves citizens of a new country.

Again the island was divided, but now between two independent republics. This division was more than geographical; already separated by a deep sense of distrust and antipathy, as the two nations entered into a lengthy period of instability and foreign interference, they were often to be the worst of neighbours. ❏

LEFT: Spanish Haiti applied to join Bolívar's federation.

Toussaint L'Ouverture

Paintings and engravings of the period show a dashing figure, usually on horseback, clad in Napoleonic military finery, a true leader of men. Other contemporaries described him as short, ugly and ill-shaped. In his lifetime, Toussaint L'Ouverture was idolised by worldwide progressive opinion as a heroic freedom fighter; when he died, writers such as William Wordsworth and Victor Hugo commemorated his achievements. But others detested him. Napoleon vowed to crush him, and he made many enemies among his own people.

Born a slave around 1742, François Dominique Toussaint Bréda was an unlikely revolutionary. Apparently of noble descent, he was singled out by his master for privileged treatment and another slave, his godfather, taught him to read. Toussaint rose to the trusted position of coachman on the Bréda plantation, near Cap Français, then livestock steward – a position normally held by a white.

But despite his status, Toussaint was receptive to the revolutionary mood growing among the slaves. When the insurrection broke out in 1791, he first protected his master's family and ensured their escape to Cap Français before joining the rebel armies. By now, he was almost 50 and known as "old Toussaint", but he was also widely respected for his learning and wisdom. His years as a senior foreman had given him leadership qualities, but what was more unexpected was his mastery of strategy and tactics.

Throughout the decade of constant unrest that followed, Toussaint transformed an ill-disciplined and ill-equipped rabble into a lethal fighting force. His men, he said, were "as naked as earthworms", but they became formidable exponents of guerrilla warfare, hiding in the mountains. His tactical instincts led him to join forces with the Spanish against the French, only to abandon them when the French republicans abolished slavery. He allowed an epidemic of yellow fever to take its toll on the British invasion force, patiently biding his time while the disease won the war. And he outmanoeuvred his rivals and enemies, earning the nickname *l'ouverture* after the opening or weak spot that he would inevitably find.

Gallant, courteous, even something of a ladies' man, Toussaint had weaknesses as well as strengths. He enjoyed power and authority and was quick to silence critics. As governor-general, he ruled with a firmness bordering on ruthlessness. The plantations resumed production, the former slaves returned to work, any hint of further revolutionary activity was suppressed. At the same time, Toussaint was conciliatory towards the remaining whites, too much so, said his more radical critics. When his nephew, Moïse, led an uprising in protest at the continuing exploitation of the black majority, Toussaint had him shot.

According to historian C.L.R. James, Toussaint finally lost touch with the revolutionary masses, the people whom he had so successfully led and

inspired. When Napoleon's intimidating force finally arrived in late 1801, James depicts Toussaint watching the fleet approach from a mountain peak. "We shall perish. All France is come to overwhelm us", he says. From that moment onwards, the formerly self-confident leader seemed crippled by indecision and in June 1802, he was seized and bundled on to a ship bound for France.

Within a year Toussaint L'Ouverture was dead, found slumped in his chair one morning in his freezing prison cell in the Fort-de-Joux in the Jura mountains. He had written several pleading letters to Napoleon, but never received a reply. "The Black Napoleon", wrote Chateaubriand sardonically, "imitated and killed by the White Napoleon." ❏

RIGHT: a portrait of the skilful Toussaint L'Ouverture.

THE AGE OF DICTATORS

On both sides of the border, political power remained in the hands of despots,

whose tyrannical rule was driven by ferocious self-interest

Bullets have long played a larger part in Haitian and Dominican politics than ballots. Elections in December 1990 were the first to be free and fair in almost two centuries of Haitian history. In the Dominican Republic, it took until 1962 for truly democratic voting to take place – only for the military to step in and overthrow the elected government. So, in both countries, democracy is a recent, and still fragile, commodity.

The roots of dictatorship lie partly in the two nations' transition to independence, a prize won by force of arms rather than negotiation. In both cases, military men were quick to grab the reins of government and the riches that went with political power. The result was chronic instability as electoral niceties went largely ignored. Throughout the 19th century and into the 20th, a succession of strong men or *caudillos* wrestled for control of the Dominican Republic, while in Haiti, only two out of 21 presidents between 1843 and 1915 managed to complete their terms in office. This volatile situation was worsened by the constant interference of foreign powers, a factor which was instrumental in creating two of the Caribbean's longest-lasting and most brutal dictators.

Years of chaos

The history of 19th-century Haiti is one of grinding poverty and perennial political turmoil. The crises that shook the country at regular intervals followed a pattern of sorts: an aspiring president would gather together a mercenary army, march on Port-au-Prince, the capital, and overthrow the existing government, only to be overthrown himself some months or years later.

The vast majority of Haitians knew little, and cared little, about such events, for the political intrigues of Port-au-Prince bore little relevance to their harsh lives, and to them all governments were synonymous only with taxation and

oppression. Occasionally, individual presidents made reforming gestures, but these were rare and usually short-lived. Some tyrannies were worse than others. The regime of Faustin Soulouque (1847–59), for instance, is remembered for its longevity and brutality. Ruling with the support of a paramilitary militia, the

zinglins, Soulouque had himself crowned Emperor Faustin I and twice tried to invade the Dominican Republic, in 1848 and 1859.

At the heart of Haiti's malaise was the old conflict between the mulatto minority and the black majority. Some 19th-century presidents were mulattos, but many more were blacks, mostly emerging from the black-dominated military. They often ruled under the watchful eye of the coloured power brokers, who made sure that no government threatened their monopoly on trade and other economic activities. However, most presidents were mainly interested in self-enrichment, with a complete disregard for the welfare of ordinary Haitians.

LEFT: Rafael Leonidas Trujillo Molina in 1955.

RIGHT: Faustin I and the Republic in the 1851 battle.

In the Dominican Republic, the situation was little better. After the idealistic leaders of La Trinitaria had been swiftly sidelined, the new nation was dominated by a handful of regional strongmen, backed by private armies. One such *caudillo*, Buenaventura Báez, had five terms in office between 1848 and 1878, specialising in extorting money from the country's tobacco-growers and, failing that, in printing money to meet government expenses.

As a result, the Dominican Republic – like

> ## No Thanks!
>
> Only a "no" vote by the Senate in Washington prevented the Dominican Republic from becoming part of the US in 1869, after the country was offered to President Ulysses S. Grant.

Haiti, with its vast compensation payment to France – suffered from rampant inflation and became increasingly indebted to foreign creditors, such as the French, Germans, British and Americans, who controlled an ever-growing slice of Haiti's coffee-exporting economy.

Spain steps in

Relations between Haiti and the Dominican Republic, meanwhile, were hardly cordial, especially during Soulouque's reign of terror, and this hostility led to one of the most extraordinary episodes in 19th-century Caribbean history.

The leaders of the Dominican Republic had long been interested in securing some sort of foreign protectorate over their territory in order to discourage Haitian expansionism, and Báez and his rival, Pedro Santana, approached France, Spain and the US with requests for annexation. In return, they offered the magnificent natural harbour at Samaná as a military and coaling installation. Finally, Spain agreed to re-annex the territory in what was the first and only voluntary process of re-colonisation in the Americas. In 1861, Spain declared the territory a protectorate.

But the arrangement was a disaster. As before, the Spanish ruled arrogantly and incompetently, discriminating against Dominicans and monopolising state jobs. A second independence war began in 1864, fought largely by black peasants who feared that the Spanish would re-introduce slavery, and by June 1865 the Spanish troops had left for Cuba.

American occupation

It took several more decades of economic chaos in Haiti and the Dominican Republic for the US to become directly involved. As the two countries sank deeper into debt, European powers, notably Germany, began to exert influence on their internal politics. Much of Haiti's coffee was shipped to Hamburg, as were many Dominican cigars, and this burgeoning trade encouraged a large German presence on the island. When German nationals were mistreated or debts were unpaid, Berlin was prepared to dispatch gunboats to seek redress, and Imperial Navy ships appeared in Haitian waters several times between 1897 and 1911. In the Dominican Republic, the unusually long-lasting dictator Ulises Heureaux (1882–99) even offered the Germans a coaling station at Samaná.

None of this was likely to please the Americans, who, since the Monroe Doctrine of 1823, had made it plain that European interference in the region was strictly unwelcome. Anxiously watching the political turmoil on both sides of Hispaniola, the US was determined not to let potentially hostile nations like Germany establish a toehold in the Caribbean. In the wake of Heureaux's assassination, the economic chaos deepened and in 1905 the Americans decided to take control of the Dominican customs (the only source of state revenue), first paying off debtors and then giving the rest to the Dominican government.

The outbreak of war in Europe and opening of the strategically vital Panama Canal in 1914 merely heightened US suspicions regarding Germany. And as Haiti slipped into near anarchy from 1911 onwards, Washington began to view the country as an unacceptable regional security risk. After President Guillaume Sam was murdered in Port-au-Prince, US Marines landed in July 1915. Almost a year later, US troops were disembarking in Santo Domingo to restore order and "protect American lives".

In the event, the Americans remained in the mantled, providing US exporters with captive markets. In the Dominican Republic, the antiquated sugar industry received a large injection of American investment.

If the political élite in Port-au-Prince and Santo Domingo were happy to collaborate in this "modernisation", the rural poor were not. Peasant guerrilla armies fought against the occupation forces in both countries and were gradually defeated by superior firepower.

The experience of US occupation, tainted by racism and human rights abuses, was instrumental in reinforcing nationalist feeling, especially in Haiti, where the occupation lasted

Dominican Republic for nine years, in Haiti until 1934. In that time they could point to certain achievements: an infrastructure was put in place, while primary health care improved.

Peasant backlash

But these were by no means humanitarian missions. The more direct motive was to turn the two countries into client states: suitable for US investment and politically friendly. As a result, land reforms enabled American corporations to displace peasant farmers, and tariffs were dis-

LEFT: Roosevelt and the US entered Dominican domestic politics. **ABOVE:** America later invaded.

longer and involved the humiliating imposition of forced labour upon peasant communities.

Papa Doc and the Chief

The Americans left behind them specially-trained military forces in both territories, intended to provide stability. In reality, they were breeding grounds for aspiring dictators, such as Rafael Leonidas Trujillo, an ex-petty criminal who rose through the ranks of the Dominican *Guardia Nacional* to take power in 1930. The first truly totalitarian dictator in the Caribbean, he ran the country as his private fiefdom for 30 years, seizing sugar estates and ranches for his own use. When an American journalist asked who owned a particularly fine bull, a startled farmhand replied, *"Es del Jefe"* (it's the Chief's). Murdering and torturing opponents, *El Jefe* was supported by the US, even when he ordered the massacre of some 15,000 Haitians in 1937 in a "cleansing" operation aimed at stemming immigration across the border. Not a modest man, he had Santo Domingo renamed Ciudad Trujillo and adopted such titles as "the Benefactor". If Trujillo provided a semblance of stability, it was

> ### PAPA DOC'S PRAYER
>
> "Our Doc, who art in the National Palace for life, hallowed be Thy name…Give us this day our new Haiti and forgive not the trespasses of those anti-patriots who daily spit upon our country."
>
> – *1960s Haitian school prayer*

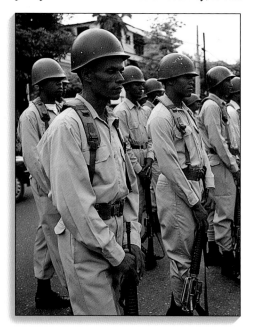

at the immense cost of tens of thousands of lives.

In Haiti, the departure of the Marines was soon followed by a resumption of hostilities between the coloured minority, who had done well out of the occupation, and the black majority. President followed president until in 1957 the military installed a myopic, softly-spoken country doctor called François Duvalier.

Yet "Papa Doc", as he was nicknamed, soon showed himself to be nobody's puppet. A militant advocate of African-descended culture and self-styled champion of the black masses, he capitalised on Haiti's resurgent mood of nationalism. Forming a loyal militia, the Tontons Macoutes *(see page 69)*, he reduced the power of the military and proclaimed himself president-for-life. The notorious Fort Dimanche prison was soon full of political prisoners, while thousands fled into exile. Under Papa Doc, Haiti became a byword for poverty and repression, a country memorably described by the novelist Graham Greene as the "nightmare republic".

But Papa Doc had his supporters, too, not least the new black middle class of government workers and political cronies. Before he died in 1971, he simply handed over power and the "family business" to his overweight and slow-witted son, Jean-Claude, better known as "Baby Doc".

Elusive democracy

The grotesque excesses of Trujillo came to an end in 1961 when the CIA and the Dominican military conspired to murder the ageing dictator, whose greed and violence had become an embarrassment. But hopes of a democratic new age were to be frustrated. After a series of short-lived interim governments, a popular social democrat, Juan Bosch, was elected in December 1962 in the nation's first free elections. He promised land reform and greater equality, quickly earning enemies among the armed forces and Church, and was overthrown after less than a year.

As pro-Bosch and anti-Bosch factions in the military looked set to engage in full-scale civil war and angry crowds demonstrated in Santo Domingo's slum districts, Washington feared "another Cuba". In 1965 the US Marines arrived once more to keep the warring sides apart and to make sure that a "safe" politician won subsequent elections. Joaquín Balaguer, formerly Trujillo's *confidant* and a man versed in political survival skills, was the chosen one.

For 35 years Balaguer dominated Dominican politics, winning elections in 1966, 1970, 1974, 1986, 1990 and 1994. In each case, allegations of fraud were rife and real democracy seemed as remote as ever. Even though a short economic boom, based on bauxite mining and tourism, brought some relief in the 1970s, a growing population faced poverty and exclusion in urban slums or backward rural communities.

By the mid-1980s, the regime of "Baby Doc" Duvalier was also at crisis point. Many who had supported Papa Doc saw his son as weak and incompetent as well as spectacularly corrupt. Mounting discontent shook the country in 1985, and in February 1986 Duvalier was flown into exile in France, leaving the army to take control of a ravaged and expectant country.

With the Duvaliers gone, the Haitian generals expected to fill the void as the country's real rulers. But popular pressure for real change made a military-dominated Haiti effectively ungovernable, and a series of juntas and civilian puppet presidents held ephemeral power during five turbulent years. Finally, however, free elections were held in December 1990 and

US-led military mission restored Aristide to the presidency. Alarmed by the prospect of massive Haitian migration to Florida, the Clinton Administration had no choice but to return the radical to power and unseat the generals.

As a result, the Haitian military was disbanded and political violence waned. And in 1996, Aristide was able to hand over power – for the first time in Haiti's history – to a democratically-elected successor. That same year the 89-year-old Balaguer was finally edged out of the Dominican hot seat by domestic and US pressure. A youthful Leonel Fernández took over, promising a fresh approach. ❑

were won overwhelmingly by Jean-Bertrand Aristide, a radical Catholic priest, whose *lavalas* (landslide) movement pledged to cleanse Haiti of its oppression and inequality. The army and the economic elite were horrified. As Aristide's rhetoric became more strident, in 1991 the armed forces moved in and sent "Titid" into exile.

What followed was one of Haiti's darkest periods, as a vicious junta, backed by terrorist gangs, held the country hostage, defying international opinion and victimising Aristide's supporters. It was not until October 1994 that a

LEFT: the military eventually turned against Trujillo.
ABOVE: Jean-Claude "Baby Doc" Duvalier.

WHATEVER HAPPENED TO BABY DOC?

On leaving Haiti in 1986, Baby Doc packed an estimated US$50 million to add to the fortune he had salted away in foreign bank accounts. He then retired to a palatial villa on the Côte d'Azur, in France. But his plans for a comfortable future were thwarted when his wife, Michèle, decamped with their lawyer and a large part of his wealth. Much of the rest was frozen in various accounts, as Haiti tried to recoup the embezzled funds.

Baby Doc had to move into a smaller house and, rumour had it, seek work as a gardener. In 1998, he bizarrely offered to return to Haiti to give the country leadership. After that, he disappeared from view.

TROPICAL ARCHITECTURE AND MONUMENTS

Hispaniola reveals the early influence of its settlers and colonists from the Amerindians to the Spanish, and from the Africans to the French

The religious icons displayed in the houses of worship in the Dominican Republic and Haiti reveal a fascinating blend of African and European culture. Catholic Spain and Latin America are important influences of the two countries, hence the richly decorated images of the Virgin Mary. Beautiful cathedrals made of stone are furnished in gold and gemstones, with works of art hanging on the walls, ceilings and altars.

FANCY FRETWORK

In Haiti a few examples of traditional gingerbread architecture survive. Named after the intricate designs of 16th century German pastry-makers, gingerbread style is based on elaborate wooden latticework. Originally hand-carved, it appeared as a decorative trim to the roofs and verandas of prosperous townhouses. The introduction of the mechanical fretsaw in the 1860s led to the mass production of designs. The fanciful trims, decorative balustrades, shutters and doors of the Oloffson Hotel in Port-au-Prince *(see pages 71 and 282)* are the most elaborate examples of a varied architectural landscape. The wide galleries wrap around the house. Built in the 1880s by a French architect, the hotel served as a hospital during the American occupation at the end of the 19th century.

▷ **ICON RESTORED**
Sculptures adorning the Catedral de Santa María la Menor in Santo Domingo were commissioned as part of a 1990 restoration.

△ **HOUSES ON THE SEA**
Land for building homes is precious in Haiti and therefore any open space such as this islet between the mainland and Île de la Gonâve could be appropriated overnight.

△ **VICTORIAN DESIGN**
The historical town of Puerto Plata is a good place to see Victorian and neoclassic buildings constructed from wood with cooling verandas.

△ **COLONIAL LEGACY**
Balconies with delicate iron fretwork add charm to the colonial style of Jacmel in the south of the DR and Cap Haïtien in the north of Haiti.

FROM CATHEDRAL TO COTTAGE

The Catedral de Santa María la Menor *(see page 183)* is believed to be the oldest cathedral in the Americas. It was built between 1514 and 1544 of gray limestone in an ornate architectural style and originally included sculptures of the apostles. The building was badly damaged during an attack by Sir Francis Drake in 1586 and it was not until 1990 that the beautiful house of worship was restored.

In the countryside many homes – most commonly in Haiti – still resemble those built by early settlers using techniques inherited from Africans and Indians. Farmers braid palm trunks covered with clay for walls and use palm fronds as thatch for roofs. Modern roofs are usually made of corrugated iron and steel.

▽ **DOOR DECORATION**
Brightly coloured and detailed decoration of the doorways which line the streets of Cap Haïtien in northern Haiti are some of that city's treasures.

△ **EUROPEAN STYLE**
Jacmel has a wonderful collection of European-inspired architecture, with walls made from stone and corrugated iron roofs.

▷ **COUNTRY COLOUR**
Even the most modest of country homes are adorned with fanciful trims and bright colours that are evocative of the Caribbean.

THE DOMINICAN REPUBLIC TODAY

*The future is looking brighter for Dominicans as the tourism industry
expands, but there are plenty of creases still to be ironed out*

Thirty-two kilometres (20 miles) southwest of Barahona on the Caribbean coast stands the rundown town of El Paraíso. Not quite paradise, the beach is littered with debris from the surrounding palm trees, while gangs of scruffy children search for "treasure" along the tide line. The multinational tourism industry, already evident in Barahona's new airport and hotel complex, has yet to arrive here. Back from the beach, a cluster of low-level apartment blocks, built in the 1970s and already slightly decrepit, are covered with fading insignia and slogans. "Balaguer again 1994–1998", says one, "Balaguer gave us these homes", proclaims another. All around the initials and symbols of the former president's Social Christian Reformist Party, the PRSC, are stencilled on to every home.

Personality politics

This everyday scene is testimony to the political system that has shaped the Dominican Republic and which was operated to perfection by the veteran Joaquín Balaguer. Homes for votes, jobs for votes, land for votes; the deal was straightforward. In return for electoral loyalty, Balaguer and his party machine handed out favours and distributed resources.

At countless ceremonies, the president personally handed land titles to grateful peasants or front door keys to those families who had been chosen to occupy new housing developments. *L'état, c'est moi* was Balaguer's guiding principle, as he controlled up to half of the national budget and sacked ministers at whim. The Dominican economy boomed briefly in the 1970s and fell into recession in the 1990s before recovering again in the 1990s. Balaguer controlled inflation, but the national debt, now estimated at nearly US$4 billion, rocketed as he spent millions on his pet projects.

It was this old-style personality politics that Leonel Fernández pledged to abolish when he

took power in 1996. After several controversial elections and three decades dominated by Balaguer, the country seemed ready for a fresh start. And yet, ironically, this new beginning was itself largely the work of Balaguer. Unable to stand in the 1996 elections he had urged his supporters to vote for Fernández. Fearful that

his old adversary, José Francisco Pena Gómez of the PRD, might at last take power, Balaguer cynically joined forces with Fernández in yet another manipulation of the system. Balaguer even managed to stand in the elections of May 2000, although he came third in the voting. The PRD, led by Hipólito Mejiá, finally returned to power after 14 years in opposition.

Party games

Party politics are an obsession, a matter of life and death in the Dominican Republic. Loyalties run deep, since electoral victory spells opportunity. When a party loses power, its supporters can expect to lose their government jobs, just as

---

PRECEDING PAGES: Punta Cana is a tourist magnet.
LEFT: Judith Egger, Coyamar hotel owner, Las Terrenas.
RIGHT: Joaquín Balaguer ruled with an iron fist.

the winning party rewards its rank and file. Members of the three main parties have fought lethal battles in the past, not just against one another but among themselves. The country seems to be in the grip of a permanent electoral campaign. No sooner has a presidential election been settled than congressional campaigning begins. At the same time, the parties look forward to the next presidential contest, starting the drawn-out and usually bitter process of selecting their candidate. Almost every wall and lamppost in the country is festooned with posters, streamers and slogans from the last election, soon to be covered with those for the next.

Juan Bosch was suffering from Alzheimer's disease. That same year, the PRD's Pena Gómez was the target of an intense racist campaign, suggesting that as a black Dominican of Haitian ancestry he was conspiring to allow Haiti to take over the country. Ominous television commercials, featuring frenetic drumming and vaudou ceremonies, were intended to alert voters to the supposed threat from across the border.

When not engaged in character assassination, politicians are just as likely to enter into the most unlikely and opportunistic alliances. The three-party structure means that there is constant strategic manoeuvring between those in

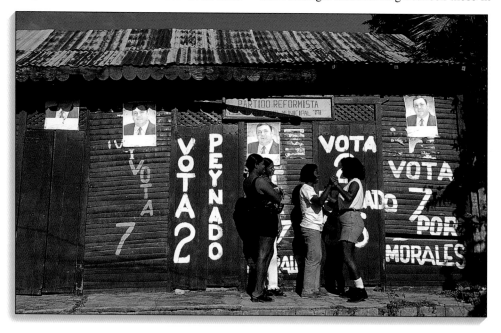

From the early days of independence, politicians have been expected to be charismatic and hard-hitting. Some, like Balaguer and Juan Bosch, ran their parties as vehicles for their own ambitions, establishing a sort of personality cult. *"Lo que diga Balaguer"* ("Whatever Balaguer says") was a PRSC slogan in the 1990s, emphasising the party's unconditional loyalty to *El Jefe*. When Juan Bosch left the PRD in the 1970s to form a new, more radical, organisation, a fierce battle broke out over his succession – even resorting to shoot-outs.

Dirty tricks are part and parcel of the Dominican political scene. In 1994 a bogus medical report was leaked to the media, suggesting that

and out of power. A familiar tactic is the congressional boycott, in which a president such as Fernández finds himself confronted by a hostile and obstructive majority in the two chambers of Congress. Under these circumstances, presidents find it hard to pass the smallest item of legislation, and quickly become unpopular.

Privatisation and corruption

One of the most obvious legacies of the Trujillo dictatorship is the extent of the state sector. The *Generalísimo* literally owned most of the country, and when he was murdered, his land, business interests and assets passed to the state. This centralisation of economic power proved very useful to politicians such as Balaguer, who could fill the boards of the sugar or electricity companies with cronies, and provide unskilled jobs for party stalwarts. But most state corporations were spectacularly unprofitable, draining the government's coffers.

If Balaguer resisted calls to privatise the key industries (sugar, electricity, banking, insurance), Fernández seemed more receptive to the idea of modernising the economy and divesting the state of some of its biggest loss-makers. Here, however, he faced the wrath of the opposition majority in Congress, who claimed that he was selling the national patrimony for short-term gain. As a result, progress in privatisation has been painfully slow.

The existence of a huge state sector, however bankrupt, has also been an irresistible magnet for the country's less honest politicians and businessmen. Hand-outs and kickbacks proliferate at every level of Dominican society, from multi-million dollar frauds to bribe-taking police officers. And the military establishment has been persistently accused of involvement in the lucrative drug transhipment business, enabling South American cocaine to reach the US via Dominican ports and airfields.

From plantation to vacation

Despite the vested interests of the old-style politicians, the Republic's economy has undergone a revolutionary transformation since the 1960s. Then, the country was almost entirely dependent on sugar exports, with a tiny manufacturing sector and very little tourism. Today, the canefields are rapidly giving way to golf courses and hotel complexes, while purpose-built factories have sprouted around Santo Domingo and other towns. Once-deserted idylls like the Samaná Peninsula or Punta Cana now welcome tens of thousands of visitors each year.

Agriculture still has a role in the Dominican economy, especially the deluxe cigar industry, which brings in annual sales exceeding US$400 million. The country also has important gold deposits (as Columbus guessed) and is a major

NO QUALMS...

President Fernández discovered that Balaguer's associates had been selling land destined for small farmers under an agrarian land reform project to developers for tourist complexes.

exporter of ferronickel. But the biggest money-spinner is tourism, accounting for revenue of US$2 billion or more each year and employing more than 150,000 people. The Republic averages over 2½ million arrivals. Most go to the large all-inclusive resorts, operated by multinational chains, but many are beginning to see the attraction of the scattering of smaller, independent hotels.

The tourist invasion has changed the face of the country, particularly the north coast around Puerto Plata where inten-

sive development has brought ecological and social problems in its wake. Tourists complain of over-persistent hustling and mounting crime, while some Dominicans are unhappy about the way in which hotels monopolise land and scarce water. But the benefits in terms of employment and income are so obvious that critics are in a small minority.

More controversial has been the spread of "industrial free zones" – manufacturing plants set up to assemble goods for the North American market. Since the 1970s, Dominican governments have encouraged foreign companies to establish factories, offering tax concessions and a supply of extremely cheap labour.

LEFT: political dissent around Lago Enriquillo.
RIGHT: local news.

Conditions in the zones are often harsh, but workers and managers alike are aware that other countries, such as Haiti and Mexico, also attract investors with low wages. In the late 1990s the export manufacturing sector produced goods worth US$3 billion annually, but most of this was taken as profits by the foreign corporations.

Pastures abroad

Walking the streets of New York's Washington Heights district, you could believe yourself to

be in Santo Domingo – apart from the climate. Dominican restaurants offer chicken, rice and ice-cold Presidente beer; *merengue* music blares from shop fronts, postal agencies guarantee next-day delivery of money transfers anywhere in the Republic – the regular influx of US dollars is a lifeline for many families.

About a million Dominicans live in America, mostly in and around New York, and they send an estimated US$1.4 billion home each year. They are now the second largest immigrant community – after Mexicans – and the fastest growing. Most are legally there, engaged in conventional, if often ill-paid, jobs, but a small minority has earned the majority an

---

CHEAP LABOUR

For as little as US$20 a week, a largely female workforce assembles clothing and electrical goods for North American and Asian companies who take the profits.

---

undeserved reputation for lawlessness. Drug-dealing and other criminal activity is part of the expatriate scene, but only a part. Many are there for educational and professional reasons: Leonel Fernández himself was brought up and educated in New York.

Dominicans are prepared to take huge risks to reach the promised land if official channels are closed. Queues for US visas are endless, so some prefer to board the rickety boats that ply the shark-infested Mona Passage between the Republic and Puerto Rico, from where they furtively make their way to the US mainland. Many die in the process. The sight of wealthy returning Dominicans, sometimes enviously known as *Dominicanyorks*, inspires more young people to take the gamble.

Caribbean role

The Dominican Republic has often seemed contradictory in its regional identity, sometimes slavishly pro-American, sometimes stridently nationalistic. Its animosity towards neighbouring Haiti is all too well known, but it has not enjoyed easy relations with other Caribbean nations, identifying more with other Hispanic states in Central and South America.

For many years, the English-speaking Caribbean distrusted the Republic, suspicious of its volatile politics and separated by language and culture. But the widespread fear of economic marginalisation in the region has prompted better relations as leaders across the region see the future increasingly in terms of cooperation and a common market. In 1998 President Fernández signed a landmark trade agreement with members of the Caribbean Community (CARICOM) promoting free trade and investment in the region.

The Republic looks towards Europe and the US for trade and aid. As a member of the Africa-Caribbean-Pacific group of developing countries, it is entitled to special treatment from the European Union, and also enjoys preferential trade status from the US. The potential for economic success is there; the problem, as Dominicans will tell you, is the politicians. ❑

LEFT: Punta Cana resorts provide entertainment.
RIGHT: a touch of luxurious living on the beach at Arena Gorda on the Costa del Coco.

MODERN HAITI

Although the overthrow of the military and the restoration of constitutional order

opened up political freedom, social conditions have been slow to improve

Dozens of US helicopter blades beat away the last of the darkness, as the sun began to make its way in the sky above Port-au-Prince on 19 September 1994. The helicopters circled the white presidential palace and the army's mustard-coloured headquarters as a delegation of American officials, headed by the former US president Jimmy Carter and including General Colin Powell, shuttled between the two buildings, trying to squeeze an agreement from Haiti's military men to leave peacefully, and allow the country's democratically elected president, Jean-Bertrand Aristide, to return.

Three years earlier, the Haitian militia backed by the rich upper echelons of society and led by General Raoul Cédras had staged a coup that sent Aristide into exile in America. They said they did not trust the former priest's "liberation theology" brand of politics.

Punishing economic sanctions by America did not destabilise the new government, as Haitians, particularly the military, earned small fortunes running food supplies, fuel and other goods through the Dominican Republic. A right-wing militia called FRAPH was doing the military's bidding, hacking Aristide's supporters into silence. Tensions were high. Every day, radio stations were reporting another mass grave on the Route Nationale 1 to the north.

Not one shot was fired

After three years, the Americans had lost patience. More and more Haitians were fleeing to the US, mostly illegally in boats that were barely seaworthy. They wanted Aristide – who had been living in exile in Washington – returned to power. They told the Haitian military to put an end to the theatrics. They were bringing the helicopters full of troops to back them up.

Following a three-week transition, during which time 20,000 US troops arrived and no

shots were fired, Aristide returned to Port-au-Prince in October to gigantic street celebrations. And it was the military leaders' turn to flee into exile – Cédras went to Panama, where he still lives in relative comfort. The chief of police, renowned for his brutality, is now in Honduras, which has refused several requests to

extradite him. Others are scattered about in Florida, New York and elsewhere.

They did not leave Aristide a country in great shape. Foreign businesses that had taken advantage of Haiti's cheap labour, particularly the fabric assembly industry and baseball makers, had all left during the embargo. More than 40,000 people had lost their jobs, shooting the unemployment rate to catastrophic heights. The few paved roads had become deeply rutted, and tourism, once a major source of revenue, was dead. What the junta had left Aristide was a broken toilet in the president's office, along with a heap of social ills.

One of the agreements with the Americans

PRECEDING PAGES: baby's baptism is an important day.
LEFT: the locals travel by brightly-coloured *tap-tap*.
RIGHT: the army continues to be a powerful force.

was that Aristide would only serve a year as president – the remainder of his term. To eliminate the threat of long dictatorships, the constitution of 1987 had been changed so that no president could serve more than one five-year term at a time. So in early 1996, Aristide handed over the presidency to his democratically elected former prime minister René Préval. Haitians say Préval and Aristide were *marassa,* Creole for twins, and critics say that Aristide remained behind the scenes pulling Préval's strings.

THE CREOLE PIG

Until the early 1980s, Haiti had 1.7 million indigenous Creole pigs, but due to an outbreak of swine fever, every one of them was killed and a whole breed was wiped out.

Catholic radio station, Radio Soleil, and by February 1986, Baby Doc had lost the support of his army and the United States. On 7 February, an American plane landed at the Port-au-Prince airport, and for several hours, truckloads of Louis Vuitton suitcases were taken from the presidential palace to the plane. Later that morning, Jean-Claude, his wife Michèle, his mother and other family members were taken to exile in France *(see page 51)*.

The next day, and for several weeks after-

High hopes with Baby Doc

During Jean-Claude Duvalier's dictatorship (1971–86), Haitian hopes had run high as he courted international aid by easing repression. As a result, foreign businesses started to establish factories in the country, creating more jobs. But the economy took another dive in the early 1980s after Baby Doc's extravagant US$7 million wedding to a high society mulatto woman which lost him a large chunk of support from the black middle classes.

So the Tonton Macoutes, the freewheeling thugs his father had set up, were put back into top gear. Tourism went into decline, civilian unrest escalated, egged on by the Roman

wards, a mixture of happiness and chaos pervaded the capital. Truckloads of revellers waving tree branches as a symbol of peace crossed the streets of the capital. In the alleys, however, it was time for revenge, and the targets were the Macoutes who had been left powerless.

The irony was that Jean-Claude's father, François "Papa Doc" Duvalier had stood above the crowd as one of the most respected men of his generation. He had been elected in 1957, taking over the presidency from an army colonel named Paul Magloire, who had installed himself as president without a vote. Civil liberties had been eliminated and arbitrary arrests had been on the increase.

Papa Doc's regime

Duvalier was a country doctor and a poet whose popularity had been increasing among the masses. A black man in a country ruled by a light-skinned elite who spoke French, this quiet-spoken man set out to shift the balance of power. His model was Toussaint L'Ouverture, who fought the revolution so that blacks like himself could govern themselves.

He painted himself as a descendant of those slaves who nearly 200 years before took an oath in a clearing at Bois Caiman to end the white man's cruelty and slavery on the island. He believed that the same spirit that fuelled the

see his "Duvalierist Revolution" take root.

After several coup attempts, Duvalier tightened the noose on his critics, declaring himself an "authentic leader of the Third World". His goal, he said, was to fight against social inequities and encourage Haitians to believe in themselves. It didn't take long for him to shift his programme into gear. By 1958, he had invalidated the regular army by creating the Volontaires de la Securite Nationale (VSN), better known as the Tontons Macoutes (see below) – a force that would respond only to him. He no longer trusted the light-skinned army officers who were still loyal to Magloire.

slaves to revolt would push Haitians to remake their country. In telling his own story later on, images of his face were superimposed on a map of Africa. Americans, he said then, had pilfered the country during the occupation from 1915 to 1934. Later, he would establish an on-off relationship with Washington, as the Americans were playing a tug of war with Moscow over Cuba. Duvalier made his people believe that the US were about to invade Haiti, and warned them away from anyone who did not want to

LEFT: a mural celebrates Aristide's return in 1994.
ABOVE: Haitian people feared the Tontons Macoutes' but dreamed of rising against them.

PAPA DOC'S HENCHMEN

François Duvalier was determined not to be the puppet of the military élite and created his own private armed group to protect his position. They took the name Tontons Macoutes from a character in Haitian folklore who carries off "bad" children in his "macoute", the Creole word for a bag made of palm leaves. They wore denim shirts and pants with a red bandanna, and at first they could be seen with a machete tucked into their belt. Then they began to carry guns.

Fiercely loyal to Duvalier, the Tontons soon did away with the denim uniforms and became the stereotype henchmen in shades portrayed by Graham Greene.

Mulatto power

Only about 5 percent of Haiti's nearly 8 million people were mulattoes (people of mixed black and white ancestry). But these light-skinned people controlled politics through the army and the economy, and set the intellectual and social calendar for the country. They had their own clubs, which were closed to blacks and their children were trained in France as doctors or lawyers. They controlled the debates as well, as they mostly spoke French, while everyone

> ### COUP ATTEMPTS
>
> There were nine attempts on Papa Doc's regime, the last being by a coastguard officer in 1970, the year before he died. All rebellions were quickly put down.

was the beginning of another dark period in Haiti's history. All civil rights were revoked; family members became suspicious of each other; open critics of the regime were beaten up, imprisoned or killed. The British writer Graham Greene *(see page 128)* expertly captured the country's mood in his 1966 novel *The Comedians*, in which an idealistic young doctor who complains about the brutality of the Macoutes is gunned down in the pool of the Hotel Oloffson.

Duvalier set out to usher Haiti into the

else spoke Creole. Duvalier, a *noiriste*, wanted to reduce their power substantially and started by attacking the Church, a heavyweight in the balance of Haitian politics. He demanded, and the Vatican ceded, that the European clergy in Haiti be replaced by a black archbishop and three black bishops. Duvalier's partisans defined Duvalierism as the end of privileges for a minority class that was exploiting the masses and the middle class.

On the streets, they said that Papa Doc had re-edited the 1804 revolution. He declared himself Haiti's eighth president for life, promising to bring changes to workers and farmers, with the Tontons Macoutes as his private army. It

modern age, promising a new airport and port, and a dam that would bring electricity to the countryside. Symbols were equally important to him, and he commissioned a large statue to the unknown slave and had it placed opposite the palace.

Failed promises

Some of his promises for a better life came true, but failures littered the landscape. One of them was a city for workers outside the capital that he aptly named Duvalierville, which has fallen into disrepair.

Haitians' hopes were deflated. He closed ports throughout the country, routing all traffic through the capital. He centralised all aspects of Haitian life, leaving the smaller towns to their own devices. Companies closed as nepotism ruled. The only people who could get jobs in government were related to someone in the Tontons Macoutes.

The brain drain

That period saw one of the greatest migrations of Haitians overseas. Intellectuals, teachers, engineers, accountants and others began to flee to the newly independent French-speaking countries

AWAY FROM IT ALL

Around 1½ million Haitians live abroad – mainly in Florida, New York, Boston and Montreal – and send more than US$300 million a year to their families at home.

islands, less than 80 km (50 miles) from the Florida coast in some parts, would become the launching point for the Haitians who would later settle in Florida, whose tropical climate and strong economy makes it a popular choice.

Bachelor prince

The only fact Haitians knew about Jean-Claude, when his father, on his death bed in 1971, bestowed upon him the role of president-for-life, was that he drove fast cars and owned a stable of European sports machines in the

in Africa, or to Canada. A few left for France, too. As work dried up further, and the grip of the Tontons Macoutes on the country got tighter, middle-class Haitians began to head to New York, Chicago and Boston, where they have settled in large communities.

That flow of Haitians to other shores continues at both ends of the spectrum. Throughout the 1970s and beyond, poorer Haitians went to the Bahamas, where they found work in the hospitality and construction industries. Those

palace. Baby Doc was the 19-year-old bachelor prince, with his father's private army of volunteer thugs still the power behind the presidency.

His administration brought some breathing room for Haitians, with foreign companies that manufactured baseballs and clothing coming to Haiti to take advantage of the country's cheap labour rates. Life was getting better, especially for the middle class. The diaspora was travelling to the homeland, bringing money and goods. They seemed to be willing to forgive the past, albeit grudgingly.

All that turned sour when Jean-Claude took a mulatto, light-skinned wife who, along with her family, became an icon of rapaciousness in a

LEFT: on parade at Fort Dimanche, Port-au-Prince.
ABOVE: Hotel Oloffson, Port-au-Prince.
ABOVE RIGHT: statue of the *Le Marron Inconnu* .

country known as one of the poorest in the Western Hemisphere. Haitians began to take notice of her shopping trips overseas, which they considered obscene. She appeared to be Haiti's Marie Antoinette and Imelda Marcos rolled into one.

And Michèle was not the only one in her family to profit from her elevated position. Her father, well-known business-man Ernst Bennett, became the sole distributor in Haiti for cars and agricultural goods, amassing a fortune.

BIG SPENDER

It is said that Baby Doc's wife, Michèle, would hold parties in the palace, turning up the air conditioning to its coldest so that she and her friends could wear their fur coats.

named Henri Namphy. He became head of the Government, tried to disband the remaining Macoutes and failed. Several other military personnel followed, but with equally poor results. A consti-tution adopted in 1987 provided for presidential and national assembly elections by the peo-ple, but the Government still tried to shift control to the army.

Presidential elections that were going to be held on 29 November that year had to be cancelled after a massacre by right-wing militias of more

The outspoken priest

Haitians kept their grumbling pretty low, going with the flow. But one person who could not keep quiet was Aristide, a young priest who began to win a loyal following among the poor for his candour and courage in the pulpit. He spoke about children dying of malnutrition, half the population still without access to education, clean water and decent roads, endemic poverty, and he railed against corruption. Public demon-strations at the time were violently crushed, until finally, in 1986, the pressure that had been bottling up for 40 years erupted and forced Baby Doc into exile.

The first to fill the void was an army general

than 30 voters at a polling station. In January 1988, new elections were held and a civilian president took power.

But not for long. Namphy grabbed his posi-tion back in June, only to be ousted three months later by officers of Haiti's Presidential Guard. While Namphy was in power, it is believed that cocaine worth around US$700 million was processed through Haiti each month, of which many senior officers reaped the benefits.

Prosper Avril, a Duvalierist general, then declared himself president and began to rule as a dictator, until March 1990 when, as protests and violence shook the country anew, he fled the country. And in December 1991, Haitians elected Aristide ("Titid") when he stood for the presidency at the last minute, giving him a landslide victory.

Aristide in exile

After Aristide was overthrown in September 1991, the Organisation of American States (OAS), an association of North and South American nations, led a trade boycott against Haiti designed to force Aristide's return to power. And the United Nations followed with its own boycott. It was important that he be returned to stop the flood of refugees arriving in America, which was causing an embarrassment to the US government.

Eventually, on 3 July 1993, Cédras, the military leader, agreed to allow Aristide to return to office and restore a democratic government by 30 October. But he failed to carry out the agreement and barred Aristide from returning, despite demands from the UN and the United States. In September 1994, the US began sending troops to Haiti to enforce the agreement and Cédras caved in. A combination of 500 US and UN soldiers remained in Haiti after Aristide returned, to help keep order and rebuild the country's infrastructure. At the end of 1995, René Préval, a member of Aristide's Lavalas coalition, was democratically elected president.

An anarchic society

Between the end of 1999 and March 2000, the peace-keeping forces finally left their base beside Haiti's international airport, terminating a presence that has bitterly divided Haitians. The troops had worked in healthcare and construction projects while they were there, but although some say they provided a stabilising presence in a still unstable nation, others say the invasion did little for the country, as Haitians were still poorer, hungrier, less literate and still getting shot down in the streets.

As Max Cherie, an unemployed mechanic, said, "When they came, we thought things would get a little better. Instead, people are still being killed all the time. Maybe they built a couple of schools, but I think considering all the people who are dying, they could help us more with security. People can't walk safely to

go to market, you can't have five cents on you, you can't carry a watch, can't have nice clothes, or the thieves will rip them off."

The 6,100-strong Haitian National Police force has been receiving training from UN civilian police trainers for more than four years, but few consider the force capable of combating crime. Tainted by drug scandals and human rights abuse, it has been caught within a power struggle by political parties vying for its control. Since April 1999, groups close to Aristide's Fanmi Lavalas have set up barricades of burning tyres in numerous street protests calling for the resignation of Secretary of State for

THE BOAT PEOPLE

Haitians took to small boats and left in their thousands in 1994 soon after the military takeover that sent Aristide to exile. Heading for Florida, they were fleeing repression, no prospect of jobs, and land that could no longer produce food. The US Coastguard picked up as many as 30,000 people from the sea that year and held them at the Guantanamo Bay naval base in Cuba. Others died due to their flimsy craft.

At first, the refugees were sent back to Haiti, but later many were resettled in Florida. Today, Haitians are still trying to escape hardship – 400 tried to sneak into Miami in one boat at the end of 1999 under cover of Millennium Eve.

LEFT: view from fisherman's wharf in Port-au-Prince.
RIGHT: a political mural criticises foreign intervention.

Public Security Robert Manuel and Police Director Pierre Denize.

In May 1999, police shot 11 detainees in Carrefour-Feuilles, a neighbourhood south of the city centre. A former Port-au-Prince Police Commissioner and several other officers were arrested in connection with the killings. Haiti's justice system is in shambles, prison escapes are common, and fair trials rare.

New political parties

The overthrow of the military and the restoration of constitutional order, however, did open up political freedom in Haiti. More than 60

legal political parties sprang up almost overnight and countless other parties are not registered. But intimidation remains a troubling aspect. On 1 March 1999, Senator Jean-Yvon Toussaint of the Organisation of People in Struggle party (OPL) was gunned down outside his house. In the April, three OPL lawmakers sought asylum in the Chilean embassy before fleeing Haiti for the US and Canada.

In September 1999, gunmen fired shots at OPL's Secretary General Sauveur Pierre-Etienne, in an assassination attempt believed to be meant for its party leader Gerard Pierre-Charles. "It is very hard to say that right now Haiti is on a more positive path than it was on the first day of the US invasion," Michel-Rolph Trouillot, professor of anthropology at the University of Chicago, said not long afterwards.

US Ambassador Timothy Michael Carney admitted Haiti was not the success story that most in the world had hoped for. "Haiti has not met the unrealistic expectations of the international community since 1994," he explained. "The modest advances in the economy, the real, but still fragile improvements in the police force, and the spotty record in the transition toward democracy reflect Haiti's history and political style."

Deep parliamentary divisions

For much of Préval's presidency Haiti has been embroiled in a political crisis that led to the resignation of his prime minister in 1997, and the near total shut-down of Parliament in 1999. The deep division was caused by Préval's prioritisation of the International Monetary Fund's (IMF) structural adjustment programme, or "Paris Plan", which Aristide had reluctantly agreed to, to facilitate his return, but had subsequently opposed.

The plan included the privatisation of nine state-owned companies. The flour mill and cement company have already been privatised, and the seaports are also to be sold. But the Government has not made any noticeable headway in improving social conditions. Instead, Haiti's annual per capita income has sunk to US$250. Illiteracy is over 70 percent, and unemployment remains between 60 and 70 percent.

"I think that the presence of US troops in Haiti saved lives, but served as a short-term solution to allow Haitian politicians to forget about long-term solutions," Trouillot said. "Some of the problems that were there in 1994–95 have now been exacerbated."

As Haiti prepared for legislative and municipal elections at the end of 2000, there were fears of an escalation of political violence and an inappropriate Government response to it. But Aristide remained the most popular politician in the country, and was expected to become Haiti's first new president in the 21st century. He said so himself in a recorded message to his Lavalas party, who were set to take control of parliament if he won the 2000 elections. ❑

LEFT: market politics.
RIGHT: Haiti relies heavily on agriculture to survive.

PEOPLE

*Despite the many cultural and racial divisions between ordinary Haitians and
Dominicans, they share a common heritage in their African-inspired beliefs*

Although the Dominican Republic and Haiti share the same land – the island of Hispaniola – their peoples are markedly disparate. The differences are displayed in the language, the physical features – more importantly race – and most of all in the culture. The historical influence of the Spanish and the more recent North American influx has shaped the Dominican Republic, while France – and to a greater degree Africa – has influenced Haiti.

The last "pure" native Taíno in Hispaniola probably died before the end of the 16th century, but today many Dominicans still like to classify themselves as *indio* or "Indian". This might seem like nothing more than a quaint and harmless affectation, but it points to a more serious issue in the country's collective psychology – that of race and colour. The problem is that the vast majority of Dominicans are of at least part African descent, and many are quite obviously black. But in Haiti, more than 90 percent of the population is black, and ancestral suspicions of the neighbouring state mean that blackness tends to be equated with all things Haitian, and hence disparaged.

In the Dominican Republic, "good" hair is straight hair, "regular" features are European ones. Women spend hours straightening their hair and trying to lighten their skin, since the country's popular culture values non-African looks and promotes an image of light-skinned beauty. TV commercials and advertisements depict almost exclusively pale-skinned models, while black people are normally portrayed in menial roles. A whole vocabulary exists to describe skin colour and ethnic identity in this most race-conscious of countries: most desirable is to be *blanco* (white), followed by *trigueno* (olive-skinned). Further down the social hierarchy come *mulatos* (mixed white-African) and *morenos* (meaning dark or

swarthy), and at the bottom is *negro*, sometimes used affectionately but more often than not as a mark of disapproval or even as an insult.

Hence the term *indio*: historically absurd, but revealing in the way that it provides a non-African racial category for coloured people. Many Dominican identity cards describe their

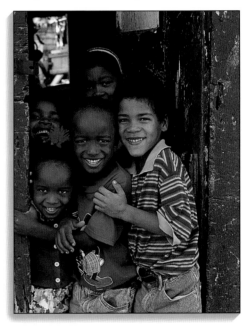

bearers as Indians, colour-coded as *oscuro* (dark), *quemado* (burnt), *canelo* (cinnamon) or *lavado* (washed). The important thing, irrespective of colour, is not to be African, and by extension, Haitian. Consequently, Dominicans have looked back into the country's past to find a cultural identity that explains their colour but denies an African heritage. Many Dominicans would deny any prejudices, but attitudes are deep-rooted, particularly towards the nation next door.

Us and them

More than a range of mountains separates the Republic from Haiti. The frontier is largely a psychological and cultural one, in which most

PRECEDING PAGES: a little Haitian girl with clever hair decoration; an old lady watches the world go by.
LEFT: selling oysters in Puerto Plata.
RIGHT: welcome to San Pedro de Macorís.

Dominicans tend to view Haitians as everything that they are not – and do not want to be. The official ideology suggests that the Dominican Republic is an Hispanic, Catholic nation, European in composition and Western in outlook. Haiti, on the other hand, is considered to be African, Creole-speaking and Vaudou-worshipping, with an alien set of cultural values. As a result, Dominicans have been taught to see their neighbours as potential invaders, who pose the threat of diluting the Republic's identity. This perception often borders on a sort of racist paranoia, in which Haitians are portrayed as being inferior, barbarous and biologically dangerous.

used to specialise in rounding up "illegal" (and often legal) Haitian migrants and expelling them in times of political tension. In theory, anyone born in the Republic is entitled to Dominican citizenship, but children of Haitian ancestry have often been expelled and sometimes separated from their parents. Haitians have few rights and face constant harassment, yet thousands are prepared to take their chance across the border each year since any kind of work, however badly paid, is preferable to the unemployment and hunger at home.

The 1937 massacre of 15,000 Haitians by President Trujillo's *Guardia Nacional* was the

Take, for instance, the best-selling *La Isla al Revés* (The Upside Down Island), written by Joaquín Balaguer during his eight years out of office and published in 1983: "The Black... left to his own instincts and without the restraints which higher living standards impose in all countries on reproduction, multiplies nearly as rapidly as plants."

Racism of this sort has fuelled a long history of violent discrimination and exploitation. About half a million Haitians are thought to live in the Republic, mostly employed in low-wage agricultural jobs or in the informal sector, but they are vulnerable to abuses, including arbitrary arrests and deportations. Balaguer

worst episode in this dark history, but injustices continue. Many Haitians are still confined to ramshackle and insanitary barracks (*bateyes*) in the sugar-producing areas, where they carry out back-breaking work for as little as $5 a day. International human rights organisations have long criticised the Dominican authorities for tolerating this exploitation, but reforms have been slow in coming.

Migrant nation

Although present-day Dominicans may like to romanticise a long-gone indigenous heritage, in reality most of the country's 8 million people are descended from later arrivals, most notably

Spanish and Africans, but also some other, smaller groups of incomers. The first Spanish settlers were hardly numerous, and many were only too eager to abandon the colony for greener pastures elsewhere. It was only at the end of the 18th century that the colony's population stabilised, helped by a large influx of immigrants from the Canary Islands. Subsequent European migration came in fits and starts, encouraged by government efforts to "whiten" the population; some Spaniards stayed after the

RACIAL CENSUS

Some 15 percent of Dominicans regard themselves as black in official census forms (the same percentage define themselves as white, while the great majority are of mixed race).

forced many landowners to let their slaves go free as they simply could not afford to feed them. By the end of the 18th century, some 30 percent of the population officially comprised of slaves, with many more blacks classified as free citizens. The 22-year occupation of the territory by Haiti inevitably added to the black population, as large numbers of Haitians married and stayed across the border. More recently, migrant cane-cutters from the smaller English-speaking Caribbean islands of St Kitts, Nevis

brief recolonisation of 1861–65; a significant Italian community began to arrive from the 1870s onwards; and a small, but conspicuous mix of Europeans settled in the 20th century, some escaping persecution by Nazi Germany.

The black population has always been small compared to Haiti's, yet despite Dominican delusions of racial superiority, people of African descent have been present in large numbers since the mid-1550s. But whereas French Saint Domingue owed its prosperity to half a million black slaves, Spanish Santo Domingo's poverty

LEFT: a family in Las Salinas.
ABOVE: friends.

and Anguilla came in the early 20th century to work on plantations around La Romana. Traces of an English dialect and distinctive musical forms left behind by these *cocolos* can still be heard around San Pedro de Macorís.

Immigrant impact

Several small migrant communities have made a significant impact on Dominican society. From the late 19th century a substantial group of Syrians and Palestinians, commonly known as *turcos*, established themselves as traders in Santo Domingo and the main towns. Mostly Maronite Christians, they rapidly earned a reputation as shrewd business operators, and several family names – Majluta, Wessín y Wessín, Isa Conde – now have strong political connections. A Jewish community has also contributed to Dominican life – firstly the Sephardic Jews who settled in the early colonial period, and more recently refugees from Hitler's Germany who put down roots in the northern town of Sosúa. But perhaps the oddest experiment in immigration policy involved some Japanese farmers brought over by Trujillo in the 1930s to populate the territory adjacent to Haiti. This

banks of the River Ozama, visible from Santo Domingo's main bridges, and face the constant threat of flood. Tiny huts of wood and corrugated iron are crammed together without sanitary facilities or services of any sort. It is here that crime, often drug-related, reaches epidemic proportions.

Yet in the past few decades literally hundreds of thousands of Dominicans have willingly moved into slum areas in the capital, leaving behind a life of poverty and boredom in the countryside. Outside the large export-orientated

> ### CITY OF CONTRASTS
>
> In Santo Domingo, the wealthy live in the northern suburbs, the middle classes share the city centre, and the poorest inhabitants have been forced out towards the edges.

attempt to create a *cordon sanitaire* around the border failed due to government neglect, and the disgruntled Japanese soon moved on.

Haves and have nots

A few residential districts of Santo Domingo or Santiago rival the plushest suburbs of Florida or California. TV satellite dishes and swimming pools can be glimpsed behind high walls, while armed guards and trained dogs protect lavish mansions. But just a few miles away, in areas like La Ciénaga (the Swamp) or Capotillo, are some of the Caribbean's worst shanty towns, where poverty, crime and disease are all too common. Some of these slums cling to the

farms producing bananas or pineapples on an industrial scale, agriculture is neither profitable nor sustainable. Young people, in particular, are not prepared to accept a life of rural drudgery. For them, the move to the city is a search for employment and excitement, and perhaps a first step towards their dream of life in the US.

Average per capita income in the Republic is about $1,600 per year (compared to under $500 in Haiti), but this average conceals a sharp difference between the wealthy top 10 percent, who account for 40 percent of income, and the bottom 10 percent – who receive less than 2 percent. The rich are a mix of old and new. "Old money" takes the form of ranching, sugar and tobacco interests, controlled by traditional light-skinned families, some of whom can trace their lineage back to the *conquistadores*. These are mostly the lucky ones, who avoided expropriation by the insatiable Trujillo clan. "New money", on the other hand, is more likely to derive from tourism, the new manufacturing sector and the sometimes dubious activities of Dominicans in the United States. Needless to say, the old élite despises the *nouveaux riches*, who are not welcome in traditional upper-class establishments like the Country Club.

For the majority of Dominicans, education and migration offer the only escape routes out

Visa for a dream

Migration provides the slim prospect of upward mobility that is lacking in the Dominican Republic. In his song *Visa para un Sueño* (Visa for a Dream), the Dominican *merengue* singer, Juan Luis Guerra expresses the fears and yearning felt by so many of his compatriots as they balance separation and homesickness against the hope for a better life. Often it is the youngest and brightest who leave in search of fame and fortune, thereby impoverishing the country's future. Conversely, their remittance payments sustain families and communities that would otherwise find it hard to survive.

of poverty. Unfortunately, education is in short supply, especially in the rural districts, where schools are usually overcrowded and under-equipped due to lack of finance. As a result, large numbers of children do not manage to complete even their primary education and an estimated quarter of adults cannot read or write. The wealthier Dominican families face no such difficulties, however, since they can afford to send their children to privately funded schools and to universities in North America.

LEFT: cooking for Haitian cane-cutters.
ABOVE: large cruise ships dock in the harbour near the Zona Colonial, Santo Domingo.

The reality of life in the US often fails to match up to the dream, but North American culture continues to exert a strong fascination for many Dominicans, especially the young. Ever since the country's early independence leaders tried to sell their sovereignty to Washington, the Republic has had a love-hate relationship with a nation that has twice invaded it. Older Dominicans may remember the humiliations of the 1965 occupation, when Marines searched passers-by at checkpoints, but younger generations are attracted by the fast lifestyle that they see daily on satellite TV. To some extent, this generational difference is reflected in the personalities of Joaquín Balaguer, proud of his

Spanish parentage and attached to a Hispanic cultural model, and Leonel Fernández, who promised in an election speech to "turn the Dominican Republic into a little New York". As more and more Dominicans experience life in the US, so American tastes and habits become increasingly commonplace.

But the Dominican Republic is not yet entirely Americanised. While baseball and Coca-Cola are almost ubiquitous, the popularity of rum and cock-fighting points to another cultural dimension, both Hispanic and Caribbean.

Regional identity also remains important; many people in Santiago, for instance, consider of religious faith in a society that claims to be 90 percent Catholic. While Catholicism is an important element in Dominican cultural identity, in reality the Church is politically weak, conservative and in desperate need of priests and money. As elsewhere in the region, Protestant churches are making gradual in-roads and competing with traditional Catholicism, but the Church still has influence in education and social welfare. In some of the most deprived areas, priests have also been at the forefront of organising community self-help groups.

But if devout Dominicans deride their Haitian neighbours for their Vaudou practices,

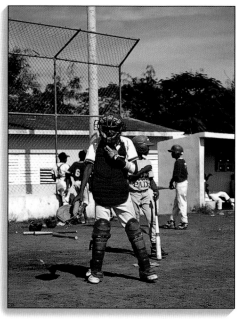

themselves different in a variety of ways from those who live in Santo Domingo. A Creole mixture of many influences, *dominicanidad* (Dominicanness) may be under threat from North American cultural dominance and remain overly fearful of Haiti, but it has strong roots in its own history and experience.

Acts of faith

Every year on 21 January thousands of pilgrims make their way to the vast modern cathedral in the eastern city of Higüey to pay tribute to Our Lady of Altagracia, patroness of the Republic since 1922 and reputed to perform healing miracles. It is one of the strongest manifestations they cannot deny that large numbers of their compatriots are also attracted to African-inspired beliefs. *Brujería*, which encompasses worship, spiritual magic and even witchcraft, has many followers, although generally their activities are not widely publicised. Dominicans of all backgrounds consult *brujos* – priests and medicine men – who offer advice and sometimes spells to counteract the effects of *mal de ojo* or the evil eye.

Ironically, then, while the Dominican Republic officially proclaims its Catholicism and its Hispanic heritage, it is precisely in folk religion and popular beliefs that its common culture with Haiti is most clearly revealed.

The Haitians

A world away from the relative prosperity of the business centres and fashionable cities in the Dominican Republic are the steamy and crowded slums along Port-au-Prince's waterfront. The anxieties are more basic here. They are about jobs, food, healthcare and education. Despite their poverty, most Haitians will do their utmost to secure an education for their children and get them through school: it is seen as their ticket to an easier life in this country of eight million people, where 50 percent of the population is considered illiterate. Families from the countryside see it this way: the child

women from all over the country go through the ritual of taking a national high school exam. The students with the highest grades gain admittance to the school of their choice. It's an investment in human capital for the future.

A crucible of all things good and bad in Haiti, Port-au-Prince best illustrates the disparities that exist in the country, with pockets of wealth surrounded by vast expanses of poverty. Pétionville, as well as dozens of suburbs that have mushroomed in the hills above the capital city, seems to be fenced off from the rest of the country. The conception of the people who live in these enclaves is that although they speak

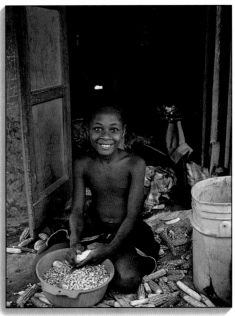

who goes to school might be able to secure employment in Port-au-Prince. That child will then become an example of what is possible and will be expected to give help to everyone else within that family.

There are no universal retirement benefits in Haiti. For countless families, the only welfare is to have one of their children attend medical or law school, or one of the professional colleges. Every year, thousands of young men and

Creole, just like everyone else, they prefer to use French or English and have probably studied abroad. Their homes are larger, their schools are better, and every night they watch American and European programmes on satellite TV.

Racial divisions

Most of the surburbanites belong to Haiti's light-skinned élite, scions of a world where colour meant everything. It wasn't too long ago, years after the Revolution of 1804, that Haitians were classified by how much white blood was in their veins. The original slave owners, from small towns in France, settled in places like Jacmel, Cap Haïtien. More than

FAR LEFT: religious icons at Santiago market.
LEFT: baseball is big business for the Dominicans.
ABOVE: education is seen as a way out of poverty.
RIGHT: preparing maize.

7,000 families fled to New Orleans a few years before the slave revolt, but many others stayed behind. At the turn of the 20th century, a few German adventurers settled in Haiti, along with some North American whites who stayed on after the US occupation of Haiti in 1919.

The Arabs, mainly Christians from Syria and Lebanon, were the last to arrive on the island, mostly after the 1940s. Refugees from a French-speaking country, they began doing business where "educated"

PORT-AU-PRINCE

It is difficult to find your way around Port-au-Prince and street maps are hard to find in advance. However, once there, good maps published by the Shell Oil Company can be bought at Shell petrol stations.

New York, Miami or Paris, speak of the "name-game" they have to play whenever they return home. Someone from an older generation will invariably try to place them by reference to their family name. Who was your grandfather? Who's your mother?

Life on the affluent hills is a world away from where most Haitians call home. Out of Haiti's total population, about 2 million currently live in Port-au-Prince. Except for the tiny proportion of the élite there, most live in cramped housing or in

Haitians would not dare venture, in downtown Port-au-Prince. Today the Arabic community have earned a reputation as successful entrepreneurs and they now own banks and factories, among various other thriving businesses.

Class divisions

Over the years, the strict racial divisions have given way to class partitions based to some extent on education and family ties. Black people who benefited from François "Papa Doc" Duvalier's black revolution began to buy homes in the hills, setting themselves apart from the millions of poor and uneducated Haitians living below. These distinctions still exist. Young Haitians, now living in

slums on the city's waterfront, such as Cité Soleil, La Saline and Boston.

The majority of Haitians, who are descendants of the African slaves brought to the island in the 15th century, still live in the countryside, where they scratch a living from small plots of land. Arable land is increasingly in short supply in the mountainous regions, as the population increases and deforestation spreads like wildfire. They live in one of the secondary cities like Gonaives, Jacmel, Cap Haïtien, Les Cayes, or in small municipalities such as Las Cahobas, a town on the border with the Dominican Republic where Michel Laguerre spent the first few years of his youth.

"I never heard of Paris or New York," said Laguerre, now a professor of anthropology and sociology at the University of California at Berkeley. "We were one step above La Saline." Haiti's turbulent past should explain this kind of disparity. Like natives of a country that has been forcibly fenced off from the outside world, Haitians spent many years looking inward. They were isolated after the Revolution, as countries with their own powerful slave-owning communities such as the United States, England, Spain, and especially France, did not want it made public knowledge that a band of slaves had indeed defeated the great general,

and multiple-channel television. In their world, the small-town grocer becomes the synthesiser of neighbourhood news, continually repackaging it as the day wears on.

Growing diversity

Until the end of World War II, Haiti was practically a homogenous country, with a shared culture. Everyone in the countryside practised Vaudou, and though city folk attended church, they were familiar with the gods worshipped by their servants. (Although Vaudou has been portrayed in literature and the arts, it is still considered as belonging to the working classes.)

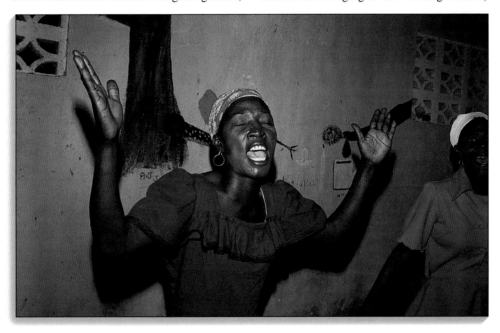

Napoleon Bonaparte's men – at the time one of the most powerful armies in the world.

"We spent too many hours looking at each other instead of looking at other people." Laguerre says. "As a country, we had a small-town mentality. It's all about gossip. People only talked about each other."

This introspective world still exists in many rural localities in Haiti today, and in plenty of neighbourhoods in the capital, too. These places have yet to join the global village, untouched as they are by Internet technology

LEFT: washing in the river.
ABOVE: Vaudou is a powerful influence in Haiti.

THE BIG BAND SOUND

Everyone loved the music of celebrated composers Nemours Jean-Baptiste and Weber Sicot, big-band leaders of the 1950s. They introduced a special kind of recreational dance music called *compas direct* or *cadence rampa* with a beat that refuses to die. At carnival time, the Jean-Baptiste and Sicot float always attracted the biggest crowds who would dance to their music and follow the float as it wound its way through the city. "There was common understanding, a common bond," Michel Laguerre, professor of anthropology and sociology at the University of California at Berkeley, says. "We were on the boat together."

When François "Papa Doc" Duvalier rose to power in 1957, Haiti became more complex, more culturally heterogeneous. In among the islanders who never left, there are those who lived abroad and have now returned – along with their own distinct backgrounds – from the United States, Canada, France, Africa, and the Dominican Republic. There are an estimated one million Haitians overseas, mainly in the United States and Canada.

In the late 1950s and early 1960s, as Papa Doc was tightening his grip on power, many French-speaking intellectuals left for teaching positions in Canada and the newly independent countries of Africa. Now they are returning, and common references are often up for negotiation. When someone who lived in New York – which has the largest Haitian community anywhere overseas with 600,000 people – talks about democracy, and a native islander talks about democracy, they're often discussing two very different things.

Looking to the US

In the past, ambitious Haitians in the countryside could climb up the social ladder by moving to Port-au-Prince, where there were job opportunities and good schools. Now, they're looking to America. Well-off Haitians send their kids to American schools, such as Union School, or Quisqueya, where they learn English. In less well-off families, children pick up English wherever they find it: on television, in books and from advertisements.

"They're getting ready for Miami," Laguerre says. Over the years and through the often difficult changes, the Haitians have remained warm and fundamentally honest. Hospitality is a strong feature of their culture. In villages, more so than in Port-au-Prince, Haitians are likely to welcome foreigners into their home for a meal and a place to rest their head.

They're hard-working people, with strong family ties and extended linkages overseas. Many families live on money sent from relatives overseas. Contact with abroad has fundamentally changed Haiti, moving it towards being a transnational culture. Television and music comes from powerful cultures in the US, Canada and France.

End of the diaspora

Now Haitian children worship the same icons as children from elsewhere around the world: Coca-Cola, Michael Jackson and Michael Jordan. More people, especially in the cities, are speaking English – the lingua franca of computers and business – and this trend is even reflected in the political system: it is attempting to retain human resources, and people who want to serve in government are being asked to turn over their other passports. Effectively they must choose between Haiti and the United States and Canada. ❏

ENVIRONMENTAL PROBLEMS

Environmental problems are very difficult to solve in Haiti. Overpopulation and poverty have resulted in severe stress on the land, and while some limited agricultural plans are being put into operation, more agrarian reform is needed, including technical and financial assistance for the peasant class. Irrigation systems need to be built to increase the export of legitimate crops, but there are obstacles in the form of massive deforestation and much corruption among the ruling classes. The cocaine trade has become increasingly important in Haiti, with government officials in the past often raking in huge profits, running into millions of US dollars.

LEFT: a Dominican elder.
RIGHT: at home with the family, Samaná Peninsula.

LANGUAGE

The island of La Hispaniola is linguistically diverse: Dominican Spanish has five different dialects, while on Haiti you will hear both French and Creole

From the beginning, the Spanish language brought to America by the conquerors was enriched with the characteristics of four different regions of the Iberian peninsula: Leon, Castilla, Extremadura and Andalucía. In "La Hispaniola", contact with the Taínos led to the incorporation of several indigenous words in

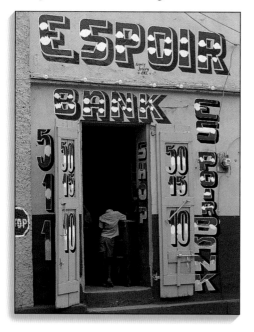

to the various Spanish dialects. Despite this, the indigenous tongues did not influence the Spanish language in a significant way, mostly because the few Indians that still survived by the mid-16th century already spoke Spanish.

The Taínos, however, left a legacy of widely used words such as *huracán* for hurricane, *hamaca* for hammock, *bohío* for house and *maíz* for corn. Even though the quantity of indigenous terms known and documented is broad, the truth is that their use and validity in Dominican Spanish is minimal.

Due to the historical circumstances of the discovery and to the geographical reality of being an island, Dominican Spanish was also influenced by the nautical terms brought by the navigators that colonised the island. Those terms were later applied to mundane objects and situations, and their sense drifted slowly from the original meaning. A good example of this is the word *tolete* which means *thole* and is used as a synonym for *stick*, *peso* (unit of Dominican currency), and even for the male sexual organ.

Dominican dialects

The Dominican Republic is currently divided into regions, each one with its own linguistic characteristics. There are five areas that can be perfectly distinguished:

● **Northern Zone** or "**Cibao**". Close to the pure-blooded Spanish brought here many centuries ago, it keeps verbs, terms and phrases that are archaic in Spain. This is especially true in the mountainous rural areas. A distinctive seal of the dialect is the vocalisation of "i" as in "faida" instead of "falda" (skirt) or "caigai" instead of "cargar" (to carry or to charge).

● **Southwestern Zone**. Predominance of the consonant "r", leading to the pronunciation "farda" for "falda" (skirt).

● **Southeastern Zone**. The assimilation of a consonant which follows another, producing "fadda", instead of "falda".

● **National District** (includes Santo Domingo). Predominance of the consonant "l" which leads to the pronunciation of words such as "puelta" instead of "puerta" (door).

● **Oriental Part of the Samaná Peninsula**. This region is more complex due to the influence of the eastern part of the Cibao region as well as the influence of the English language and the Haitian dialect.

Santo Domingo, like other parts of the Caribbean, distinguishes itself by the strong use of its Castilian vocabulary as well as its syntax. Moreover, the vocabulary used in Santo Domingo has a more phonetic similarity to the Andalucian region than to the Castilian region.

Santo Domingo was the first centre of the Americanisation of the Spanish language in the

Dominican Republic. One characteristic of the Dominicans is the use of idiomatic sayings and phrases, some of them old, and others taken from more modern media. These sayings and phrases add a picturesque and refreshing flavour to the daily use of the Spanish language.

The actual African influence on Dominican Spanish has not been significant, since the integration of the black slaves only occurred during the first half of the 16th century. This integration happened at the time when the island's earliest inhabitants – the Taíno Indians – were in the process of being exterminated.

After this there were no resources to bring black slaves in large numbers onto the island. From the beginning, a large number of these black slaves were not brought directly from the African mainland, but from Spain, where they had been acquired from Portugal and were therefore already hispanicised.

Examples of some incorporated words are *cachimbo* (smoking pipe), *can* (party), and others which also have been extended to the Antilles, such as *naqueru* (child's funeral) = *naquine* (child's funeral) in Puerto Rico; *bembe* (lip) in Puerto Rico = *bemba* (lip) in Cuba.

> **LANGUAGE LIMITATIONS**
>
> English is spoken on the island only in certain exclusive resorts and top hotels. German is spoken by staff in some of the north coast hotels.

Haitian Creole

If you want to converse with people while in Haiti, bring along both a Creole and a French dictionary. Everyone in Haiti speaks Creole, but about 10 percent of Haiti's 8 million people know French well enough to use it comfortably in any situation. The French dictionary will come in handy in dealing with any members of Haiti's élite, who sometimes are reluctant to use Creole with foreigners. Some might even be insulted if a foreigner attempts to use Creole, given the low status of the language.

Although related, Creole is not a dialect of French. It belongs to a group of languages called French-based creoles in which the majority of the vocabulary is taken from French. Other French-based creoles are found on Mauritius and the Seychelles, and in Louisiana in the US. Approximately 80 percent of Haitian Creole's vocabulary comes from French, but the words do not necessarily have the same meaning, form or function as French. For example, *neg* in Creole means a man, but in

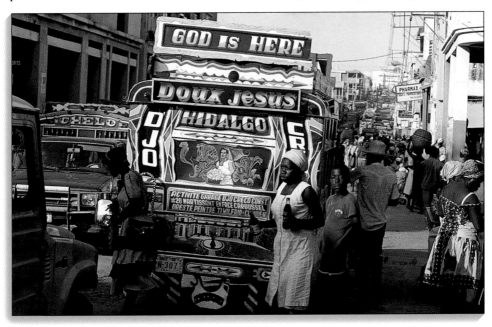

LEFT: a corner shop in Cap-Haïtien.
ABOVE: every *tap-tap* tells a story.

French *negre* means a black man, a negro. Structurally, however, Creole is very different from French, having more in common with the other Creoles. It has a simple grammar that doesn't require conjugating verbs according to the subject, as in French and English. Instead, key words are placed before a verb to indicate a tense.

French was declared the official language in the 1918 constitution, but it wasn't until 1987 that Haitians gave Creole its due by making it one of the two official languages. Until then, French was the only language in public service and in schools, and therefore only a small num-

ber of people were able to communicate with officials and educators, read newspapers and legal documents. The élite spoke French with each other, and and also used it with their children to make sure they grew up at an advantage. Creole was – and still is in some circles – reserved for family and close friends, for speaking with servants and for Vaudou ceremonies. Many classes are still taught in French, although most students are not as proficient at the language as they could be, and many of the teachers speak it badly.

It wasn't until 1964 that the government allowed people who spoke only Creole to use it for any official purpose. Because of the social stigma, many Haitians think that Creole is not a viable language, going as far as saying that Creole has no grammar, that they don't have a native language. That's because few know how Creole came to them. It came to Haiti with the Africans, who brought along about 30 languages from their homes in West Africa. Before independence, according to Michel DeGraff, a linguist at the Massachusetts Institute of Technology, Creole had prestige. There was no prejudice towards Creole, as whites preferred to deal with slaves who knew Creole.

"An African who spoke Creole commanded respect," says DeGraff. "More so than one who spoke French or one who spoke neither. Those who didn't speak Creole fast were sent to plantations." *Neg Bosal* (rough man) was the phrase used for slaves who were not acclimatised, who could speak neither French nor Creole. The Africans spoke languages that belonged to the Niger-Congo family of languages, which came into contact with the dialects of provincial France. The French slave-owners, merchants and tradespeople did not speak Parisian French, which did not exist at that time.

A common language

Over the years, the Africans took the syntax from their own languages, borrowed French words from the whites, and cobbled a common language. That ability to communicate in the same language can be partly credited for the early and successful emancipation of Haitians.

It was only after independence that Creole lost its prestige, when the neo-colonial class looked on French as a privilege; the African languages disappeared and French became a symbol of education and prestige. Mulatto businessmen, whose fathers were French, sent their children to France to study, and Creole became a reflection of the social and political situation. Language had become a symbol of class. "Creole is a disadvantage in certain places," DeGraff says. "In the countryside, people will be more than happy to speak Creole."

There are distinct regional variations in pronunciation and grammar, and it is only recently that Creole has become a written language in a meaningful way. The long-term neglect of the language means there are no "official" rules of grammar, only this one: if a native Haitian Creole speaker says it's OK, then it's OK.

Morisseau the saviour

Poet-playwright Felix Morisseau-Leroy's name burns bright in the consciousness of generations of Haitians. He made Creole "respectable" to those who thought of their language as a disreputable patois incapable of expressing much beyond the most basic human needs.

Morisseau wrote a play, *Antigone in Creole*, and performed it in Port-au-Prince in 1953. It was the first time Creole-speaking Haitians saw a play in their own language. The themes were universal: freedom, justice, equality. Morisseau was forming his ideas at a time when people like François "Papa Doc" Duvalier was talking about black power. Creole was as good as classic French, he said. Morisseau's adaptation of the Greek tragedy was a revolutionary act, the tremors from which can be felt today in the words of populist activists like singer Manno Charlemagne, the mayor of Port-au-Prince and priest-turned president Jean-Bertrand Aristide.

Morisseau, who died in Miami in 1998, became an almost mystical and mythical figure.

"He was the inspiration who allowed me and others to continue the work he started doing," said Jan Mapou, a friend who started a cultural group called Sosyete Koukouy in Miami and has directed Morisseau *Antigone in Creole* for Haitians abroad. Now, several more works, including teaching manuals and other reading material are available in Creole, as Haitians continue to debate whether children should be taught in Creole instead of French. At the same time, universities in the United States and elsewhere offer doctorate programmes in Creole. Several dictionaries are available, including *Creole Anglais* by Joel Laguerre and Bryant Freeman and a Haitian-English dictionary by Albert Valdman of Indiana University.

As a young language, Creole has absorbed words from several other languages besides French. A smattering of English words have made their way into Creole, including:
- shoe black (*choublak*), the common name for hibiscus. It comes from the American occupation of 1915 when hibiscus was used to shine shoes and American soldiers requested "shoe black" when they wanted their boots polished.
- coat (*kot*) – also jacket (*jaket*).
- many words derived from brand names, such as *Clorox* for bleach, *Delco* for generator, *frijide* for refrigerator, and *kleneks* for tissues.
- the ubiquitous hotdog, as well as "chips" for potato crisps.

Getting a feel for Haitian Creole

Most words don't change their form, meaning there are no endings to signal grammatical distinctions such as singular or plural for nouns, or tense for verbs. For example, "the book" is translated as *liv la* and "the books" as *liv yo*.

Grammatical relations between words are signalled by the order in which the words are put together. For example, the order for a declara-

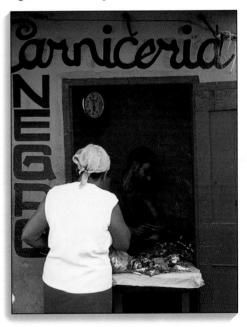

tive sentence is: subject, verb, indirect object, direct object. Other examples of word order include: Yves *renmen* Marie means Yves loves Marie (possession is shown by placing the possessor immediately after the thing possessed); and *Kay* Marie, which translates as Marie's house. To express negation in Creole, the marker "*pa*" comes immediately before the verb.

As in English, there are three persons in the singular (*mwen*, *ou* and *li*) and two in the plural (*nou* and *yo*). The first person *nou* corresponds to we and you, and can refer to more than one person, if at least one of them is a participant in the conversation. *Yo* is more than one person or thing *not* participating in the conversation. ❑

LEFT: Vaudou images adorn a building.
RIGHT: butcher's store front in San Cristobal.

HAITIAN ART

Local paintings lie covered in dust while talented artists go hungry. But, despite the difficulties faced by the art trade in Haiti, the future is looking brighter

When a country has very little in terms of material wealth, art is not just a vibrant means of expression, it's an affirmation of identity, the hard currency of hope, and a potent agent for social change. As one of the richest resources of this poverty-stricken nation, Haitian art is recognised throughout the world by its bold primary colours and its primitive motifs, and is traditionally regarded on the island as a symbol of the long, tumultuous struggle of the country's soul.

Art in Haiti is present everywhere: at the airport, in restaurants and hotels, on *tap-taps* (buses) and street corners, inside markets and modest homes. But at Port-au-Prince's teeming Iron Market, colourful oil paintings, covered with a layer of dust, sit stacked in piles as high as the ceiling while hungry vendors wait for customers and barely earn a living. The Iron Market was once a popular shopping stop where cruise ship passengers loaded up on Haitian art, but now, along with many art galleries on the island, it has fallen on hard times.

Dwindling sales

"In the past, Haiti depended on upper-class, well-educated and liberal tourists, who were very good buyers of our art," explains Michel Monnin, a Swiss-born art critic and dealer who has lived in Haiti for almost 50 years. "When tourism fell off back in the 1980s, the day-to-day dealing of art fell off with it. We also have the problem of collectors who are stuck on one image of Haitian art. Art in Haiti, like art everywhere in the world, is in constant evolution. Often, when buyers see the new art being produced by some of our young artists, they say, 'This isn't Haitian art. We want the real thing.'

"There are a few big name artists who are able to sell their work to collectors in Europe,

and lesser-known artists who sell their work to diplomats, journalists and UN employees, but in general, Haiti today is a country full of artists and most of them are starving."

Whether most artists in Haiti are actually starving is debatable, but Monnin is right in saying that Haiti is a country full of artists. Whether rich or poor, almost every family has at least one member who works as an artist. It is commonly said that Haiti has more artists and poets per capita than most other countries on earth.

Georges Nader Jr, owner of an art gallery in Petionville, paints a more promising view of the current status of art in Haiti. "In our gallery, a bunch of modern painters – Alix Roy, Calixte Henry, Galland Semerrand, Gesner Armand, Luckner Dasmangles, Lyonel Laurenceau, Henry Jacques and Bernard Segourne – are getting the highest prices ever for their work, and I believe that we are entering a period when we are going to see another great boom in Haitian art."

PRECEDING PAGES: rich colours and imagery of naïve art.
LEFT: *Mariage D'interet* by Rigaud Benoit in the Musée d'Art Hatian, Port-au-Prince.
RIGHT: a symbolic metal sculpture.

The early masters

The history of the first Haitian art boom can be traced back to the early 1940s when American teacher and aspiring artist DeWitt Peters went to Port-au-Prince to teach English. A conscientious objector during World War II, Peters was awed by the "self-taught and instinctive" artists he encountered in the cities and throughout the countryside of Haiti.

In 1944 he opened the Centre d'Art in Port-au-Prince, still in existence today. The Centre's

VAUDOU INFLUENCE

Vaudou has been a major factor in Haitian art. Inextricably linked to the unseen world, Haitian artists served *Vaudou* spirits by decorating temple walls and flags used in ceremonies.

Other great artists who came out of the Peters era included Philomé Obin and Riguad Benoit, who both died in 1986; Castera Bazile, who died in 1964; Wilson Bigaud; Préfète Duffaut; Jasmin Joseph; Georges Liataud; and André Pierre, who still produces exuberant art in the yard outside his Croix-des-Missions home, some of which sells abroad for up to US$50,000 a piece. "Haitian art is mystical because Haiti is mystical," Pierre once told *Art & Antiques* magazine. "Everything comes from the spirits."

goal in the early days was to arouse Haitians' interest in the arts, provide needed supplies, and nurture the talent of hundreds of impoverished artists on the island. Peters is credited with "discovering" Vaudou priest Hector Hyppolite, the legendary Haitian master whose dramatic paintings were marked by Vaudou rituals, symbols and gods, along with prominent Christian figures amid Caribbean landscapes. Before he met Peters, Hyppolite was an obscure artist and financially strapped house painter, so poor that he used chicken feathers as paint brushes. In the last three years of his life, with the financial assistance of Peters, he produced over 250 paintings. He died in 1948.

Throughout the late 1940s and 1950s, this early generation of Haitian artists attracted international acclaim and put Haiti on the world map for its visual arts, making the genre widely popular. French surrealist André Breton and Cuban master Wilfredo Lam also helped raise interest by bringing attention to Haitian art in Paris and arranging European shows to highlight their work.

After buying five Hyppolites to take back to Paris in the late 1940s, Breton reportedly told Peters, "This should revolutionise modern painting; it needs a revolution." What resulted from all this international attention was a virtual art explosion of what became known in the art world as the "naive-primitive" or "instinctive" genre. Described by critics as lush, bold, pastoral, whimsical, lyrical, romantic and exotic, these naive-primitive oil paintings for the most part emphasised Haiti's African heritage, but also had an overlay of classical French influences. Lush jungle landscapes, wild animals, towering mountains, exotic flowers and plants were common themes.

Eventually, this pleasing-to-the-eye style became synonymous with Haitian art throughout the world. Isaa El Saieh, a Palestinian art dealer who has lived in Port-au-Prince all his life, started selling naive-primitive art in Haiti

Haiti and will go out of his way to help them find exactly what they want. One of his former clients was the writer Graham Greene, who, after a round of shopping for art, asked El Saieh to take him to one of Haiti's most notorious brothels for a late-afternoon tryst.

Haitian art goes commercial

During the next few decades the blossoming of art in Haiti continued, promoted by local merchants and sold under the generic "Haitian Art" label to tourists. From the start, Haitian art was created for the export market and artists were encouraged to produce work that fitted into this

in the 1950s and has never stopped. A gregarious old man with a thick moustache and barrel chest, he has a stable of modest-to-good artists from whom he regularly buys work. His home in Port-au-Prince, a rambling hillside mansion on Avenue Chile that also serves as a gallery, has a massive storage area that's always packed with canvases. Along with claiming to know more about Haitian art than "all the so-called experts in the world", El Saieh still makes himself available to tourists shopping for art in

LEFT: André Pierre at work in Croix-des-Missions.
ABOVE: the painting of wild animals at a jungle watering hole by Blanchard reveals common themes.

mould. Although credited with "discovering" naive-primitive art in Haiti, what DeWitt Peters actually did was create a mass market for Haitian art, much of which was clone-like and predictable, the product of a formula that worked and easily made money. Haitian art became stereotyped in the process, assumed to be of interest only to folk art collectors or souvenir-hunting tourists. In essence, it turned into a clichéd art form marked by commercialism and tailored to feed tourist consumption.

Haiti's upper classes never considered their own art valuable, and looked instead to Europe to decorate the walls of their plush, tropical homes. There are few Haitian collectors of

Haitian art; most of the work of the early masters, such as Hyppolite and Obin, is in the hands of private European collectors. Obin, however, spawned an art revolution in his own family, and today there are dozens of his close and distant relatives producing art in Haiti and abroad.

Throughout the 1960s and 1970s, the Haitian art market thrived on a constant flow of well-heeled tourists. The galleries in Port-au-Prince, Petionville and Jacmel prospered. In addition to the paintings, fine mahogany wood carvings, beaded flags and iron sculpture crafted from oil drums, became common art commodities.

But when the tourist market collapsed in the

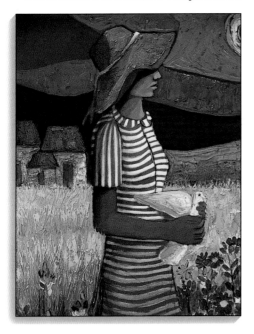

1980s, so did many of the country's galleries. And when the hardships of the post-Duvalier/ economic embargo years followed, the art scene in Haiti got even worse. There were shortages of food and fuel, as well as paint, canvases and brushes. Some artists had only latex house paint, which cracked on their canvases in about two years. Others worked with just a few colours, and their art, referred to as "embargo painting", was evidence of the scarcity of supplies. Some gave up painting altogether and turned to sculpture, using scrap metal, tin cans and wire found on the streets.

After the election of Jean-Bertrand Aristide in 1990, the streets of Haiti saw a proliferation of street art, political graffiti in the form of joyous murals. Bold and provocative, most appeared as a spontaneous celebration of political and social liberation unleashed by the downfall of the Duvalier regime. Rich with the patriotic colours of red and blue, the common themes of these murals included the number 5, Aristide's number on the ballot; a crushed guinea head, a bird that once symbolised the Duvalier regime; and the horrific practice of "necklacing" – placing a petrol-soaked tyre around a victim's neck and setting it on fire.

After the 1991 coup forced Aristide into exile, most of these murals were obliterated by the Haitian military. When Aristide was returned to power in 1994, Haiti's political street art came back to life. And today, although democracy remains fragile, the country is seeing a renewed cultural vitality, and an intense period of expression that is relatively free of fear.

The new generation

"Artists are a tormented species, no matter where you come from," said Edouard Duval-Carrie, a prominent Haitian artist who divides his time between Miami, Florida and Port-au-Prince. "And artists in Haiti for generations have been tormented by what they saw around them."

Among the new generation of Haitian artists, Duval-Carrie is one of a handful – including Burton Chenet, Philippe Dodard, Mario Benjamine, Lionel St Pierre, and metal sculptors Serge Jolimeau and Gabriel Bien-Aimeó – who have gained international recognition for their work, and who have also been able to earn a decent living from it.

This young generation is exploring Haitian roots and culture with a new, freer form of expression, transcending the stereotypical image of naive-primitive art usually associated with their country. Most have been educated in Europe or North America, are well-travelled, multi-lingual, urbane, and willing to take greater risks in their work.

Now in his forties, Duval-Carrie creates lush, colourful and intense paintings that are definitely Haitian, but far from being clichéd. Full of both beauty and despair, they are portraits of paradise with a hint of violence and a tinge of terror. The subjects of his work range from mythical gods to bourgeois matrons, Vaudou spirits, political brutality, and even Jean-Claude Duvalier in drag. Like his contemporaries,

Duval-Carrie resists being categorised. "One look at me and you can see that I am neither primitive nor naive," he explains. "I am a contemporary Haitian artist with a political agenda who is trying to analyse my country and figure out why it is in such a mess.

"My biggest complaint about Haitian art today is that it is still lumped together under this one broad category. We have had several great artists who should have received recognition as individual masters, not just regional or Haitian painters. And we have never had a retrospective show at a major museum, or even a catalogue collection of our masters."

hundreds of fine artists in Haiti today who have little choice but to sell their work to dealers for a few dollars, he is optimistic about the future in the new millennium: "The years ahead look very promising for Haitian art. We have a democratically elected government, the organised terror has gone, artists are no longer afraid to express themselves politically, and there is great demand for the discussion of our country's problems. And even though the tourist market is very weak, all of the current circumstances will mean that a finer quality and more original form of art will be coming out of Haiti in the years to come." ❑

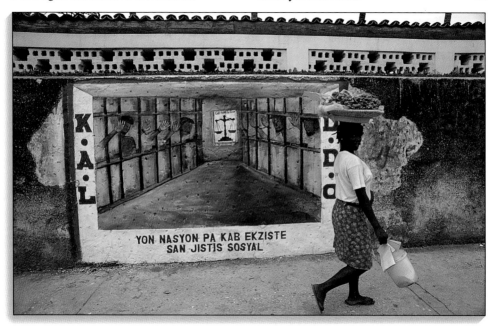

Calixte Henry, a Haitian artist in his sixties, echoes Duval-Carrie's sentiments. "There has always been a problem with Haitian painting because of the concentration on Vaudou," he once told *Art & Antiques* magazine. "I say there is more: there is what the painter feels within. I'm not going to do Vaudou just because it sells." Instead, he has turned to European Impressionism for inspiration, while resolutely expressing scenes of Haitian life.

Although Duval-Carrie admits that there are

LEFT: *Paseo a las 10am* by Candido Bido.
ABOVE: many political murals carry a strong message and so some are destroyed during political unrest.

DANGEROUS ART

Artistic censorship has always existed in Haiti, especially during such turbulent times as the post-Duvalier years. Musicians whose music challenged the status quo have been jailed and executed, their performances threatened or halted by a spray of bullets.

Because visual artists don't regularly make public appearances like musicians, they have fared somewhat better, but they too have been threatened by the powers that be. Over the years, many have left the island out of fear and now live and work in Paris, Montréal, New York, and Miami, where controversial and political art is usually tolerated and often actually encouraged.

THE ORIGINS OF VAUDOU

*Outlawed as dangerous superstition, it has taken hundreds of years
for Haiti's most popular religion to gain official recognition*

The saying that "Haiti is 80 percent Roman Catholic Vaudou" may be close to the truth, rather than an exaggeration. What started out hundreds of years ago in west Africa as simply ancestor and spirit worship has developed in Haiti into a unique syncretic religion, with its own world view, philosophy, healing system and artistic expressions. As the Vaudou master drummer and emperor (high priest) Aboudja Derenoncourt says: "Vaudou is not just a religion, it's a way of life."

A misunderstood religion

Vaudou permeates the Haitian psyche, operating at all levels of society, from peasants to city intelligentsia. Along with Kwéyol, it is fundamental to cultural identity and for any kind of insight into this extraordinary country. Vaudou has been a significant factor in Haitian history since the first slaves arrived in 1503, inspiring fierce resistance, which culminated in the final rebellion against France.

Jean-Jacques Dessalines, the rebel slave leader who declared independence in 1804, was an *oungan* (priest) who would be elevated to the Vaudou pantheon after his assassination. Despite prescriptive legislation and a series of anti-superstition campaigns aimed at wiping it out, Vaudou has survived and was officially recognised by the state in 1987.

Yet the Vaudou of Haiti is a far cry from the sensationalised, spine-chilling version of the movies in which bug-eyed zombies roam the land and possessed devotees wreak havoc with voodoo dolls riddled with pins. This stereotype resulted from confusing Vaudou with the magical practices of the *bocor* or sorcerer, which were not part of the religious system. The misrepresentation of Vaudou and the paranoia this caused was fuelled by the precedent set when the slaves won their independence in 1804. The

Haitian revolution sent tremors of fear through all the slave colonies of the Caribbean as well as the southern slave-owning states of America.

The plantocracy of the entire Americas felt threatened, and the fear of similar uprisings was transferred to Vaudou – certainly a unifying factor among the rebel armies. Besides the isolation which followed independence, Haiti has also suffered from misconceptions about Vaudou. Some of these, based on the taboos and mystification of the past which sought to maintain the survival of Vaudou, unfortunately contributed to its negative image.

But Vaudou is essentially a polytheistic religion of harmony and tolerance, based on the relationship between the natural and supernatural worlds and the ties between the living and the dead. Since State recognition, there has been a movement, in Haiti and elsewhere, to give Vaudou more positive exposure. As Aboudja Derenoncourt points out: "This is a tradition open to the world. Everyone can come and look

LEFT: a popular Vaudou ceremony on All Saints Day, Port-au-Prince.
RIGHT: Vaudou flags with their symbols and detailed beadwork are considered by some to be works of art.

into Vaudou and see the positive things we're doing and see we're not hanging people upside down or eating soup with fingers in it."

Vaudou originated in the religious practices of the Fon, Yoruba and Ewe tribes in the area of west African which now covers Ghana, Nigeria, Togo and the Republic of Benin, formerly Dahomey. The word Vaudou (the preferred spelling among Haitians) comes from Vodu, the Fon word for God. *Loa* – the Congo word for spirit – survives in the Haitian Creole *"Lwa"* – a term

NEW WORLD SURVIVAL

Uprooted from their different tribal homelands and shipped off to St Domingue, the west African slaves took their beliefs with them as a means of survival in a hostile world.

deliver their messages, would possess or "ride" a dancer, hence the term "horse" for an initiate who is possessed. Regular communication with the ancestors and spirits meant the living could benefit from the accumulated tribal wisdom of the past and contact with supernatural forces.

For slaves arriving in the new world, Vaudou evolved as much as a system of survival and resistance as a link to "Guinee", the ancestral homeland. The spirits of the various tribes or nations were accepted into the Vaudou pantheon

used interchangeably with *les mystères, les anges* and *les saints* to mean "the spirits".

Although the African religions recognised a supreme being and creator, he was considered beyond human affairs, so the living turned for guidance to the dead and the spirits. The soul of a recently deceased family member would in time reach the status of ancestor and could later become a spirit and eventually come to represent an archetype. The *vodun* or "ancestors and spirits" were honoured and summoned by ceremonies of drumming, dance and song, while animal sacrifices were offered to solicit their help and guidance. Priests mediated between the initiates and the spirits who, when ready to

with the same characteristic tolerance as were the Roman Catholic saints. The French Code Noir, introduced to regulate slavery in 1658, required slaves to be baptised as Catholics and banned all other religions. Vaudou embraced the saints and assimilated them: the Virgin Mary became Erzulie, goddess of love; St Patrick was equated with Dambala, the life force, and St Joseph with Loko, spirit of healing.

While the deities of the culturally dominant Kingdom of Dahomey and the Dahomean Rada rites formed the African tradition which survives to this day, a new nation of aggressive spirits was born in St Domingue as a response to the intolerable conditions of slavery.

Spirits of rebellion

The Petro nation of spirits was born from the meeting of runaway slaves (*marrons*) and surviving Taínos, the indigenous Amerindians with whom they shared many common beliefs and a hatred for the genocidal European colonisers. The Petro spirits expressed the rage and subsequent rebellion of the slaves, which the benign, protective Rada deities were unequipped for. Although it was a Petro ceremony at Bois Caiman in 1791, presided over by the Jamaican *oungan* Boukman, that signalled the start of the rebellion against France, it is the Rada rites that are still celebrated annually at Souvenance, a

towards the temple. Some are already in a state of trance induced by hours of chanting inside one of the temple's inner rooms. Led by the *oungenikon* (chorus leader) – a hunched old man whose voice still has amazing vigour – the *ounsis* break into songs of welcome. Cowskin drums begin to charge the night air with surging polyrhythms that change with each song. By the end, one man has collapsed, possessed, falling to the floor. Catching himself he rises, brushing the dust from his head, and joins the other *ounsis* who have gathered at a small building at the entrance to the Lakou. Fernand Bien Amie, the grey-haired, stately high priest

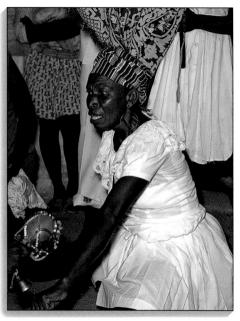

few miles from the northwest town of Gonaïves, where independence was declared in 1804.

Imagine it is Easter Saturday night. The darkness engulfing the Plain of Gonaïves signals the start of an ancient ceremony, which will continue day and night until the following Thursday. In the Lakou Souvenance, a spiritual compound revered as the seat of the Dahomey rites – Haiti's oldest surviving Vaudou tradition – white-clad *ounsis* (initiates) make their way from mud-walled, millet-thatched huts

FAR LEFT: food offerings on an altar.
LEFT: a painting of the black virgin in a temple.
ABOVE AND RIGHT: Vaudou flag and ceremony.

or Serviteur stands solemnly erect. In one hand a candle, which flickers in the night air, in the other, a large enamel mug for pouring libations.

The *ounsis* begin to chant for Papa Legba, the spirit who guards the gate to the realm of the *Lwas*, the spirits who will be invoked and to whom sacrifice will be made over the following days: "Papa Legba open the gate for us."

The Serviteur steps slowly out into the dusty track leading to the Lakou, pouring a libation to Legba in the dirt. Re-entering the compound he pours a libation before the "admirals of the drums" – the master drummers whose inconceivable energy will keep the *ounsis* singing and dancing for the following five nights. The ceremony has now begun and in the peristile, the communal room of the *ounfor* (temple), the *ounsis* dance until long after midnight.

By five in the morning they are back in an inner room, emerging after dawn, their white vestments – worn to summon energy and power for the ceremonies – splashed with the blood of slaughtered goats, ready for a day of sacrifices to the *Lwas* of the compound.

Various spots in the compound represent towns in the ancient kingdom of Dahomey. The ceremonies and dances performed at each of the locations are those of the *Lwa* associated with each town. Many of the songs are sung in

intense, as the ceremony becomes a beautiful fusion propelled by the drums, sustained by the call-and-response songs. Many *ounsis* and spectators alike have been possessed by the different *Lwas*, yet in this context of devotion and joyous celebration, possession is the norm and not in the least intimidating.

The fact that the Souvenance ceremony has survived (some think for over 200 years) is proof of how deeply rooted Vaudou is. The religion of the slaves retains its validity for their descendants, the Creole-speaking peasants who account for 90–95 percent of the Haitian population. Yet although Vaudou has played such a

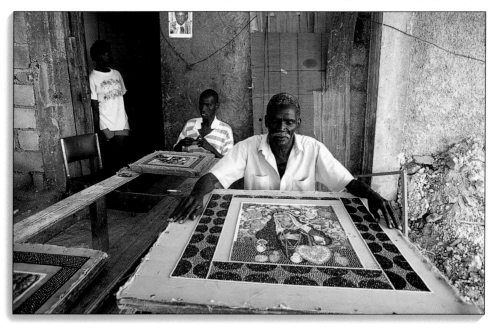

langaj, an African devotional language that is no longer understood. By dusk, the sacrifices to Ayison, Ogou, Zamadonn, Atchasou and Dambala are complete, and the *ounsis* have exchanged their white vestments for a riot of individual colour.

The crowd in the compound has been growing all day and there are several thousand people packed tight to see the Serviteur – dressed in his satin sash of blue and red, fringed with gold, flanked by the Haitian flag and the pale blue flag of La Société Belle Etoile, the Souvenance congregation – lead a procession round the tamarind tree of Ogou, the warrior spirit. In the failing daylight the colours are vibrantly

significant role in Haiti, it has also suffered the same oppression meted out to similar African-derived belief systems in the Caribbean.

While it was a motivating force in the war of independence, when the slaves believed that if they died in battle, their spirits would return directly to the ancestral homeland of Guinee, Vaudou soon became an embarrassment to both the mulatto and black political élite. These two factions, which temporarily put aside their hatred and rivalry to defeat the French, only to resume hostilities after victory, still shared the 19th-century belief in the supremacy of European culture and the backwardness of Africa.

So while politicians could speak of Haiti as

"the cradle of African independence", their sons were educated in France and the Roman Catholicism of their former French masters remained the official religion.

Vaudou was allowed to flourish under black presidents like Soulouque but was subsequently suppressed by the mulatto president Geffrard, who signed a concordat with the Vatican in 1860 as part of his attempt to "remove from our land these last vestiges of barbarism and slavery, superstition and its barbarous practices."

These sentiments are echoed in the position of fundamentalist Protestants who are now making inroads in Haiti, just as charismatic Christian sects are throughout the Caribbean. It was the period of American occupation from 1915 to 1934 which saw the start of the ideological shift away from cultural Eurocentricity, the eventual re-evaluation of Africa, and Vaudou's rehabilitation. Faced with US political and cultural imperialism, writers like Justin Dorsainvil and Jean Price-Mars founded the ethnological movement which defended both the relevance of Vaudou and west African traditions.

State recognition at last

Although ideology was shifting, Vaudou was still suppressed or exploited. Declared illegal in 1935, the Protestant convention established with Haiti in 1949 led to massacres of *oungans*, the destruction of *ounfors* and sacred trees.

The last massacre of Vaudou priests occurred in the 1986 "Deshokage", or uprooting of Duvalierists, following Baby Doc's flight to France. State recognition under Article 30/1 of the new constitution of 1987 finally gave Vaudou official recognition. The Nacyonal Zantray, founded in 1986, is an organisation of Vaudou institutions with a government mandate to promote the re-evaluation of the sacred cult and to equip it as an agent of social, economic and environmental development. Projects have been set up aimed at making rural Vaudou communities self-supporting, establishing *ounfor*-based primary schools and literacy schemes, as well as much-needed reforestation schemes.

Despite the harsh realities Haiti still faces, the official recognition given to both Vaudou and Creole shows a new mood of embracing essential elements of the nation's identity. Vaudou rhythms and songs play an important part in the repertoire of a whole new generation of "racine" or roots groups disseminating Haitian culture to a World Music audience.

As the religion of the majority, Vaudou has consistently been tolerant of Catholicism and other Christian sects (all Vaudou ceremonies begin with Catholic prayers). The Catholic and Anglican church in Haiti now view Vaudou in a more favourable light, and it is only the growth of evangelical Protestantism – which often holds out the lure of employment – which continues to condemn the sacred cult.　❑

LEFT: Vaudou priest and flag maker Edgar Jean-Louis.
RIGHT: a painting of Jean-Claude Duvalier on the side of a temple; he used Vaudou to maintain power.

DEFENDERS AND EXPLOITERS

Price-Mars' seminal collection of lectures *Ainsi parla l'oncle* argued that Vaudou could not be dismissed as mere superstition but was in fact a religion of "dynamism or animism". The *noiriste* writers of the Griot group (including the young François Duvalier who would later become the notorious Papa Doc) founded after the US occupation, developed this re-evaluation, calling Vaudou "the transcendent expression of racial consciousness before the enigmas of the world". The Duvaliers, father and son, exploited Vaudou connections to maintain power. Papa Doc especially, manipulated peasant sensibility, dressing at times like the spirits of death and rebirth.

MORE THAN *MERENGUE*

*They may not be politically in tune, but Haiti's African-rooted beats and the
Dominican Republic's eclectic dance music provide a musical bond*

The musical spectrum of Hispaniola ranges from Haiti's neo-African forms, some of the Caribbean's oldest surviving African music, to the manic mayhem of *merengue*, the Dominican national music, which is a serious contender for the fastest music in the Caribbean.

At first glance, these uneasy neighbours appear to have totally different musical traditions and styles (Haitian French and Creole influenced as opposed to the distinctive Latin sound of the Dominican Republic), but there are musical bonds linking the two political entities.

A common link

Periods of occupation by the French and then by independent Haiti did not endear Dominicans to Haitians. Consequently, despite their equally antagonistic relationship with Spain, Dominicans have always identified culturally with Spain or other Latin American countries. Their African heritage, symbol of the Haitian enemy, was rejected to the extent that blacks even now often refer to themselves as "Indios oscuros" (dark-skinned Indians).

Yet the west African heritage is there, both indigenous and imported by thousands of Haitians who came, and still come, to cut sugar cane. The Dominican folk religion, with its worship of west African spirits, drum-led songs, dances and spiritual possession, is close to Haiti's Vaudou, while *gaga* (a Dominican version of Haiti's *rara*, a raucous Lenten street procession music featuring bamboo and zinc trumpets) is popular on the western border with its large Haitian immigrant community.

Even *merengue* links the two. Ironically it is still the national dance of both countries. The Haitian and Dominican versions both originated in the first half of the 19th century. These were only two variants of a whole family of creolised European dance forms based on the

---

LEFT: playing the maracas at a beach bar on the Samaná Peninsula.
RIGHT: Feet of Rhythm reveal the importance of dance to the culture.

contredanse, mazurka, polka, quadrille and waltz, which were fairly popular throughout the Greater and Lesser Antilles.

As might be expected, controversy and rivalry surround the origins of the *merengue*, with the Haitians claiming they introduced it east of the border during the 1822–44 occupation. During

the 20th century, the Dominican form became so dominant it was borrowed in the 1950s to form the basis for Haiti's enduringly popular *konpa* dance music.

Caribbean interaction

Another significant yet more subtle musical bond between the two countries comes from their constant exposure to other Caribbean styles of music. The migratory experience of both populations has involved them in cultural interaction in neighbouring Cuba and Puerto Rico and throughout the greater Caribbean. In the past, Cuban *son*, *bolero*, *guaguanco* and *mambo*, and more recently *salsa* from Puerto

Rico, influenced both Haitian and Dominican music, while the Haitian-derived *tumba francesa* became a distinct genre in Cuba's Oriente province, and *merengue* has been a huge hit as far south as Venezuela.

Beyond these links, however, the two countries have their own distinctive music. What is so surprising initially is that both countries (especially Haiti, the poorest nation in the whole of the western hemisphere) have produced such vibrant, powerful music, considering their long histories of oppression and devastation.

Haiti is unique for its sacred Vaudou drums and vast repertoire of songs and dances (many

Vaudou evolved as a clandestine and syncretic religion under colonialism. The slaves came from an area in west Africa stretching from Senegal to the Congo River basin and on arrival in St Domingue, members of the same ethnic group were deliberately separated in order to prevent communication and rebellion.

The ancestral spirits and deities of the many different tribes were integrated into a new, extended pantheon, which also embraced the Roman Catholic saints of the French slave masters. In the isolation of the plantations and the mountain communities of runaway slaves, the religion and its music developed some regional

still undocumented and unrecorded) performed to worship and invoke the *Lwas*, or spirits. Although similar neo-African religions exist throughout the Americas, (Santería in Cuba, Kumina in Jamaica, Shango in Trinidad and Candomblé in Brazil and other South American countries) Haiti's early independence in 1804 meant the survival of African musical forms to an extent unparalleled elsewhere.

Some of these forms are now unknown in Africa. It has been suggested that their survival is not due simply to the conservatism of religious music but rather to the fact that specific rhythms are used to summon the spirits. If those rhythms are altered, the spirits do not answer.

variations. Even the sacred drum – the voice of the spirits – comes in many shapes and sizes, from the 3 metre (10ft) tall *asoto* to the bongo-sized *tanbou kout*. Most of the other instruments are percussive (rattles, bells and tambourines), but the European violin and flute are used by southern *menwat* (minuet) groups, a legacy of the days when slaves played in orchestras at the colonists' concerts, operas and balls.

Among the many different rites, the Rada of Dahomey (the oldest African tradition in Haiti), the Kongo, Petwo (a new nation of militant spirits called into being to combat slavery) and Bizango (secret society) are best known. All these rites have their own specific instruments, rhythms, song and dance cycles. Rada instruments include three, single-headed cowskin drums: the largest, the *manman* (mother drum) is played with one hand and the hammer-shaped *agida* stick. The *manman* leads the dance with its low-register rolling, indicating choreographic or song changes by breaking against the rhythms of the other drums. The midsized, middle-register *segon* is played with one half-moon-shaped *abara* stick and a straight stick, answering the *manman* with intricate patterns, between drums and call-and-response songs, is the most sophisticated Vaudou music.

For Westerners accustomed to the concept of sheet music, the experience of listening to the master drummers leading the five-days-and-nights Rada ceremony at Souvenance which begins on Easter Saturday *(see page 107)*, is incredible.

The rhythms, passed down from generation to generation, are never repeated and there are no scores to play from. Sera Jean-Baptiste, one of the Souvenance

MERENGUE FESTIVAL

Santo Domingo's annual Merengue Festival is held in the last week of July and the first week of August, featuring a selection of the world's best merengue bands and dancers.

while the smallest, high-pitch *boula* – played with two straight sticks – continues a regular beat in time with the *ogan* (bell). The *ason* (rattle) can only be handled by *oungans* and *mambos* (priest and priestesses) or the *oungenikon* (chorus leader). Occasionally, a *bas* (large tambourine) supports the *manman*.

The foremost Rada rhythms are the trilogy of *yanvalou*, *mayi* and *zepol*, and the *nago gwan kou*, *kongo-rada* and *dyouba-matinik*. Rada music, with its beautiful interplay

LEFT: the brass section of L'Orchestre Septientional play at home and abroad.
ABOVE: Kanpech on stage.

"admirals of the drums", jokingly admits, "You have to know how to play drums here. You really have to know what you're doing, otherwise they'll eat you!"

Marathon ceremony

The main rite for the Kongo spirits is the marathon 15-days-and-nights ceremony at Sukri Danache. The Kongo rhythms of *kita* and *boumba* are played by hand on two single-headed goatskin drums, which answer each other call-and-response style, while *tchachas* (rattles) play in counter rhythm and the bell maintains a continuous time. Southern Kongo groups may use up to eight drums in an ensemble.

Besides the sacred music of Vaudou, Haiti also has a rich folk tradition and a variety of urban-based European and Caribbean influenced dance styles. The traditional folk song "*Choucoune*" provided the melody for "*Yellow Bird*", a long-time favourite throughout the English-speaking Caribbean.

Many of the folk forms, work songs of the *konbits* (communal field gangs), play, story, praise, protest and political songs are simply continuations of African traditional forms. *Mizik twoubadou* (troubadour music), which is performed by small ensembles of guitar, maracas, *gwaj* (scraper), *tanbou* drum and *marimba* (a wooden

trumpets), *big* (bugle), *gwaj*, *tchacha* and occasionally saxophone and trumpet. Those without instruments beat time on empty bottles.

The most significant dance music since the 19th century has been the *meringue* or *mereng*, a creolised version of an old European dance, although other forms, such as the *mascarón*, *quadrille* and *contredanse* have also enjoyed popularity. Based on the quintuplet, a five-note rhythm, the *mereng* originally developed in two forms: one for the salon and one for the streets.

European-trained Haitian composers like Occide Jeanty, Ludovic Lamothe and François Manigat wrote *merengs* for piano, sometimes

box bass fitted with metal keys which are plucked by the player who sits on the box), was introduced by cane-cutters returning from Cuba.

Rara music

Another folk form which is just as popular as carnival music in countryside and city alike, is *rara*. This exuberant music, which has Vaudou connections, accompanies the vividly costumed bands that parade through the streets from Ash Wednesday to Easter day. While the bands sing songs with themes ranging from topical events to political satire and the outrageously obscene, a skilled hooting accompaniment is provided by *vaksins* and *kones* (bamboo and pressed zinc

using violins or woodwind. The Afro-Parisian sound is reminiscent of ragtime and Puerto Rican dances of the same era. The street *mereng* was especially popular with the 19th-century carnival crowds, as it was used to mock and ridicule prominent or powerful figures.

As a popular dance, the *mereng* acted as a barometer of musical and ideological fashion, absorbing any number of influences. During the American occupation of 1915–34, dance bands began incorporating jazz into their repertoire and from the 1920s onwards Cuban *son* was a major influence. Aspects of Vaudou music were introduced as part of the movement rejecting US culture and affirming Haitian values.

While classical composers like Justin Elie and Werner Jaegerhuber utilised Vaudou-inspired melodies, the dance bands, now in a big swing band format, introduced Vaudou ceremonial instruments to their line-up and Vaudou rhythms and melodies to their compositions. The Super Jazz de Jeunes, the most famous of the Vaudou-Jazz bands, dressed in colourful folk style and their stage show included dancers moving to the well-known *yanvalou*, *kongo* and *ibo* Vaudou rhythms.

By the mid-1950s, the craze for the accordion- and sax-led Dominican merengue swept Haiti, altering the course of its cousin for ever. In 1955, saxophonist Nemours Jean-Baptiste introduced his new dance rhythm, *konpa-direk* (direct rhythm), which, while slightly altering the beat, owed much to the merengue.

This was the start of *konpa*, which would dominate Haitian popular music until the 1980s and which is still played by foreign-based bands, notably, Tabou Combo and the Magnum Band. In 1958, Weber Sicot, Haiti's leading saxophonist, produced his *Kadans-rampa* (rampart) rhythm (identical to *konpa* except for a minor variation in beat) in direct competition with Nemours. It was the contrived rivalry between the two bandleaders, which marked the start of modern commercial Haitian music, lasting until Sicot's 1965 song of truce, *"Polemik Fini"*.

Mini-djaz bands

In the early 1960s, the influence of US and British rock and pop spawned a proliferation of Yeye combos (after The Beatles' *Yeah Yeah Yeah*) among the children of middle- and upper-class Haitians. Although the Yeyes were popular at youth concerts, the non-contact dances which went with the music were too much of a break with the traditional *tet kole* (heads glued together) dance style. Combos began including *konpa*, with its close-couple dance style, in their repertoires. These groups were known as *mini-djaz* (big dance bands were known as *djaz*, while *mini* referred to the miniskirt craze).

With the success of *mini-djaz* bands like Shleu-Shleu and Tabou Combo, the established *konpa* bands scaled themselves down in order to compete. Through the 1970s, *konpa* – with

LEFT: a variety of percussion instruments on sale at mercado modelo, Santo Domingo.
RIGHT: Tabou Combo.

its guitar and percussion sound augmented by sax or organ – was a major influence in the French Antilles, French Guiana, and Dominica and St Lucia (both English-ruled islands with Creole-speaking populations).

But with the emergence of hi-tech *zouk* in Martinique and Guadeloupe in the early 1980s, that influence waned as it did back home where *konpa*, the popular music of the repressive Duvalier era, made way for a new cultural thrust. One of the few island-based *konpa* bands to survive the change was Coupé Cloué, led by the late great troubadour Gesner Henry.

The most significant development in the past

PUERTO PLATA FESTIVAL

The second largest merengue festival in the Dominican Republic is held during the first week of October in the large town of Puerto Plata, on the northern edge of the country – the Amber Coast. It is the largest town on the Atlantic side and also capital of the province. During the festival, the malecón is closed to vehicles so that a multitude of stalls can be assembled along both sides of the wide seafront street. A large stage is erected, on which famous merengue singers perform songs and dances. The carnival is also a harvest festival and includes a traditional arts and crafts fair where local artisans exhibit their wares.

two decades has been the *mizik rasin* (roots music) movement, which some see as a development from Vaudou-jazz of the 1940s. *Mizik rasin* was produced by the generation who, at the end of the 1970s, were influenced by roots reggae, funk and rock.

While the novel *generayson* cultural movement of the 1980s stressed the importance of the Creole language and utilising rural music as inspiration, *mizik rasin* explored Rara and ceremonial Vaudou music. Foula, led by the Vaudou master drummer Aboudja,

POPULAR PERFORMER

Manno Charlemagne is a witty and satirical troubadour who began singing protest songs in the Duvalier era. He has spent many years in exile and is now mayor of Port-au-Prince.

following. Their live performances, with Hendrix-like guitar soaring over the battery of Vaudou drums, are intense and cathartic. It's not unusual for audience members at a Boukman Eksperyans concert to become possessed. Theodore "Lolo" Beaubrun, founder and leader of Boukman explains: "This music is engaged, for the revolution. We have to go back to the spirit level, beyond intellect, ideology, religion."

The contemporary music scene reflects some of the current trends in the Caribbean and the

experimented with a fusion of both Vaudou drumming and American-influenced jazz.

Bands like Boukman Eksperyans, Sanba-yo, Sakad, Boukan Ginen, Kalfou Lakay and more recently Koudjay, Ram, Zobop, Alowi Jaweh and Kampech use traditional songs and Vaudou rhythms in a vibrant new fusion incorporating transnational influences from rock, funk, jazz and more recently rap and hip hop. The *rasin* bands are probably the first Haitian representatives on the World Music scene.

With conscious lyrics which champion the poor and oppressed in Bob Marley style, the *rasin* bands, who have suffered their share of persecution at the hands of the military, have built a huge

US. *Zouk*, *salsa*, *merengue*, soca and especially reggae and ragga from neighbouring Jamaica are all popular. King Posse, the young dancehall band even sing in convincing Jamaican patois. Rap and hip hop artistes have been on the scene since Master Dji's 1987 "Sispann", a call for the end of political violence. This style has received a tremendous boost from the success of Haitian-born Wyclef Jean, one time Fugee, whose debut CD *The Carnival* included four Creole tracks.

Although they do not belong to the world of super hype, there are two young guitarists who are highly respected at home and around the world. Beethova Obas for his gentle troubadour songs which draw on traditions from Brazil and the entire Caribbean, and the composer Amos Coulange for virtuoso renditions of his new arrangements of folk themes from Haiti and the French Antilles. The young tropical flamenco trio Strings are also acquiring an international reputation.

A few hours on the bus takes you from the home of Vaudou rhythms across the border to the capital of merengue, the northern provincial town of Santiago de los Cabelleros, which is the Dominican version of Nashville.

Musically the Dominican Republic may be synonymous with merengue, but there are instrument with purely African origins is still used in parts of the DR, where it is known as a *gayumba*, and the tall *palo* drums of the Afro-Dominican folk religion which are played throughout the Republic, are Yoruba in design.

The *palo*, which is carved from a single piece of wood and then hollowed out, comes in two sizes: the *mayor* is 1.5 metres (5ft) -tall and 30 cm (1ft) in diameter across the single goatskin head; the *menor* is nearly 1 metre (3ft) -tall and 23 cms (9 inches) across. While one drummer beats the skin with bare hands, another hits the body of the drum with a stick, a recognisably African practice.

many other styles to discover. These range from the distinctly African style *cantos de hacha*, chopping songs of the south and *plenas*, or work songs, to the almost pure Spanish *tonadas* and *salves* of the Cibao Valley, whose melodies resemble those of ancient Castille.

African influences

Even though the African heritage has been denied or rejected by the cultural mainstream, it survives. The mosquito drum or earthbow, an

LEFT: Lolo Beaubrun, the lead singer of Boukman Eksperyans, one of the most popular *racines* bands.
ABOVE: Richard Marx of RAM.

Fiestas celebrating Saints' days often feature *palo*-driven music, which takes the form of call-and-response song and dance. In the north coast town of Samaná, where many of the black American immigrants who arrived in 1824 were settled, the feast day (21 January) of the Republic's patron saint, the Virgin of Altagracia, is preceded by the *Novenas* – nine nights of celebration. The festivities start at 9pm each night, finishing at six the following morning, and the focus of these all-night parties is the *palo* drumming, with its accompanying Dance of the Palos (a circular couples dance) and improvised songs, sung by a lead singer with call-and-response chorus. In Samaná, the *bambula*, an Afro-Caribbean dance widespread throughout the Caribbean, is also performed.

Another obvious example of African and Roman Catholic syncretism is the *saradunga* festival, held for John the Baptist on the night of 23 June in the southern town of Baní. Here the *Capitana*, *Bomba* (the major African dance of Puerto Rico) and the *Jacana* are all carried out to the accompaniment of the double-headed, barrel-shaped *tambora* drum, the *guira* (metal scraper) and the characteristic and ubiquitous call-and-response singing.

Only 19 km (12 miles) from Santo Domingo in Villa Mella, a popular legend exists explain-

imported by immigrants from the English Leeward and Windward islands and the Momise dance dramas, Creole versions of the English Mummers plays, were brought from St Kitts and Nevis in the 1920s. In San Pedro, *la danza del padre invierno* (a Father Winter dance based on the St George and the dragon legend), *la danza salvaje* (wild dance) and *la danza del Codril* are performed on St Peter's Day (29 June) and at other festivals on the island.

Even the basic five-note rhythm of the merengue probably has African origins. This rhythmic pattern is common to much of the black music of the Americas, from the Cuban

ing the arrival of the *palo* drums, which are used by the congos del Espirutu Santo, who play at the feast of the Holy Ghost and throughout the year at wakes and secular dances. Folklore has it that in the mid-19th century a saint was found playing the drums in a guava field. A more mundane theory is that this tradition derived from the African *kalinda* dance, which was banned a century before.

Other folk rhythms, like the *mangulina* from the mountains and the *carabine,* may well have African origins. One unique Afro-Caribbean tradition, the *ritmo guloya* of the San Pedro de Macoris region on the south coast, deserves special mention. The *guloya* dances were

habanera, Puerto Rican *danza* and Argentinian tango, to the early Trinidadian calypsos.

The origins of merengue are undocumented. One theory suggests that the original dance was based on the popular *upa* from Cuba, which travelled to Puerto Rico where it was banned as immoral in 1848. After adapting steps from the *contradanza*, it was then referred to as the *merengue*. An account of its first performance in the Dominican Republic goes back to the 1844 war against the Haitians, when the victorious Dominicans sang and danced a song about a deserter: *Toma' Juyo con la Bandera* (Thomas Fled with the Flag).

Despite its obscure beginnings, merengue

developed from folk forms before going on to establish itself not only as the national dance music but as an international genre, which even eclipsed salsa as *the* Latin dance sound of the 1980s. Of the many Creolised European dance forms to originate from the Caribbean, *merengue* has probably travelled the furthest and certainly moves the fastest.

In its early form the merengue was played by ensembles of guitar (or smaller four-string cuatro), *guira* (a perforated metal cylinder scraped with a metal stick, a modern

> **UBIQUITOUS SOUNDS**
>
> The big band sound of merengue can be heard all over the DR – in the streets, restaurants, taxis and bars – and mostly played at full volume. You'll either love or hate it.

of vibrant rhythms and the call-and-response final section of the accompanying songs, with their wide-ranging topics. Predictably spurned by the white and mulatto élite as being vulgar, merengue was enthu-siastically embraced by every-body else.

By the end of World War I, the modern form of merengue had been established: the short introductory *paseo* followed by the two longer sections, the *merengue* or song section which segued into the call-and-response, improvised *jaleo*. The structure of the two main

version of the gourd scraper still used in Cuba), *tambora* (double-headed barrel drum, the left head made from male goatskin played by hand; the female goatskin right head played with a stick), and *marimba* (a metal key box bass).

By the 1870s, the guitar had given way to the melodeon, the button accordion brought by German immigrants, which was to give the merengue its defining sound.

What began as a very restrained European dance soon took on the Afro-Caribbean features

LEFT: merengue was made for dancing.
ABOVE: music can be heard everywhere – in the bars, restaurants, clubs and on the street.

parts is very similar to Afro-Cuban forms like the rumba or *guaguanco*, where the melodic European-style first part is followed by some percussion-led improvisation.

Of all the regional variants the *merengue tipico* of the Cibao region has became the most influential. This classic style known as *Perico Ripiao* (after The Ripped Parrot bar in Santi-ago's red-light district) was popularised by bandleaders like Nico Lora and Tono Abreu in the 1920s. Galvanised by the runaway tempo of the *tambora*, the accordion is played with staccato stabs to the harmonising saxophone. A late addition to the line-up, the sax would blare out *merengue*'s international success, but the accordion-led style is still very much alive in Santiago with players like Francisco Ulloa and Fefita de la Grande.

The American occupation of 1916–24 fuelled growing nationalism and with it bourgeois acceptance of the merengue. Although the DR has little to be grateful to Rafael Trujillo for, during his bloodthirsty dictatorship merengue was elevated to the status of national music and dance by a 1936 decree. Urban dance bands were legally required to incorporate merengue in their swing band repertoires. These bands, heavily influenced by Cuban *mambo*, added the exhilarating

trumpet and sax arrangements which still feature in contemporary merengue.

Ironically, Trujillo's 1961 assassination was celebrated with the merengue "*El Muerte del Chivo*" (Death of the Goat). While the 1970s saw merengue competing with salsa and US pop, the emergence of bandleaders like Johhny Ventura, Cuco Valoy and Wilfredo Vargas pioneered the speed-defying modern version of *merengue* which would sweep the heartlands of salsa in Puerto Rico and New York City.

Ventura, with his James Brown-like stage presence, pared down the ensemble, giving the lead role to the sax and the horns, replacing the accordion with guitar and keyboards or synthesizer, and emphasising the automatic fire of the *tambora*. Vargas has made the merengue a truly Caribbean mélange of drawing-room *konpa*, *zouk*, reggae and even rap.

Rival to merengue

The most outstanding figure of what some would call neo-*merengue*, is the extraordinary singer/songwriter Juan Luis Guerra. After training at the National Conservatory and studying jazz at Boston's prestigious Berkley College of Music, he returned home to form the vocal quartet 440, performing Manhattan Transfer-style jazz songs.

In the 1990s, Guerra tackled both merengue and *bachata*, traditional, sentimental, guitar-based country music. With influences ranging from The Beatles to the great Panamanian salsero Ruben Blades and the Cuban *nueva canción* singers, particularly Silvio Rodriguez, Guerra's nasal delivery perfectly matches the popular timbre of the Latin style. His vocal sophistication, intelligent and often socially conscious lyrics, and command of diverse styles, make him – along with the brilliant jazz pianist Michel Camilo – the Dominican Republic's most significant contribution to international music.

Although it has not yet gained the international exposure of *merengue*, *bachata* (songs of bitterness) is the highly popular soul music of the Dominican barrios, the voice of the displaced rural peasant driven by poverty to the slums of Santo Domingo, New York City or any major Caribbean port. It is easy to identify a Dominican bordello in Antigua, Curaçao or the Virgin Islands by the steady stream of sweet melancholic *bachata* drifting from it at all hours of the day and night.

Bachata developed from the guitar-led folk ensembles of the 19th century, which by the 1950s played a repertoire of Cuban *sons*, *boleros* and Mexican *rancheras*, with their sentimental appeal. Although dismissed by the middle classes, who in the 1970s labelled it *bachata* after the raucous lower-class fiestas, singers like Luis Segora and Julio Angel popularised the form to the extent that it now rivals the *merengue* at home. ❑

LEFT: innovative band leader Johnny Ventura has been compared to James Brown on stage.
RIGHT: Emeline Michelle gets in the groove.

HAITI'S LITERARY ART

Haitian authors are making their mark at home and abroad with serious
novels written in various languages, including Creole

The new voices in Haitian literature are speaking in different languages: English, French and Creole. In the US, the strongest of those voices belongs to Edwidge Danticat, a young Haitian American author who has earned the respect of literary critics and a devoted following among lovers of new Caribbean feminist literature *(see page 126)*. Her short story collection, *Krik? Krak!*, was nominated for the prestigious National Book Award in 1995.

In French-speaking Canada, it's the voice of Dany Laferriere that's being heard. His *How to Make Love to a Negro* – the fanciful musings of an immigrant out of place – caused a sensation when it hit the bookshops of Montréal in the autumn of 1985. Most of Laferriere's work has now been translated into English.

Immigrant voice

A lot of serious literature is being created in Haiti as well, by authors such as Rodney St Eloi, Yanick Lahens, Margaret Papillon, Paulette Poujol and Lyonel Trouillot, who all write in French. Among them is Gary Victor, who served as a deputy minister under former president Jean-Bertrand Aristide, before the military coup of 1990. Vaudou, politics and acerbic social comment are blended in his novels.

Danticat's stories, however, have struck a chord that resonates deeply among women and immigrants in the United States. Her voice is fresh, honest, caring and respectful of the past. She speaks eloquently and realistically about the experience of moving to a new land.

Danticat grew up in New York City, but all her stories have deep roots in the Haitian soil of her childhood. It is in Haiti that she began to notice, and nurture, the magic of storytelling – as much a part of the Haitian landscape as its mountains and blue seas. "In telling stories to my mother and me, my grandmother gave us a gift, a treasure trove of beautiful memories..."

LEFT: reading at Hostal Nader Hotel, Santo Domingo.
RIGHT: Vaudou rituals continue to be a common theme in Haitian storytelling.

Danticat writes in the foreword to *The Magic Orange Tree and other Haitian Folktales*, a collection by Diane Wokstein. "For once you are granted the remembrance of a story, it never stops with you. You find yourself anticipating your next opportunity to retell the tale."

It is in that spirit that she wrote her recent

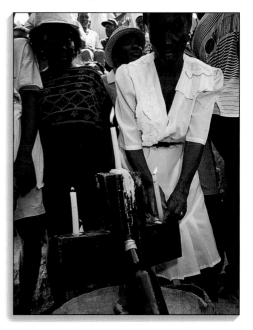

novel, *The Farming of Bones*. Set in 1937 in the Dominican Republic, the story turns over soil that has been soaked over decades with Haitian blood. It is the story of one kind of immigrant, Haitians too poor and unable to find work in their own country who cross over to the other side of the island to cut sugar cane. Danticat creates characters that could have walked out of any history book, or any painting depicting that migration. *The Farming of Bones* is fiction, but it could have been fact.

Set on the comfortable plantation of Alegria, not far from the border with Haiti, the novel begins on an August morning in 1937. The protagonist is Haitian-born Amabelle Desir, who serves as light housekeeper and companion to Señora Valencia, Alegria's young matron. Amabelle and Señora Valencia have been friends since they were little girls, since the day Valencia's father found Amabelle in tears on the banks of the Massacre River. Amabelle's parents, herbal healers, perished after they were caught in the river's current and swept away

So the girls grew up together, Amabelle sharing a room with Valencia, but that changed when Valencia married the ambitious Pico Duarte, a rising star in the army of dictator Rafael Leonidas Trujillo Molina. What united them in the past is now forgotten. Their blood and class differences are now all that matters. Amabelle is banished from Valencia's bedroom, and shares a room with a sugarcane worker who arrived looking for work after a hurricane destroyed his home in Haiti.

When Valencia gives birth to twins, a boy and a girl. The boy, light-skinned, is named after the dictator. The girl's skin is deep bronze. "Amabelle, do you think my daughter will always be the colour she is now?" Valencia asks. "My poor love, what if she's mistaken for one of your people."

Against this background begins one of the most appalling chapters in Dominican history.

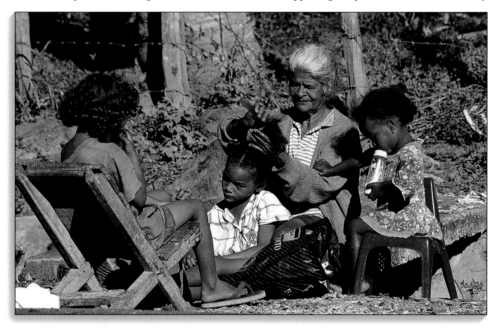

THE ART OF STORYTELLING

Darkness falls in Haiti, and everything turns to magic. Around the countryside, the only visible light is a yellowish glow from small kerosene lamps inside small huts. Mothers put their babies to bed. Everyone whispers as they move around, large shadows on the walls. The only noises are the mournful sounds of livestock bedding down for the night.

There are no TVs here, only a storyteller who gathers children around him to hear his folktales. "Crick!" says the storyteller, a signal that the story is about to begin. "Crack!" they answer, meaning they're ready. And so the story begins.

Haitians believe that nightfall is the right time for stories. Telling a story in daylight only brings bad luck. Tonight, maybe they'll hear about the *loupgarou*, the werewolf who eats children alive. Or they'll hear about Bouki, a dumb character who gets into all kinds of trouble, or Malis, the smart fellow who gets Bouki out of those troubles.

Some stories are about the church and God, others are about Vaudou. In Haiti's oral tradition, these stories occupy an important place. Watching the faces of the children and their wide, bright eyes, they certainly entertain. They're also used to educate, to tell right from wrong. They've been passed along through the centuries, often with little change. Some tell what life was like during slavery, and others go all the way back to Africa.

In October 1937, thousands of Haitian labourers are shot by Dominican troops and police. The killings go on all over the country. Dominicans support the effort. Haiti's president, Stenio Vincent, remains silent in the face of such horror. "The poor man, no matter who he is, is always despised by his neighbours," someone tells Amabelle. "When you stay too long at a neighbour's house, it's only natural that he become weary of you and hate you."

As a child, Danticat lived through her own

THE 1937 MASSACRE

President Trujillo was angry at the number of Haitians settling in the DR. Thousands were herded up in courtyards, forced to lie face down, then shot in the back of the head.

Luckily, she survived that dark period in history, joining her family in New York three years later. Like all young immigrants of that age, Danticat spent a period floating between languages – in her case, Creole and English.

It didn't take her long to find her voice, though. In her first published work, an essay that appeared in a New York newspaper, she talked honestly about her immigrant experience. Graduating from Barnard College with a degree in French literature didn't leave many options. It was either teaching

version of madness and terror under Jean-Claude Duvalier, who was named Haitian president for life after his father François Papa Doc Duvalier died in 1971. Danticat was nine years old at the time. Dissent was not tolerated.

When Danticat first started writing down her poems in her little schoolgirl notebooks, "a lot of people who were in jail were writers. They were journalists, they were novelists, and many of them were killed or 'disappeared'. It was a very scary thing to think about," she said.

LEFT: many remember hearing stories at their grandmother's knee.
ABOVE: imagery in art is mirrored in literature.

or nursing. She chose writing, translating her experiences into tales of universal appeal.

Danticat was only 25 years old when *Breath, Eyes, Memory* was accepted for publication. Next came *Krik? Krak!*, which includes stories about life in Haiti during the Duvalier years. Characters range from a man attempting to leave the island in a faulty boat to a woman who doesn't want her son to discover she's a prostitute.

The well-received collection competed for the National Book Award with works by writers such as Madison Smartt Bell, whose own *All Souls Rising* explored the Haitian revolution in all its gory details.

Edwidge Danticat

There's no mistaking Edwidge Danticat's voice. It's strong, immigrant, female and black. And, it's unsettling. In her novel, *The Farming of Bones*, she leads readers through a nightmarish landscape of brutality, where labourers from Haiti are treated as less than human on the sugar cane plantations of the Dominican Republic.

Danticat may be the most celebrated Haitian-American writer of her young generation, but she knows about pain. She was only an infant when her father left the family's native Haiti for New York,

in search of a better life. Her mother followed soon after, leaving her to be raised by an uncle. Danticat hardly knew her family when she and a younger brother were reunited with their parents in America more than eight years later. A shy 12-year-old, her accented English stood out at Clara Barton High School in Brooklyn. She quickly assimilated.

Raised in a culture that teaches its women to be mute and obedient in a male-dominated world, Danticat now lays bare painful issues once taboo in her homeland. In her first novel, *Breath, Eyes, Memory*, Danticat shares a young twisted world, between love and sexual deviousness, as she traces the mental steps a young girl goes through as her mother tests her virginity. Is this sexual abuse? Would she have

thought those thoughts in Haiti? The US creates the space that makes it possible to raise those questions, and Danticat's character, Sophie, begins to distance herself, from her family and her culture.

Her recent novel, *The Farming of the Bones*, also explores the great divide of exile, this time between families and between countries. Seminal moments in the story take place along the Massacre River, which separates Haiti and the Dominican Republic. Generations of Haitian farmers have crossed over to cut sugar cane, live on plantation-style shacks, and get miserable wages. Those who have stayed behind illegally live in fear of border-town army patrols that can send them back to Haiti at any time. Haitians say that as black Creole speakers, they are treated shabbily. Some elderly Dominicans tell their grand-children stories of legendary cruelty from Haiti's army of freed slaves who occupied the Spanish side of the island for 20 years after their revolution.

It is against this background that Haitian-born Amabelle Desir, the protagonist in *The Farming of Bones,* serves as light housekeeper and companion to Señora Valencia, a plantation's young matron. Amabelle's parents drowned in the swirling waters of the Massacre, where the plantation owner picked up the orphan. The girls grew up together, but worlds apart. Amabelle's Haitian roots in 1937 force her to flee the house where she was raised, as Rafael Leonidas Trujillo's army leads a pogrom against Haitians in his country. More than 30,000 Haitians are said to have died at the hands of Dominican soldiers, militias whipped up into a frenzy, the waters of the Massacre flowing red.

Sixty years on, the genocide continues to find deep resonance in Haiti, a country still seeped in blood and tears. Danticat's voice has found a res-onance in international circles, her work getting the attention it deserves, both in her adopted coun-try and in her homeland. Her collection of short stories, *Krik? Krak!*, was nominated for a National Book Award and in 1998 the *New York Times Mag-azine* picked out Danticat as one of America's most promising young artists. She was an honoured guest at Haiti's Festival of the Diaspora in 1999.

Although she writes about deeply hurtful episodes, Danticat draws readers in with sparse words presented in a gentle style. But don't mis-take that gentleness for anything less than what it is: a writer of exceptional talent sharing a rich her-itage with her fellow Haitians and opening a new world to readers throughout the globe. ❑

LEFT: Edwidge Danticat: a novelist who knows pain.

Dany Laferriere made his mark as a writer early on, too. His satire *How to make Love to a Negro* became wildly popular in Canada and was quickly adapted and made into a film when he was still in his early 30s. Like Danticat, Laferriere was born in Port-au-Prince, but left Haiti for exile in North America for different reasons.

He was working as a radio journalist in the mid-1970s at a time when the younger Duvalier was actually creating more openings in Haitian society for press

GUEST OF HONOUR

Although she writes in English, Danticat's fame has reached her homeland. She was a guest of honour at the 1999 Festival of the Diaspora in Haiti.

him long to produce *How to Make Love to a Negro*, a book about an immigrant determined to move ahead in a new culture without losing his identity.

The beauty of Laferriere's writing is that he didn't swallow this new culture whole. He set out to look at it with a critical eye. David Homel, who has translated Laferriere's works into English knows the author well. "That first novel," Homel says, "is not what one would expect to find by just reading the title. It is much more complex.

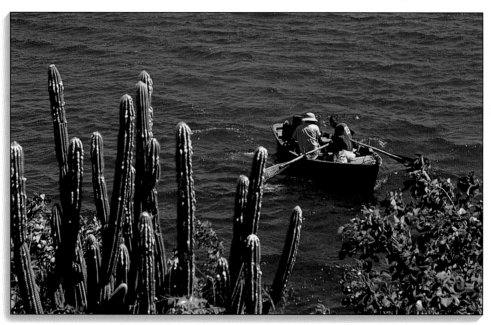

ABOVE: escape is a common theme in literature.

freedom. However, Laferriere soon saw the door of opportunity firmly closed when he stumbled upon the body of a murdered colleague on the side of the road. He decided it was time to move on and headed to Montréal. The year was 1978.

He followed the well-trodden immigrant path and found work as a labourer in various factories throughout the city. By night, he wrote about his experiences as a black man who grew up in Haiti, whose professional life took a curve, and who now was living among a minority in a city of French Canadians. It didn't take

"Once one gets past the effective teaser title," he continues, "sex becomes mostly an indicator of class, ethnic and historical conflict. When the hero fails to score, it is because he has committed not a romantic but a historical gaffe. Whether it is his praise of carbohydrates to a Scarsdale dieter, or his admission that, in his country, people eat cats, the results are hilarious and usually result in the hero sprinting out of his prospective lover's apartment to try to catch the last subway of the night. Even in the most sensual moments, the hero's calm, collected consciousness is evaluating the acts of love-making in terms of class and colour."

The book became an international best-seller,

making Laferriere Canada's best-known Haitian writer. He went on to work as a journalist for Canadian TV, while continuing with his fiction. Other works include: *Why Must a Black Writer Write About Sex?*, a look at race, sex and class in America; *Dining With the Dictator*, a tale of a young boy's foray into the lives of daring and beautiful women in Port-au-Prince; *An Aroma of Coffee*, the magical story of a 10-year-old boy spending the summer with his grandmother in a small town in Haiti, listening to her stories; and *Eroshima*, a contemplation on sex, death, beauty and the Bomb.

Laferriere and his family live part of the year in Canada – where he has a loyal following – and part of the year in Miami.

Many other young Haitian writers are finding their literary voices in exile, too, some even writing in Creole, which has been gaining wider acceptance as a written language in Haiti and elsewhere around the world.

A wider audience

In Haiti, most writers trying to reach an international audience continue to write in French. Among them is Marguerite Papillon, whose novels about class, colour and child abuse, among other issues, are gaining a small fol-

GRAHAM GREENE

In his 1966 novel, *The Comedians*, Graham Greene revealed Haiti's descent into a terrifying orgy of lawlessness under François "Papa Doc" Duvalier and his Tontons Macoutes. On one of his frequent visits to Haiti he took a room at the Hotel Oloffson, a creaky building in Port-au-Prince. A former "summer home" for a vice president, then a hospital during the American occupation, the hotel was later immortalised by Greene in his novel. As a small recompense, one of the rooms bears Greene's name. That tradition has been followed for several other artists who have graced the old hotel with their presence, such as the Rolling Stones' Mick Jagger.

lowing among Haitians in the United States and Canada. Papillon has written a selection of short stories, along with a novel for adolescents. She's married to the famous Haitian painter Albert Desmangles, and is reportedly also a talented painter herself.

The issues Papillon raises in her novels were first brought up by another female writer, Marie Chauvet. She was nurtured by the same egalitarian principles that were the hallmarks of other authors, such as Seymour Pradel and Jacques-Stephen Alexis, who rang the bell for writers of their generation to become engaged in the immediate world around them through their writing. Alexis' work laid the groundwork for the school of writing that would later be known as negritude.

Chauvet, who grew up in a world where women had limited roles, wrote passionately against all kinds of abuse committed against women and the poor. All her novels are dominated by the question of equality and justice. Her writings didn't have many fans, including her second husband, who apparently bought all remaining copies of *Amour, Colère et Folie*, (Love, Anger and Madness) – published in 1968 – and immediately had them burned. Chauvet died in New York City in the early 1970s.

These young writers, whether in exile or still

reproduce French literature in the Caribbean, with the subject of Haitians themselves being worthy of only cursory interest.

It took the US occupation in 1915 to change that. White US Marines from the American South did not deal in subtle racial categories. To them, Haitians were black, whether mixed race or pure Africans. And that included the writers, who were treated as blacks who spoke French.

This state of affairs spurred Haitian authors to begin looking at themselves differently. Led by Jean Price-Mars, they began to seek their identity in Haiti's African roots. They began to write about the people of Haiti, the peasants

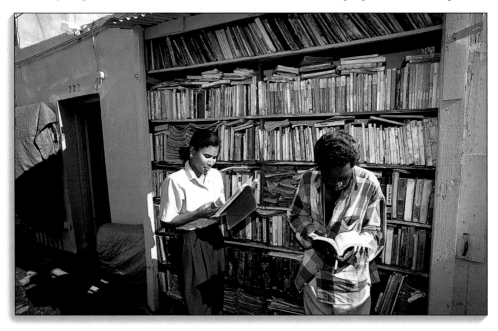

living in Haiti, are following a path first laid out at the turn the century by others like Jean Price-Mars. He put down the demarcation line in 1919 with his essay "Thus Spoke Uncle" about the need to recognise Vaudou and Creole as the essence of Haitian life.

There was no Haitian literature to speak of before Price-Mars. The Haitian experience was limited to writers of mixed race who had turned their backs on their African roots. It was part intellectual snobbery – they were trying to

LEFT: Hotel Oloffson in Port-au-Prince, made famous by Graham Greene's novel, *The Comedians*.
ABOVE: read in French, Creole, Spanish and English.

who live *en deyo* – a Creole term for "in the countryside" – away from the snobbery of city life. Creole words and Vaudou began to appear alongside each other in their books.

Political writers

Soon, some of these writers started dabbling in politics. In 1922, Price-Mars wrote a poem calling on Haitians to resist the occupation, which ended in 1935 with the withdrawal of US troops. Price-Mars became a national figure and later went on to occupy important positions in numerous administrations, including Minister of Foreign Affairs and Ambassador to France under François Duvalier in the 1960s.

But it would take writer Jacques Roumain to humanise the countryside Haitians, the pure descendants of Africans, who spoke only Creole and practiced Vaudou rather than Catholicism. Born in 1907, Roumain belonged to the same generation as Price-Mars. He founded the Haitian communist party, and died at the young age of 37. His novel, *Gouverneurs de la Rosée* (*Masters of the Dew*) may be the best-known Haitian novel of all time, translated into countless languages around the world and the subject of a feature film.

It is a universal story: a family's small plot of land turns into hard dirt from a brutal dryness that has gripped the land. Crops are dying. The prodigal son crosses the border into the Dominican Republic – just like Danticat's characters in *Farming of the Bones* – where he can work as a labourer on a sugar plantation. He keeps his family alive by sending money home, and on his return, actually brings them life itself, by going on a quest to find water. In the end he succeeds, and the whole community blossoms once more.

Besides *Masters of the Dew*, few other works by Roumain have been translated into English, although there are some famous poems of note, including *Langston Hughes*, *Madrid*, and *When the Tom-Tom Beats*.

While *Masters of the Dew* celebrates the power of the human spirit over environment, Roumain the doctrinaire Marxist seethes with anger in his other work. Listen to the opening section of his poem *Filthy Negroes*, when he says, "we filthy negroes, we won't take any more, that's right we're through being in Africa, in America, your negroes, your niggers, your filthy negroes, we won't take anymore, that surprises you, to say: yessuh, while polishing your boots, oui mon pe to the white missionaries, or master, while harvesting your sugar cane, coffee, cotton, peanuts, in Africa, in America, poor negroes, filthy negroes, that we were, that we won't be anymore, we're finished, you'll see…"

Passing on the torch

When the Catholic Church and the Haitian government began their campaign against Vaudou in the mid-1930s, with soldiers going about from village to village destroying altars and sacred symbols, Roumain was one of the first writers to oppose it. Strangely enough, he recognised the important place of Vaudou in Haitian culture, but was opposed to Vaudou itself. As a communist, he regarded it as a superstitious religion.

Roumain's literary activism didn't die out with his death. He passed the torch to other poets and novelists, such as Felix Morisseau-Leroy and René Dépestre. Morisseau-Leroy stunned the Haitian élite with his *Antigone in Creole*, an adaptation of the Greek tragedy to Haitian conditions in a language that other intellectuals of his time had deemed incapable of conveying complex ideas. ❏

WRITERS' RETREAT

The tranquil port of Jacmel, with its wide streets and the faded splendour of its grand townhouses, is undergoing a renaissance as a refuge for writers and artists. It is the birthplace of the renowned poet René Dépestre *(see opposite)* and also of the talented painter Préfète Duffaut, whose art work not only adorns the town itself but can also be seen in the Eglise Sainte Trinité Episcopal in Port-au-Prince. Both the government and the private sector are now investing in this town that was once a busy trading post and has traditionally had a long-standing link with the arts. There is also a strong tradition of Vaudou here.

LEFT: a rural image of rice harvesting.

A Writer in Exile

René Dépestre is arguably one of Haiti's greatest living writers. A political activist, Dépestre has lived in Cuba, where he used to broadcast communist propaganda targeted at Haiti. He has since renounced communism and now lives in France.

He came from a poor family in Jacmel, a city southwest of Port-au-Prince that has produced its fair share of writers and is currently becoming a refuge for artists from all over Haiti, the United States and even Europe.

Dépestre's parents could barely afford to send their children to school. But within the grinding poverty of their existence, there was also a certain dignity. And his family's dire economic condition did not stop the young poet from enjoying the beauty of the world around him.

He published his first work as early as 1946, when he was only 19 years old. His circle of friends include the Cuban poet Nicolas Guillen and Aimé Césaire of Martinique, and he once served as secretary to the famous Spanish poet, Pablo Neruda.

Dépestre's love of life shines through all his poems. They're filled with a sensuality, a love of things around him and of living beings.

His novel, *Closed for Dezombification*, takes an overt stab at the François "Papa Doc" Duvalier regime. The main character, Henri Postel, owns a small shop in a working-class neighbourhood of Port-au-Roi. He's 49, of mixed race, a former senator and political agitator.

He drinks too much. The president condemns him to death – by boredom. He's expected to fall apart in this process of internal zombification, but he manages to resist.

Life becomes interesting when Postel enters the annual contest of climbing the greasy pole, which takes place in the national park. President Zoocrates Zachary sees Postel's challenge as a personal threat to his own control, and decides to face him head-on.

Dépestre was transparent in his attempt to ridicule Papa Doc Duvalier's closest supporters, giving the characters in the book cover names that anyone living in Haiti at the time could easily match to the real people: Clovis Barbotog, Angel Boipiraud, the president's married daughter, the local bishop, Monsignor Wolgonde, and even the revolutionary Jean-Jacques Brissaricq. Haiti's infamous Fort Dimanche (Fort Sunday) becomes Fort Samedi (Fort Saturday).

Postel puts up his morally courageous battle against the forces of darkness and attempts to wake the Haitian people from the lethargy of their long-term hopelessness.

Dépestre has said in the past that the novel is not an historical chronicle, a *roman à clef*, or one based on his own life.

However, he was also quoted as saying that, "The events and the characters of the narrative

therefore belong to the realm of pure fiction.

"Any resemblance to persons, animals, trees, living or having lived, any similarity, close or distant, to names, situations, places, systems, cogwheels of steel or fire, or to any other scandal in real life, can only have the effect, therefore, of coincidence that is not only accidental, but downright scandalous."

Dépestre writes with passion and profound insight into the politics of Duvalierism and the penetrating influence of the practice of Vaudou on everyday Haitian life.

Like others before and after him, what he does best is simply, but beautifully, expose the fun and eroticism of what it means to be Haitian. ❑

RIGHT: René Dépestre spent many years writing in exile, unable to return to his homeland.

SPANISH AND AFRICAN CUISINE

*The fusion of European and spicy African influences have created
Dominican and Haitian cookery with their own distinctive flavours and colours*

Dominican cuisine owes much to its rural roots. Indigenous, African and Spanish heritages encouraged a varied harvesting of foodstuffs and cooking techniques which still flavour today's tastes. Rosy images of peasants farming homesteads or *conucos*, cultivating the staple crops of yam, plantains and sweet potato often romanticise a bucolic culinary past. But the severity of the colonial plantation system and the associated slave trade has similarly been a catalyst for contemporary Dominican dishes. Many modern-day food crops arrived from Africa on the slave ships, while the ill-fated indigenous groups already propagated plants such as the yucca.

Similarly, the lineage of traditional agricultural produce can be traced directly to the experimental dabbling of early Spanish settlers. Cattle, goats and chickens were domesticated, and the introduction of coffee and cocoa beans and their subsequent cultivation occurred only after the mid-18th century.

Perhaps the most significant new crop during colonial times was sugar cane. The arrival of Columbus on his second voyage with two bundles of cane later fuelled a sugar-based economy that not only shaped the historical development of the Caribbean region as a whole, but also redirected established trade routes. First cultivated during the 16th century, sugar cane remains the dominant crop. The failure in recent times, however, to stem the challenge of high fructose corn syrup and artificial sweeteners threatens to knock sugar off its throne. New pretenders are encroaching, and reinforcing their status as consumer and economic staples. Many of the former canefields are now carpeted by pineapples or forested with citrus and banana plants. The cultivation of traditional and arriviste foodstuffs closely parallels national development and forms the basis for the current *comida criolla* (Creole cuisine).

LEFT: a *fritay* vendor preparing *banan peze* fried plantain for sale, at the market in Charlette.
RIGHT: chickens on the way to market.

La bandera Dominicana

If invited to dine at a Dominican home, you will more than likely be treated to one of several favourite platters. Stories of *merengue*, politics and national pride will be nourished by *la bandera Dominicana*: flying the flag at dinner refers to the national dish of rice, beans,

chicken or meat, with avocado, plantain, yucca and salad. Tasty, wholesome and heavy. Rice and beans, *arroz con habichuelas*, form the foundation of most meals – good news for vegetarians. However, chicken, chicken and chicken is the other staple ingredient. No self-respecting restaurant leaves *arroz con pollo* (chicken and rice) off the menu.

Sancocho, a delicious meat and vegetable stew, is frequently employed in more poetic parlours as a metaphor for Dominican society. The pleasing potpourri of sausage, pork, chicken, beef, goat, vegetables, herbs and spices parallels the social blending of Spanish, indigenous and African influences. Conjured up for family occasions and friendly reunions, *sancocho* is a tasty potion for togetherness.

Another standard, *mofongo*, is a plantain-based dish served as a Dominican classic. A word of warning – many culinary adventurers have confused *mofongo* during their à la carte forays and ordered substantial helpings of another traditional favourite, *mondongo*, an action-packed stew of tripe and entrails.

Not so easily confused, *pipián* is another favourite stew, this time presenting the roaming palate with goat's offal. Goat (*chivo*) is served in a variety of forms and often makes an interesting variation for the visitors' tastebuds.

The less adventurous may settle for *asopao de pollo*, a deliciously filling chicken and rice soup. Extras include chicken's foot – a delicacy in the republic. Many dishes are served with green plantains, either boiled and mashed as *mangú*, or sliced and fried as *tostones*. Ripe or yellow plantains are also fried, but are much sweeter. *Ropa vieja*, "old clothes", generally fails to live up to its name and is usually a tasty dish of seasoned fried beef served with rice and a side salad of lettuce, shredded cabbage, tomato and avocado.

Festivals are an excuse to eat, particularly during *Las Navidades*, the Advent run-in of

How to Avoid Food Poisoning

Hotel food in the Dominican Republic won an unenviable reputation in the late 1990s when British newspapers reported a spate of food poisoning outbreaks among tourists on package holidays to the country. They alleged that food hygiene and sanitation were poor, even in some of the fancy hotels, and the Consumer Association's respected magazine *Holiday Which?* claimed that 90 percent of hotels inspected by them served contaminated food.

Fearing loss of revenue, the Dominican Republic Ministry of Tourism installed a team of inspectors to monitor all hotels and restaurants. Today the tourist chiefs claim that there have been no serious food poisoning outbreaks

recently and that hygiene standards are closely monitored.

Here are a few tips to help visitors avoid the kind of stomach upsets that can ruin a holiday:

● Make sure that all drinks and – just as important – the ice you put in them are made from boiled or bottled water.

● Avoid raw food, salads and fruit that may have been washed in tap water.

● Make sure all cooked food is served piping hot.

● Avoid cooked food that has been allowed to stand in the open for several hours.

● Be cautious of food from street vendors unless you have a strong stomach.

food, booze and merriment. Yuletide excess commences in earnest on Christmas Eve for those who can afford the season's festivities. *Lechón asado* (roast pig) traditionally draws family and friends together at house parties. *Pasteles en hoja*, savouries wrapped in plantain leaves, and *niños en vuelta*, minced meat swaddled in rice, complement the feast.

A sweet tooth is more than catered for by the sugar-laden range of desserts. Traditional cakes – *bizcochos* – combine sweetness with a highly adhesive and delicious white cream-like topping. *Dulces de leche* materialise as sweet dreams after liquidising milk with a variety of filled pastry turnovers) and *quipes* (ground beef encased in cracked wheat) provide a good entrée. *Chimichurris* are more substantial pork sandwiches off the spit.

After a few roadside fry-ups, even the most reticent of healthy eaters will be scrambling for an appointment with the nutritionist. Fortunately, they come to you. The itinerant fruit stalls (greengrocers on tricycles) offer a luscious cascade of fresh produce – mangoes, pineapples, oranges, *guineos* (bananas) – all peeled and presented for you. *Quenepas* may provide a handy new taste sensation. Sold in bunches, the brittle green skin of the fruit is

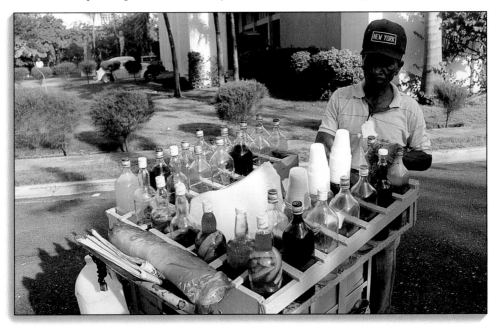

fruits then solidifying them in syrup. For those wishing to keep the sugar-rush at bay, *queso de hoja*, a moist white cheese from Bonao served with flat cassava bread, *casabe*, acts as the perfect antidote.

On the hoof

Much of Dominican culinary life occurs on the street. Fried foods are readily served up from mobile vats. A sampling of *yanniqueques* (Johnny cakes), *pastelitos* (meat or cheese-

broken open, revealing a white pit surrounded by a sweet pulp.

When the heat takes its toll, *frío fríos* provide temporary relief. Shavings of ice are scooped into a cup and topped with a variety of fruit syrups. Sliced coconuts provide a refreshing gush of *agua de coco*, and the gentle purr of a miniature mobile thresher will guide you to an energy-restoring glass of sugar cane juice.

Bars and cafés

Café society has found its tropical home in the Dominican Republic. Cafés cater for all tastes – coffee-fuelled morning reviews of the newspapers, sober afternoons of delicious ice creams

LEFT: Sunday lunch includes fried plantain.
ABOVE: a *frío frío* stand in the Dominican Republic offers temporary relief from the Caribbean sun.

and outrageously divine fruitshakes, or rum-soaked cocktail evenings. *Batidas con leche*, a rich mixture of condensed milk, sugar, crushed ice and a bewildering range of fruits will keep you nourished until supper. *Lechosa* (papaya), *zapote* and the unusually named orange-based *morir soñando* ("to die dreaming") are particular favourites. If fruit juice alone suffices, then *jugos* will be the order of the day. You may wish to ask the waiter to go easy on the sugar, or leave it out all together. *Jugo de china* and *chinola* – orange and passion fruit – frequently top the taste polls.

People-watching on a central plaza, such as

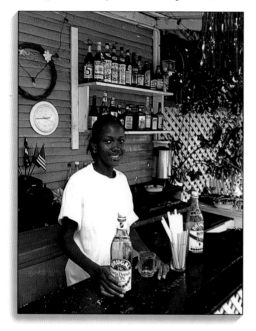

the capital's Plaza de la Hispanidad, provides a relaxed start to an evening's café entertainment. Whether cruising later to swish downtown bars, or meandering quietly homewards and stopping off at a *colmado*, the choice of beverages for the evening will be either the excellent domestic beer or locally-produced rums. The former option is ruled by Presidente, by far the most popular bottled beer and of outstanding quality. Attentive brewing and razor-sharp marketing has made this beer a national icon. Always served ice-cold, Dominicans will view with distaste anyone who accepts a lightly-chilled bottle.

Rum is sold in three general categories – *blanco*, *dorado*, and *añejo*. The former lighter rums are used in cocktails and with mixers. The darker blends are more suited to less vigorous adulteration. True *añejos* are best taken neat. *Un servicio* consists of a bottle of rum, a bucket of ice and *refrescos* (soft drinks) as mixers. Given the strength, quality and abundance of Dominican rums, the ability to hide alcohol within sweet fruit flavours, as exemplified by the ubiquitous *ron ponch*, is a dangerous trait among Dominican bartenders. Many a happy hour at sunset can slip smoothly through to a melancholic dawn.

Unmissable Haitian griyo

It's hard to miss the smell and sight of *griyo*. If Haiti had to have a national dish, griyo would carry the banner, and proudly. It's everywhere. It is part of what Haitians call *fritay* – Creole for fried food. There is no better word to describe those pieces of pork, sweet potatoes, bony fish, *akra*, fried plantain and *taso*, on sale on street corners throughout Haiti. Customers pick up a dollar's, or a few cents' worth, of *griyo* or *banan peze* (fried plantain) as a snack on the way to the Champs de Mars across from the National Palace in Port-au-Prince.

Fritay vendors are invariably women. They travel far and wide to get the best prices on *malanga* and *patates*, pork and snappers. To cook, they dip the flour-coated meat and vegetables into a vat of hot oil bubbling over a charcoal fire. On offer are tempting morsels including crispy pork rind, sweet potato, blackened fish, rice and beans. To accompany griyo ask for *pikliz* – shredded cabbage, carrots and peas pickled in hot peppers, although it's not advisable to order griyo if your stomach is not used to eating street food in Haiti.

HERBAL CURE-ALLS

Traditional remedies for a variety of maladies make full use of hundreds of local ingredients growing in the wild and widely available throughout Hispaniola. There are alleged natural cures for everything from the common cold to catarrh.

● To combat colds, a tea made from mint, limoncilla and guanábana (custard apple) leaves with lemon slices cut into the shape of a cross is recommended.

● For stomach aches, a tea of aloe leaves or cloves, cinnamon and aniseed will ease troubles away.

● Catarrh can be counteracted by a powerful concoction of shark and cod liver oil, chives and honey.

Nearby, a man, usually the fritay vendor's husband, sells pieces of sugar cane, another sort of fast food.

In the city, most Haitians seem to eat on the run during the day. This is odd in a country where unemployment, or under-employment, is the highest in the Caribbean. But the night belongs to the fritay vendors – a good business for thousands of women. Their twinkling lamps are sometimes the only lights visible on the streets at night, even in the capital.

The demise of the Creole pig

Griyo is a good, cheap protein alternative to beef: there is very little grazing or arable land in mountainous Haiti. Fish, too, is pricey due to deforestation, silt running down hills during the rainy season covers the reefs. As a result, fishermen need to go further afield to find a good catch.

Pigs, on the other hand, are good business in Haiti. Low-maintenance animals, they roam freely, foraging for vegetable and fruit scraps. To use a cliché, the little *cochons* are a piggy bank of sorts for Haitians. Valued highly, children are given piglets as gifts. Others buy a few animals, fatten them and sell them for a hefty profit. There's always a demand, so there's always plenty of money to be made.

Back in the early 1980s, though, it was difficult to find any pigs in Haiti. They were all slaughtered as part of a US government project to prevent the spread of swine disease. After scientists discovered some of the Creole pigs in Haiti carried porcine fever, they feared the disease would spread to the Dominican Republic, and eventually to the hog population of North America. Although those pigs have since been replaced (by a different breed), Haitians complain that varieties introduced from the United States are more finicky eaters and don't taste the same as their old Creole pigs.

Local produce

There are no farms in Haiti, just garden-sized plots that dot the mountainous landscape. Most rural Haitians work these smallholdings raising beets, aubergines, carrots, hot peppers, tomatoes, corn, millet, beans, plantains, okra, spinach, tomatoes, avocados, manioc and other tubers like *malanga*. Fruits include mangoes,

papayas, oranges and mandarins. Spices are also nurtured wherever there's a space to grow them.

Saturdays at the vegetable market could be from a scene in a Haitian painting. Women balance bright baskets of fruits and vegetables on their heads, and sway their hips as they come down the hills. Some catch the *tap-tap* (the bus) from the mountains to the towns and cities, where they offer their colourful produce for sale. In Port-au-Prince, one of the biggest markets is held on Avenue John Brown, not too far from where the roads crosses Martin Luther King. The air is cooler down here, quite different from the wilting heat of downtown Port-au-Prince.

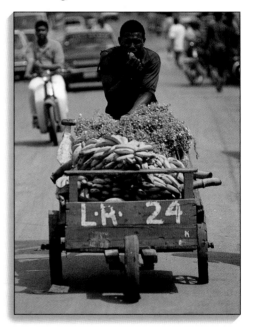

GRIYO: ALMOST A NATIONAL DISH

The ingredients: 2 lb cubed boneless pork
¼ cup of olive oil, ¼ cup of water
1 cup of chopped onion, ¼ cup of chopped shallots
1 small hot pepper (minced), 1 tsp of black pepper
1 cup of fresh orange juice, ¼ cup of fresh lime juice
1 tbsp of chopped thyme, ½ teaspoon of salt
Marinate the pork. Heat oil in a heavy skillet; add the pork, turning frequently to brown evenly. Stir in onions, shallots, orange and lime juice, water, thyme, salt, pepper and hot pepper. Bring to the boil, cover, reduce heat and simmer for 30 minutes. Uncover and turn up the heat, stirring constantly to prevent burning, for 10 minutes.

LEFT: Dominican Brugal rum is sold in most bars.
RIGHT: a greengrocer on wheels.

Haitian farmers also raise chickens, goats and some cows, although they don't eat them. They are raised with the specific intention of selling them on to fritay vendors. The majority of rural Haitians only butcher their livestock for very special occasions such as baptisms or weddings. And a few use them in animal sacrifices to their Vaudou gods.

When they can find it, Haitians love to eat fish, crabs and conch – the latter is a delicacy that Haitian men believe helps their sexual performance. Mounds of the huge shells are piled high in coastal villages, testament to their great popularity. The conch, known as *lambi*, is either grilled, or simmered in a tomato-based creole sauce. Restaurants also serve conch fritters, a Caribbean favourite that requires chopping or grinding the conch meat, mixing it with onions, celery, green pepper, hot pepper, thyme, tomato purée, salt and pepper in a soft batter, then frying it in golfball-size pieces.

Imported foodstuffs

Most foodstuffs in Haiti are imported, including the very popular codfish. Prepared in a batter with onions and hot peppers, then fashioned into a ball, the *akra* as the dish is called, is fried.

Haiti has been awash with imported dark

A TYPICAL CREOLE LAMBI

The ingredients, to serve 4 people:
- 1½ lb conch, shelled, cleaned and skinned
- 2 limes, juice and grated rind
- 1 onion, sliced
- 3 cloves garlic, minced
- 2 shallots, minced
- ¼ cup of butter
- 1 tomato, peeled, seeded and chopped
- ¾ cup of water
- 2 tsp of thyme, chopped
- ¼ tsp red pepper flakes
- salt and pepper, to taste

Pound the conch meat into 3mm (⅛-inch) thickness with a wooden mallet. Cut into 4cm (1½-inch) square pieces. Place in a bowl and squeeze over the lime juice. Add the lime rind and completely cover with cold water. Refrigerate for approximately three hours.

Sauté the onion, garlic and shallots in a heavy saucepan until soft and opaque, keeping the heat low and taking care not to brown them. Stir in the tomato, water, thyme, red pepper flakes and conch meat. Bring to a vigorous boil, then reduce the heat. Simmer, partially covered, stirring occasionally, until the conch meat is fork-tender (about 1 hour). Season to taste with salt and pepper.

chicken meat from the US, which has been discarded from the fast food outlets. Local chicken farmers can't compete. Rice, one of the staples in the Haitian diet, is shipped from overseas, competing with the native variety produced in the Artibonite Valley. And all processed food comes from either the Dominican Republic or the US. However, most Haitians cannot afford such products, maintaining a daily diet based on locally grown food.

Much of a muchness

Variety is not the spice of life in the Haitian kitchen. The only experimentation to be found in their cuisine is believed to be taking place in the large Haitian communities in Miami, New York City and Montréal.

For those who can afford it, the Haitian menu does not vary much from week to week, or from home to home. It is usually a two-course meal, starting with beef either grilled on charcoal, or cooked in tomato sauce, mixed with cabbage and other vegetables. Every meal is accompanied by plantain, either boiled or fried. Wealthier middle-class families also eat goat meat, which is cooked in a similar way to beef.

The second course is either rice and beans, or cornmeal and beans. The beans are either red, or white, and are cooked in a sauce, or stirred into the rice. Some Haitians serve up rice and beans with every meal.

There are only subtle geographic variations in the Haitian menu, for example: cooks in the northern part of the country cook their rice and beans with a head of clove, while in southern areas they don't. Haitians are not big beer drinkers – they prefer their meals accompanied by a local sweet cola drink or freshly-squeezed fruit juices.

Outside influences

Slowly, as a result of contact with the Syrians and Lebanese who have settled here over the years, some Haitians have began to incorporate Arab dishes such as stuffed vine leaves into their dishes, but this practice is limited to a few restaurants and a small number of homes.

Besides picking up a piece of griyo from a street vendor, Haitians don't eat out much.

FAR LEFT: a Haitian girl carries grapefruits to market.
LEFT: fresh fish is not always easily available.
RIGHT: a colourful fruit stand.

Those who can afford it will go out for exotic food such as pizza or hamburgers. These can be found in Pétionville, the wealthy suburb above Port-au-Prince with bars, cafés and clubs. They cater mostly for wealthy Haitians, as well as tourists and foreign workers.

Pétionville has enough multi-star French restaurants to satisfy the most sophisticated palate. Restaurants such as Chez Gérard and Plantation serve a menu that would rival any European four-star establishment. Restaurants that have managed to combine the two cultures have achieved remarkable results. Just don't expect to find a plate of griyo in these places.

Haitian homes come alive on special occasions, such as a child's first communion and New Year's Day, when pumpkin soup is usually served. On Christmas Eve, the favoured dish is griyo, prepared with rice and beans, *lambi* and other sweet-tasting food. Christmas is also one of the times to bring out the *Rhum Barbancourt*, locally produced from sugar cane. A bottle of five-star aged Barbancourt is reserved for special occasions and is mixed with lime juice, sugar and crushed ice. No festive occasion is complete without sharing a bottle of *cremasse*, a home-made concoction of rum and sweet, thick condensed milk. Before you know it you'll be feeling mighty happy. ❑

SPORTING PASSIONS

*Baseball dominates, but golf, horse racing, polo and watersports
are all popular. So, more controversially, is cockfighting*

There is one great passion which runs through all classes of Dominican society, and that is baseball. This is a game in which two teams of nine players each try to win points by hitting a small ball so hard with a bat that the one or more runners spread out across the field – in a diamond marked by white cushions – can manage to run to safety before the opposing team recovers the ball. The movements on the field will long remain a mystery to the uninitiated spectator, but the Dominicans, just like the North Americans, love the game.

Baseball remains without doubt the nation's favourite sport. Six teams compete for the national championship: two each from the Cibao Valley and Santo Domingo and one each from La Romana and San Pedro de Macorís. They compete six days a week, and the main season runs from October to January.

In winter, the *Quisqueya* in Santo Domingo and the other stadiums on the island are often sold out for weeks in advance. In summer, baseball fans settle down in front of the TV to follow the competitions of the American Major League. After all, many of their compatriots can be seen running, hitting and catching across the flickering screen. No other South American country can claim as many top-rate players in the US as the little half-island in the Caribbean. More than 50 Dominicans currently take to the field for the Major League teams, and another 500 or so play for the Minors.

An American import

In the early part of the 20th century, from 1916 to 1924, US troops occupied the Dominican Republic for the first time, in support of the Monroe Doctrine. The "Americanos" brought their favourite game with them to the island – baseball. It seems that the young islanders took to the game as well, for it wasn't long before

they had formed a team which was good enough to take on the international competition. During the 1950s the first Dominicans successfully played the game in the Major League of the United States. The Alou brothers and Juan Marischal are famous names to this day.

The Dominican Republic has now become

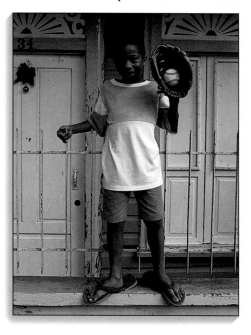

a paradise for talent scouts working on behalf of the Major League clubs. Every winter, American scouts occupy the stands of the islands baseball stadiums, on the lookout for future home-run record-breakers. The Los Angeles Dodgers, Cleveland Indians, Chicago Cubs, Boston White Sox and other clubs run training camps in many locations throughout the Dominican Republic. In some of them, the young hopefuls undergo intensive training for three months without a break, while other US clubs send coaches into schools every day, where they spend their afternoons teaching boys how they can best hit the ball into the invisible strike zone.

LEFT: Manny Ramirez in action.
RIGHT: baseball has been a national sport in the Dominican Republic since the Americans arrived.

A large number of the players who have made it to the top in the United States grew up in the *bateyes*, the impoverished barrack-like settlements around San Pedro de Macorís where the sugar-cane workers live. There, as small boys, they played on uneven ground with sugar-cane bats, an unripe orange and gloves made from old cement bags or milk cartons. On Sundays, these same children would flock into the Tetelo Vargas Stadium to learn a few tricks by watching the *Estrellas Orientales* (the Stars of the East). Sammy Sosa, Pedro Martínez, Raúl Mondesí, José Martínez, Tony Peña, Tony Fernandez and Manny Ramirez are all top stars in the baseball firmament of the US. The legendary Matty Alou once joked about the remarkable success of the Dominicans: "It must be the water".

No doubt the warm climate on the island plays a part by supplying ideal conditions for year-round training. But probably the most important incentive for the youthful talents is

> ### YEAR-ROUND BASEBALL
>
> Six baseball teams compete for the national championship during the winter season which runs from October to January. In the summer Dominican fans can follow the US Major League on TV.

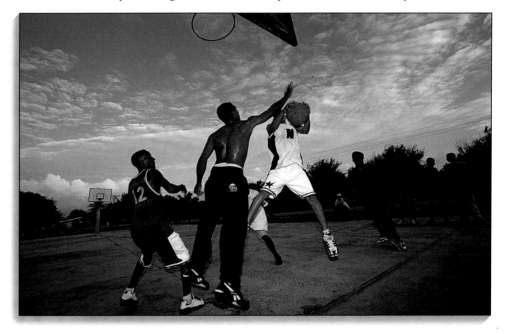

"SLAMMIN" SAMMY SOSA

For 37 years, the baseball legend Roger Maris held the single-season home run record – until 1998, when Mark McGwire and Sammy Sosa had a neck-and-neck race on the long run home. "Big Mac" of the St Louis Cardinals was the first to make it, and a few days later, "Slammin' Sammy" of the Chicago Cubs also broke Maris's record.

Sammy Sosa, the enterprising boy from the Consuelo slums near San Pedro de Macorís, contributed to his family's income as a shoe-shine boy. Today he is a multi-millionaire sporting superstar whose international fan club has been growing ever since he began his career with the Texas Gulf Coast in 1986. His sporting prowess and winning smile have resulted in several magazines voting him Sportsman of the Year and he was invited to watch the US president, Bill Clinton, light the Christmas Tree at the White House.

Sosa also donates a percentage of his earnings to good causes. In December 1997, as "Sammy Claus", he toured schools and hospitals in the US and the DR, distributing gifts to thousands of children. A father of four, Sosa founded the bi-national Sammy Sosa Foundation for underprivileged children. Sosa, who reputedly gave his first contract payment of US$3,500 to his mother Lucrecia, save a few dollars which he used to buy his first bicycle, incorporates the universal dream of the poor boy made good.

the fact that a sports career in the US still remains the best way of realising the American Dream. Stars like Sammy Sosa earn millions of dollars every season in the US, and plenty of pesos in their homeland as well, by flickering across TV screens in advertising campaigns or appearing in a newspaper or magazine. Every boy dreams of following in Sosa's footsteps.

Hoop dreams

Basketball occupies the second position in the Dominican sports league. Most schools have a basketball court, and many professional baseball players started life playing basketball. A few

Golf

It cannot be denied that golf is enjoying a boom in the Dominican Republic. As elsewhere in the Caribbean the grassy sport is in season all year round, unlike in parts of Europe and the US. At the end of the 1980s there were only four golf courses in the republic; today there are almost two dozen with more planned. Many of them enjoy lovely locations near the seashore, where one can hit a ball clear across the cliffs, ravines and bays.

Locals and visitors alike are in agreement that the best courses on the island are the Pete Dye course, known as "Teeth of the Dog", in

years ago, if you'd asked a young Dominican what he liked best about the United States, the most likely answer would have been Michael Jordan. Today though the popularity of basketball has diminished in the face of the huge success of Dominican baseball players. However young local hopefuls can still be seen frequently aiming the ball into the net. Felipe López, who plays for the Vancouver Grizzlies, provides the island's basketball fans with an internationally famous star to admire.

LEFT: basketball has been somewhat overshadowed by the success of baseball.
ABOVE: polo at Casa de Campo.

the grounds of Casa de Campo, and the Playa Grande course on the north coast near Río San Juan, designed by Robert Trent Jones Senior.

Sport of princes

Prince Charles plays it, as do a whole galaxy of the world's aristocracy and everyday folks too. Devotees of the ancient sport of royalty – polo – are varied. Perched on horseback, they wield long sticks which they use to try to manoeuvre a small white ball into the opposing team's goal. Polo is one of the fastest team games in the world. It is played by two teams of four on a field which is more than three times the size of a football pitch. Each game lasts about an hour, for which each player will need five or six polo ponies (hence the great expense), because according to the Hurlingham Rules, which originated in the English club of the same name, the horses have to be changed every seven-and-a-half minutes.

There are four polo fields within the grounds of the luxurious Casa de Campo resort near La Romana. Champions from around the world look forward to meeting here during the season, which runs from November until May.

The Maharajah Jabbar Singh brought the game to the Caribbean. Porfirio Rubirosa, a famous Dominican playboy, had met the Indian

A windsurfing paradise

Canadian windsurfer Jean Laporte discovered the Dominican Republic in general, and the Bay of Cabarete in particular, for the sport in 1984. "One of the best windsurfing places in the Caribbean," was the champion's verdict. Before long, his international fan club arrived hot on his heels.

In the early days the people of Cabarete were torn between admiration and amusement for Laporte and his companions, whom they christened *mariposas* (butterflies); nowadays, large numbers of young Dominicans compete with the visitors on their narrow boards. The pre-

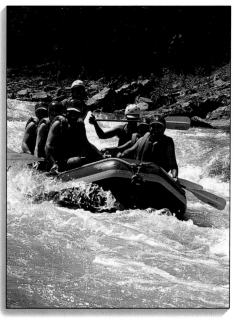

aristocrat in Europe and encouraged him to visit the Antilles in 1954. Singh was an excellent polo player with a handicap of nine, who brought with him his knowledge of the game as well as trainers and horses and soon built up a pretty good team. Since his death in 1986, his sons have been in charge of the polo played at Casa de Campo.

For spectators who did not grow up in the saddle, an amusing variation on polo proper is offered at Casa de Campo: donkey polo. In this version, the ball is considerably larger. The game can severely tax the laughter muscles of the spectators and participants, due in part to the antics of the notoriously stubborn creatures.

vailing wind in the Bay of Cabarete is an invigorating northwest trade wind measuring force five or six on the Beaufort scale. The entire Atlantic coast of the island also provides excellent conditions for the sport.

Deep-sea fishing

Boca de Yuma in the southeast Dominican Republic is the traditional angling centre. It was the place where international fishing competitions were held every year until Hurricane Georges more or less blew away the little village at the mouth of the Río Yuma. So the fishermen planning to hook sea-dwelling creatures, such as the blue and white marlin, sharks and tuna, currently have to make a detour to Cabeza de Toro in Punta Cana. High season runs from January until June, but fishing continues throughout the year. Further information can be obtained from the *Clubes Naúticos* or *Actividades Acuáticas*.

On Avenida de la Salud

In Santo Domingo it seems incongruous that, in the heart of a metropolis of 3 million people, a city where traffic chaos reigns, there should be a smooth, wide tarmac road running through the middle of the *Parque Mirador del Sur* on which not a single car can be seen. The Avenida

ple-watch look out for the former president Balaguer who has been known to enjoy a Sunday constitutional in the park.

Cockfighting

Before baseball conquered the country, cockfighting was the most popular spectator sport in the Dominican Republic. Even today, there is scarcely a village without its own *galera* or *club Gallistico*. Every weekend, an air of excitement with a hint of scurrility pervades the windowless circular wooden or concrete buildings which contain the arenas. The fighting cocks are weighed and measured to deter-

de la Salud, the "Avenue of Health", is out of bounds to all motorised vehicles. Here, sportsmen whose lives would be at risk on the other roads of the capital can get rid of their excess energy: joggers, inline skaters, skateboarders, roller skaters, cyclists, walkers. The extensive parkland means that the air here is considered to be better than elsewhere, and the little drinks stalls by the wayside provide welcome refreshment. Dominican sportsmen flock to the park, especially on the weekend. If you prefer to peo-

LEFT: windsurfing and white water rafting are popular watersports in the Dominican Republic.
ABOVE: there is a cockfighting arena in every town.

mine which birds should be pitted against each other, then the proud owner attaches spurs of metal or bone to the claws of his bird and ensures the requisite adrenaline rush by repeatedly propelling the creature across the 6-metre (20-ft) -wide arena towards its opponent.

Meanwhile, the bookmakers clamber across the rickety spectator stands, accepting bets, which are placed in a mysterious sign language. The sums of money involved are often quite large; a man will sometimes wager a whole month's wages. A successful fighting cock can cost between US$500 and US$1,000.

Violent pecking and scratching with razor-sharp claws results in a bloody battle during virtually every encounter, although it is by no means always a fight to the death. The struggle often ends when one of the sparring partners gives up; sometimes both animals refuse to fight on.

Cockfighting, which was invented over 3,000 years ago in Asia, has been the subject of much controversial debate in the Dominican Republic, but so far the attempts to ban the bloody sport have been no more than half-hearted. It remains a popular sport supported by Dominicans from every walk of

US Sports in Haiti

Young Haitians only started playing basketball seriously towards the end of the 20th century – even though US troops occupied Haiti for a longer period than they did the Dominican Republic.

yard) track. The system is based on the American one, and the regular race goers are usually happy to help novices fill out betting slips. They may also offer useful (or not so useful) racing tips and information about the hot favourites or outsiders in the upcoming races.

No sporting paradise

Haiti is not exactly a sportsman's paradise. For example, the country has only one golf course, the *Pétionville Club* near Port-au-Prince. In this

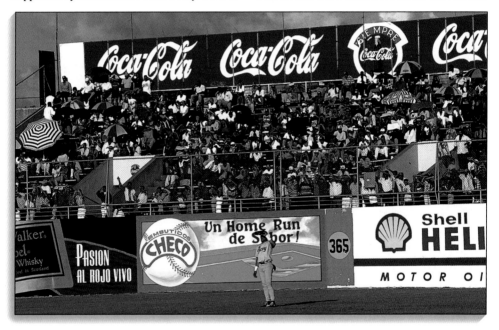

life. Once forbidden from attending, women, are still rare visitors to the arenas.

Horse racing

No blood flows on the race track which lies between Santo Domingo and the airport, but the atmosphere is just as exciting and lively as a cockfight. At weekends punters flock to the *Hipódromo Qinto Centenario*, and whole families also come to enjoy an afternoon at the track with a carnival atmosphere among the snack and drinks stands. Even those who speak no Spanish and have no idea how the betting works can enjoy a visit to the modern, spacious racing complex with its 1,600-metre (1,750-

desperately poor country, sporting activity remains a privilege of the upper classes. Their favourite forms of exercise include – apart from golf – horse riding and tennis. Ronald Agenor has even provided Haiti with a player who has competed on an international level in what some consider to be a white sport – tennis.

The ordinary people satisfy their competitive instincts primarily through cockfighting. As with their next door neighbour, there is virtually no village without its own arena constructed of wooden planks. In the bigger towns, there are large circular stone buildings where even wealthy Haitians can be seen taking their place in the stands to watch the fray.

In Haiti the cocks fight without spurs. At the beginning of each fight, the birds are intoxicated with *Clairin*, an alcoholic beverage consisting of partially distilled rum which is passed directly from the owner's mouth. He forces the liquid through his lips so that the cock is enveloped in a fine, mildly inebriating mist. Bets start at 1 gourde (15 cents) and a fighting cock can cost up to an average month's pay, around US$30.

Ball skills

Football (soccer) can't compete with baseball across the border, but in Haiti it causes many a

goal was the only one scored by the Haitians in Munich and the moment of glory is remembered in Haiti to this day. Patrice Dumont, author of *Haiti to Munich – 20 Years On* marked the anniversary by recounting every detail of that sensational event. Today, the Haitian national side takes on other teams from the Caribbean and fans follow their favourite teams – Brazil and Argentina – on the TV screen. There is little interest in the football skills of their former colonial rulers, France. When Brazil was defeated by France in the final of the 1998 World Championship, Haiti was engulfed in mourning. ❏

heart to beat faster. You will see a leather ball being kicked around everywhere – in school playgrounds, along a path through the fields, and of course in the major stadiums, the Sylvio Cator in Port-au-Prince and the Parc St Victor in Cap Haïtien.

The last major international victory of the Haitian football team was many years ago in 1974, when the national team qualified for the World Championship in Germany; they even managed to score a goal against Italy. The Italians may have won the game, but that famous

LEFT: large crowds turn out for local baseball games.
ABOVE: A game of chance on a Haitian street corner.

A GROWING SOCCER SCENE

Despite the lack of financial investment in football in Haiti, there are many small clubs who play unofficial contests all over the country. The National League of 57 teams is divided into three divisions. Only league finals and international games are played at the refurbished Sylvio Cator Stadium. The atmosphere is loud with lots of singing and drumming, just as you'd find in Brazil. The official league season runs from November to May, while the other games are played during the summer. There is also a project called Athletique d'Haitiand, which trains talented young players from the slums. It is next to the motor racing track 4 km (2 miles) from the centre of Port-au-Prince.

BACK TO NATURE

The tourist brochures focus on the beaches. But this fertile, mountainous island

has much to offer outdoor enthusiasts and the ecologically aware

Hispaniola offers eco, nature and adventure tourists some of the Caribbean's most exciting prospects. Haiti is the region's most mountainous country and the Dominican Republic is home to the region's highest mountain, Pico Duarte, at 3,087 metres (10,128 ft). The north coast of the Republic is also one of the world's major whale-spotting and windsurfing destinations. The country already has a well-developed eco and adventure tourism infrastructure with many established tour operators and activities ranging from hiking and diving to kayaking, rafting, tubing, climbing, abseiling, caving, canyoning, cascading, paragliding, mountain biking and horse riding.

The Dominican landscape is both dramatic and varied: spectacular mountain ranges; long rivers winding through forests or rushing through ravines and over high waterfalls; fertile valleys; mangrove swamps and white sand beaches fringed by the clear blue waters of the Caribbean.

Wildlife

Flora and fauna are abundant with over 5,600 plant species (including more than 300 endemic orchids); 258 bird species (including the Hispaniolan parrot and parakeet); four species of sea turtles and two freshwater species; reptiles like the American crocodiles of Lake Enriquillo and the rhinoceros iguana; 33 land mammals (among which are the endangered *solenodonte* and *jutia*) as well as the endangered Antillean manatee and the humpback whale.

Both of these marine mammals come to the Silver Bank 140 km (87 miles) off the north coast during the breeding season from December to March. The Silver Bank is the most important humpback sanctuary in the Atlantic, with up to 3,000 whales visiting annually. From January to March there are day trips out to the Silver Bank from Puerto Plata and shorter

excursions to Samaná Bay further east, where pilot whales, bottlenose, spinner and spotted dolphin can also be seen.

With 16 national parks, six scientific reserves, natural monuments, protected areas (islands, bays, river estuaries, lagoons) and ecological corridors, the Dominican government is taking

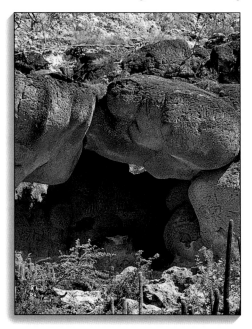

a systematic approach to preserving the environment. Construction is forbidden in the 67 protected areas. Establishing the central parks of Armando Bermudez and José del Carmen Ramirez has saved the last extensive areas of forest, and the Plan Sierra reforestation project is onstream at nearby San José de las Matas.

The Dominican national park system covers the republic's range of bio diversity and offers many adventure options, from the relaxation of camping to the more strenuous activities of climbing, hiking and river sports.

Los Haïtises park on the south coast of Samaná Bay has mangroves, wet forest and subtropical rainforest, and is a major habitat for

PRECEDING PAGES: devastating deforestation on the road to Forêt des Pins, Haiti.
LEFT: a humpback whale in the waters at Silver Bank.
RIGHT: Taíno petroglyphs at Las Caritas.

the Hispaniolan parrot, owls and gannets. Some of the caves here are decorated with Taíno petroglyphs and pictographs.

The highest peaks in the Caribbean (Pico Duarte, 3,087 metres/10,128 ft, La Pelona, 3,070 metres/10,072 ft, La Rucilla, 3,045 metres/9,990 ft and Pico Yaque, 2,760 metres/9,055 ft) are found in the central region in the Armando Bermudez and José del Carmen Ramirez parks, where temperatures can fall below freezing point in December and January. Besides the Dominican Republic's national bird – the *cigua palmera* – there are woodpeckers, kestrels and other rare species.

62 species of birds, including the tiny *manuelito*, the great hummingbird and the *cu-cu*.

Jaragua, further south, is the largest park and includes Beata and Alto Velo islands. Geological formations discovered here date back 50 million years. The Oviedo Lagoon is home to the country's largest population of flamingoes. Also in the southwest is the Sierra de Bahoruco highland park where more than 50 percent of the orchid species known in the Dominican Republic can be found. One of the most important national monuments is the Bahía de Calderas, established to protect the great Las Salinas sand dunes.

Coniferous trees provide vegetation on the lower ground, while pine covers the higher slopes. Mammals include wild pigs, while lower down, savannah snakes make their home. This area is also the source of Yaque del Sur River.

In the southeast, the Eastern National park, includes Saona Island and supports subtropical wet and dry forest. Saona is the habitat of the rare, white-headed dove and the manatee. Its extensive cave system also features many examples of pre-Columbian art.

The smallest park is Isla Cabritos in Lake Enriquillo in the south west. The 12 km (7½-mile) long island is below sea level and supports a large crocodile population, 10 species of cactus and,

The north coast

The north coast is a haven for divers, windsurfers, mountain bikers and horse riders. Cabarete is classed as one of the best windsurfing beaches anywhere, and hosts World Cup competitions. A protective reef and varying wind conditions make Cabarete ideal for both beginners and worldclass windsurfers.

Neighbouring Sosua, with its shallow reefs, has the best diving for beginners, but there are also sites for the more advanced, such as Las Palmitas, the Airport Wall and the interconnecting tunnels of La Piramide. In the south, close to Santo Domingo, La Caleta National Underwater park has reef and wreck dives as well as freshwater cave diving. Saona Island is a good site for spotting big fish and Punta Cana on the east coast has the DR's longest coral reef, nearly 30 km (19 miles), which is protected by an active preservation programme.

The north coast and the northern mountain range have mountain bike trails ranging from easy to advanced off-road or single-track mountain passages. Those who prefer to tackle mountains on foot can try the strenuous hike up Pico Duarte (or cheat by riding a mule)

SUBMERGED TREASURE

West of Sosúa there are wrecks to explore off Cofresi and Montecristi. Qualified divers can join salvage parties that are searching more than 20 shipwrecks, including those of the 1563 Spanish treasure fleet.

cading sites are El Salto del Jimenoa, Cascada del Limón, Cascada Ojo de Agua and El Salto de Baiguate. Canyoning takes you up the wall of a river gorge with rope and harness. When you're high enough you jump into the river. The best sites are in La Damajagua in Imbert and the Jarabacoa area. You can paraglide over mountains and rivers from any convenient ridge, given the appropriate wind conditions. (Ecosport packages are offered by Rancho Baiguate in Jarabacoa in the centre of the coun-

and the easier climbs up Pico Yaque or Mt Isabel de Torres in Puerto Plata.

If you want to get wet, try rubber rafting on the Rio Yaque del Norte in Jarabacoa. You can go solo without a paddle in an oversized rubber tube on the same river, or the Rio Jamao al Norte or Rio Isabela in Santo Domingo.

For the truly adventurous there's cascading and canyoning. Cascading involves climbing to the top of a waterfall and then abseiling down the middle of the cascade to the bottom, where you jump into the water. The best cas-

---

LEFT: riding in the Dominican Republic's countryside.
ABOVE: rafting down the Río Yaque del Norte.

try and by Iguana Mama Adventure Tours, situated in Cabarete on the north coast.)

Despite extensive deforestation, soil erosion, crippling political and economic problems, Haiti is making slow steps to arrest its ecological decline. There are a number of reforestation and eco-tourism projects already onstream aimed at preserving and developing the natural heritage.

UNESCO and the UNDP, in conjunction with other international organisations and the Haitian Institute for the Protection of the National Heritage, has already initiated the Route 2004 project. This will celebrate the bicentennial of independence, with a programme restoring and preserving major natural and cultural resources with tourism in mind. The first stage has focused on the historic area from Fort Liberté to Cap-Haïtien on the north coast, with its national history parks, where tours have been developed.

While Haiti cannot compete with its neighbour as yet in terms of organised ecotourism, there is still a wide range of activities available and sites to visit. Besides the peaks of La Selle (2,674 metres/8,770 ft) southeast of Port-au-Prince and Pic de Macaya (2,347 metres/7,700 ft) in the southwest peninsula, there are the Forêt de la Visite and pine forests above Port-au-Prince. There are caves in the north on Ile de la Tortue and Dondon; and in the south near

Les Cayes at Camp Perrin, Port-a-Piment and Île-a-Vache, and Les Iles Cayemite, Vol Drogue, Anse d'Azure and Anse Duclerc near Jeremie.

Coral reefs can be found on the Côte des Arcadins and Labadie north of Port-au-Prince, Île de la Gonâve and south at Cayemite near Pestel and Île-a-Vache. In contrast to the lush central Artibonite Valley and most of the southwest peninsula, parts of the area from Gonaives stretching northwest to Port-de-Paix is virtually desert. There are waterfalls at Seguin in the Pine Forest; the famous Vaudou pilgrimage spot at Saut D'Eau; Artibonite in the centre of the country; and at Etang Pichon and Belle Anse in the southeast near Jeremie.

Although the best beaches are found on the Atlantic coast in the north (Labadie), or on the Caribbean coast near Les Cayes (Port Salut, Port-a Piment), or near Jacmel (Mouillage, Raymond les bains, Cyvadier Plage), the marine park of the Arcadin cays 3 km (2 miles) off the Côte des Arcadins, has excellent diving.

Ecological degradation has destroyed many wildlife habitats and adversely affected fauna but there are two mountain parks which eco-tourists will want to visit. Parc La Visite is on the high Massif de la Selle, a five-hour hike from the hilltop resort of Kenscoff. Covered in pine and montane cloud forest, the park is home to 80 species of birds and endemic mammals – the *nez longue* and the Hispaniolan *hutia*. The black-capped petrel nests here and the migratory North American warbler winters here.

Virgin cloud forest

The Macaya National Park at the tip of the southwest peninsula is the site of Haiti's last virgin cloud forest. There are pines 45 metres high, 141 orchid species, 102 fern species, 99 moss species and 49 species of liverwort. There are 11 species of butterfly, 57 snails, 28 amphibians, 34 reptiles, 65 birds and 19 bats.

The most spectacular fauna are the Grey-crowned Palm Tanager and the Hispaniolan *trogon*. The endangered peregrine falcon also winters here. From Les Cayes it takes about half a day to reach the University of Florida base at the edge of the park, where there are camping facilities.

Etang (Lake) Saumâtre east of Port-au-Prince is the habitat for more than 100 species of waterfowl, flamingoes and crocodiles. Although organised tours and activities are few, both the national parks are good birdwatching sites and there is horse riding in La Visite Park and the Bassin Bleu near Jacmel. The University of Florida runs a project for those wishing to scale Pic Macaya.

Contact the Destination Djondjon organisation which will put you in touch with a country-wide network for alternative tourism. Djondjon has regional affiliates who offer accommodation ranging from rural homes to luxury hotels and who organise ecological and cultural trips. This is an excellent way to travel the country and experience rural Haitian lifestyle. ❑

LEFT: coral around Île de la Gonâve.
RIGHT: relaxing by the stunning Salto Aqua Blanco.

THE HUMPBACKS OF THE SILVER BANK

The mating season of the rare, majestic humpback whale is a major attraction for nature-loving visitors to the reef around the Samaná Peninsula

In the Bible, there is a story about Jonah who is swallowed by a whale, taken on an adventure and eventually delivered back to land unharmed by the creature. Whales have fascinated people for generations and today there are tours of their various habitats around the world from Canada to the USA, from Mexico and the Caribbean to Hawaii. The Dominican Republic is home to the only humpback whale sanctuary in the eastern Caribbean, the Silver Bank Marine Sanctuary.

ON THE BANCO DE LA PLATA

Several thousand North Atlantic humpback whales head south during the winter months from December to March in search of warmer climes to mate and calve. These migratory animals are cetaceans: marine mammals that are warm-blooded, give birth to suckling young and breathe air. In the waters around the Banco de la Plata (Silver Bank) in the Dominican Republic one can witness fantastic visual displays during the mating season because much of the activity is played out on the surface of the water. The humpbacks communicate with one another, with a song-like call used between adults as they search for a mate, and between mother and calf. Males compete in loud groups for the right to mate with much breaching (breaking through) of the water, lobtailing and fin slapping, which can become violent toward the end of the mating season. Visitors to the Silver Bank Sanctuary will see that the animals can be gentle giants too, allowing the adventurous to float in the ocean alongside them in what is known as a soft-in-water encounter.

△ **SEARCHING**
A growing number of tour operators run well-organised whale-watching tours in the Caribbean where humpbacks head during the winter.

▷ **HEADS AND TAILS**
A humpback whale (megaptera novaeangliae) lobtailing in the waters around the Silver Bank Sanctuary.

WHALE-WATCHING EXCURSIONS

△ SPECTACULAR DISPLAY
To capture the amazing sight of a humpback whale tail breaching in the waters around Silver Bank Sanctuary be sure to take a camera and waterproof clothing.

◁ ON THE LOOK OUT
The clear Antillean waters off the Dominican Republic's coast are a treasure trove for snorkellers on the look out for humpback whales, dolphins and other exciting marine life.

◁ BAYWATCH
Whale Watch Bay on the Samaná Peninsula is a great spot on dry land from which to observe the great mammals in the ocean.

▷ GOING BELLY-UP
A Caribbean humpback whale swims belly-up just below the surface as a swimmer looks on in a soft-in-water encounter.

Whale watching tours are popular in the warm waters around the Banco de la Plata, which lies within the Silver Bank Marine Sanctuary, about 100 km (60 miles) north of Puerto Plata. Visitors can also observe whales off Bahía de Samaná (Samaná Bay) in the northeast of the Dominican Republic. Both places offer breathtaking sights of migrating humpback whales. With powerful binoculars the whales' mating rituals and calving can be seen from dry land at Bahía de Samaná, but it is nothing like the view from a whale-watching boat.

An adult can grow up to 12 metres (40 ft) and weigh about 40 tons. So it is an impressive sight when the animals (usually male) breach – rush out of the water at great speed, hit the surface and fly through the air. Access to the protected Banco de la Plata is severely restricted. For tour details contact Oceanic Society Expeditions (tel: 800 326 7491 or 415 441 1106), which has soft-in-water encounters. Alternatively call Aquatic Adventures (tel: 409 291 1210) or Victoria Marine, which has an office on the malécon in Samaná (tel: 809 538 2588).

THE DOMINICAN REPUBLIC

A detailed guide to the entire country, with principal sites clearly cross-referenced by number to the maps

Think of the Caribbean island of the Dominican Republic and visions of palm-fringed strips of wide golden sand lapped by warm water are sure to appear. Indeed there are many miles of fine beaches to enjoy from the Costa Caribe in the southeast to the Costa del Coco in the far east and elsewhere – though not all have escaped the nastier effects of mass tourism. But scratch the surface of this mountainous land and there is so much more to see.

Protected within the national parks are cascading waterfalls, rivers and vast forests – the habitats of varied flora and fauna. The wildlife includes some found exclusively on the island within its fertile valleys and dry, arid desert conditions in the west around Lago Enriquillo. The highest points in the Caribbean are here too and some visitors are attracted by the challenge of hiking through the mountain ranges and scaling the peaks.

In the tranquil northwest, the agricultural Cibao Valley and the lush hills of the Cordillera Central, country life continues in much the same way as it always has. Sugar cane and fruit plantations, paddy fields and fragrant alpine forests dominate the landscape, while the hills offer relief from the tropical temperatures inland.

Experience the hurly-burly of the nation's colourful capital city, Santo Domingo. Rich in the historical monuments of the founding fathers, beautiful centuries-old architecture stands side by side with modern structures. The capital is the commercial and cultural centre of the Republic, where local people rush about their everyday business. But typical of the Caribbean and Latin America, there is always time to stop, relax and chat in the pretty squares and parks.

Elsewhere in the Republic there are interesting sights, including the ruins of La Isabela in the north between Puerto Plata and Monte Cristi: this was the first permanent settlement in the Americas. There is also evidence of the effect of a rapid rise in tourism development with luxury resorts and crowds of sun- and fun-seeking visitors. All-inclusive hotels jostle for space along the coast from Boca Chica to Punta Cana, the Samaná Peninsula to the Amber Coast. Sosúa and Cabarete on the north coast have some of the best scuba diving and windsurfing and the infectious rhythms of merengue music, played at ear-splitting volume, can be heard almost everywhere. ❑

PRECEDING PAGES: the lush Constanza farmland; a pony and mule trek through the Cibao Valley; girls running through the clear waters that lap Isla Bonita beach, Las Terrenas on the Samaná Peninsula.
LEFT: Carnival characters in La Vega.

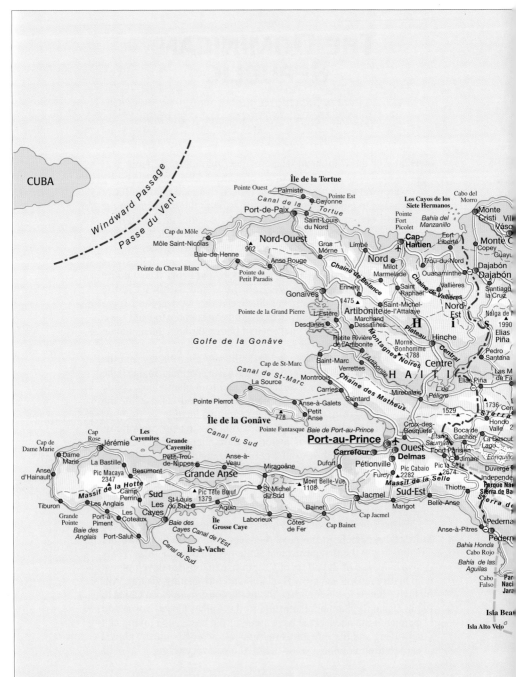

CUBA

Windward Passage
Passe du Vent

Île de la Tortue
Pointe Ouest
Palmiste
Pointe Est
Cayonne
Canal de la Tortue
Port-de-Paix
Saint-Louis du Nord

Cap du Môle
Môle Saint-Nicolas
902
Baie-de-Henne
Pointe du Cheval Blanc
Pointe du Petit Paradis
Anse Rouge

Nord-Ouest
Gros Morne
Limbé

Los Cayos de los Siete Hermanos
Pointe Fort Picolet
Bahía del Manzanillo
Cabo del Morro

Monte Cristi
Vása
Monte C
Copey
Guayu

Cap-Haïtien
Fort Liberté
Trou-du-Nord
Dajabón
Dajabón
Santiago la Cruz

Nord
Milot
Marmelade
Ouanaminthe
Saint Raphaël
Chaîne de Valliéres
Vallières

Gonaïves
1475
Saint-Michel-de-l'Attalaye

Pointe de la Grand Pierre
L'Estère
Artibonite
Marchand Dessalines

Nalga de
1990
Elias Piña

Nord Est

Desdunes
Petite Rivière de l'Artibonite

H I S

Pedro Santana

Golfe de la Gonâve
Morne Bonhomme 1788
Montagnes Noires
Plateau
Hinche

Centre
Las M de Fa

Elías Piña

Cap de St-Marc
Canal de St-Marc
Saint-Marc
Verrettes
La Source
Montrouis
Carries
Saintard
Centre
HAITI
L de Péligre

Pointe Pierrot
Anse-à-Galets
Petit Anse
778
Mirebalais

1529
1736 Cer

Sierra

Hondo Valle 2

Île de la Gonâve
Canal du Sud
Pointe Fantasque
Baie de Port-au-Prince
Port-au-Prince
Croix-des-Bouquets
Boca de Cachón
La Descut
Lago

Cap de Dame Marie
Cap Rose
Jérémie
Les Cayemites
Grande Cayemite
Anse-à-Veau
Carrefour
Ouest
Delmas
Étang Saumâtre
Fond Parisien
Jimani
Enriquill

Anse d'Hainault
Dame Marie
La Bastille
Pic Macaya 2347
Beaumont
Petit-Trou-de-Nippes
Grande Anse
Miragoâne
Dufort
Pétionville
Pic Cabaio 2282
Pic la Selle 2674
Furcy
Massif de la Selle
Thiotte
Duverge
Independe
Parque Na
Sierra de Ba

Tiburon
Grande Pointe
Baie des Anglais
La Hotte
Camp Perrin
Les Anglais
Sud
St Louis du Sud
1379
Aquin
Mont Belle-Vue 1108
St Michel du Sud
Bainet
Jacmel
Marigot
Belle-Anse
Sud-Est
Sierra de

Massif de
Port-à-Piment
Les Coteaux
Les Cayes
Baie des Cayes
Laborieux
Île Grosse Caye
Côtes de Fer
Cap Bainet
Cap Jacmel
Anse-à-Pitres
Pederm

Port-Salut
Canal de l'Est
Île-à-Vache
Canal du Sud
Pederi

Bahía Honda
Cabo Rojo
Bahía de las Aguilas
Cabo Falso
Par Naci Jara

Isla Bea
Isla Alto Velo

CARIBBEAN SEA

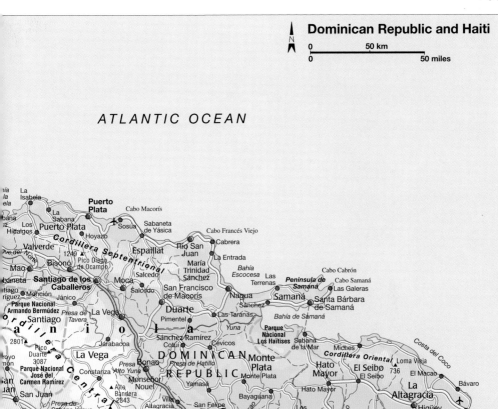

Dominican Republic and Haiti

N

0 — 50 km

0 — 50 miles

ATLANTIC OCEAN

Puerto Plata
Cabo Macorís
La Isabela
La Sabana
Los Hidalgos
Puerto Plata
Sosúa
Sabaneta de Yásica
Cabo Francés Viejo
Valverde
1249
Pico Diego de Ocampo
Espaillat
Río San Juan
Cabrera
La Entrada
Bisonó
María Trinidad Sánchez
Mao
Salcedo
Bahía Escocesa
Las Terrenas
Cabo Cabrón
Península de Samaná
Cabo Samaná
Las Galeras
baneta
Santiago de los Caballeros
Moca
Salcedo
San Francisco de Macorís
Nagua
Sánchez
Samaná
Santa Bárbara de Samaná
tiago
ríguez
Mahción
Jánico
Parque Nacional Armando Bermúdez
Presa de Tavera
La Vega
Duarte
Las Tarénas
Bahía de Samaná
Santiago
Pimentel
Yuna
Parque Nacional Los Haïtises
2801
Cordillera
Pico Duarte
3087
Jarabacoa
Sánchez Ramírez
Cotuí
Cévicos
Sabana de la Mar
Miches
Cordillera Oriental
Loma Vieja
Costa del Coco
royo
ñón
La Vega
Bonao
Presa
Alto Yuna
Presa de Hatillo
Monte Plata
Hato Mayor
El Seibo
El Seibo
736
El Macao
Parque Nacional José del Carmen Ramírez
Constanza
Monseñor Nouel
Monte Plata
La Altagracia
Bávaro
San Juan
Alta Bandera
2843
Villa Altagracia
Yamasá
Bayaguana
Hato Mayor
La Romana
Higüey
Punta Cana
Presa de Sabana Yegua
2581
San Cristóbal
San Felipe
Los Llanos
La Romana
Juanillo
Hato Nuevo
Azua
San José de Ocoa
Distrito
Nacional
San Pedro de Macorís
Boca de Yuma
Cabo San Rafael
Azua de Compostela
Peravia
Presa de Jiguey-Acuate
San Cristóbal
La Caleta
San Pedro de Macorís
Santo Domingo
Cabo Caucedo
Isla Catalina
Bahía La Altagracia
Parque Nacional del Este
Vicente Noble
B. de Ocoa
Las Carreras
Baní
Punta Ocoa
Punta Palenque
Isla Saona
B. de Neiba
Punta Martín García
Barahona
ruco
ahona
Enriquillo

CARIBBEAN METROPOLIS

*Sprawling out from the Zona Colonial, Santo Domingo, the
Dominican Republic's capital city, is a vibrant, noisy place.
Its parks, palaces and museums offer some respite*

Map
on page
170

Santo
Domingo

More than 2 million Dominicans live in the sprawling metropolis and bustling hubbub of the nation's capital. At any one time, the bulk of residents seem to be out and about – negotiating cracked pavements or gushing along the arterial roads which crisscross the city and lend a semblance of order to the urban bustle. Street corner sentinels, neighbourhood regulars and observers on home turf decorate the vibrant streetscape, diligently watching fellow citizens fly by. Santo Domingo is alive and kicking.

The combustion engine, in all its various stages of evolution, provides the background growl that accompanies every roadside chat and shopping transaction. Infrequent lulls of activity are readily dissipated by the fleets of overloaded buses or *gua-guas, carros públicos,* thundering trucks and private cars which career along the main drags. Internationally flavoured avenues – Abraham Lincoln, Winston Churchill, John F. Kennedy and Bolívar among others – hold the key to unlocking citywide travel. While much can be covered on foot, some places will require a taxi fare or a double-dime adventure in the *públicos* – the mainstay of the popular transport system. These cars traverse the city along fixed routes, stopping to pick up and set down on request.

At the mouth of the Río Ozama, the **Zona Colonial** peacefully reflects its important historic past behind ancient thickset walls *(see pages 183–190).*

LEFT:
"El Macho" obelisk.
BELOW:
guarding the
Palacio Nacional.

Monument to liberation

The western limit of the old city is marked by the solid stonework of the **Puerta del Conde ❶**. Originally built in the mid-17th century to commemorate the successful repulsion of British troops from Spanish territory, the former city entrance evokes stronger emotion in Dominican hearts as the site of the declaration of Dominican statehood in 1844, signifying the population's imminent liberation from Haitian control. In front of the arch, an underfoot brass plate marks "kilometer zero"– the locus for measuring inter-provincial distances and the starting point from which to explore a hectic, vibrant city which always seems to be on the edge of chaos.

While the Puerta del Conde heralds the colonial chapter of the tour, the past is never far away outside the imposing gateway. The old city walls on either side form the eastern edge of the **Parque de la Independencia**, a popular spot for resting and people-watching. Surrounded by swirling traffic, which re-groups and warms up for the westward race along Avenida Bolívar, or an eastward dash down Avenida Mella, the park's relaxed atmosphere is all the more apparent and welcome. The occasional shoe shiner or street vendor seem almost amateurish in their persistence compared

Santo Domingo

with the well-practiced assault of those garrisoned in the colonial quarter. Perhaps the presence of the **Altar de la Patria** (daily; free) exudes an element of tranquillity and respect for the three famous founding fathers enshrined in the park. Built in 1976, the mausoleum houses three towering white marble statues and the remains of the statesmen who engineered the fledgling republic during the 19th century: Francisco del Rosario Sánchez, Juan Pablo Duarte and Ramón Matías Mella. Stern-looking military sentries guard the monolithic solemnity of the site seven days a week.

Leaving a shady park bench induces a change of pace, not least while negotiating a crossing of the Avenida Bolívar on the north side of the park, then heading east along the consumer-driven Avenida Mella. Before plunging into the shopping mêlée, you can recall the past at the **Fuerte de la Concepción**. The contrast between old and new is never clearer than after a visit to the ruins of this fortress, built in 1543 at the corner of Avenida Mella and Calle Palo Hincado. Formerly the northwest outpost of the colonial city, a morass of brightly-coloured overhead signs greets today's gaze along the Avenida Mella.

The **Mercado Modelo ❷** lies a short walk down this heaving, jumbled concoction of clothes stores, tourist trinket marts, superstores, banks and camera shops – markedly more up-beat than the parallel pedestrian strip of El Conde in the Zona Colonial. This busy covered craft market focuses largely on the tourist trade, but it is also used by locals. A plethora of stallholders eagerly divert passers-by, proffering woodcarvings, paintings, T-shirts, amber jewellery, dolls, ornaments, ironwork… a veritable lion's den, treasure trove and old curiosity shop combined. Be prepared to bargain, be seduced and leave with a purchase. Beyond the indoor maze of merchants is Little Haiti where vegetable and fruit sellers pack the back streets, jostling for space with the colourful Haiti-bound buses or *tap-taps* and several *botánicas* – bright, perfumed shops selling religious icons, potions, candles and images for the faithful.

Down along the Malecón

Avenida George Washington, otherwise known as the **Malecón ❸**, which skirts the seafront from the port, is a welcome escape from the buzzing throng of shoppers and pedestrians. A 20-minute seaward stroll down Calle Santomé from the market takes you through the Zona Colonial to the **Ciudad Nueva**, a neighbourly mixture of 19th-century town houses, noisy mid-street baseball games, sociable corner shops and beautiful glimpses of a dilapidated architectural past. Gingerbread lattices lace their way through tumbling balconies. Rocking chairs creak on stone-tiled floors. Approaching the sea, the imposing statue of the indigenous peoples' rights petitioner, **Fray Antón de Montesinos** *(see page 34)*, looms to the left, overlooking the harbour entrance and marking the head of the Malecón. A healthy walk westwards follows the contours of the rocky seashore, usually refreshed by a welcoming sea breeze and occasional mists of spray. The rocks are perennially manned by expectant fisherfolk, while youngsters bob between the waves on inflated inner tubes.

Map on page 170

You will not be permitted to pay your respects to the three national heroes in the Altar de la Patria if you are in shorts.

BELOW: liquor for sale.

Merengue can be heard in restaurants, bars, even taxis and is usually played at full blast.

The relative inactivity of the afternoon rolls over to the dusk arrival of the jogging set, to be replaced by a busy nightlife clientele. Roadside bars spring up and *merengue* blasts forth from straining stereo systems at the weekends. The volume increases impressively for the annual *merengue* festival during the last week of July and first week of August *(see page 111)*. Thousands gather on the Malecón to dance, drink and party some more. *Carnaval (see page 111)*, at the end of February, is another occasion for a boisterous seafront gathering. The pre-Lent celebrations coincide with the anniversary of Dominican independence, fuelling vivacious parades, non-stop music and the copious flow of rum.

A westward trek along the 3-km (2-mile) long Malecón leads past two self-congratulatory obelisks erected by Trujillo and winds up at the uninspiring **Centro de los Héroes**, renamed to commemorate those who fought the former dictator. Once the site of the Free World Fair for Peace and Fraternity during the 1950s – another of the dictatorship's ironic financial follies – the area now houses a green-painted concrete forest of government buildings. For those wishing to play postal roulette, the main Post Office is located nearby.

The first university of the New World

Inland, sandwiched between the Zona Colonial and Avenida Abraham Lincoln, the neighbourhoods of Gazcue and Ciudad Universitaria provide interesting glimpses of city life. Both areas house a variety of educational and cultural centres, mixed within pleasant residential zones.

Gazcue lies directly west of the Parque de la Independencia *(see page 169)*. Formerly the home of the city's élite before they headed for the hills of the newer northern suburbs, this catholic cluster of architectural styles dates from

BELOW:
directing the traffic in Santo Domingo.
RIGHT: service with a smile.

Map on page 170

the 1930s. Beautiful leafy streets and the distinguished array of homesteads wrapped in a veil of sleepy decay lay the foundations for a pleasant ramble. Occasional modern apartment blocks juxtapose urban designs, while the arrival of several fashionable restaurants, cafés and businesses have threatened to wake up this twilight zone in recent years. The relatively lively thoroughfare of Calle Santiago leads to the **Ciudad Universitaria ❹**, the adjoining residential neighbourhood that is home to one of the oldest universities in the Americas.

It may lack funds and architectural longevity, although originally founded in 1538, but the Autonomous University of Santo Domingo (UASD) makes up for material shortfall with a proud reputation and a history of vigorous student activism that consistently challenges the political and social inequalities evident in Dominican society. A range of concerts, films, and theatre productions, not to mention demonstrations, are regularly held on site.

The **Palacio de Bellas Artes ❺**, an impressive building that dominates the intersection of avenidas Máximo Gómez and Independencia, architecturally it promises more than it offers culturally. There are occasional events and art exhibitions held in the spacious halls, but generally little happens on the inside. The grand stairway murals of José Vela-Zanetti are worth a peek, though.

A concentration of culture

The **Plaza de la Cultura ❻** (the museums are open Tues–Sun; separate entrance fees), just a few blocks to the north on Avenida Máximo Gómez, soon provides a feast of opportunities to satiate the cultural appetite. Set amid pleasant lawns and landscaped gardens, the complex was constructed during the 1970s in the finest modernist style, and houses the most important arts institutions

TIP

Carros públicos – old minivans or cars, which traverse fixed routes – can take you from one area of the city to another and sometimes beat the taxi! Flag down a ride for the princely sum of three pesos *(see Travel Tips, page 351).*

BELOW: the impressive Palacio de Bellas Artes.

Exhibition of pre-Columbian artefacts plot the early history of the Dominican people.

BELOW:
the interior of the Museo del Hombre Dominicano.

in the country. Fronting the main entrance, the **Teatro Nacional** *(see Travel Tips, page 111)* is the imposing home of classical arts in the Dominican Republic. National and international artists regularly perform ballet, opera and orchestral performances here. A smart dress code is expected and enforced for all performances. At the top occasions, the well-to-do descend, bib-and-tuckered, from their gated uptown villas to join a who's who *soirée* of social flurrying.

The **Museo de Arte Moderno** (tel: 685 2153) houses an excellent exposition of contemporary Dominican art which more than compensates for any shortcomings of the Palacio de Bellas Artes. Even sceptics cannot fail to be aroused by the vivacity, depth and quality of the work on display. Representations of country life, evolving from the 1930s *costumbrismo* movement headed by Jaime Colson, Darío Suro and Yoryi Morel, provide a feel for the rural traditions that infuse longstanding notions of *dominicanidad*, which can seldom be experienced during a short stay in the country. Between museum hops, the café by the side of the Museo de Arte Moderno, provides a well-stocked retreat for a reflective drink or meal.

The **Museo del Hombre Dominicano** (tel: 687 3622) has fascinating exhibits of pre-Columbian artefacts and illustrates the history of the Conquest and slavery, demography, folklore, rural life and religious beliefs. The *Carnaval* display includes brightly-coloured masks and garish costumes, and offers a good taste of the festive atmosphere. Unlike many aspects of Dominican society, the museum provides a reasonably balanced and unbiased amalgam of Hispanic, African and indigenous influences.

The two remaining museums ignite fewer sparks of enthusiasm. The **Museo Nacional de Historia y Geografía** (tel: 689 0106) constructs a loose chrono-

DOMINICAN JEWS

The author Peter Furst describes his arrival by boat on the north coast of the island: "We glided past a shanty-town whose roofs of corrugated iron, catching the sun's first rays, exploded into a roaring, mind-expanding van Gogh of Dominican parentage" (*Don Quixote in Exile*, 1996).

Similar tropical landscapes greeted the 300 Jewish families who, like the writer, were fleeing Nazi Europe for the promised sanctuary of Dominican shores. Centuries earlier Jewish moneylenders had financed Columbus's first expedition, while the advent of Sephardic Jews during the 19th century consolidated interests in the island's import and export trade. It is the later arrivals, however, who have charted the most apparent changes to Dominican society.

A Jewish enclave was established in Sosúa, east of Puerta Plata (*see page 211*), following moves by Trujillo to encourage European immigration in the late 1930s. Though many of the settlers remigrated overseas during the 1960s, they left behind a thriving dairy and meat industry that still serves the island. Few visible remnants of the Jewish presence remain, but the Sinagoga de la Comunidad Judía de Sosúa (synagogue) and the Museo de la Comunidad Judía de Sosúa (Museum of the Jewish Community of Sosúa) survive as records of their time here.

Map on page 170

logical journey around 19th-century Haitian-Dominican tussles, and the assorted memorabilia and personal effects from the two longest-lasting dictatorships of Ulises Heureaux (1886–99) and Leónidas Rafael Trujillo (1930–61). The **Museo Nacional de Historia Natural** (tel: 689 0106) similarly hawks a lacklustre display of gems, rocks, basic ecology lessons and a stuffy array of taxidermists' treats. Additional enlightenment is restricted to those who are able to understand the Spanish display notes. Finally, and also of more interest to Spanish readers, the neighbouring **Biblioteca Nacional** (National Library) houses a significant collection of books encased in an impressive modernist block.

Wander eastwards along Avenida Dr Pedro Henriquez Ureña for about five blocks to refocus the tour on the nitty-gritty of everyday political reality, headquartered in a pink, domed baroque fantasy at the intersection of avenidas Doctor Delgado and México. The **Palacio Nacional** ❼ combines neoclassical style, presidential grandeur, regal decadence and keen security. It was designed by Italian architect Guido d'Alessandro during the late 1940s to match the magnificence of the dictatorship, and Trujillo's troubled ghost allegedly whisks through the ornately mirrored and heavily furnished salons, haunting present incumbents.

Around the city parks

Santo Domingo is fortunate in having its fair share of well-maintained, attractive and accessible park space. Bordered to the north by affluent suburbs and adjacent to the foreign diplomatic missions dotted along Avenida Anacaona, the **Parque Mirador del Sur** ❽ (daily), in the western reaches of the city, is a popular location for in-line skaters, cyclists, runners, and people out for a stroll. The elderly former president Balaguer traditionally takes his afternoon promenade

TIP

The Palacio Nacional is not generally open to the public, but free guided tours can be arranged on Monday, Wednesday and Friday by calling 686 4771. If you are given a tour, you are expected to be smartly dressed.

BELOW: the Palacio Nacional.

Schedule park visits to avoid the afternoon heat and regular rainy season downpours – early morning or evening visits will prove more pleasant, especially during the summer.

BELOW: the shuttle shades visitors from the heat.

in the park. A helicopter hovers overhead and an entourage of personal assistants and wired-up bodyguards on the ground mimic the "men-in-black" routine, while *El Ex-Presidente* shuffles along the path under the hot sun. The 7-km (5-mile) stretch of paths and lawns is a much appreciated retreat away from rush-hour traffic fumes. Police close the through road to vehicles during morning and evening peak hours (6–9am and 4–8pm). The park lies along a limestone ridge that hides a series of caves: the Cueva del Paseo de los Indios has a notable bat population, but perhaps the best-known cave is the **Guácara Taína** on Avenida Mirador del Sur. Converted into a lively subterranean music venue, this is where *capitaleños* dance and make merry until dawn at the weekends.

The **Jardín Botánico Nacional** ❾ (tel: 567 6211; Tues–Sun; entrance fee) on Avenida República de Colombia is fair reward for journeying to the north-western edge of the city. Nestled among Santo Domingo's wealthiest households in the residential suburb of Arroyo Hondo, the botanical gardens cover 180 hectares (450 acres) and exhibit a wide variety of tropical and aquatic plants, ferns, a herbarium and 200 species of palm. Within minutes of arrival, the buzz and belch of distant traffic is easily discarded for a tranquil few hours among the vegetation. The Japanese garden receives worthy praise, but perhaps just as striking are the floral and faunal national emblems. A pavilion houses the famous collection of over 300 indigenous orchid varieties. Fine examples of the national plant, the *caoba* or mahogany tree, have survived recent hurricane damage and the national bird, the palmchat, is often visible among the royal palms. A huge floral clock adds a note of eccentricity – more reliable and useful perhaps is the shuttle that ferries visitors around the gardens when the heat distracts even the most avid gardening enthusiasts.

A natural companion to the botanical gardens and a short drive east along Avenida los Reyes Católicos, the **Parque Zoológico** (Tues–Sun; entrance fee; tel: 562 3149) is another undervalued and undervisited nugget in the northwest of the city. Enhanced by its relative isolation, the 160 hectares (400 acres) of landscaped gardens and sensitively housed animal inmates provide an unexpected attraction. A focus on African wildlife immediately transports you beyond the confines of the zoo. Pink flamingos stand on sentry duty around the lagoon, while tigers stalk their relatively open enclosures. Rare Dominican fauna, the hutía and solenodon, find refuge here, and again, a shuttle saves legwork for the walk-through aviary and reptile houses.

Map on page 170

Where's the smallest "P" on a bottle of Presidente beer? Scouring the label will generally not reveal the tiny golden letter printed alone below the writing. But if you find it, you'll have the chance to impress, even the regulars, with your local knowledge.

Across the Río Ozama

Beyond the **Río Ozama**, the eastern section of the capital is noticeably less affluent than many of the western suburbs. The low-income settlements along the river bank are alarmingly worlds away from the city's wealthy neighbourhoods. Crossing over on Puente Mella, the Zona Colonial downstream on the west bank seems an ever isolated patch of urban antiquity.

The rainbow-striped **Molinos Dominicanos** are eye-catching kaleidoscopic silos that have gained their own prominence on the city's low-level skyline. A great sight for homesick prairie folk, the huge canisters also mark the way towards and cast their shadow on one of the first churches constructed in the Americas. The **Capilla de la Virgen del Rosario** ⓫, at the end of Avenida Olegario Vargas, is a quiet drop-in chapel en route to the capital's latest and largest architectural venture, Columbus's lighthouse or the **Faro a Colón** ⓬ (Tues–Sun; entrance fee; tel: 592 5217), a five-minute walk to the east. Dreamed

BELOW: pink flamingos around the lagoon at the Parque Zoológico.

Map on page 170

People need to wear shoes, but they also need to wear a tie. The lighthouse is that tie.

— ATTRIBUTED TO JOAQUÍN BALAGUER ON THE CONSTRUCTION OF FARO A COLÓN

BELOW: guarding Columbus's tomb at the Faro a Colón.
RIGHT: a manatee (*trichechus manatus*) can be seen at the Acuario Nacional.

up in the 1920s to honour the conquistador's arrival in the Americas, original plans were penned by British architect, J.L. Greave, who won the international competition for its design. Funding and interest languished for almost six decades, until President Balaguer resurrected the idea to construct the Faro a Colón in order to commemorate the 500th anniversary of Columbus's landfall in 1992. Originally to be financed with donations from around the Caribbean, the Dominican government eventually dug deep into national coffers.

Material expenses aside, controversy has engulfed the project. Hundreds of low-income families were forcibly removed to clear space for construction, or later shovelled aside to hide unscheduled human shabbiness. The lighthouse itself is an 800-metre (875-yard) long concrete edifice, shaped as a recumbent cross which projects a laser image of the crucifix into the heavens – when funds allow it to be lit. At the centre, the tomb of Columbus is guarded by a military vigil. In addition, reproductions of documents and colonial artefacts and exhibitions from other countries highlight the path of the Conquest.

Built as a mausoleum, ongoing debate contests the veracity of its namesake's remains. A great voyager in life and in death, Columbus's relics were shipped on a variety of occasions between Cuba, Spain and Santo Domingo, after an initial Spanish burial in 1506. Custodians of a tomb in Seville, however, also lay claim to his remains, and Italian and Cuban petitions have similarly jockeyed for pole position as the final resting place on the Grand Navigator's celestial cruise.

The Three Eyes and an orphaned manatee

The lighthouse is situated at the western end of the **Parque Mirador del Este**. Heading across the 5-km (3-mile) long narrow park (a short taxi ride), similar in layout to its western twin, the paths and perimeter roads eventually lead to three sinkhole caves called **Los Tres Ojos** ⓭ (Tues–Sun; entrance fee). Flanked to the north by the *Autopista de las Américas*, the main thoroughfare to the airport, "The Three Eyes" is a popular stop for coaches making rapid detours en route to the airport. If time permits it is worth hanging back from the crowds to savour something of the beauty of the underground caves and the three deep lagoons. Roughly hewn steps lead down to these karst sinkholes, adorned by stalagmites and stalactites, while a raft (extra cost) assists passage between the lagoons. Humidity levels soar as the day progresses, so arrive early, beat the crowds and enjoy what should be a natural wonder.

Another popular venue is the **Acuario Nacional** ⓮ (Tues–Sun until 8pm; entrance fee; tel: 592 1509). Located a few blocks to the south of the Parque Mirador del Este on the Avenida España, the aquarium is well worth an extended trip. The star of the show is Tamaury, an orphaned manatee rescued off the southwest coast of the island near Barahona. While information is given only in Spanish, non-Spanish speakers can still enjoy the aquatic venture and its associated breeding programmes. An underwater walkway allows visitors to watch the sharks playing overhead, while a host of fish swim alongside in the massive transparent tank. ❏

THE OLD COLONIAL CITY

Map on page 187

At the heart of Santo Domingo is the Zona Colonial, the preserved reminders of Columbus's first town in the New World. A tour of the old quarter provides a sense of life in those early days

This is where life in the New World began – in the narrow streets of colonial Santo Domingo on the west bank of the Río Ozama, and it is here that you can experience the vibrancy and grandeur of 16th century living in the New World as you walk around the Zona Colonial, the first colonial town to receive a royal charter from the Spanish Crown. Founded in 1498 after several false starts, the old city has a rich colonial past with many beautiful buildings still intact. Authentic and atmospheric, colonial Santo Domingo is not only a joy for the history buff, but for shoppers, art lovers and, in fact, lovers of all kinds, who stroll the romantic cobblestone streets, dine in fine restaurants and chance upon delightful historic attractions on every corner. Santo Domingo was laid out in a grid pattern, and this pattern became the model for town-planning in North America. The logic of this layout makes a walking tour of old Santo Domingo an easy and pleasurable experience.

A good place to start a walking tour of the Zona Colonial is at **Parque Colón ❶** on the corner of the bustling, pedestrian shopping street, Calle El Conde and Arzobispo Meriño. The park is named for its bronze statue of Christopher Columbus made in 1897 by the French sculptor, Gilbert. This is where you can opt for a guided tour or a bus tour of the old city. But, with map in hand, discovering the delights of the old city of Santo Domingo on your own is a breeze.

The first of many firsts

On the south side of the park, east of Arzobispo Nouel stands the **Catedral de Santa María la Menor ❷** (daily, 9am–4pm; no shorts). Built between 1514 and 1544, it is believed to be the first cathedral in the Americas. From the outside, the grey limestone cathedral is a majestic sight with massive gates which were originally carved with sculptures of the apostles. When Sir Francis Drake attacked the city in 1586 *(see page 36)*, these were destroyed – as was much else in the building he used as his headquarters – and it wasn't until 1990 that they were replaced with sculptures representing the indigenous people.

Inside, the newly restored cathedral is a dizzying mixture of Gothic, Spanish Renaissance and baroque architecture that's surprisingly harmonious. The beautiful stained glass windows have been recreated by the contemporary Dominican artist, Rincón Mora using the original 12th-century method, and other treasures include the 18th-century carved mahogany altar, the silver carillon created by Italian sculptor Benvenuto Cellini (1500–71) and the oil painting by the 17th-century Spanish artist, Bartolomé Murillo; 14 distinct chapels line the interior of the cathedral, and the treasury contains, among other riches, the

PRECEDING PAGES: an aerial view of the old city and the Río Ozama.
LEFT: altar detail inside the cathedral.
BELOW: chess on the Calle El Conde.

Religious icons were often crafted from gold and precious stones.

emerald-studded crown of Queen Isabela. The queen was forced to pawn her precious crown to meet the expense of Columbus's first voyage.

Facing Parque Colón on the east side of Calle Isabel la Católica, is the 19th-century **Palacio de Borgellá**. Once the home of the governor, today it houses government offices and a conveniently situated post office. A half block south of the palace, and a right turn on to Calle Padre Billini, brings you to the **Casa de Tostado** ❸ (Thurs–Tues, 9am–2pm; entrance fee) the home of the writer, Don Francisco Tostado. The first university professor born in the colony, he was murdered by Sir Francis Drake's raiding party in 1586. Later the graceful house became the Archbishop's Palace, and the double Gothic windows are the only surviving examples in the New World.

Today, inside the well-restored palace, the **Museo de la Familia Dominicana** (Museum of the Dominican Family) portrays how a typical well-to-do Dominican family lived in the 19th century. The lovely inner courtyard is a good place for a rest.

First seat of learning and some early churches

The majestic **Convento de los Domínicos** ❹ (Tues–Sun; free) stands at the corner of Calle Padre Billini and Calle Duarte Macoris another block to the west. Founded in 1510, the convent was visited by Pope Paul III in 1538, and, impressed by the theology lectures that he heard here, he granted it the title of university, making it – you've guessed it – the oldest university in the New World. Its unusual ceiling depicts both the classical gods and the Christian saints and angels in a single pantheon. The Sun represents God while Mars, Mercury, Jupiter and Saturn are the four evangelists.

BELOW:
the Convento de los Domínicos.

The **Iglesia de la Regina Angelorum** (Mon–Sat), two blocks further along in Calle José Reyes, was constructed in 1537 and is a delicate plateresque-style building that was badly damaged during Haitian rule from 1822 to 1844, but some of the original structure survives. Today, the church of the Queen of the Angels is a small convent which has an exquisite wood altar inside the simple chapel and a wall made of silver. On the same street, half a block north at No. 6 is the **Museo de Porcelana** (Tues–Sun; entrance fee). Built in the 19th century and modelled on the Alhambra in Spain, this very small museum has a lovely collection of antique porcelain.

Around the corner, and one block to the west on Calle Arzobispo Nouel, is the **Iglesia del Carmen** (open at varying, unscheduled times). Built around 1615 at the side of Capilla de San Andrés, the chapel contains a lovely wooden sculpture of Jesus. A 10-minute detour down Calle Sánchez with a right turn on to Calle Arzobispo Portes will bring you to the **Puerta de la Misericordia** ❻. Forming part of the old wall of Santo Domingo, its name "the Gate of Mercy" was bestowed upon it because the local population always fled to this point for protection during hurricanes and earthquakes. It was at this site, on 27 February 1844, that Ramón Matías Mella, one of the country's founding fathers, fired the shot that began the struggle for independence from Haiti after 22 years of occupation (*see page 46*).

Lovely Ladies Street

Directly east from the Gate of Mercy, after about 800 metres (just over ½ mile), the lovely **Calle Las Damas** leads northwards parallel to Río Ozama. This Street of the Ladies is the oldest in the western hemisphere and its name honours

The Museo del Ambar, which has a gift shop, can be found at 452 Calle Arzobispo Meriño and is open every day until 6pm; admission is free. See pages 207–215 for more information about this amazing gem.

BELOW:
a tobacco shop on Calle Las Damas.

TIP

When visiting the Fortaleza Ozama, if you decide to hire one of the many guides offering their services at the door, make sure that you agree on a fee before you start.

the elegant noblewomen of the Spanish Court who promenaded along it in their finery each evening. Today it is the visitors who promenade, delighting in the street's beautifully restored colonial buildings.

The imposing buildings of the **Fortaleza Ozama** ❼ (Tues–Sun; entrance fee) dominate the southeastern end of the Calle Las Damas. Also known as the Fortaleza Santo Domingo, it was built in 1503 to protect the eastern border of the city overlooking the mouth of the Río Ozama, and it forms the oldest military complex in the New World. Inside the massive stone walls is a pleasant garden with the munitions building to one side, guarded by a statue of the Virgin Mary. At the opposite end of the garden is the **Torre de Homenaje** (Tower of Homage), built in 1505 which, despite its name, was the cruel holding pen for condemned prisoners. Today it is a museum and gallery with changing exhibits, and from the roof, at the top of a spiral staircase, there is an all-embracing view of the city.

Situated to the north of the fort, the **Casa de Bastidas**, (Tues–Sun; free) was constructed in the early 16th century for Don Rodrigo Bastidas, the king's tax collector. Bastidas went on to found the city of Santa Marta in Colombia. The house has a neoclassical portal and an inner court resembling a cloister. Inside, there are two pretty gardens, as well as two fine art galleries and a gift shop well worth a visit.

Across the street is the Gothic **Casa de Francia** ❽, which today is occupied by the French Cultural Alliance, part of the French Embassy. It was originally built in 1503 and is where the famous explorer and conqueror of Mexico, Hernán Cortéz, is supposed to have planned his conquests. The Alliance often holds art exhibitions of modern Dominican artists.

BELOW:
guard of honour at Panteón Nacional.

ADVENTURER EXTRAORDINAIRE

Hernán Cortés (1485–1547) was only 19 years old when he arrived in Santo Domingo from Spain in 1504. Desperate for adventure, he was intelligent, ruthless and ambitious. His prayers were answered when he met the conquistador Diego de Velázquez, who helped him in his successful expedition to conquer Cuba in 1511.

Fired with the conquering spirit, Cortés was given the command of an expedition to Mexico in 1518. After founding Vera Cruz, he arrived at the magnificent Aztec capital of Tenochtitlán in 1519 with fewer than 400 Spanish soldiers, 16 horses – never seen before in the New World – 10 heavy guns, four lighter pieces of artillery and plenty of ammunition. The Aztec emperor Montezuma II thought Cortés was a messenger from the god Quetzalcóatl, and welcomed the explorer with many gifts, but the Spaniards repaid the emperor by taking him prisoner and attacking the city. Forced to retreat, Cortés didn't conquer the city until 1521, when he completely destroyed it and laid the foundations for Mexico city.

In 1522 he became governor of New Spain. After more conquests he went back to Spain in 1528 and was returned to Mexico City as Captain-General in 1530. In 1540 he went home a sick man, where he died.

A few steps more on the opposite side of the street is the elegant **Hostal Nicolás de Ovando**, once the home of the city's first governor and where Christopher Columbus himself was a guest. Enter the lobby and you'll see that the newly restored house is now a hotel just oozing olde worlde ambience. Next door is the **Capilla de Nuestra Señora de los Remedios** (Mon–Sat; Sun for Masses beginning at 6am). Rebuilt in 1884, the Chapel of our Lady of the Remedies is where the Spanish colonists first worshipped before the cathedral was constructed, and has Castillian-Romanesque style blind arches and a barrel-vaulted ceiling.

Resting place for real heroes

The neoclassical grey limestone façade of the **Panteón Nacional** ❾ (Mon–Sat; free, but it's customary to tip the guide; respectable dress required) dominates the opposite side of the street. Constructed between 1714 and 1745 as a Jesuit monastery, the building was given to the Spanish Crown in 1767 when the

Map below

CALLE ARZOBISPO MERIÑO

Behind the Panteón Nacional is the Plaza María de Toledo, named for Diego Columbus's wife. Here is an art gallery, restaurant and outdoor café, where you can enjoy a tropical drink or a meal and a chat with veteran Tennessee owner, Bettye Marshall.

Jesuits were expelled from Hispaniola and it has served as a tobacco warehouse and a theatre since. In 1955, the dictator Trujillo mandated that the building be transformed into a memorial to the country's national heroes, thinking that he himself would one day be interred here. Ironically, it now contains the remains of the martyrs who assassinated him. In fact, on the ceiling above the altar a commemorative scene of the assassination is painted. Note the sculpted Dominican coat of arms that graces the entrance and the exquisite copper chandeliers, a gift from Spain's own dictator, General Franco (1892–1975).

Just around the corner in Calle Luperon is the **Casa de los Jesuitas** (Mon–Fri 8am–4.30pm; free), which houses not only the Institute for Hispanic Culture but also an excellent library of colonial history.

Spanish treasure – a royal inheritance

A fascinating treasure chest of eclectic, colonial objects fill the **Museo de las Casas Reales ⑩** (Tues–Sat and Sun morning; entrance fee) across Calle las Mercedes on the other side of the Panteón. In two 16th-century Renaissance-style mansions, the Museum of the Royal Houses was where the Royal Court or *Real Audiencia (see page 33)* for the colony sat. On display are antique coins (pieces of eight) and dolls, coats of armour, coaches, a Royal Court room, treasure from shipwrecks, gilded Spanish colonial furniture, an apothecary shop and Taíno Indian artefacts. In the cartography room, an enormous map marks the voyages of Columbus. The museum also puts on exhibitions of contemporary Dominican art.

To know the time of day, the judges sitting in the *Real Audiencia* in the Casa Reales merely needed to glance out of the window at the **Reloj del Sol (sundial)**

BELOW: interior of Museo de las Casas Reales.

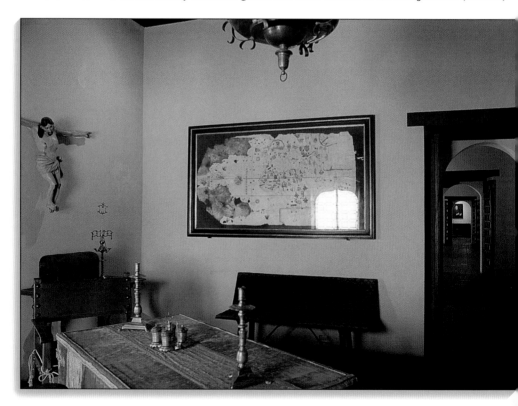

across the Calle Las Damas, to find out the time. The strategically placed timepiece was built in 1753 and is a perfect spot for a pause to savour the fabulous view of the Ozama River.

Map on page 187

Colonial splendour in the Plaza d'Espagne

The Calle Las Damas enters the **Plaza d'Espagne**, where you come face to face with the **Alcázar de Colón** ⓫ (Wed–Mon; entrance fee; guided tours in English), the most spectacular colonial site in the city. This was the palace of Christopher Columbus's son, Diego, who succeeded Ovando as governor of Hispaniola in 1509. Diego lived here with his beautiful wife, María de Toledo, King Ferdinand's niece, until 1523. After that the Moorish villa was the home of the Spanish Court for more than 60 years and it is where Pizarro, Cortez, Ponce de León and Balboa charted their future conquests. The coral-stone palace's graceful arched façade is magnificent, and each of the 22 rooms has been carefully refurbished with period furniture and paintings donated by the University of Madrid.

In the 18th century, the Alcázar de Colón was in such a bad state that it was used as the city's unofficial dumping ground. It has since been restored three times.

The palace also houses the **Museo Virreinal** (Viceregal Museum) that displays religious items and furnishings of the colonial period, and from the second floor you can enjoy a grand view of the river and the entire Zona Colonial. Venture around the back of the building and you'll come to the **Puerta de San Diego**, the original gate to the city which still stands in a part of the old city wall built to discourage a riverside attack.

A flight of steps down from the front of the Alcázar takes you to a narrow street called **La Atarazana** (Royal Mooring Docks), which was once the colonial commercial district and where naval supplies used to be stored. Today, the

BELOW:
playing dominoes on the plaza at the Alcázar de Colón.

Map on page 187

The ruined fortress and church of Santa Bárbara (Mon–Fri am, Sun for Masses starting at 6am) lie in the northernmost part of the old city. Completed in 1574, the church is a mishmash of architectural styles including baroque and Gothic.

BELOW: cathedral gateway detail.
RIGHT: a beautiful bride at Hospital de San Nicolás de Bari.

small white houses lining the street are home to craft shops, art galleries and restaurants, providing the ideal spot for rest and refreshment and relax. Here you'll find **Drake's Café**, a convivial bar, and **Museo del Jamón** which, despite its name, is *not* a ham museum, but a lively delicatessen and bar.

A little way north along La Ataranza, stands the 17th-century **Atarazanas Gate** and the **Museo de las Atarazanas Reales** ⑫ (Mon–Sat and Sun morning; entrance fee). This maritime museum tells the story of the most famous shipwrecks around the Dominican coast, along with some marvellous exhibits of recovered treasure such as silver and gold coins, porcelain, antique bottles and all manner of interesting contraband.

Duarte – father of the *República*

One of the Dominican Republic's founders was born in 1813 at the house which now contains a museum in his honour. The **Museo de Juan Pablo Duarte** ⑬ (Tues–Sun 8am–noon and 2–4.30pm; entrance fee) can be found at 308 Calle Isabel La Católica, two small blocks to the west of La Atarazana. The national hero liberated the Dominican Republic from Haitian domination in 1844, only to see it come under Spanish rule again in 1861. He fought hard against it but was eventually forced to leave the country and died in Venezuela in 1876. The museum is dedicated to the life of Duarte who is considered to be the father of the Dominican Republic.

Just two blocks south down Calle Isabel La Católica, on the corner with Calle Emiliano Tejera, stands the **Casa del Cordón** ⑭ (daily; free) where Diego Colón first lived when he arrived in 1509. Built in 1500, it is the oldest European-style residence with two floors in the New World. On the façade, the sculpted sash and cord is the symbol of the rope-belt worn by the Franciscan order.

Overlooking a small hill, another two blocks to the west, lie the evocative ruins of the **Monasterio de San Francisco** (daily; free). Built in 1508, it was the first monastery in the New World, but Drake destroyed it in 1586 *(see page 36)* by setting it on fire. After rebuilding, it was then levelled by an earthquake in 1673. Restored again, it was damaged by a hurricane in 1751 and converted into a lunatic asylum in 1881 – the chains that used to hold down the hapless patients can still be seen. Just as poignant, during the 20th century, artists took refuge here from the Spanish Civil War. Today the ruins often serve as a venue for cultural events.

A couple of minutes' walk south on Calle Hostos and Calle las Mercedes are more ruins. The **Hospital de San Nicolás de Bari** ⑮ was ordered to be built by Nicolás de Ovandó, to serve the city's poor, and was the first hospital in the Americas. You can still make out the shape of the hospital in the form of a cross, the configuration of all colonial hospitals.

The church of **Nuestra Señora de las Mercedes**, three blocks west on the Calle las Mercedes, was built between 1555 and 1576, but after being plundered by Drake and suffering earthquakes and hurricanes, the cloister is the only original feature that remains. The baroque carved wooden altar is a masterpiece. ❏

FROM CARIBE TO COCO

Rural primitiveness rubs shoulders with luxurious holiday resorts around the southeast coast, offering stunning beaches, an underwater world and a national park teeming with exotic birds

Map on page 198

Provincial peacefulness and professional power-tourism? The island's beautiful southeast coast is living proof of such a strange marriage. Peasants driving their cattle alongside fields of waving sugar cane are just as typical as tourists relaxing in high-end luxury resorts.

However, it is a big mistake to categorise the eastern part of *La Dominica* as mainly a "mecca for charter tourists". True, the endless white sand beaches of the Costa Caribe in the southeast and Costa del Coco in the far east are skirted by hundreds of hotels, some of them small and picturesque, some of them lavish and ready to be featured in design bibles like *Elle Decoration*. Every month or so another new complex is on the drawing board of some European, yes European, architect. But the eastern interior, especially in the provinces of San Pedro de Macorís, Hato Mayor and La Romana, is still dominated by rural simplicity. Raising cattle and cultivating fields of grass-green sugar cane are major aspects of Dominican life and many a *campesino* may be seen riding a horse against a backdrop of pale purple mountains. In contrast, the industrial cities of **San Pedro de Macorís** and **La Romana** are abuzz with *motoconchos* (taxi motorcycles). Here are the nation's largest sugar processing plants, providing a fat portion of the Western hemisphere with the beloved "sweet crystal".

Nevertheless the east *is* a major destination for package tourists and backpackers alike. The Government is proud of its supply of more than 13,000 hotel rooms in the region. The scenic Costa Caribe has at least 50 beaches – half of which are clustered with fancy accommodation. Yet there are plenty of inexpensive inns as well, where individual travellers prefer to stay and don't need to book in advance. The spectacular Costa del Coco (40 km/25 miles of pure white sandy beaches), on the other hand, caters solely to charter tourists. Punta Cana's up-market beach resorts resemble one gigantic satellite village, where the all-inclusive set-up satisfies every need possible. It's heaven for both beach bums and sports enthusiasts, but for the more adventurous traveller it might just seem like wasted time in an isolated golden cage. Except for some tiny hamlets, the area is sparsely populated and therefore poor in infrastructure, the next large city is 50 km (30 miles) away.

PRECEDING PAGES: boats tied-up at Playa Bayahibe. **LEFT:** fun in the sun at Punta Cana. **BELOW:** Jesus and Sammy Sosa.

The world's largest bathtub

East of **Santo Domingo ❶** on the bumpy *Autopista Las Américas* (watch for those potholes), it takes about 45 minutes to reach the small beach at **La Caleta ❷**, where the Parque Nacional Submarino lies beneath the waves. Here is an intact reef teeming with exotic fish and colourful corals, and three wrecks at this popular spot provide a fascinating day's diving. To reach

At the small Museo Ceremonial La Caleta (daily, free), near Boca Chica, a variety of Amerindian ceramics are on display, alongside a Taíno burial site.

BELOW: sleepy fishing villages dot the coast.

the park's waters, it's necessary to take either a rather scary dinghy ride from the beach or go by speedboat from Boca Chica, a 10-minute drive away.

Beyond Las Américas airport lies the stronghold of Euro-Canadian party-tourism. **Boca Chica ❸**, also dubbed the "Rimini of the Dominican Republic", offers all the hustle and bustle a fun-hungry person can desire – 24 hours a day. At the weekend, when the city dwellers join the foreign visitors and descend into the "world's largest bathtub", the reef-protected **Playa Boca Chica** resembles one crazy MTV-style beach party. Panhandlers offer everything from manicures to fake amber jewellery to hair-braiding – in every language. *Mariachis* serenade the crowds with hits like *Bambolero*, while revellers practise their clumsy merengue steps until the dawn.

Founded as a port for exporting sugar cane in the 1930s, this one-time idyllic *pueblo* gained fame when the gruesome dictator Trujillo built a beach villa here. After his dispatch in 1961, Boca Chica grew into a fancy and exclusive resort earning itself the name "Playa St Tropez". Nowadays, every business-savvy local rents out rooms, and the busy **Calle Duarte**, the main strip, is lined with souvenir shops, cappuccino bars and open-air restaurants. At night though, it reverts to a red light district with persistent girls trying to lure even the most devoted family man through their doors. Watch out for their exuberant hugs – most of the time it's a trick to pick your pocket.

In a way, Boca Chica is a crazy human zoo. Yet away from the all-inclusives and the seedy Calle Duarte, you can still enjoy its simple attractions and low-price guesthouses. In Bahía de Andrés, the beautiful and inviting lagoon does not go beyond 1.5 metres (5 ft) deep and is ideal for children. At low tide you can wade all the way to the island **La Matica** just offshore.

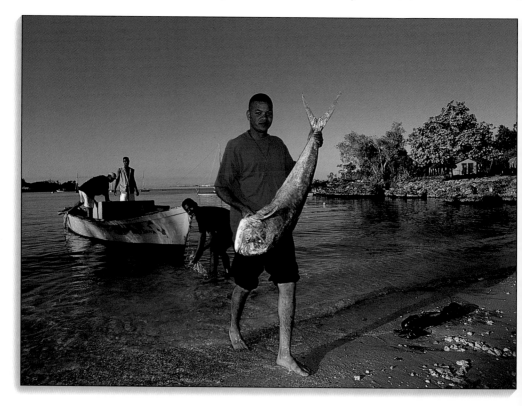

All-inclusive isolation

About 14 km (9 miles) eastwards along the coast is the all-inclusive settlement of **Juan Dolio/Villas del Mar** overlooking the flawless white coral beaches of the Caribbean and presenting quite a mishmash of architectural styles. Busy at weekends, this 10–12-km (6–7-mile) stretch is completely isolated from Dominican life and is quiet out of season. The many luxurious all-inclusive hotels dominate the beaches, and the cheaper guesthouses are closer to the Las Américas highway with a 10-minute walk to the shoreline.

Juan Dolio was created as a tourist development in 1987 and, with construction sites for hotels and condominiums to your right and left, it is steadily growing into a super-neat fantasyland for the wealthy. Today there is no village *per se*, just a long road with lots of speed bumps and shopping malls. Traces of true Caribbean life can only be found in remnants of the original dusty fishing village of Juan Dolio, where the pizzeria El Sueño offers home cooking just like *Mama Italia* serves it *(see Travel Tips, page 354)*.

The drive to **San Pedro de Macorís** ❹ (pop. 212,000) is smooth and should not take longer than 45 minutes. Crossing the large bridge over the **Río Iguamo**, the industrial clouds hang like tinted cotton balls above the country's fourth largest city. San Pedro is still synonymous with sugar cane, yet the real money comes from the baseball team Estrellas Orientales and their permanently sold out stadium **Tetelo Vargas** during the season from February to October. Sammy Sosa, North America's current *beisbol* hero *(see page 142)*, is one of the many players exported from the San Pedro team.

The port town, named for the Macorís Indians, was founded in 1822, and it soon grew into a centre for the sugar processing industry. With the outbreak of

Map on page 198

TIP

In the old fishing village of Juan Dolio you can stay in the Fior di Loto, an East Indian-style guest house reminiscent of an Indian temple in Calle Central. Tel: 526 1146; fax: 526 3332.

BELOW:
friendly chat at the salon in San Pedro de Macorís.

World War I, sugar prices shot up, turning San Pedro into a prosperous haven for entrepreneurs. European and Arabian immigrants swarmed into the so-called "Sultan of the East", American sugar honchos landed in Pan Am seaplanes on the Río Iguamo, and majestic villas with neoclassical and Victorian ornamentation started to spring up. Nowadays, their splendour has almost entirely flaked off – yet it's still worth having a look at the neo-Gothic church of **San Pedro de Apóstol** (1913) on the river bank, and the **San Pedro fire station** and mansions near **Parque Duarte**. However, this university town is loud and rather unfriendly towards visitors. Be prepared for heavy traffic caused by the *zona franca*. Unfortunately, the road out to La Romana leads right through the chaos.

Map on page 198

Cockfighting is a popular pastime in the south.

La Romana – a friendly sugar town

Autopista No. 3 shoots like an arrow across the flat landscape, through fields of swaying sugar cane and grazing cows, reminiscent of a classic Dominican oil painting. Taking the little dirt road to your right, after the village of **Soco**, the local *playas* **Soco**, **La Sardina**, **La Rata** and **Cumayasa** appear languidly behind the fields. In the distance, **La Reina Cumayasa** *(see Travel Tips, page 352)*, one of the most stunning hotels of the southeast, stands aloft like a Mediterranean castle above the mouth of **Río Cumayasa**.

La Romana ❺ (pop. 101,350) is the financial capital of the southeast, a friendly little town, where visitors can hang out in appealing Euro-style cafés or shop at the **Mercado Municipal** for souvenirs and fresh herbs. The well-kept town and the affluent-looking locals indicate that the country's biggest sugar mill plant (Central de la Romana) still operates successfully here. Colourful gingerbread houses front the **Avenida Libertad** and in the centre is the large, open **Parque Central**. Close by the pretty church of **Santa Rosa de Lima** overlooks a smaller park.

BELOW: market day in La Romana.

La Romana, established as a port by the Spaniards in 1502, is named after a Roman scale there, used for weighing sugar. But it was only in the 1920s that the town came into its own, when the American company Gulf & Western invested in the sugar production industry and poured US$20 million into La Romana in an attempt to turn it into "the showcase of the East". In the 1970s, the company built the billionaire's playground, **Casa de Campo** ❻ (the "house in the country"), just 10 km (6 miles) along the coast.

One of the most sumptuous holiday resorts in the Caribbean, the complex spans over 30 sq km (12 sq miles) with more than 950 palatial villas and smart *casitas* (cabins). The Dominican-born couturier Oscar de la Renta designed the interiors and has one of his own next to such celebrities as Sharon Stone and Julio Iglesias. Oiling this leisure machine are three golf courses, a marina, a polo club, 15 swimming pools, 17 tennis courts, a riding stable with several hundred horses and dozens of private beaches.

Sitting on a plateau in a spectacular position above the "house in the country" is the international artists' village of **Altos de Chavón** ❼. Spoilt Europeans used to sympathetic architecture might trash this mock-Andalusian settlement, yet, undeniably, the beauty of the picturesque limestone buildings and panoramic

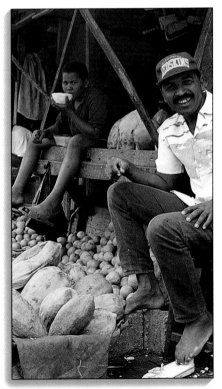

view over the **Río Chavón** has to be an inspiration to all. Part of this US$40-million project, created in the mid 1980s, is the **Museo Arqueológico Regional** (daily; entrance fee), which houses an extensive collection of Taíno artefacts. A branch of the **New York Parsons School of Design** is also here, as well as a 4,000-seat amphitheatre, where international stars often top the bill (Frank Sinatra was the first) and fancy boutiques and restaurants. Be warned, however, the prices are exorbitant.

TIP

The artists' enclave of Altos de Chavón can be reached by a free bus service that leaves Casa de Campo every 30 minutes.

BELOW:
an aerial view of Altos de Chavón.

A Robinson Crusoesque isle

Lying in an idyllic bay, backed by the Parque Nacional del Este, **Bayahibe** ❽ (pop. 2,400) is a sleepy fishing village only 30 minutes drive away from La Romana. Yet it is only a question of time before the construction-crazy tourism-honchos wake it up for ever, and the pastel-coloured huts and seafood restaurants by the water will turn into museum pieces. The locals rent out their homes as guesthouses for as little as US$25 a night, making it popular with backpackers, while the owners live in extensions at the back. They also offer boat rides to **Playa Dominicus**, further around the coast, to neighbouring lagoons and to the Robinson Crusoesque **Isla Saona** (pop. 1,000) off the southern tip of the island.

Part of the Parque Nacional del Este and fringed by virginal, coral sand beaches, the mangrove-lined lagoons of the beautiful 117-sq km (45-sq mile) Isla Saona are home to endangered birds such as the Hispaniolan lizard cuckoo and zillions of mosquitos (insect repellent is a must!). Ironically, many travellers prefer the quicker ride (about 45 minutes) on one of the catamarans or speed boats that leave Playa Bayahibe every morning. One company offers rum and *merengue* dancing girls on board and the party continues on the island.

OSCAR DE LA RENTA

Fashion designer Oscar de la Renta was born in 1932 in Santo Domingo where he studied art. He left the Dominican Republic at the age of 18 to study painting at the Academy of San Fernando in Madrid. While in Spain he landed a job at the world-famous fashion house of Cristobal Balenciaga, whose elegant gowns were the coveted apparel of the 1940s and '50s. In 1937 Balenciaga moved his operation to Paris but de la Renta remained in Spain until 1961 when he too moved to Paris to join the house of Lanvin-Castillo as a couture assistant. By 1963 he had settled in New York, designing the couture collection for Elizabeth Arden.

Unable to let his imagination run wild with his designs, he started his own fashion company in 1965 and throughout the 1960s he built up a reputation – and a fortune – for his opulent, ornate evening dresses.

Although he is an American citizen, he has remained loyal to his roots in the Dominican Republic, and spends most of the year at the beautiful beach villa he built in the exclusive Los Corales in Punta Cana. He and his great friend, Spanish crooner Julio Iglesias, have not only invested in the Casa de Campo resort, but also co-own the Punta Cana airport and much of the town.

An Amerindian stronghold

The **Parque Nacional del Este ❾** covers most of the Dominican Republic's southeastern peninsula and incorporates a total area of 41,900 hectares (103,500 acres). Established in 1975, the Eastern National Park is one of the newer conservation areas of the Dominican Republic. Bird watchers and nature lovers who are not bothered by the intense and dry heat can explore the park's tropical deciduous forest for glimpses of around 112 exotic birds. Wild olive, mangroves, Hispaniolan mahogany and coconut palms give shelter to rhinoceros iguanas and all sorts of reptiles and endemic mammals, such as the endangered solenodon and hutia.

The few beaches can only be reached by boat, and you may spot gentle manatees and bottlenose dolphins playing in the waters. In the **Guaraguao** area there are several pre-Columbian caves with Taíno carvings and drawings on the walls, and many artefacts have been found at La Aleta, once a large ceremonial site that was discovered in 1997. It is believed that this was the settlement that the priest Bartolomé de las Casas *(see page 34)* witnessed being destroyed in 1503.

The northeastern entrance to the park is near **Boca de Yuma ❿** which was reduced from a quaint fishing village to a deserted ghost town by Hurricane Georges in 1998. Ruined hotels and tourist villas are up for sale and the seafood restaurants overlooking the splendid Bahia de Yuma have been swept away. The famous deep-sea fishing tournament, which attracted blue marlin hunters from all over the world every June, had to be moved to Playa Cabeza de Toro further north, and the dirt road to the Taíno Cueva de Berna is inaccessible. But restoration work is in progress.

Map on page 198

A 5-minute boat ride from La Romana port takes you to the picture-perfect Isla Catalina. Belonging to an Italian shipping company, the icing sugar-beaches serve as a spring board for divers to a magical underwater world.

BELOW LEFT: Playa Saona.
BELOW RIGHT: the entrance to Parque Nacional del Este.

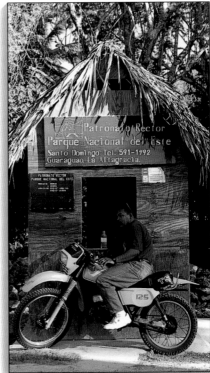

Higüey – a miracle town

Carretera 4 provides a smooth trip north through wide swathes of sugar cane and vegetable fields to **Higüey** ⓫ (pop. 120,000), 32 km (20 miles) away. *Motoconchos* buzz like flies through the streets of this thriving town, which has a lively market and a rum factory nearby. Founded in 1494 by Spanish *conquistador* Juan de Esquivel, the capital of the province of La Altagracia developed in the early 1500s under the rather infamous governor of Santo Domingo, Nicolás de Ovando, who chose Ponce de Léon (1502–08) as his administrator.

The true attraction of this drab city is the **Basílica de la Nuestra Señora de la Altagracia**. Built as the cathedral *de la Merced,* this imposing structure is where Columbus's forces planted their cross while fending off an Indian attack. The soil is attributed with mysterious miracles: the story goes that Columbus and his posse were on the point of defeat by the Taínos when a vision of the Virgin appeared on the cross allowing the Spaniards to repel the attack. In 1922, *La Altagracia* (Virgin of the Highest Grace) became the country's patron saint, and, ever since, pilgrims have been coming to the site on 21 January and 16 August. In 1952, the French architect André Jaques Dunoyer de Segonzac built the existing modern church. With a 60-metre (200-ft) high round arch and the tallest bell-tower in the Americas, the cathedral is easy to spot from miles around.

Beautiful beaches of Costa del Coco

Vamos a la playa? No problem in **Punta Cana** ⓬, 45 km (28 miles) east of Higüey on the 60-km (37-mile) long Costa del Coco, as this stretch of coastline has the most stunning beaches in the Dominican Republic. Each and every one of them could be a film set for *The Blue Lagoon*. Thanks to the coral reefs that

TIP

No one is allowed in the Basílica de la Nuestra Señora de la Altagracia wearing shorts or a mini-skirt.

BELOW LEFT:
Higüey's "new" cathedral.
BELOW RIGHT:
sailing in the waters around Punta Cana.

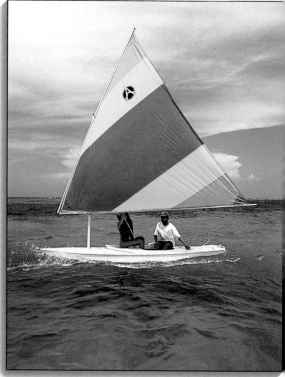

protect the bays from the might of the Atlantic, the conditions are ideal for swimming, with bathtub temperatures (77°F/25°C), and the forests of coconut palms behind give the desired shade. The idyllic **Playa Punta Cana** stretches for over 2 km (1 mile) and, apart from two all-inclusives and a luxury villa, the tourism magnates have so far kept their hands off it. The lesser-known **Playa Juanillo** further south is a meeting point for local youth.

Cabo Engaño, the easternmost point above Punta Cana, provides ideal conditions for both surfers and windsurfers. The cape juts out into the dangerous **Mona Passage**, which separates Hispaniola from Puerto Rico – and the wind whips around it. Northwards, the mega-luxurious hotel resorts along the 24-km (15-mile) coastal stretch between Bávaro and Punta Arena Gorda are a complete contrast to the poverty-stricken local life outside the fences. These palatial satellite villages (up to 1,200 rooms each) offer everything from psychiatrists to casinos to shopping malls. Their architecture is akin to "New Mexican Adobe meets Sheraton 2000". The pools resemble fantasy renditions of Michael Jackson's *Neverland Ranch*, and a plethora of sports are on offer, from water skiing, surfing and sailing to horse riding, golf and tennis, and more. Children are well catered for in "kiddie clubs" and can play in the clear, warm, shallow sea.

The **Bávaro Beach Resort Complex** *(see Travel Tips, page 352)* is the biggest and most popular on the Costa del Coco. With the areas' only 18-hole golf course and an Ibiza-like nightlife, its five hotels are categorised by their names (Palace, Golf, Garden, Beach, Casino). Higüey, more than 50 km (30 miles) away, is its nearest town, so the international-style restaurants and bars in the resort are the only alternatives. Shopping is restricted to the **Plaza Bávaro** shopping mall – with prices reaching dizzy heights. The **Manatí Park Bávaro** ⓭ (Plaza Bávaro, daily; entrance fee; tel: 552 0807) is popular with visitors to the Costa del Coco, being the only attraction in the area. The zoo houses almost every indigenous animal of the *republicá*: flamingos, manatees, rare birds and spiders, crocodiles and performing parrots. And for an additional fee, you can swim with the dolphins.

Dream bays and Atlantic waves

North of **Playa Arena Gorda**, the charter meccas are left behind glinting like shiny oyster pearls in the sun, and the Atlantic waves provide lots of fun. From here, there is one lonely dream bay after another – **Playa El Macao**, **Boca de Maimón**, **Punta Sabena** and **Playa del Muerto**. The enchanting lagoons of Boca de Maimón are postcard material, where you can walk for hours without seeing any other visitors except dozing sea turtles. The numerous potholes on the shabby coastal road are the only setback – without a four-wheel-drive the trip is not recommended.

Passable, but not much better is the drive further north to the **Reserva Científica Laguna Redonda y Limón** ⓮, where you can watch magnificent seabirds stalk through the mangroves and experience the sensation of being deep in the jungle. About 20 km (12 miles) further on lies the quiet little unspoilt port of **Miches**. From the beach you can watch the fishermen while lunching on fresh grilled fish. ❑

Map on page 198

On the Costa del Coco, wealthy Dominicans craving fresh seafood eat at Capitán Cook (Playa del Cortecito, tel: 552 0646). The Spanish owner serves up delicious paella, lobster and devilish caipirinhas.

BELOW: beautiful beaches stretch along the Costa del Coco.

THE AMBER COAST

Rich in precious amber, the northeast coast is blessed with beautiful beaches, coral reefs and rolling countryside which attracts both sun worshippers and adventure tourists

Maps:
Area 212
Town 208

The Dominican Republic's northeastern region is every bit as varied as its topography – fertile valleys with forested, inland mountains soaring to breathtaking vistas, and 120 km (75 miles) of dazzling beaches. Known as the Amber Coast because of its extensive deposits of the ancient resin, the area's amber is among the most desirable in the world.

The north coast has the Atlantic Ocean for its front door and a chain of majestic mountains as its backyard. In between are some of the most beautiful beaches in the Caribbean, interspersed with historic towns and modern resorts.

With such a felicitous natural environment, the north coast offers a range of active and high adventure sports. The exhilaration of the Atlantic's strong currents and on-shore winds makes for excellent windsurfing at Cofresí, Playa Dorada, Playa Grande, Sosúa, and Cabarete. Scuba diving is outstanding all along the north coast thanks to the many protected bays and clear water. Opportunities abound for diving among beautiful reefs, underwater pinnacles, walls with swim-throughs and a number of historic wrecks. Popular dive areas on the Amber Coast include Sosúa, Río San Juan and Cabrera and the Samaná Peninsula in the far east. West of the main city of Puerto Plata are Costambar, Luperón, and Monte Cristi *(see page 222)*.

Other northern adventures include traditional mountain climbing, horse riding and caving (exploring the extensive cave networks in the area – some with prehistoric drawings). The largest concentration of caves in this region is between Río San Juan and Cabrera. There are fascinating pictographs (drawings) and petroglyphs (rock carvings), depicting the lives of the Taínos. To get the adrenalin pumping why not try cascading? It involves plunging down a 55 metre- (200 ft-) high waterfall. Canyoning afficionados climb high into the steep rocks, then jump into a river far below. Exciting white water rafting is available at Jarabacoa in the nearby "Dominican Alps", within the Cordillera Central, so called because of its mountains, rivers, waterfalls and fragrant pine forests.

Golfers paradise

There are numerous golf courses on, or near the coast. The two regulation 18-hole courses are **Playa Dorada**, a championship course designed by Robert Trent Jones (tel: 320-3344/4262), and **Playa Grande** at km 9 on the Rio San Juan-Cabrera road, with 10 spectacular holes along the reef-lined shore (tel: 248-5314). There are also several 9-hole courses including: **Los Mangos** in Coastambar, mostly used by residents and guests of Hacienda Resorts (tel: 970-7143); **Costa Azul** between Sosúa and Cabarete (tel: 571-2608) and **Loma de Chivo** in the far east on the

PRECEDING PAGES: a a ride on the beach at sunset, Cabarete. **LEFT:** poolside playtime, Sosúa. **BELOW:** rollerblading on the Malecón, Puerto Plata.

The teleférico is the best way to reach the summit of Pico Isabel de Torres.

Samaná Peninsula (tel: 538-3111). Further afield in Jarabacoa, there is a 9-hole course in the pines of La Vega (tel: 573-2474) and Las Aromas has 18-holes in the hills of Santiago (tel: 276-5396).

Puerto Plata

Outside the confines of the popular all-inclusive resorts which pepper the coastline there is plenty to discover. Historically significant the city of Puerto Plata, literally "port of silver", is the natural starting point for a tour of the Amber Coast. The early Spanish settlers are believed to have named the town after discovering the water in the bay sparkled like silver.

Founded in 1502, **Puerto Plata ❶** is the largest city on the Atlantic coast and a focal point of the north. It is steeped in history dating from the arrival of the conquistadors, who came in search of gold, and events in the 16th century to the harsh Trujillo years and beyond. A number of restaurants and hotels line the lively *malecón* (seaside promenade) which extends about 6 km (4 miles) along the waterfront from Fortaleza de San Felipe at the tip of the peninsula, past the downtown area as far as Long Beach at the eastern end (Avenida Circunvalación Norte). The *malecón* is the venue of some of the city's biggest annual events including Carnival (February or March) and the Merengue Festival in October.

BELOW: view of Pico Isabel de Torres.

The city was once an important port because of its close proximity to the neighbouring agricultural region of the Valle del Cibao (Cibao Valley) and the northwest. **Fortaleza de San Felipe Ⓐ** (daily 9am–5pm; entrance fee) at the end of Avenida General Gregorio Luperón (part of the *malecón*) is believed to be the oldest fort in the New World. It was built between 1564 and 1577 on **Bahía de Puerto Plata** as a northern defence against invasion by sea. In recent history the fortress has been a prison during the Trujillo years and home to the Brugal rum factory. Today it is a museum with a historical photographic exhibition and a display of guns and canon used in independence battles.

The **Brugal Rum Factory** (daily tours 9–11.45am, 1–3.45pm; free; tel: 586 2100) is now on Avenida Luis Ginebra just inside Puerto Plata, west of Playa Dorada. Established in 1888, the factory bottles 360,000 litres (634,000 pints) of rum every day, of which only 5 percent is exported.

Pico Isabel de Torres B towers 850 metres (2,800 ft) above the city and the **Parque Nacional Pico Isabel de Torres** (daily; tel: 586 2122). Known locally as Loma Isabel de Torres the peak can be reached by the **teleférico** (cable car). Out of order for a long period in the 1990s the *teleférico* began running again early in 2000. For a small fee the cable car carries visitors from the city to the extensive **Botanical Gardens**, providing a spectacular view of Puerto Plata Bay below. Queues for the cable car can be long during high season and it may not run if there are high winds. At the summit of Pico Isabel de Torres is a 16-metre (52-ft) statue of Jesus Christ similar to the one on Sugarloaf Mountain in Rio de Janeiro, Brazil. Hiking to the top is possible, but difficult as there are no cut trails. Visitors can also access the peak by four-wheel drive vehicle, or grab a ride from a local (unofficial) guide on the back of a motorbike.

Back in the centre of Puerto Plata, the beautifully restored Art Deco **Catedral San Felipe Apóstol C** on Calle José del Carmen Ariza stands opposite **Parque Independencia** – also known as Parque Central – a pretty park bound by Calles Beller and Duarte. At the centre of the park is an attractive two-story Victorian-style wooden structure called **La Glorieta**. Many of the other charming gingerbread buildings which line the streets, house restaurants, bars, shops and offices.

The Museo del Ambar Dominicano in Puerto Plata has tours in several different languages.

BELOW:
the pretty Parque Independencia is known locally as Parque Central.

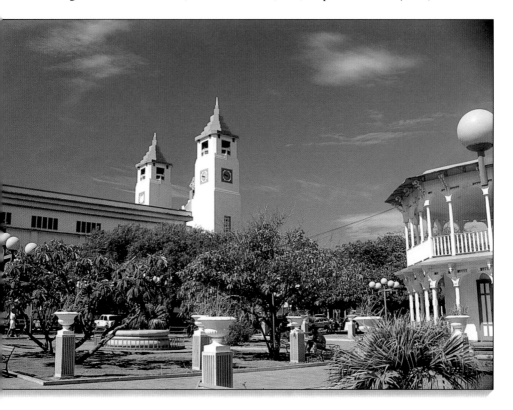

Maps:
Area 212
Town 208

Masks from the time of the Amerindians are still used at carnival time.

The mountains around Puerto Plata contain the world's richest deposits of amber believed to be up to 25 million years old. A lustrous vegetal resin containing prehistoric fossils, it is often fashioned into jewellery and ornamental items *(see page 215)*. The close proximity of the amber deposits makes this the ideal home for the **Museo del Ambar Dominicano** ❶ (Mon–Fri 9am–6pm, Sat 9am–5pm; entrance fee; tel: 586 2848), a private museum in a beautiful Victorian mansion southeast of Catedral San Felipe Apóstol at No. 61 Calle Duarte. The first floor is a large shop, one of the best places to buy amber with confidence. Exhibits on the second floor include extensive examples of the most prized prehistoric animal and plant specimens encased in honey-coloured resins. Dominican amber comes in a rainbow of hues from translucent, golden-yellow, green, red and brown to a deep blue. The rare blue amber is found only in the east of the Amber Coast and is unique to Hispaniola. It contains no inclusions (fossilized insects).

Displaying replicas of items made by the first inhabitants of Hispaniola, the small **Museo de Arte Taíno** (tel: 586 7601) is virtually unknown. It offers a look at the culture of the Amerindians who lived peacefully on the island for 1,500 years before the Europeans arrived. An excavated tomb provides fascinating insight and Taíno art reproductions are on sale.

An exclusive playground

BELOW: fun in the sun, Sosúa.

The private gated resort complex of **Playa Dorada** is around 5 km (3 miles) east of Puerto Plata. It consists of 14 large oceanside all-inclusive hotels sharing a substantial strip of sandy beach and featuring casinos, discos, numerous restaurants and bars, a shopping plaza, swimming pools and a wide variety of sports

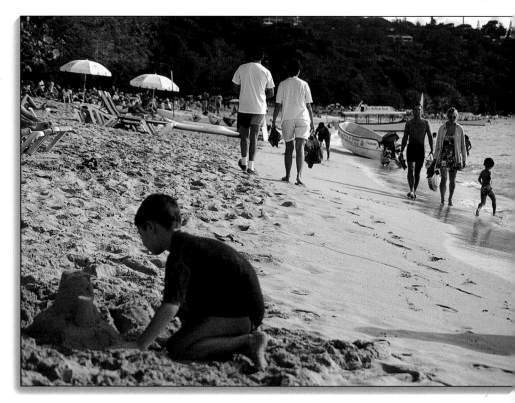

facilities available to hotel guests only. In addition there is a championship 18-hole golf course. Guests can (and some do) spend a whole week here without leaving the compound. They don't appear to be bored or curious about exploring the outlying areas to see a very beautiful part of the Dominican Republic.

Heading east along the Amber Coast, pretty beaches in the suburbs and villages stretch around tranquil bays and coves. An extensive selection of first class resorts and casinos, mid-sized hotels and guest houses is available all the way around the eastern end of the coast. Just before Sosúa, on Carretera Sosúa, 20 km (12 miles) east of Puerto Plata, **Columbus Aquapark** (daily 10am–6pm; entrance fee; tel: 571 2642) beckons children of all ages. There are five Olympic-size swimming pools and a diving tower, a slow flowing "river", water slides, volleyball courts and places to eat. Lockers can be rented for the day and the park is popular with local families, especially on Sunday.

Sosúa

A sleepy hillside fishing village only 10 years ago, **Sosúa ❷** has morphed into a hotel-laden tourist mecca, albeit more relaxed than other Caribbean mega-resort complexes. The beach is lined with rows of bars, restaurants, cafes and souvenir shops. Popular activities include sailing, scuba diving, and snorkelling around the coral reefs just offshore. A favourite with European travellers – many of whom have stayed or returned to the Dominican Republic to open guest houses, cozy restaurants, and open-air bars along Calle Pedro Clisante – Sosúa is actually divided into two neighbourhoods, separated by a sheltered bay with a distinctive half-mile long, white sandy beach.

Los Charamicos, to the west, has grown into a business and residential area

Maps:
Area 212
Town 208

Pretty pastel-coloured buildings line the streets of the Amber Coast.

LEFT:
Sosúa synagogue.
RIGHT: on the
beach at Cabarete.

The flag of the Dominican Republic in rich, mosaic tile, symbolizing the mix of people who make up the nation.

for the many Dominicans who moved here to work in the local tourist industry. It has a typically Dominican ambiance, its centre filled with crowded, rambling streets lined with old characterful buildings and noisy *motoconchos* constantly running up and down. Most restaurants serve local dishes, and some are well-known for their excellent fish specialities.

El Batey, across the bay to the east has blossomed into a tourist centre with hotels, bars, cafes, souvenir shops and other attractions located mainly along Calle Pedro Clisante. It was founded by Jewish refugees in 1940 *(see page 174)*. After the Dominican dictator, Trujillo, ordered the massacre of 15,000 Haitians in 1937 *(see page 52)*, he tried to repair his international image during World War II (1939–44) by offering political asylum to Jewish refugees fleeing persecution by the Nazis in Germany. A small group of settlers began the areas' now famous dairy and smoked-meat industries that continue to flourish today. Some on the Jews intermarried with their new neighbours, while maintaining their religious customs. But over the years most of the original group of refugees left the island. Ironically, many German expatriates took their place, together with migrants from Austria and Eastern Europe.

Although few of the descendents of the original settlers remain, the Jewish community in El Batey maintain the one-room **Sinagoga de la Comunidad Judía de Sosúa** (synagogue) on Calle Dr Alejo Martínez near Calle Dr Rosen. Next door the small **Museo de la Comunidad Judía de Sosúa** (Museum of the Jewish Community of Sosúa; Mon–Fri 9am–1pm; tel: 571 1386) chronicles their sojourn. Exhibits include photographs from the 1940s and the first telephone in the town.

Sosúa's lively nightlife encompasses packed dance floors in town (which don't get crowded until around midnight), plus casinos, bars, restaurants and more discos in the large hotel complexes nearby. The whole area hots up in October during the annual Jazz Festival which attracts performers from the United States and throughout the Caribbean.

After dancing the night away many visitors want to spend some of the daylight hours relaxing on the sand. The beautiful neighbouring beaches of **Puerto**

Chiquito, **Playa Chiquito** and **Playita** are ideal, and they also provide a plethora of water sports including sailing, waterskiing, jet-skiing, and surfing. **Sosúa Bay** is considered to be one of the best areas on the north coast for scuba diving thanks to the vibrant coral reef which lies close to shore. A little further from the beach, outside the bay, a second reef referred to by local divers as the Tropical Garden offers more experienced divers an interesting area to explore. New divers can arrange to take lessons in Sosúa which can lead to a PADI certification.

Cabarete, the windsurfing capital

About 10–15 minutes drive east of Sosúa **Cabarete** ❸ is one of the Caribbean's (and the world's) premier windsurfing locations. Trade winds here produce the tremendous waves that attract the sport's best amateur surfers from around the globe for the annual **Cabarete Race Week** in June. The town has also hosted the Professional Windsurfing Association's World Cup several times, also held in June – the best month of the year for excellent winds ideal for windsurfing and sailing. Some of the greatest windsurfing is believed to be at Playa Encuentro, west of town, where local surfers have named the waves.

Cabarete was a sleepy fishing village until the tourist industry took hold in the Dominican Republic in the 1990s and transformed the place into a well-developed, busy leisure centre. However, the easy-going friendliness of the townspeople remains. In addition to sites for advanced scuba divers other active sports include tennis, body boarding, horse riding and mountain biking. With its national parks, mountains perfect for hiking, 15 km (9 miles) of beach and sheltered sandy bays Cabarete and its neighbours are a hub of activity during the peak holiday season.

Ecotourism is growing. A few local companies offer adventure tours that don't cause long term damage to the environment, including Iguana Mama (tel: 571 0908; *see page 357*) and Freddy Tours (tel: 571 0829). Both have offices in town. Cabarete is the starting point for guided tours to Pico Duarte, Jarabacoa and a fantastic trip around the north coast.

See delicate fretwork on the balconies of gingerbread-style buildings.

Map on page 212

The dancing and partying start late (typical for this part of the world), sometimes in the wee hours of the morning and continue until breakfast. The bars are often brimming with a happy mix of local people, holidaymakers and windsurfers all enjoying the loud *merengue*, a speciality cocktail or two and discussing the events of the day. There is often live music on the sand and regular beach parties and barbecues.

Rio San Juan and Cabrera

Continuing east from Cabarete some of the Dominican Republic's most spectacular, virtually deserted beaches unfold. Long stretches of powdery sand meander around Bahía Escondida. Picturesque **Río San Juan** ❹, about a one-hour drive southeast of Sosúa, is home to the cool mangrove shielded **Laguna Gri Gri** ❺ where visitors can explore a series of mysterious marine caverns during a leisurely 2-hour boat trip. Board the boat at the end of the main street, Calle Duarte. The caverns were formed by erosion of the soft karst layers and the largest one contains striking stalagmites and stalactites. Scuba diving offshore is excellent. The boat passes **Cueva de las Golondrinas**, a 10-metre (32-ft) deep 12-metre (39-ft) high cave, and stops at **Playa Caletón**, a popular beach known locally as La Playita. The village of Río San Juan has notable fishing and dairy traditions.

The restful atmosphere of Río San Juan is exemplified by the main street which is lined with pretty pastel-coloured gingerbread-style architectural gems. After dark activities centre around the art galleries, small restaurants, ice cream parlours, swinging jazz clubs and discos where visitors can learn the *merengue* – the vibrant national dance. The communities of Río San Juan and its neighbour Cabrera were jointly re-named **Costa Verde** in 1999, a sure sign that this will probably be one of the next areas to receive mega-resort treatment and tourist related development.

About 5 km (3 miles) outside Río San Juan is one of the most beautiful beaches in the country, **Playa Grande**. This is also the home of the Playa Grande golf course, opened in 1997 with its beautiful links overlooking the reefs. There are plans to develop the whole area with hotels, resorts, holiday villas and sports facilities, but for the moment the beach remains free for public access. There is a tiny nature reserve nearby, and local people have set up small food and drink stalls along the beach. The seafood on sale is definitely worth a try.

Continuing along the coast towards Cabrera look out for a small park. **Parque Nacional Cabo Francés Viejo** ❻ preserves precious rainforest with a variety of flora and fauna. The area has extensive freshwater caves where advanced scuba divers with proper training can dive through the wide tunnels. At Cabrera in the province of Maria Trinidad Sánchez is **Cuevas de Lago Azul**, three beautiful lagoons which flow underground to the sea. The water is clear, blue and cool, ideal for swimming. The next main town is **Nagua**. There is little of note in the town, or along this route, until one reaches the Peninsula de Samaná (*see page 227*) at the far eastern tip of the country. ❏

BELOW: the steamy mangroves at Laguna Gri Gri.

Amber

Amber was formed out of sticky resin from the flowing sap of a now extinct tree called *Hymenaea Protera*. Over the passage of time, the resin hardened, creating the amber as it is today. The *Hymenaea Protera* grew in prehistoric times, up to 50 million years ago. Tiny lizards, flies, spiders and other creatures were trapped in the sap and their fossilized remains, known as "inclusions," are preserved intact in the hard, translucent material. The rarest amber specimens are embedded with these fossils.

Amber from the Dominican Republic is not as well known as the amber that comes from the Baltics, but experts now consider it to be among the best and most valuable in the world because of its translucence and wide variety of colouring.

The amber deposits are found in a grey sandstone and seashell mixture in the mountains along the northeastern coast (eponymously named "The Amber Coast"). This is mined by hand to protect the delicate contents. Then skilled craftsmen carefully extract and examine the amber to see if it contains any fossils.

If they find fossils in the resin, the craftsmen use special cutting and polishing techniques to best display minute details of the creatures inside the translucent material of the gemstone. Amber that doesn't have inclusions is processed into jewellery. Some of the unusual shades of amber are blue, green, red and a beige-yellow, called cognac.

Although varicoloured amber is found in many countries all over the world, the colours from the Dominican Republic's northern mountains are among the most desirable. Collectors around the world put the highest value on the rare blue amber and on pieces containing animal fossil inclusions. Some dealers claim that even sapphires can't match the distinctive purple amber from the Dominican Republic.

Paolo Costa, director of the Amber Museum in Puerto Plata, said, "Amber has an important history, which many people aren't familiar with". Indeed, American movie director Stephen Spielberg conducted background research into amber in the Dominican Republic for his movie blockbuster *Jurassic Park*. The film featured a mosquito preserved in amber which had fed on dinosaur blood. The blood provided the DNA which the fictional scientists used to recreate the prehistoric dinosaurs.

Before 1950, Dominican amber was not very well known. When the Soviet Union lowered the Iron Curtain and shut down the Baltic supplies, suddenly everyone turned to the Dominican Republic. That was when the world's experts and European dealers first discovered the high quality and beauty of Dominican amber.

For 30 years, this amber dominated the market. Then the Soviet Union collapsed and newly independent Baltic countries – Latvia, Estonia and Lithuania – started exporting large quantities of amber from their mines. Consequently, Dominican production dropped drastically in the early 1990s, but it is now, again, the predominant source of this beautiful "transparent gold." ❑

RIGHT: amber with a fossilized inclusion.

THE QUIET NORTHWEST

Christopher Columbus chose this coast as the location for his first colonial town in the New World in 1493. Outside the confines of a holiday resort, not a great deal has changed

Map on page 212

The extreme northwestern corner of the Dominican Republic, to the west of Puerto Plata, is bordered in the south by the magnificent mountain range of the Cordillera Septentrional. Only two main roads (*Carreteras* 1 and 5) serve the region with any efficiency, passing through small ramshackle towns and villages on the way. In between the mountains and the Atlantic coast the rolling landscape provides grazing for cattle and goats alongside fields of tobacco and sugar cane. Wild orchids grow in profusion on the old trees of the sub-tropical dry forest that covers large areas particularly in the Parque Nacional Monte Cristi in the far northwest. This stretches almost as far as the colourful border town of Dajabón, a crossing-over point to Haiti.

Protected by wide stretches of coral reef, busy with marine life, the Atlantic coast beaches are mainly grey and gravelly and not up to "paradise" standards, apart from a few in resorts such as Cofresí, where scuba diving, fishing and other watersports are good value. This is the coast where Columbus decided to settle his first group of New World colonists, and remains of the historical site can be seen in the Arqueología Parque Nacional Historico La Isabela. Out in the ocean, dolphins and humpback whales can sometimes be spotted during the months of January and February. Very little has changed in this undeveloped region and the people, many of whom are descendants of immigrants from the Canary Islands in the 18th century, are as friendly as ever.

PRECEDING PAGES: country life in the northwest. **LEFT:** on the road to Monte Cristi. **BELOW:** ready for the beach.

Waterfalls and a sheltered bay

It may be difficult to leave the comforts of a holiday complex where everything is at your fingertips, but it's worth venturing outside the resort gates where you may experience the sensation that time has stood still for decades. In a taxi or hired car, organised through your hotel *(or see Travel Tips on page 351)*, take the *Carretera* 5 southwest out of **Puerto Plata** *(see page 208)* towards the mountains. After about 10 minutes, take a left turn at the crossroads and continue to Imbert 22 km (14 miles) away.

Surrounded by sugar cane fields and farmland, the little town of **Imbert ❼** is named for José Maria Imbert, a hero of the Restoration of the Republic and is mainly a busy intersection for picking up transport connections – be they *motoconchos*, *gua-guas*, buses or taxis – to surrounding areas and the south. The town has a restaurant and a gas station and nearby at **Damajagua** is a spectacular series of 20 small waterfalls each with a pool, eight of which are accessible to the public. Here you can wallow in the cool waters before heading west to Luperón, 25 km (15 miles) away on the *Carretera* 30, just off the road that brought you into Imbert.

This plaque at the Arqueología Parque Nacional Historico La Isabela commemorates the first colonial town in the New World. However, there are a couple of villages nearby that also call themselves La Isabela, which can cause confusion.

BELOW: the ruins at La Isabela.

Luperón ③ is a small fishing village set in a beautiful and natural bay of the same name, which is well protected from the hurricanes that can strike between June and October. For this reason, the bay has become a haven for yachts from all around the world. The local people mainly earn their living from farming and fishing in the Atlantic waters, making it a good place to stop for a lunch or dinner of seafood and the delicious Dominican speciality of creole fish in any one of the little *comedors* (restaurants). Just outside the village is the modern **Luperón Beach Resort**, an all-inclusive hotel complex which has a lovely beach and offers a wide range of watersports.

La Isabela – Columbus's first colonial town

After Columbus had returned to Hispaniola in 1493 to find the Spanish garrison at Puerto La Navidad obliterated *(see page 28)*, he established the town of La Isabela – named for the queen of Spain – further along the coast, 12 km (7 miles) west of where Luperón is today. But it was doomed from the start, as the first colonists succumbed to disease and the strains of hard manual labour, or became disillusioned and returned to Spain when no gold could be found. Violence and discord, hurricane and fire all added to the demise of the town and by 1498, the remaining colonists had left to start Santo Domingo *(see pages 169–190)*.

Some of the remnants of this short-lived town have been unearthed and preserved in the **Arqueología Parque Nacional Historico La Isabela ④** (daily 8am–5pm; entrance fee). Here you can see the foundations of Christopher Columbus's original house, and a cemetery containing both Taíno and Spanish burial chambers. Unfortunately some of the site has fallen into the sea, including parts of Columbus's house. A museum contains some interesting artefacts, believed to have belonged to those early colonists, and provides information about the Taínos in the pre-Columbian days, although only in Spanish.

Excavation of La Isabela began in the 1950s and archaeologists have attempted to reconstruct parts of the stone walls of the main buildings. The reconstructed **Templo de las Americas** (Temple of the Americas) is on the spot where the first Mass in the New World was celebrated on 6 January 1494. La Isabela is also believed to have had the first City Hall in the Americas (1494).

Estero Hondo – battleground for liberty

Further along the coast to the west you come to **Estero Hondo**, which has a quiet, undiscovered beach. However, in 1959 the peace was broken when a boatload of exiled Dominican anti-government activists disembarked here in an attempt to bring down Trujillo's regime. The dictator learned of the rebels' plans and sent the army to ambush them, resulting in a bloody battle. Since then Estero Hondo has remained a symbol of the Dominican struggle for liberty and democracy.

A short distance further along the rough coastal road, on the border of the province of Monte Cristi, is the small fishing village of **Punta Rucia** where brightly coloured fishing boats lie on the pretty, sandy beach. Framed by coconut palms and shallow waters, it may not the cleanest but it is one of the favourite beaches on what Dominicans call the *Línea Noroeste* (Northwestern Line); on Sundays it comes alive with picnickers and the sound of *merengue*.

Because the roads on the coastal side of the mountains are generally poor, it may be best to go to Monte Cristi via Imbert and take the *Carretera* 5 south to *Carretera* 1. This road is one of the best in the Dominican Republic and runs for

Map on page 212

From Punta Rucia boat trips go to the Laguna Estero Hondo mangrove swamps and the white sandy island of Cayo Arenas, 10 km (6 miles) off shore.

BELOW: a mural for Maximo Gómez y Báez.

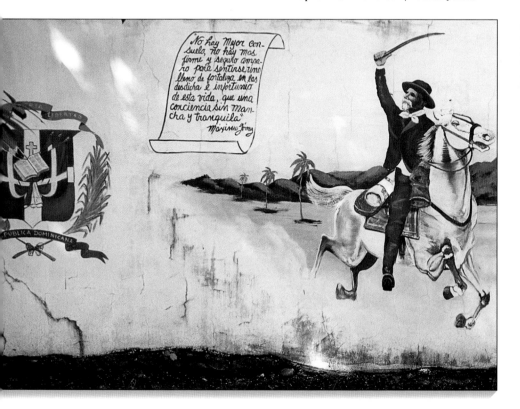

90 km (55 miles) along the southern slopes of the Cordillera Septentrional above and almost parallel to the Río Yaque del Norte.

The rises and falls of Monte Cristi

As you approach the town of **Monte Cristi ⑩**, the capital of the province of the same name, the landscape becomes much drier, dotted with scrub, cacti and xerophyles due to a combination of low rainfall in the region and scorching temperatures which can reach 35°C (95°F). Flattening out into the delta of the Yaque del Norte, the only relief to the northwest of town is the peak of **El Morro**, washed by the sea on one side and waterways with mangroves on the other.

Founded in 1533 by 60 farming families, the original village of Monte Cristi, along with other towns on the northwest coast, was evacuated in 1606 by Hispaniola's governor Antonio Osorio in order to end illegal commerce between the villagers and foreign pirates. For 150 years Monte Cristi lay abandoned until it was resettled by farmers from the Canary Islands. It then became an important seaport, handling goods such as timber, honey and tobacco that were carried down the Río Yaque del Norte from Santiago *(see page 239)* and La Vega *(see page 245)*. The city flourished, attracting European businesses, until the construction of the railway which connected Puerto Plata to the towns of the Cibao Valley and the Restoration War in the 1860s caused its downfall as a centre of commerce.

The Victorian buildings lining the streets of Monte Cristi reflect the town's European influence and include a large French clock dating from 1895 in the Parque Central. Here too, in the Plaza del Reloj is the former house of Baní-born Maximo Gómez y Báez, where he and José Martí signed the manifest for Cuba's independence, alongside the historic homes of Restoration War generals.

The old colonial shipwrecks and reefs off the beaches of La Granja and El Morro, just north of Monte Cristi, provide good diving. Deep sea fishing expeditions can be organized through Club Nautico Monte Cristi Inc. (tel: 579 2530). Every June a blue marlin fishing tournament is held.

BELOW: a one stop shop for a taxi or a refreshing drink.

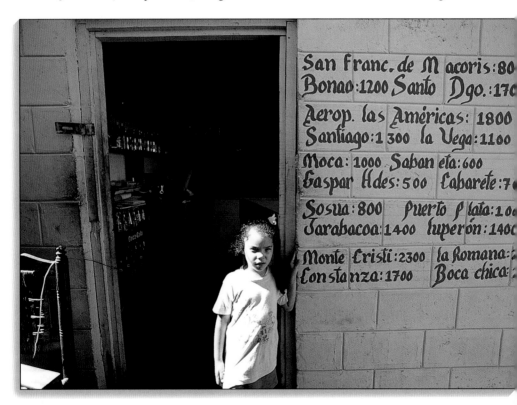

The beaches, El Morro and the waterways and lagoons either side of town form the **Parque Nacional Monte Cristi** along with the **Los Cayos de los Siete Hermanos** ⓫ (Islands of the Seven Brothers). These seven tiny islands provide a sanctuary for seabirds and turtles who come here to lay their eggs, sadly poaching has taken its toll. Closer to the shore in front of Juan de Bolaños beach, and just a five-minute boat ride away, lies **Cayos Cabras** (Cabras Key), lapped by the Atlantic Ocean it provides a window on a world of tropical fish and starfish. An old lighthouse and a salt pond can be seen on the western side of the key.

Dajabón – a colourful border town

A 30-minute drive south from Monte Cristi through subtropical dry forest and bush, past coastal lagoons, is **Dajabón** ⓬, right on the border with Haiti. Only the **Massacre River** (Río Dajabón) which can easily be crossed on foot, separates the two nations. Founded on 4 July 1776 by a Spanish soldier named José Solano, Dajabón became an important point of commercial traffic between the colonies of French St-Domingue and Spanish Santo Domingo after the Aranjuez Treaty was eventually signed by France and Spain in 1777, defining the boundary between the two.

Today hundreds of Haitians pour across the border every day to sell their wares at the market here on Monday and Friday, at really inexpensive prices. Pots and pans and other kitchen utensils, secondhand clothes and shoes, and perfumes are all spread out on colourful cloths on the dusty ground for people to inspect. Then with their day's takings, the vendors buy rice, beans, plantain and other produce before crossing back to Haiti. Here in one small town, the differences and contrasts between the two countries are plain to see. ❑

Map
on page
212

TIP

The road between Monte Cristi and Dajabón can be travelled at night as long as you use common sense. The dry forest and bush either side of the road is said to be a hiding place for runaway Haitians and Dominicans.

BELOW: the sun sets over the cemetery at La Isabela.

THE SAMANÁ PENINSULA

Fringed with soft white beaches, this beautiful peninsula juts out into the clear blue Atlantic Ocean, making it an ideal vantage point for whale-watching

Map on page 231

Santo Domingo

Dense forests of palm trees shading a carpet covered with bromeliads and orchids clothe the gently rolling green hills; little vegetable gardens frame the brightly-painted cottages; rivers and waterfalls plunge through lush tropical vegetation. On the Samaná Peninsula lie lonely beaches of sand as fine and white as confectioner's sugar, where the sea is warm and as blue as a picture postcard. Here, seeing the world through rose-coloured spectacles does not require the assistance of a rum cocktail.

More than 80,000 people live in the villages and little towns of Samaná, which covers both sides of the Bahía de Samaná. The Dominicans like to live on the street, and much of everyday life is carried out in the open air, for all to see. *Merengue* blares out of the open-sided bars; elderly men click their dominoes in front of a *colmado*; a group of boys in baseball shirts play pool under a leafy roof; a grandmother, sitting in a rocking chair on her veranda, peels a mango, and a couple of teenagers have their hair braided in the shade of a huge tree next to the cocoa beans and coconut shells spread out on the asphalt to dry in the hot Caribbean sun. Samaná seems a peaceful place, remote and like a small universe on its own.

For a long time the region was separated from the rest of the island by a broad area of marshland. It was necessary to take a boat trip in order to reach the main island, which was 60 km (38 miles) long and 20 km (13 miles) wide, until the waterway was turned into dry land in the last century. For hundreds of years after the arrival of Columbus, Samaná remained uninhabited until, during the 18th century, a few migrants from the Canary Islands settled here. At the beginning of the 19th century, during the Haitian occupation, land was made available to former slaves from North America and the English-speaking islands of the West Indies. The descendants of these settlers spoke a strange mixture of English and Spanish known as *inglés del muelle*. Reminders of the origins of the inhabitants of Samaná can still be seen in the large numbers of Smiths, Kings and Greens in the telephone directory, and the handful of Protestant sects, not to mention such culinary specialities as *yannikekes* (Johnny Cakes).

An individualistic approach

Samaná is still a place for individualists. Some visit the peninsula because of the picturesque beaches on the north coast, while others take delight in the Parque Nacional Los Haïtises and its seabirds, mangrove swamps and secret caves across the bay. Between January and March, humpback whales gather near the *Banco de la Plata*, 60 km (38 miles) north of the coast, and can often be seen in the bay. The huge

PRECEDING PAGES: fishing boats off Playa Bonita. **LEFT:** colourful column, Las Terrenas. **BELOW:** a milliner selling his wares in Sabana de la Mar.

TIP

Part of the Sanctuary
for the Marine
Mammals of the
Dominican Republic,
Samaná Bay is an
ideal jumping-off spot
for whale watching
tours (see pages
156–7). For details, call
(409) 291 1210 or
email: whales@
aquaticadventures.com

BELOW: a hillside
view on the road
between Sanchez
and Las Terrenas.

marine mammals migrate each winter southwards from the cold North into warmer waters, to mate and give birth to their young, which would freeze instantly if they remained in the chilly North Atlantic.

The Government in Santo Domingo is aiming to establish a high-class, luxury tourist industry in Samaná, and therefore a lot of energy is being put into the establishment of a working infrastructure. The airport of Arroyo Barril on the peninsula's south coast has been open to international traffic since 1999, although the runway is still too short and the concrete surface too thin for the large transatlantic aircraft. However, a good quality tarmac road now leads from Sánchez at the entrance to the peninsula as far as Las Galeras on the northeastern tip. Las Terrenas, on the north coast, is also easily accessible. Improvements are also being made to the track across the mountains to Santa Bárbara de Samaná.

Victorian cottages and spectacular views

Sánchez ❶ is usually considered no more than a stopover by visitors but it's worth taking time out for a stroll past the brightly-coloured wooden Victorian cottages down to the harbour of this little port. The railway line which once ran from La Vega to Sánchez no longer exists, and the tracks are completely overgrown with vegetation. In the town itself you can see the remains left from the early years of the 20th century, when the bustle between the railway station and the port brought a little life to this remote corner. At the harbour, try the fried crabs in **Las Malvinas** restaurant.

A steep and winding road climbs northwards from Sánchez into the hills, which reach an altitude of over 400 metres (1,300 ft). From **Naranjita** – the

RAINFOREST AND MANGROVES

The Parque Nacional Los Haïtises covers an area of more than 200 sq km (nearly 80 sq miles) on the southern side of the Bahía de Samaná, opposite the peninsula. The karst soil is covered with tropical rainforest, bordered by extensive woodlands of red and white mangroves. The natural habitat of frigate birds, vultures, sea swallows and pelicans, the park is accessible only by boat and as you approach it you pass a number of *mogotes* – overgrown karst islands – which rise out of the sea like emerald-green mushrooms. Young fish, crayfish, crabs and mussels abound in the shallow water between the mangrove roots.

The excursion lasts about five hours – three hours in a speedboat, and two on land – and includes a visit to the park's karst caves. In the Cueva de la Linea are some fascinating rock carvings left by the Taínos – sadly interspersed with modern-day graffiti. La Arena offers stalactites and bats, while the San Gabriel impresses by virtue of its size, its bizarrely-shaped stalactites and stalagmites and a subsidiary cave, open to the sky. Sometimes you can swim along an underground river. Drinks are served on board, and often a meal in a restaurant is included *(see Travel Tips, page 357)*.

highest point on this stretch of road – there is a spectacular view of the largest continuous coconut palm forest in the whole of Hispaniola, as well as sweeping panoramas of the shimmering green meadows that billow out as far as the Atlantic coast and the three tiny offshore islands known as **Las Ballenas** (literally meaning the whalebones). Their form, as the name indicates, is reminiscent of the back of a whale as it rises out of the sea.

A few dozen bends later, after a total journey of 17 km (11 miles), you reach **Las Terrenas ❷** located on the north coast. It was only at the end of the 1980s that the first houses were built alongside the beach. Today, the approach road, the Calle Principal, is flanked over a distance of around 2 km (over 1 mile) by souvenir shops, cafés and bars, and bureaux de change. Numerous small hotels, restaurants and diving stations are mushrooming along the lovely beachfront from where you can walk out to the coral reefs at low tide.

Since **Cacao Beach**, which was the first all-inclusive resort, was opened, the little town has grown into Samaná's main holiday centre, and the number of inhabitants has expanded rapidly as a result, with the international community now comprising some 14,000 residents – many of the well-heeled arrive by private plane. The French make up the largest minority group, then Italians, Swiss and Germans.

Las Terrenas is the place for those people who are not at ease among large crowds of holidaymakers, but like to be kept occupied. Distractions of all kinds are available around the clock: diving, snorkelling, sailing a hobie cat or riding a horse. As night descends, you can relax over a sundowner in a beach bar, such as the **Casa Salsa**. Discos – **Mambo, Nuevo Mundo** or **Tibidabo** – are open until the early hours.

Map on page 231

 TIP

In Las Terrenas' recently-completed El Paseo de la Costanera shopping complex, you can not only go shopping, but also get a new hairdo, a beauty treatment, air tickets or even have a tooth crowned.

BELOW: a mobile shoe salesman, Las Terrenas.

Peace and quiet at Punta Bonita

Gerard, the chef at the Hotel Atlantis (tel: 240 6111) in Punta Bonita, once served as chief chef to President François Mitterrand of France. Today, he ensures that not only fine food, but also fine French wines, are served in the restaurant.

The road west out of Las Terrenas, is currently in a lamentable state. But it is worthwhile enduring the 5 km (3 miles) of bumps and ruts to get to **Punta Bonita ❸**, the perfect destination for those in search of complete peace and the opportunity to do nothing more than relax beneath the palm trees. Pretty little hotels – from the new **Coyamar** to the long-established **Acaya** – nestle under palm trees in tropical gardens, and from time to time a horse canters along the sandy track by the beach, or a *motoconcho* rattles past. (Of late, so too does the occasional Caoba Tours coach.) Further along lies the magnificent **Playa Coson** and a string of unnamed beaches, where you can walk along the shore for miles on the soft white sand in the shade of the coconut palms without encountering a soul. In the opposite direction, you can walk along the beach all the way back to Las Terrenas.

En route to Santa Bárbara de Samaná

There has long been a road link between Las Terrenas and the provincial capital of Santa Bárbara de Samaná about 30 km (19 miles) away on the south coast, but it is only recently that is has begun to be improved. Travelling eastward out of Las Terrenas, after a few kilometres you pass **El Portillo Beach Club**, an attractive all-inclusive holiday resort offering a wide range of sporting facilities, which also possesses a grass runway for small charter planes.

The road continues for about 5 km (3 miles) into the hills and eventually reaches a little village where, at the **Casa Berca** (tel: 240 6261), you can lunch on spicy Creole specialities before setting out on mules or horses with a Dominican guide to the **El Limón** waterfall. The ride takes about one hour, crossing

BELOW: the inviting pool near El Limón.

alarmingly steep hills, bridle paths and muddy cattle tracks. The water plunges over 40 metres (130 ft) into a pool which provides an inviting opportunity to cool off. Depending on the season and the weather conditions, the ground may prove to be quite slippery, making this ride correspondingly adventurous.

The route through the hills is just one of three ways of reaching **Santa Bárbara de Samaná** ❹. Another way is by ferry across the Bahía de Samaná from Sabana de la Mar, which affords the most attractive view of the little port as it chugs into the harbour. However, the ferry is for foot passengers only.

Should you approach the capital along the coastal road from Sánchez, then pause briefly at **Las Garitas**. On the left-hand side is the **Balneario La Fuente**, a natural swimming pool beside a little stream, where you can plunge into the refreshing green water and then enjoy a snack or an iced drink on the shady terrace. At weekends the *balneario* belongs to the Dominicans, and loud *merengue* music is likely to drown out the birdsong. And during the week, tour groups sometimes stop here for light refreshment; it is usually busy but the decibel level is lower.

Motoconchos which pull small trailers are ideal for taking the shopping home.

New developments

Samaná, as the provincial capital is invariably known, is booming. For many years, yachts from all the corners of the world have dropped anchor in the little bay, overlooked by the port that clings to the shore between two hills. These international sailors added a touch of worldly flair to the provincial charm. Now a five-year project has been initiated, during the course of which the sea bed is being dredged to accommodate a harbour for cruise ships and a marina with berths for 600 yachts. Perhaps by then the four-lane Malecón with its

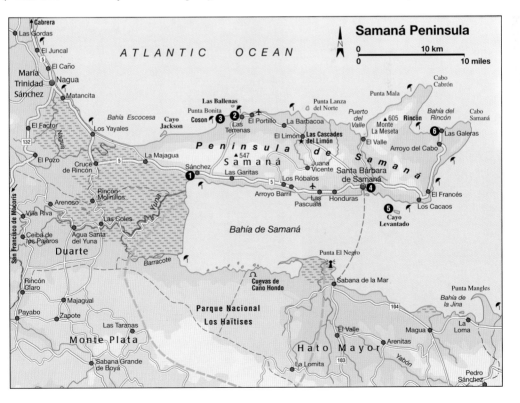

When work on Arroyo Barril airport was delayed by the Government in 1996 for technical studies, the local people got tired of waiting to get their jobs back and formed the Comité Samaná se Cansó de Esperar *(Samaná's Tired of Waiting Committee).*

BELOW: whales tailing in Samaná's waters. **RIGHT:** relaxing on the beach.

numerous roundabouts, built during the 1970s under the Balaguer government, will seem more suited to the dimensions of this modest township.

The history of Samaná – or at least, what is known of it – is soon told. On 12 January 1493, Columbus and his fleet reached the peninsula here and discovered that the Ciguayo Indians, for whatever reason, were waiting to receive them armed with bows and arrows rather than a welcoming smile. The *Gran Almirante* immediately christened the bay *Golfo de los Flechas*. Once all the Indians had been killed or enslaved, the remote region remained silent and abandoned for a long time. In the mid-18th century the Spanish governor, Francisco Rubio y Peñaranda, settled migrants from the Canary Islands here in order to prevent this section of the coastline being captured by pirates and smugglers. In 1946 the town was destroyed by a major fire, and only a few of the houses, which were mostly built of wood, survived the flames. One building which escaped was the 19th-century Methodist church, **La Churcha**, as it had been built of materials imported from England. Today, most of the houses are concrete.

The **Malecón**, the harbourfront promenade between the Hotel Cayacoa on the west side of the Bahía de Samaná and the pretty Hotel Tropical Lodge on the east side, is where the ferry docks, linking Samaná with Sabana de la Mar on the other side of the bay. It is from here, too, that the excursion boats start out for the idyllic island of **Cayo Levantado** *(see opposite)*, and from mid-January to mid-March the whale-watching boats also leave from here. Those wishing to observe the marine mammals in their element should contact Kim Beddall at the offices of **Victoria Marine** (tel: 538 2588), which is also on the Malecón.

Welcoming cafés and restaurants line the promenade. In the **Café de Paris** you can order delicious *crêpes*, while the **Mata Rosada**, run by a chef from

Alsace, is considered by many to be the best restaurant in town, serving French and Creole-style seafood. With the green hills behind you and the sea in front, and the islets of **Cayo Vigia** and **Cayo Linares** on the horizon, you may wonder why you hardly ever see anyone on the picturesque footbridge linking the islands with the mainland.

The colourful side of Dominican life is to be seen at the **market** at the entrance to the town, behind the garage. Fruit, vegetables, meat, fish and clothing are all offered for sale, and the locals barter, argue, laugh and play *merengue* music for all they are worth. (Here you will also find *Públicos*.)

An excursion to **Cayo Levantado 5** will carry you back to the sun-sand-and-palm-trees scenario. However, it must be admitted that nowadays this exceptionally beautiful island in the bay only lives up to the desert island idyll early in the morning, during the evening and of course at night. During the day it is not easy to find a quiet corner between the stalls of grilled shellfish and fizzy drinks, and the lobster-coloured visitors.

As well as boats from the Malecón, a shuttle service to the Cayo Levantado is operated by the hotel **Gran Bahía**, 10 km (6 miles) east of Samaná on the road to Las Galeras. A delightful complex built in the Victorian style, the private beach is relatively small, but the swimming pool is perched picturesquely on a hill.

Land's end – Las Galeras

Until recently, **Las Galeras 6**, a tiny coastal village at the northernmost end of the peninsula, was devoted exclusively to the independent tourist. This meant that your neighbour's towel on the lovely beach lay mostly at a discreet distance from your own, and that, at night, total peace reigned, except for the noises of the tropics and the sounds issuing from the village's only bar. It also meant that each new arrival was eyed with friendly curiosity. If it transpired that a newcomer was a day-tripper, they would be invited to take a seat under a palm-frond roof by the seashore where, perched on a rickety bench and with their feet buried in the sand, they would be served freshly caught fish. If they wished to stay for a while, they would have the choice between three small hotels: the **Moorea Beach**, the **Club Bonito** and the **Villa Serena**. After a few days they would know everyone in the village.

Recently, however, mass tourism has made its appearance in Las Galeras. The all-inclusive resort **Casa Marina Bay** in the neighbouring bay offers 250 rooms, two restaurants and a discotheque. The village itself is changing accordingly: a two-storey supermarket has recently opened up. And yet, Las Galeras is still the perfect setting for successfully doing nothing at all. You may go on a diving trip with **Dive Samaná** or visit **Moby's Whale Watch Restaurant** on the precipitous cliffs just before you enter the village. From here you can watch the huge marine mammals through binoculars without getting too close.

The magnificent beaches of **Rincón**, earmarked for a vast new resort, **Playa Madame**, and **Colorado**, whose sand shimmers with reddish hues, can be reached by boat, moped, on horseback or even on foot (about two hours). ❑

Map on page 231

BELOW: cooling down the midday heat.

NATURE'S HARVEST: THE ART OF THE CIGAR

The Dominican Republic is home to some of the world's finest traditional cigar makers. They have earned a reputation for producing quality smokes

Historical records suggest that the smoking of tobacco is not a modern pastime but an age-old pursuit practiced by some of Hispaniola's first settlers – the Taíno Amerindians.

Of the traditional crops grown in the Dominican Republic, including sugar, cocoa and coffee, tobacco is considered to be the oldest. And while the growing and export of the other crops has waned over the years the tobacco industry is still flourishing. The main tobacco growing and manufacturing region is Santiago in the north.

UP IN SMOKE

Cigar-making is complex and time consuming. As a rule it takes six weeks to germinate the tobacco seeds and a further six weeks before the plants are harvested. The dried out but still damp bundles of tobacco leaves are tied into bales and left to ferment in temperatures reaching as high as 60°C (140°F). This expels the ammonia and reduces the nicotine. The fermented tobacco is then left to age for up to two years, with some strains being left for as long as 10 years. A master blender creates a cocktail of aged tobacco which is hand-rolled into a cigar shape, cut and pressed into a mould. Finally the cigar is wrapped tightly in a specially selected fine tobacco leaf and secured with vegetable glue. The finished cigar is stored and aged for between one and six months before being boxed and shipped to stores throughout the country and around the world.

△ **THE PERFECT ROLL-UP**
At Don Esteban in Santiago, the tobacco is rolled by hand, pressed into a mould for an hour, before being wrapped.

◁ **CREATING A BLEND**
Sorting the tobacco leaves according to taste and strength. Up to four varieties can be blended together.

◁ **FIELDS OF GREEN**
Tobacco farmers tend their precious crop with care to avoid damage. Harvesting is a precise art with leaves picked in stages from the base up.

△ **CUTTING THE TOBACCO**
Once dried and fermented the tobacco's temperature is constantly checked. The prepared leaves are only cut when they have matured.

BIG CIGARS, BIG BUSINESS

During the 1990s the Dominican Republic became the world's largest exporter of cigars attracting tens of millions of dollars in foreign revenue. The agricultural belt of Santiago is the main growing region for tobacco because of its rich soil. There are also several cigar factories in the north. But cigars are made elsewhere and specialist stores and street vendors can be found all over the country, especially in Santo Domingo. Famous Dominican brands include Montecristo and Arturo Fuente. For a closer look at the history of tobacco the Museo del Tabaco *(see page 241)* near Parque Duarte, in Santiago, is worth a visit. The museum contains exhibits dating back to the 16th century.

Cigars and their accoutrements are big business in spite of a vociferous international anti-smoking lobby. Choosing a cigar can be complicated. Go for either a straight sided or figurado (shaped) cigar, from a corona to robusto, culebra to perfecto. Then there is the ring gauge (diameter) to consider, which affects the burn rate and smoking time.

△ **FROM GREEN TO BROWN**
Preparing the green tobacco for drying: during the process the green chlorophyll-filled leaves change to brown due to carotene production.

▽ **FAMOUS NAMES**
In the Dominican Republic some of the best-known and best quality tobacco is grown for cigar-making, using plants grown from Cuban seed.

◁ **DRYING OUT**
Tobacco leaves are hung out to dry on poles for 1½ to 2 months. Each pole holds up to 100 leaves. Once dry the tobacco is bundled.

THE CIBAO VALLEY

*The real "gold" of the island was discovered early on
in the rich, fertile soil of this northern region, where
towns like Santiago still prosper after 500 years*

Maps:
Town 240
Area 245

Santiago de los Caballeros

Santo Domingo

Paddy fields, banana plantations and fields of tobacco stretch out along both sides of the roads; cocoa trees and coffee bushes prosper on the rolling hillsides; lorries, heavily laden with sugar cane or oranges, thunder along the busy *Autopista* Duarte from Santo Domingo, heading for the bustling economic centre of Santiago. The Cibao region in the north of the island is the *República's* bread basket: between Santiago, La Vega and Salcedo in particular, a thick layer of black fertile soil covers the ground. Rainfall is heavy in the southeastern section of the valley, which runs for 200 km (125 miles) between the mountain ranges of the Cordillera Central and the Cordillera Septentrional. That there is no shortage of water is due also to the rivers Yaque del Norte and Yuna.

The fertile valley has long been settled, and many plantation families have prospered over the centuries. Christopher Columbus called the beautiful landscape *La Vega Real*, the Royal Valley, and not long after his arrival, the *conquistadors* founded two settlements here – Santiago de los Treinta Caballeros and La Concepción de La Vega. The towns grew rapidly, but were destroyed by an earthquake in the 16th century. Both were rebuilt on different sites.

The **Rua Turística** (*Carretera* 25) winds through the green hills of the Cordillera Septentrional for 50 km (30 miles) between Santiago and the north coast, passing numerous picturesque ribbon villages, and giving panoramic views over the Cibao Valley.

PRECEDING PAGES:
paddy fields
in Los Yayales.
LEFT:
rolling hills and
Constanza crops.
BELOW: Santiago
cigar makers Carlos
(left) and Don
Carlos Fuente.

Santiago – a proud city

Santiago de los Caballeros ❶ is one of the most important cities in the country, a fact which it owes to the *Autopista* Duarte, giving it a direct link to Santo Domingo *(see pages 169–190)* 155 km (96 miles) away to the south. It is an important economic and business centre, and with its population of 700,000 is also the second largest metropolis in the land after *La Capital* – there is keen rivalry between the two cities.

Described as being the "proudest" city in the Dominican Republic, Santiago seems less chaotic than Santo Domingo; the activity in the streets appears more purposeful. The inhabitants of Santiago are fond of mentioning that most of the country's presidents, along with numerous celebrities from the spheres of art and culture, have been natives of the city. The **Universidad Católica Madre y Maestra** is in an attractive spot on the southern section of the Avenida S. Estrella Sahdalá, and has an excellent reputation.

The original town of Santiago de los Treinta Caballeros was founded in 1495 by 30 Spanish aristocrats (*caballeros*), along with Columbus's brother Bartolomé, a few kilometres to the northeast of the city, near the village of **Jacagua**. The new arrivals were hoping to find more of the gold here which they

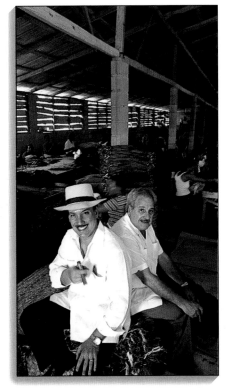

had seen in the settlements of the Taínos. However, in 1562 the town was completely destroyed by an earthquake and was subsequently rebuilt in its present position on the eastern bank of the **Río Yaque del Norte**. Pirate raids during the 17th century, further earthquakes (in 1755, 1783 and 1842), not to mention a major fire during the *Guerra de la Restauración* (War of Restoration) in 1863, hampered the town's growth until it eventually expanded to become the economic centre which it is today.

Santiago is a city to visit for business, not for a holiday. Executives from all over the world stay in the efficient business hotels such as the **Gran al Mirante**. The nightlife here is quite lively, too, and shopping is considerably cheaper than in Santo Domingo.

Fortaleza San Luís (Fortress of St Louis) **Ⓐ** was built on a hill on the banks of the Río Yaque at the end of the 19th century. It was then used as a prison; today, the complex is occupied by the Dominican army, and it is only possible to get a glimpse of the inner courtyard. The road running along the top of the river bank lives up to its name of **Avenida Mirador del Yaque**, as from here there is an attractive view of the new section of Santiago to the south. Heading north you will find yourself in the city centre, where there's a wealth of Victorian and neoclassical buildings tucked between the modern ones.

Around Parque Duarte – the central square

The tall trees of the **Parque Duarte Ⓑ** provide shade in which elderly men pass the time of day on benches, exchanging news and putting the world to rights. Ice cream, cold drinks and music cassettes are offered for sale at street stalls, and on the northern side of the square, the drivers doze in their

BELOW: view of Río Yaque del Norte.

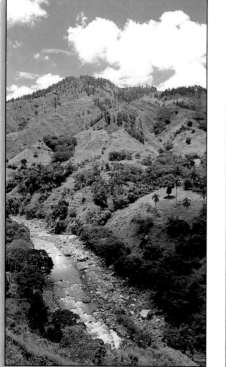

horse-drawn carriages as they wait for customers to take on a nostalgic tour of the city. In the centre of the little park is a small pavilion, behind which rises the **Catedral de Santiago Apóstol** , built between 1868 and 1895 in a style which combines classical and neo-Gothic elements. Inside is an elaborately carved mahogany altar, decorated with gold leaf, and the beautiful stained-glass windows (*vitrales*) were completed by the artist José Rincón-Mora during the 1980s.

The **Museo del Tabaco** (Tues–Fri 9am–noon, 2–5pm; Sat am; entrance fee) next door was established by Dr Salvador Jorge Blanco. The exhibits provide a wealth of information about the tobacco plant, all the more interesting because the tobacco industry is one of the most important economic factors of the region. The equipment, photographs and text are arranged in an illuminating manner throughout the museum; an English guide is available.

The **Centro de Recreo**, on the western side of the square, was built at the end of the 19th century in the Mudéjar revival style, and stands in marked contrast to the mostly Victorian buildings in the historic city centre. Today, members of a private club gather beneath the exquisitely carved beams. You may be permitted to join a bingo session held here on Sundays.

The neighbouring building is an attractive and well-maintained example of Victorian architecture. Within the **Palacio Consistorial (District Council Chambers)** , the **Museo de la Villa** (Tues–Fri 9am–noon, 2–5.30pm; Sat and Sun 10am–2pm; entrance fee) displays the history of the city.

A few steps further on stands the **Centro de la Cultura**. In addition to the 500-seat **Teatro Nacional** and music school, in which concerts by local musicians or visiting stars from North America are held. There are also rooms for

Map on page 240

TIP

To find out what's on in Santiago and the surrounding area, drop in to the Centro de la Cultura on Parque Duarte, and look at the notice boards there, or call the local tourist office on 582 5885.

BELOW: a horse-drawn carriage waits at the Plaza de la Cultural.

The white marble Monumento a los Héroes de la Restauración de la República is referred to locally as "El Monumento".

BELOW:
José Manuel Bermúdez with his collection of Trujillo classic cars.

exhibitions by national and international artists (daily 9–noon, 2–8pm; free). And if your visit to Santiago does not fall during the month of February, when you can experience the colourful pre-Lenten carnival processions at first hand, the next best thing is to see the brightly-painted masks, especially the local variety known as *lechones* with long, sharp horns, that are worn in the parades along with other folkloric items. These, at the **Museo des Artes Folklórico Tomás Morel ❺** (opening times vary; free), are displayed in a pretty Victorian wooden house in the Calle Restauración, at the corner of Lopez .

Calle del Sol – a commercial thoroughfare

On your way back to the Parque Duarte, a good place to stop for a snack is the **Bar Colón** in the Calle 30 de Marzo. Decorated in Spanish style, the café serves delicious coffee and sandwiches, but the long, curved wooden bar is often crowded, especially at breakfast time. Thus refreshed, you can face the crowds along the **Calle del Sol**. A long, straight thoroughfare, lined on both sides with banks, shops of all kinds and temporary stalls, this road is the economic centre of Santiago. In the side alleys, the dark entrances of the brightly-coloured houses conceal repair businesses and a multitude of other small shops. The **Mercado Modelo**, on the corner of Calle España, offers all kinds of souvenirs, from jewellery to basketwork. From the floor-to-ceiling windows of the restaurant on the top floor of the **Hotel Camino Real**, near the Calle Mella, there is a spectacular panorama of the city.

On a hill at the eastern end of the Calle del Sol stands the city's most prominent landmark, the **Monumento a los Héroes de la Restauración de la República ❻**. It is 67 metres (220 ft) tall and was erected by President Rafael

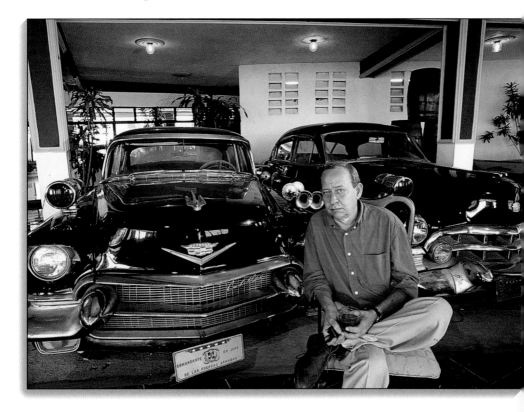

Leonidas Trujillo in honour of the heroes of the War of Restoration. Those unfamiliar with the city should be grateful to the cruel dictator, for the monument can be seen from virtually everywhere, thus making it practically impossible to get lost. In the entrance hall you can inspect the *murales* by the artist Vela Zanetti, who died in 1998; his work also adorns the United Nations Building in New York. The top of the column, surmounted by an allegorical female figure, can be reached via a staircase, and there are wonderful views. Below the monument, in the district surrounding the Calle R.C. Tolentino, numerous pubs and bars have sprung up. **Las Tres Café** and **Talanca** have live music from time to time.

Tobacco and rum, coffee and cocoa

Beyond the city centre, you can take advantage of the opportunity to investigate at first hand the production of rum and tobacco. South of Santiago, 3 km (nearly 2 miles) along the *Autopista* Duarte, stands the **Tabacos Don Esteban** cigar factory. A couple of dozen workers are employed here in the manufacture of the exclusive cigars. The German manager, Oskar Nausch, speaks fluent English and provides an authoritative and humorous account of the various stages of production. (Call for a guided tour: tel: 587 9976 or 583 3277).

Those who prefer their pleasures in alcoholic form can head for the **Bermúdez Rumfabrik ©** (tours: Mon–Fri 9am–noon, 2–3pm) in the northwestern district of the city to taste the *República*'s pride and joy for themselves and see how it is made. The rum distillery is a long building on the Avenida J. Armando Bermúdez on the corner of Blanca Mascaro.

Moca ②, the capital of Espaillat province, lies some 20 km (13 miles) to

Maps:
Town 240
Area 245

Camp David Ranch in the Gurabo district of Santiago (Carretera Luperón, km 7.5, tel: 583 5230) is a restaurant with a breathtaking view of Santiago. Veteran cars which once belonged to the Trujillo family and a state carriage owned by ex-President Balaguer are on display here.

BELOW:
Dominican rum is a well-kept secret.

THE STORY OF RUM

Christopher Columbus brought sugar cane seedlings to Hispaniola on his second voyage in 1493. The plant had spread from Asia via the Mediterranean to southern Europe, and the recently discovered "West Indies", with their subtropical climate, offered ideal conditions for its cultivation. Sugar soon became the "white gold" of the region, until the Europeans discovered sugar beet as an alternative source of sweetness.

The story of rum is almost as old as that of sugar cane itself. The principles underlying its manufacture have remained virtually unchanged, too. The best rum is made from molasses, the thick substance which remains after the crystallized sugar has been extracted. This by-product is thinned down and allowed to rest for at least 12 days. Then the rum is distilled and blended to obtain the best flavour. The blending is the most difficult part of the procedure, requiring the most skill. Before the amber-coloured liquid is bottled, it is matured in oak barrels for at least one year to allow it to mellow.

Compared with Jamaican rum, the Dominican version by Bermúdez, Barceló and Brugal has a lighter taste. But the export market is of secondary importance to Dominicans, as they prefer to keep their rum for themselves.

TIP

Time of the Butterflies (1995) by Dominican author Julia Alvarez provides a lively and penetrating portrait of the brief lives of the Mirabal sisters, who were killed by the ruthless dictator, Trujillo, in 1960.

the east of Santiago. Clinging to a hillside, the little town was founded in the 18th century; today it is a centre of coffee and cocoa production. Off the beaten track, it provides an ideal opportunity to absorb the atmosphere of a typical small Dominican town, although this one is richer than most. In the town centre there is a lovely neoclassical church, **Nuestra Señora del Rosario**, and the organ in the **Sagrado Corazón de Jesús**, whose tower dominates the region from the outskirts, is the only one of its kind on the island. Moca's Golden Age was during the early years of the 20th century, when the railway line between La Vega and Sánchez passed through it. A monument on the **Plaza Viaducto**, depicting a small locomotive on rails, recalls those years. Moca, by the way, seems to have played very little part in the history of the nation – except for the fact that, in 1899, the rebels who planned and carried out the fatal attack on the dictator Ulises Heureaux were from the town.

Murder in Salcedo

A well-maintained tarmac road leads for about 12 km (8 miles) through scenic farmland planted with bananas and cacao trees, divided up by little rivers, dotted with palm trees and trimmed with ribbon villages. **Salcedo ❸** holds a bloody chapter of the nation's history. A small metal monument at the entrance to the town, and the portraits of the *Tres Hermanas Mirabal* painted on the wall recall the fact that the three Mirabal sisters – like many other political opponents and thousands of Haitians – were murdered by the henchmen of the dictatorial President Trujillo in November 1960. In the **Plazoleta de las Hermanas Mirabal ❹**, a small square a few kilometres further eastwards near the village of Ojos de Aguaon, lies the frame of the car in which the outspoken sisters died

BELOW: monument to las Tres Hermanas Mirabal.

and a 5-metre (16-ft) sculpture dedicated to their memory. The little **Museo de las Hermanas Mirabal** (the family next door will show you around for a small fee) stands on the right-hand side of the road some 5 km (3 miles) beyond Salcedo on the way to San Francisco de Macorís. The highly respected Mirabal family, of which the present Vice-President of the Dominican Republic is a member, has dedicated the exhibition of photos and personal possessions of Patria, Minerva and María Teresa to the memory of the three young women.

Carnival in La Vega

The original La Vega, known as **La Vega Vieja** ❺, was founded in 1494 a few kilometres to the northeast of the present day La Vega. Its *raison d'être*, like that of Santiago, was gold. The *conquistadors* assumed from the tales of the Taínos that extensive deposits of the precious metal were to be found around here. The settlement rapidly grew in prosperity, not due to the modest amounts of gold discovered, but to the fertility of the valley, which enabled the Spanish to begin cultivating sugar cane right from the start. Nonetheless, towards the middle of the 16th century, many settlers abandoned the region. A number of them attempted to make their fortune prospecting for gold on the South American mainland, and in 1562 a severe earthquake almost completely destroyed the town. It was not until the 17th century that reconstruction began on the new La Vega, some 10 km (6 miles) to the south.

Today, **La Vega** ❻ (also known as La Concepción de la Vega) is a quiet provincial town despite the proximity of the *Autopista* Duarte. Its 60,000 inhabitants mostly make a living from the extensive *zona franca*, the free industrial zone to the north. The historic buildings of La Vega which are still standing –

Map below

Carnaval masks can represent good or evil.

BELOW: keeping the peace at *carnaval*.

Map on page 245

the **Palacio de Justicia**, the **Teatro La Progresista** and the fire station, the **Bombería** – all date from the beginning of the 20th century, when the railway line to Sánchez created an economic boom for the town. The most recent architectural addition is the **Nueva Catedral**, at the junction of calles Independencia and Restauración, which was built of concrete in 1992. It is a building full of pomp and circumstance in which the Biblical number 12 is of great significance: 12 doorways lead into the interior, and 12 round windows provide light.

February is the best month to visit the town, for then all hell is let loose every Sunday. Dominicans all agree that the pre-Lenten carnival in La Vega is the most magnificent in the land. *Diablos cojuelos* ("Limping Devils") in garish costumes dance through the streets. Their faces hidden behind gruesome masks, they take great delight in attacking innocent bystanders with pigs' bladders full of water.

Vision at Sacred Hill

The **Santo Cerro** ❼, or "Sacred Hill", can be found about 10 km (6 miles) north of La Vega and it is here that a legend, dating from the time of the *conquistadors*, was born. The story goes that in 1495, under the leadership of the *cacique* Guarionex, the Taínos went into battle against the Spanish. When they attempted to burn the cross which Columbus had erected, the *Virgen de las Mercedes* suddenly appeared and protected the Christian symbol from the flames. As a result the Amerindians were persuaded to accept its authority. "Is it possible that the cross was made of metal?" ask the cynics. The Dominicans deny this argument, for in the pilgrimage church of **Las Mercedes**, which was built in 1886, a splinter of wood from the historic cross is reputedly preserved

BELOW: cross detail on Santo Cerro.
RIGHT: off to *carnaval* on a *motoconcho*, La Vega.

for posterity. Whether you believe the story or not, it's worth a visit because from behind the church there is a magnificent view of the valley, the forests of palms and the amapola trees which are a wonderful sight in February when they are covered in coral-red blossom.

On the other side of the Santo Cerro, a steep road winds down into the valley towards the *Carretera* 21. At this point, if you turn left towards Pueblo Viejo, you arrive at the scant remains of La Vega Vieja. The next left turning puts you on the road to the **Ruinas Convento San Francisco** ❽, of which only a few outer walls can still be seen. You can make out the layout of the various components of the first monastery to be built on the soil of the New World: the chapel, well, cloister and enclosure. Beside the monastery is an old cemetery.

The open ruins of the **Fortaleza Nuestra Señora de la Concepción** can be found along the *Carretera* 21. The fortress was built by the Spanish after their victory against the Taínos on Santo Cerro. Not much is left of the fortress today either. The highest wall still standing is 2 metres (6 ft) tall and it was once part of a tower complete with embrasures. A tiny museum (daily; entrance fee) displays everyday items dating from about 1500, including a large mortar described as a Spanish sugar mill – a true indication that the *conquistadors* grew sugar cane in the fertile valley even in those days. ❏

CORDILLERA CENTRAL

*The Dominican Alps offer panoramic views over lush valleys,
fertile farmland and forests and rapid flowing rivers,
perfect for hikers, cyclists and eco-minded adventure tourists*

Map on page 253

Santo Domingo

The Cordillerra Central is a magnet to nature lovers, with beautiful alpine vegetation, clear mountain air and stunning panoramas of the surrounding rolling landscape. Hence it's attraction to active sports enthusiasts who flock to the area referred to affectionately as the "Dominican Alps", to hike, cycle and ride on horseback through the picturesque countryside and national parks. The Central range is vast, the largest of the five mountain regions in the Dominican Republic, running across the island of Hispaniola starting in Haiti and ending in the southern region of the Dominican Republic near **San Cristóbal**. The mountain peaks here offer cool relief from the heat inland and on the coast and have the highest elevations in the entire Caribbean. Pico Duarte *(see page 255)* rises to an astonishing 3,087 metres (10,128 ft) and La Pelona reaches 3,150 metres (10,335 ft). Nestling at the foot of Pico Duarte are the two main towns, Constanza in the southeast and Jarabacoa towards La Vega *(see page 245)* in the northeast. Bonao, in the east, is also worth a visit.

Overwhelmingly an agricultural and nature region there is some industry in the area mainly due to the presence of mineral deposits such as nickel, silver and bauxite around Bonao. Though it is a difficult task, Falconbridge nickel mine exploits the abundant mineral deposits. There are also several nature parks and scientific reserves with unique and luxurious vegetation and complex ecosystems, including the Parque Nacional José del Carmen Ramírez in the south, Parque Nacional Armando Bermúdez in the north and the Parque Nacional Valle Nuevo in the southeast.

These mountains are a dream come true for nature lovers, whether one visits simply to contemplate nature's wonders or to seek adventure in an adrenaline rush activity.

Guided excursions are available to Constanza and Jarabacoa from all the main tourist centres in the country. Jarabacoa is most commonly accessible by bus travelling northwest from Santo Domingo, which can take up to two and a half hours, or a short ride from La Vega. If you plan to drive yourself you would be best advised to rent a four-wheel-drive vehicle to cope with the rugged terrain.

Mountain adventures

Jarabacoa ❶ is a small town of 6,000 people in a lush valley 528 metres (1,732 ft) above sea level on the eastern bank of the **Río Yaque del Norte**. This is a rich agricultural and farming area producing fruits and vegetables as well as a wide variety of flowers. The valley is irrigated by the Río Yaque del Norte, the country's longest waterway and an ideal place for rafting. There are several ranches in in the area which offer water rafting tours and other action-packed

PRECEDING PAGES: the view over Jarabacoa. **LEFT:** crossing the pool at Salto de Jimenoa. **BELOW:** rafting down the Río Yaque del Norte.

Locally grown fruit is used to make tasty fresh fruit juice served in the bars and restaurants.

activities such as tubing, canyoning, hiking and excursions through the countryside on horseback or in jeeps to **El Salto de Baiguate** and **El Salto de Jimenoa** (entrance fee) 3km (2 miles) outside Jarabacoa. Both waterfalls flow from the Río Yaque del Norte, but it is El Salto de Jimenoa that is the most spectacular (and easily accessible) of the two, with waters tumbling down about 40 metres (130 ft) into a cool, rocky pool below. The route to the falls is well-signposted and served by public transport, there are also parking facilities a short walk through the forest. In town visitors will find basic accommodation, but the best deals to be had are on the outskirts where there a few hotels and cabins for rent.

North of Jarabacoa is **Balneario La Confluencia** a shallow natural swimming pool created where the Río Yaque del Norte and Río Jimenoa meet.

Popular with vacationing Dominicans, the Cordillera Central is also a great place to try your hand at active sports. Though the Río Yaque del Norte is not as fast flowing or rough as others outside the Dominican Republic, the journey down the river by inflatable raft can still get the blood pumping. Tours can be booked in town. A less strenuous way of exploring the valley is by hiking along one of the trails in the national parks to Pico Duarte.

Fruit and forests

Cutting deeper into the central region and climbing higher from Jarabacoa is another beautiful valley, **Constanza** ❷. One of the highest valleys in the country at 1,200 metres (3,940 ft) above sea level, it has a temperate climate and temperatures are known to drop below zero in winter. The direct route which connects Jarabacoa to Constanza is rough and not recommended, it should be attempted

BELOW: horse riding through the valley, Jarabacoa.

only if driving a sturdy four-wheel-drive vehicle. Therefore the longer, but more practical route would be to take the *Autopista* Duarte back towards Santo Domingo, turning off at *Carretera* 12, which affords superb views of the valley, its forests and rivers, and leads to the town of Constanza. Here the combination of a mild climate and fertile farmland produces abundant crops of fruit and vegetables (mainly garlic and strawberries) not usually grown in the Caribbean, and beautiful flowers for export.

The mountains surrounding the town are rich in timber-yielding woods such as mahogany and American pine, while the land down south to the **Parque Nacional Valle Nuevo** has a protected forest which includes cool streams and is excellent for birdwatching. Heading back along *Carretera* 12 towards Bonao is the **Reserva Científica del Ebano Verde** a small forest which contains an amazing variety of plant and bird species.

East of Constanza in the mountains is **Bonao ❸**, capital of the **Monseñor Nouel Province**. Essentially a mining town, Bonao is the hometown of famous Dominican artist Candido Bidó, an award-winning painter who has has exhibited his work, portraying women and pigeons, throughout the world. Bidó established an art school for painting and crafts, including ceramics and pottery which can be bought from roadside vendors.

Also in the district is the **Falconbridge Nickel Mine**, which for years has been one of the largest producers of nickel and iron for export. Although the mine provides the region with much needed jobs for local people, its effect on the environment has been a concern due to the pollution and degradation of the soil believed to be connected to the industry. In contrast much of the central range is being preserved in the form of national parks.

Fragrant frangipani.

Map on page 253

Most guides who lead tours through the national parks speak Spanish only, unless you book a trip through a tour group who will provide an English-speaking guide upon request. In the interest of safety carry bottled water to drink during a hike up to the peak.

BELOW: colours of Constanza.

Through the parks

The Dominican Republic has more than 20 national parks and reserves and two of its main parks are in the Cordillera Central, created in the 1950s to protect the forests and wildlife they support. The central's two main national parks, Parque Nacional Armando Bermúdez and Parque Nacional José del Carmen Ramírez are in the foothills of the Antilles' highest elevation, **Pico Duarte ❹** *(see opposite page)*, and its neighbouring peaks La Pelona (3,080 metres/10,105 ft) and La Rucilla (3,045 metres/9,990 ft).

To the north is **Parque Nacional Armando Bermúdez ❺** (entrance fee) with its steep ground covered by native pine trees. The climate is alpine with cool weather dropping below freezing point during the winter months. In December and January the temperature can reach –8°C (18°F) during the night, and the rising sun reveals frost-covered bushes and vegetation, creating a type of ghostly scenery, that is unexpected in the Caribbean.

Most organised tours begin at one of the small villages in the vicinity, including La Ciénega, where there is a ranger station at the entrance to the park. If you are travelling independently this is a good place to book a qualified guide and buy an entry permit, both essential for exploring the land. An alternative jumping off point is San José de las Matas, a small and, in parts modern, town southwest of Santiago. This is cattle country and though the roads are less than wonderful, they are passable in a four-wheel-drive vehicle.

There are a number of well trodden hiking trails leading through the park, up to the mountains and Pico Duarte. Most of the trails start at one of the many ranger stations in the valley. Among the wildlife which populates the area are a rich variety of birds such as the *cotorra*, a small parrot indigenous to Hispaniola, the woodpecker, the *cigua palmera* (palm chat) the national bird, *papagayo* and the *Guaraguao*, a rapacious bird that preys on small rodents.

The wild boar, hunted by the highlanders many years ago because they attacked domestic animals, represents the mammals. This is also the habitat of the mouse and the *hutía* a small native rodent. Small snakes can be found in the lower areas of the woods.

South of Parque Nacional Armando Bermúdez and west of Constanza is **Parque Nacional José del Carmen Ramírez ❻** (entrance fee). Together the two national parks are home to more than ten of the Dominican Republic's main river systems and therefore have the most plentiful water resources in the country. The land gives birth to the rivers that irrigate the San Juan Valley, one of the most fertile in the country, known as the "south's granary". This is also the source of the **Río Yaque del Sur**, twin brother of the Río Yaque del Norte. Together the parks' rivers irrigate around 5,000 hectares (12,400 acres) of land. The rivers also provide the nearby communities with electricity from a hydro-power plant.

Several tour groups organise river trips and treks through the parks and mountains on foot or by mule. For information about activities in the area contact Iguana Mama Adventure Tours (tel: 571 0908; fax: 571 0734) which operates out of Cabarete or Rancho Baiguate in Jarabacoa (tel: 696 0318). ❏

Climb Pico Duarte

There was no attempt to climb Pico Duarte, at 3,087 metres (10,128 ft) the highest mountain in the Caribbean, until 1944. Today there are several trails leading to it. During his term as president, the dictator Trujillo christened the mountain Pico Trujillo, but with his fall the imperious peak was renamed after the founding father and 19th-century revolutionary Pablo Duarte. Even for experienced climbers "Il Pico" is a challenge: the ascent leads through dense rainforest and extreme climate zones (from sunny and hazy to ice cold and windy).

The best time to climb is between March and October. Warm clothes, hiking boots, rain and sleeping gear, a flashlight, a medical kit and food provisions are essential. As part of the Parque Nacional Armando Bermúdez on the northern border in the San Juan province, Pico Duarte is best reached from the little village of La Ciénega, upriver from Jarabacoa. From there it is 23 km (14 miles) to the peak. Take an organised tour or employ a qualified guide (you pay the guide and provide provisions) for the trip, which will take three days on foot. The same journey by mule will cut the travelling time down to two days.

A good place to find a guide is through the small hotel Patria Muñoz, or make enquiries among the local people. To hike through the approaches and climb the peak you will need a park permit, which can be obtained from the National Parks Office in Santo Domingo, or you should be able to pick one up at the park entrance on the outskirts of La Ciénega.

At first, the trail follows the Los Tablones River. The first 4 km (2½ miles) is a lush landscape of tropical broadleaf forest interspersed with wild cane. If you are tired, you can spend the night at a cabin nearby. The path climbs to La Cotorra (namesake of the Dominican parrot), passing fragrant almond trees, sierra palms and carpets of fern as it enters a wonderfully scented pine forest. At the designated rest area look up and see the fire-red *cotorra* swing through the crisp air. The view of the La Ciénega valley is stunning.

RIGHT: ponies and mules can help carry hiking equipment, food and you, if you get tired.

Now the trail follows the ridge line for about 2 km (1 mile), after that the steep gradient reaches a side trail leading to the high mountain valley Valle Tetero. The neon-green grass meadows, reminiscent of the Swiss Alps, are an impressionist's dream. On to La Compartición, and the ascent of "Il Pico" starts in earnest. It would be wise to stop and catch one's breath before embarking on the steep and exhausting 14-km (9-mile) hike. The Aquita Fría trail passes a large bog which is the source of Río Yaque del Norte and Río Yaque del Sur. The meeting of these two rivers is a terrific sight. The final ascent should begin before dawn. After a steady climb through pine forest the path leads through the Vallecito de Lilis, an open meadow with fields of lily's and a perfect view of both Pico Duarte and La Pelona. Continue, passing between massive boulders until you reach the summit. There, a bronze bust of the national hero Pablo Duarte awaits. The views in all directions are spectacular and include the Caribbean Sea, Lago Enriquillo, the Cibao Valley and the mountains. ❏

WEST TO LAGO ENRIQUILLO

You can see life at its simplest and nature at its wildest on this as yet untouched part of the island. Mountain ranges, desert landscapes and one of the world's largest salt lakes provide stunning scenery

Map on page 262

Santo Domingo

West of Santo Domingo's glitzy hotel resorts, life is still like a fairytale from an unknown world. Here the island shows its more frugal and most varied side. Few people visit this untouched land, where the inhabitants welcome everybody as their best friend. "Nowhere", promises tourist guide Julio E. Feliz, "will the Dominican Republic surprise you more than on this magnificent stretch of the island." As the capital's skyline recedes behind you, the road cuts through a desert-like landscape reminding even the most unpoetic person of a surreal Dalí painting or a scene out of Wim Wenders' road movie *Paris, Texas*. Moody as the hot and arid west can be, suddenly lush rainforests appear, embedded at the feet of gigantic *sierras* (mountain ranges), along with deserted pebble beaches, the world's second largest salt lake – home to crocodiles and iguanas – and two huge national parks where Amerindian caves and petroglyphs are poignant reminders of the islands early inhabitants.

Besides the adventure, the poor country-dwelling Dominicans are exceedingly warm and cordial. Despite their modest, often squalid existence, they shower the foreigner with boundless hospitality. Here, most of the people find it honourable to be photographed and might hug you passionately if you give them some *pesos* for their shy smile. And don't be surprised if they invite you into their little shacks, where tasty *guisados* (goat stew) and *agua de coco* (coconut water) are served for the guest of honour.

PRECEDING PAGES: rural landscapes beckon. **LEFT:** friendly smiles in Azua. **BELOW:** statue of the great *cacique* Enriquillo.

Memories of bloody battles

History has left its scars in this region of the Dominican Republic. The biggest towns of San Cristóbal, Baní and Azua de Compostela were all founded by *conquistadors* and the statues in their little parks are carved memories of bloody battles between Haitians and Dominicans, or between Spaniards and Taínos. The deep spirituality of the Amerindians is inscribed in the landscape near San Juan de la Maguana and around Lago Enriquillo, where the great *cacique* Enriquillo fought successfully against the Spanish conquerors. The modern tyrant Trujillo left architectural (and emotional) marks in and around his birthtown of San Cristóbal.

In contrast to the east and north of the *República*, where tourism dominates the economy, money comes mainly from agriculture and mining. The "business-savvy" Dominicans are at present eagerly working on the *zona sur*, the touristic development of the southwest. Finances are still scarce though and many travellers still prefer the more "civilized" areas of the charter meccas. But it won't be long before the steel towers of hotels such as Hyatt & Co will be reaching for the azure blue sky…

*Baní town
flag mural.*

San Cristóbal – Trujillo's home town

Just take the perfectly paved *Carretera* Sánchez from Santo Domingo to the west, and the industrial clouds of the Caribbean metropolis will soon fade into the lovely scent of freshly-cut sugar cane and aromatic herbs growing on the roadside. Endless sugar-fine beaches and coconut palms are not to be found here, yet the Dominican desert of scrub and organ pipe cacti, surrounded by massive *sierras*, is fascinating in its own way.

Passing **Haina**, the main port of *la capital* which has the country's largest sugar cane mill, **San Cristóbal ❶** emerges after 15 km (9 miles) on the banks of the **Río Nigua** like a mini version of bustling Santo Domingo. The industrial capital of the southwest with a swelling population of 170,000 is notorious as the birthplace of Rafael Leonidas Trujillo y Molina. It is hectic and polluted, and not very friendly towards tourists – who knows, maybe it's the evil spirit of *El Generalísimo*, who left numerous landmarks around town.

Recognising the first Constitution of the Dominican Republic, which was signed in the early 19th century after a rebellion against the Haitians in the local **Palacio del Ayuntamiento** (city hall), the dictator officially named San Cristóbal the "Meritorious City". However, today there is not much of meritorious value left here, and its sights will take only about two hours to visit.

Close to the **Parque Duarte** stands the neoclassical church of **Nuestra Señora de Consolación** (daily 6–8am, 5.30–8pm; free) where you can see Trujillo's tomb. The corrupt Trujillo spent a fortune on his home town, building the church in 1946 at an astronomical cost of US$4 million from government funds, along with the recently renovated plaza in front where, ironically, the city cannot afford to provide the fountains with water.

BELOW: Nuestra Señora de Consolación houses Trujillo's tomb.

West of the town on a small hill lies the pompous **Palacio del Cerro**, Trujillo's lavish, but never lived in, six-storey villa, which is undergoing a slow process of restoration. You may be shown round by a devoted servant of the late dictator. Costing US$3 million from the government's coffers, the end result was so over-the-top that, apparently, when Trujillo's closest confidants criticised it for being tasteless he claimed that it was a gift from the people of San Cristóbal and declined to live in it.

Instead he lived in another of his extravagant creations, the **Casa de Caoba (Mahogany House)** ❷ tucked away 5 km (3 miles) north of the town in the thicket. This house is also being renovated and should be finished by about 2003. In the 1980s an attempt was made to restore the house to its former glory after it fell into disrepair, but concrete was used to replace the rotten wood which rather destroyed the look of it. Just a stone's throw away is the former private spring baths of "*El Jefe*", the **Balneario La Toma** (Mon–Fri 9am– 6pm, Sat and Sun 7am–8pm; entrance fee).

Petroglyphs and bats

The **Reserva Antropológica de las Cuevas de Borbón** ❸ is just another 15 minutes along a bumpy dirt road north of Caoba. This is a series of 40 interconnecting caves, which include the **Cuevas de El Pomier**, where there are more than 5,000 petroglyphs and several thousand Amerindian wall paintings. The caves, which are open all the time are also home to thousands of bats (don't forget the flashlight).

South of San Cristóbal, 15 km (9 miles) away on the coast, lies the sleepy village of **Nigua**. Right after the bridge over the **Río Nigua** are the old ruins of

Map on page 262

To avoid getting lost and to save time, it is advisable to take a taxi to visit Trujillo's Palacio del Cerro and Casa de Caoba.

BELOW: the petroglyphs near Caoba.

Southwest

Map on page 262

two sugar mills: the 18th-century **Ingenio Boca de Nigua** and the earlier 16th-century **Ingenio de Diego Caballero**. A sign in front of the old factories describes the stages of sugar production.

The scenic coastal road *Carretera* 10 leads westwards out of Nigua and passes the empty beaches of **Najayo**, where you can see the ruins of Trujillo's beach house, and **Palenque**. However, the mouse-grey sand and rotting garbage around the palms may not appeal: the locals just love to slouch in those bright blue wooden sunchairs and snack on deep-fried cassava loaves and papaya juice. If you don't want to drive in the dark, you could stay at the Swiss-run **Hotel Playa Palenque** (tel: 243 2525) one minute away from the beach.

Baní – birthplace of a liberation fighter

After a pleasant drive through a green landscape of waving sugar cane bordered by pastel-coloured huts, **Baní ❹** (pop. 40,000), also dubbed the "city of poets", is the next big town. The name Baní means abundance of water and, founded by immigrants from the Canary Islands in the 18th century, the town is friendly and sane. Except for the **Museo de Máximo Gómez** (Mon–Sat; free), which honours the native 19th-century Cuban liberation fighter, there is not much to see, although coffee junkies should check out the **Museo del Café Dominicano** (Mon–Sat; entrance fee) where the Dominican wonder bean is documented. Great pictures can be taken at the lively **Mercado Modelo** near **Parque Central**. The city beach **Playa Baní** is hard to reach, but definitely worth the bumpy ride.

From late May to early July, look out for stalls selling Baní's small but very sweet mangoes.

About 30 km (19 miles) further to the southwest, the salt gardens of the **Las Salinas Peninsula ❺** jut into the sea, and the area has been protected as a National Monument. To get there, follow the signs to Las Calderas naval base and turn left on to the dirt road. The bleach-white salt hills have a surreal note, with the windy **Bahía de Las Calderas** to the right and panoramic **Sierra Martín García** behind. The Santa Fe-inspired **Club Salinas Hotel** (tel: 471 9463) is a little-known spot for windsurfers. For a pleasant swim in a beautiful setting, take the road north to **Palmar de Ocoa**. This quaint fishing village, which holds an annual fishing tournament, has a neat grey beach and some weekend *haciendas* for wealthy city folk.

BELOW: preparing salt at Las Salinas.

Into the desert

The scenery changes to an arid landscape of scrub and organ pipe cactus once back on the *Carretera Sánchez* (*Carretera* 2) towards Azua, 55 km (34 miles) west of Baní. In the spring, acacias and mesquite bloom on the mineral-rich soil. About 15 minutes before you reach Azua there is a military post that looks more like a miniature market in the middle of nowhere. Here poor children sell freshly-roasted peanuts alongside toothless old ladies offering bundles of tasty shallots and dried chilli peppers. The wooden *pilóns* (mortars) and *cana* brooms are a particular speciality of the area.

Azua de Compostela ❻ (pop. 85,000) is another bustling city which lives off its flourishing agriculture (both honeydew and watermelons). In 1504 the

The Corral de los Indios is a large circle of stones 7 km (4 miles) north of San Juan de la Maguana, which was once a Taíno cult meeting place. In the centre is a tomb pillar, engraved with naive grimaces. La Maguana is the name of a Taíno tribe.

town was founded 17 km (11 miles) to the north by the Spanish soldier and colonialist Diego Velásquez (1465–1524), who later conquered and governed Cuba. He was granted a coat of arms by King Ferdinand in 1508. Yet the shipping metropolis, once home to the conqueror of Mexico, Hernán Cortés *(see page 186)*, regularly suffered heavy pirate attacks. Eventually, in 1791, Azua was wiped out by an earthquake, and the town was rebuilt on its present site. Several times, Azua was burned to the ground, mostly by the Haitian army, until the gory battle of 19 March 1844 brought the Dominicans their long awaited independence from Haiti. The battle, which is honoured by a monument in the **Parque Central**, took place 16 km (10 miles) away at **Puerto Viejo**, once one of the main ports of the island, where you can still see some colonial ruins, and where the great Taíno leader Enriquillo is said to be buried.

Alternatively, you can plunge into the lukewarm waves with the locals at the stony **Playa Monte Río** on the Bahía de Ocoa. Try the grilled fish there at the **Restaurante San Miguel** and enjoy the postcard-view of the lush green mountain **El Número** (628 metres/2,060 ft).

Barahona – gateway to a natural world

Returning westwards on the main coastal highway, the road gets steeper and more winding. Massive rocks as red as brick shoot up on both sides, and suddenly a breathtaking view of the **Bahía de Neiba** unfolds. Entering the fertile mouth of the **Río Yaque del Sur**, a bright green oasis of banana plants, *carata* palms and sugar cane flashes up in the otherwise barren land.

Barahona ❼ (pop. 160,000) is the next and last big town in the southwestern part of the *República* and is 80 km (50 miles) from Azua. It's hard to imagine

BELOW:
domino players can always find a game.

this provincial port town ever being an El Dorado for the all-inclusive set, or as the "Boca Chica of the Southwest", but the international airport has long been finished (though no planes land here) and the town planners are eagerly cooking up concepts for luxury resorts. It is only a matter of time before this untouched part of the island disappears under a sea of development, but for the moment there are only a few neat hotels catering to tourists, and the locals are just beginning to get used to *caritas blancas* (white faces).

The airport is actually named for one of the town's daughters, the Hollywood actress Maria Montez, whose real name was Maria Africa Gracia Vidal. Born in Barahona in 1912, she made more than 20 films throughout the 1940s, including *The Arabian Nights* and *Ali Baba and the Forty Thieves*. She died in 1951.

A favourite hideout for the notorious pirate Cofresí, Barahona was founded in 1802 by the Haitian liberation fighter Toussaint L'Ouverture *(see page 47)*. The town blossomed early as a major port for sugar export and, today, coffee, minerals such as gypsum, bauxite, wood and wax are handled here as well. There are no sights whatsoever in town, although many houses are colourfully painted, nor are there any decent beaches. But the people are extremely friendly and live life to the full, as you may see at the **Malecón** at night when the youngsters swing to *merengue* and show off their latest motorcycle acrobatics.

The real attraction of the town is its position at the top of the **Península de Pedernales** giving easy access to the beautiful national parks. Spend a day driving high up into the Alp-like mountains of the **Sierra de Baoruco** to the idyllic coffee village of **Polo** (*Carretera* 46 for 10 km/6 miles to Cabral, then turn left for 25 km/15 miles). The scenery is magnificent, as it is when you drive south from Barahona along the "Côte d'Azur of the Dominican Republic".

Map on page 262

The international airport is named for Barahona-born María Montez (above), who made it big as a Hollywood film star in the 1940s.

LEFT: street talk.
BELOW: view of the Baoruco coastline.

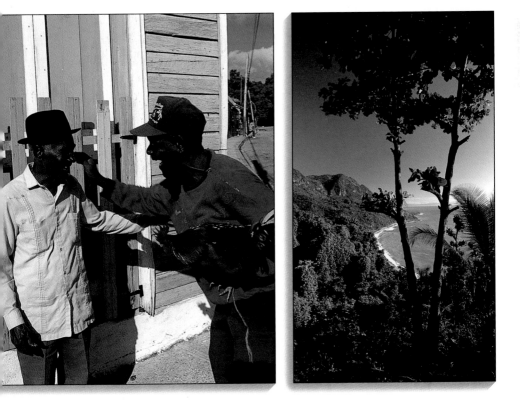

Casa Bonita, also known as the Baoruco Beach Resort in Baoruco (tel: 696 0215, fax: 223 0548) is a Moroccan-inspired resort, built in 1998, which some say offers the best food in the Dominican Republic. It also has a fantastic view of the bay.

The well paved, but winding *Carretera* 44 separates the lush green rainforest of the Sierra de Baoruco to the right, while to the left cliffs rise steeply above the azure-blue Caribbean Sea. Numerous bays with endless pebble beaches and coconut palms interspersed with fishing huts line the road. Kids cool off in the crystal-clear waterfalls and rough and tumble in the rivers. Above the pastel-coloured village of **Baoruco**, 17 km (10 miles) south of Barahona, you can see the nation's own semi-precious stone larimar being mined (Mon–Fri; free). **Playa San Rafael**, a little further on, is the most popular beach – where two freshwater pools fed by the **Río San Rafael** entice you in for a refreshing swim and *mamís* cook up tasty grilled fish in the shade.

Wildlife and archaeological treasures

At **Oviedo**, the massive **Parque Nacional Jaragua ❽** (1,400 sq km/540 sq miles) starts. The biggest national park of the *República* spreads across the whole of the southern part of the Pedernales peninsula and includes the uninhabited islands of **Beata** and **Alto Velo** to the south. Once the "biotope" of the *cacique* Xaragua, it now attracts the attention of archaeologists, naturalists and scientists. No wonder, since the park holds many pre-Columbian caves and even more archaeological treasures are still to be unearthed.

The wildlife includes 60 percent of all native birds. Even the endangered Hispaniola buzzard can still be seen gliding over the rough landscape of scrub, sharp "dogtooth limestone", cacti and desert palms. Exploring the extremely hot, labyrinthine park by yourself is prohibited. You must buy a permit at the ranger station at the park entrance (daily, 9am–5pm) at the **Laguna de Oviedo** and take an organised tour with an official guide. The Laguna, a shallow, 15-km (9-mile)

BELOW: cacti and scrub landscape.

CROCODILES IN THE PARK

Alongside the giant rhinoceros iguanas and the ricord iguanas, a large number (some say around 500) of American crocodiles (*crocodylus acutus*) can be seen basking in and around the Lago Enriquillo in the Parque Nacional de Isla Cabritos.

Since the early 1990s these prehistoric-looking reptiles have been the subject of a conservation study programme funded jointly by the Wildlife Conservation Society and the Swiss agency for Cooperation (HELVETAS). Researchers have reported that sightings of crocodile nests rose from 14 in 1995 to 51 in 1996 – three nests were robbed by people in 1993 and only one in 1995.

The main nesting grounds are on the Isla Cabritos, and, in recent years, nests have been spotted on beaches which are heavily frequented by tourists. Two nests have even been found right next to a trail on sandy ground, showing that the conservation work is helping to create a more peaceful co-existence between humans and crocodiles. After the eggs have hatched, the mother crocodile tends to ferry her newly-hatched young away from the salty lagoon, out of harm's way, to the mouths of the freshwater streams that flow into the lake from the Sierra de Neiba and Sierra de Baoruco.

long saltwater lake is the perfect spot to watch colourful flamingos, pelicans and rhinoceros iguanas at close range.

Driving along the flawless but winding *Carretera* 44 to **Cabo Rojo** ❾, 48 km (30 miles) across the peninsula on the western coast, you skirt the Parque Nacional de Jaragua on the left, with the **Parque Nacional Sierra de Baoruco** to your right. On this road you can smell the heady aromas of the herbs of the Dominican "macchia" that the Taínos used for their medicine. Named for the blood orange-red colour of its earth, which produces large amounts of bauxite, the fishing port Cabo Rojo (red cape), is the second entrance to the Jaragua National Park. Following the bumpy dirt road southwards along the shore, you will discover untouched beaches scattered with large conch shells.

The best beaches are in the **Bahía de las Aguilas** (a little-known hot-spot for scuba divers and snorkellers), which can only be reached in a four-wheel-drive or by boat. Ask the fishermen at the surreal cave-village **La Cueva** between Cabo Rojo and the bay. For a few US dollars they will take you there, as well as to the mosquito-infested islands of Beata and Alto Velo. At **Pedernales**, 20 km (12 miles) north on the border with Haiti, there are several checkpoints and little else.

A round trip to Lago Enriquillo

The extremely dry landscape surrounding **Lago Enriquillo** ❿ distinguishes the Dominican Republic from most of the other islands in the Greater Antilles. Almost every corner holds some historical value, since the legendary chieftain Enriquillo hid from the Spaniards with his men in the rocky mountains of the adjacent **Sierra de Baoruco** and **Sierra de Neiba**, waging war against them for

Map on page 262

TIP

Públicos and *gua-guas* regularly ply the *Carretera* 44 between Oviedo and Pedernales and can take you to the ranger station at the entrance to the Parque Nacional Jaragua by the Laguna de Oviedo.

BELOW: view over Lago Enriquillo.

over 14 years. In 1533, on Isla Cabritos in the middle of Lago Enriquillo, he signed the first peace treaty between the Taínos and the colonials with an envoy of the Spanish king. The treaty guaranteed his people a reservation and himself the honorary title of "Don".

If you start early enough from Barahona (6am is perfect), you can make the tour around Lago Enriquillo in eight hours. Follow the *Carretera* 44 north out of the town for 12 km (7 miles), then turn left on to *Carretera* 48. After crossing the **Río Yaque del Sur**, the road will take you through lush sugar cane plantations where you'll see the squalid barracks of Haitian labourers and children playing naked in the dust.

After the *pueblo* Galván you come to **Las Marías** where the more foolhardy can jump into the sulphur hot springs from the surrounding oak trees. Then on through **Neiba** – which has a colourful market on Wednesday and Saturday – to **Villa Jaragua** and the shores of Lago Enriquillo, a 200-sq km (77-sq mile) inland sea, three times saltier than the ocean and lying almost 40 metres (130 ft) below sea level. Framed by statuesque coconut palms, with the Sierra de Neiba to the north and the Sierra de Baoruco to the south, the lake was once part of a channel that linked the Bahía de Neiba in the east with the Baie de Port-au-Prince in the west, until it was cut off by tectonic movements of the earth's crust. You may find fossils, seashells and pieces of coral embedded in the soil.

A walk on the Isla Cabritos

The scenic road going northwest around the lake offers magnificent views, the most spectacular being at **Las Caritas** caves at the top of a steep 5-minute climb near **Postrer Río**. The caves served as a holy temple to the Amerindians

TIP

The animals at Lago Enriquillo don't like the hot sun. If you want to see them, visit Isla Cabritos in the early morning or in the evening. During the day they hide under lily pads.

BELOW: on the road to Neiba.

and Enriquillo was said to have hidden from the *conquistadors* here. The petroglyphs carved into the coral stone allude to Indians praying.

About 500 metres (550 yds) further on is the entrance to **Parque Nacional de Isla Cabritos** (daily 7am–7pm; entrance fee; tel: 224 9525). Walk through the shady tropical forest with iguanas larger than domestic cats to the boats that cross over to **Isla Cabritos** (Goat Island). But don't expect to see goats – instead the 12-km (8-mile) long island is home to some of the rarest animals in the Caribbean: crocodiles, rhinoceros iguanas and ricord iguanas, large turtles and 62 species of birds, including flamingos, Hispaniolan parrots and spoonbills.

Back at the park entrance, the *balneario* **Las Barias** in **La Descubierta** is only a 10-minute drive away, providing an ice-cold dip in a shady oak forest. The locals indulge in the oregano-spiced *chivo guisado* (goat stew) at Señora Etamila. Next stop is the border town **Jimaní**. With the permission of the Haitian Embassy in Santo Domingo you can cross over to the "Other Hispaniola" in a private car (but not a rented one) and buy fake Nike sportswear at the duty-free market. Or take a trip to the saltwater lake **Etang Saumâtre** *(see page 298)* on the Haitian side of the border.

Returning to Barahona along Lago Enriquillo's south shore on the *Carretera 46*, the bronze statue of the lake's namesake, Enriquillo, stands at an intersection near **Duvergé**. Before you reach the town of **Cabral**, the country's second largest inland lake, the **Laguna del Rincón** ⓫ (47 sq km/18 sq miles), unfolds to your left. Here visitors may find flamingos and cormorants, and perhaps the endangered *jicotea*-turtle, languishing in and around the fresh water. The price you have to pay for this treat is an annoying, some might say strenuous, 20-minute tramp to the lake through damp hot fields.
❑

Map on page 262

BELOW: taking a mule ride home, Rincón.

HAITI

*A detailed guide to the country, with principal sites
clearly cross-referenced by number to the maps*

Haiti is not a typical Caribbean destination, no picture postcard idyll of tropical charm. It is a land of startling extremes and contrasts, a place where grinding poverty is matched by extra-ordinary resilience, distressing squalor by great natural beauty, cruel inequality by individual warmth. It is a unique country, capable of provoking strong reactions and leaving few people indifferent.

Travelling within the country is a challenge; little goes according to plan. But the rewards are not measured in terms of comfort or familiarity. For what Haiti has to offer is precisely the unexpected. One thing is certain: you will not quickly forget this land of intense colours and insistent rhythms. Nor will you be able to ignore the ever-present imprint on today's nation of a proud history and a tragic past.

For a small country, there is astonishing diversity within its land-scapes. Cactus-studded desert hillsides border lush green valleys; cool mountaintop villages are within half an hour of the sweltering city centre; a bustling capital of 2 million people seems a world apart from remote rural hamlets where electricity and piped drinking water are as yet unknown. And history has dictated that the North and the South – the two great peninsulas that reach out as if to seize the island of La Gonâve – have separate traditions and identities, re-flected in their people as much as their architecture.

Port-au-Prince is the nerve centre and for a century and a half after independence the exclusive preserve of a commercial and governing élite, it is now home to a third of the population. The city is crowded, dirty and restless, but from its streets emerges a vitality born of the daily struggle. And with this comes the creativity that has made the impoverished nation so rich in artistic achievement. The capital's museums, art galleries and street markets bear witness to this creative impulse. Port-au-Prince's tireless activity is perhaps best experi-enced from the relative calm of its hillside neighbourhoods or from the mountain vantage-points above the graceful suburb of Pétionville.

The North is littered with the ruins of Haiti's momentous history: plantation houses, palaces and the the awe-inspiring Citadelle La Ferrière. The South, traditionally the bastion of the wealthier mulatto minority, is a remote region of crumbling colonial towns and tiny fishing villages. In between lie the fertile Valley of the Artibonite, once the source of fabulous colonial wealth, and the desolate moun-tains that stretch towards the border with the Dominican Republic.

In the 1930s a bestselling and sensationalist book about Haiti was published entitled *The Magic Island*. The book's merits were debat-able but the title undeniably well chosen, for that magic is still as powerful today. You may well fall under Haiti's spell.   ❏

PRECEDING PAGES: sailboat lands in St Louis du Sud bay; a busy market day in Port-au-Prince; every *tap-tap* tells a story.
LEFT: carnival is fun time.

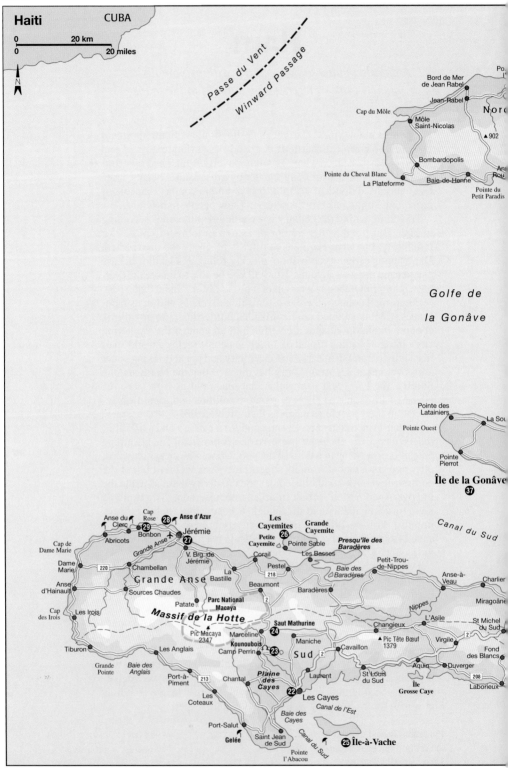

Haiti

CUBA

0   20 km

0   20 miles

N

Passe du Vent

Winward Passage

Bord de Mer
de Jean Rabel

Po

Jean-Rabel

Cap du Môle

Môle
Saint-Nicolas

Nor

▲902

Bombardopolis

Ans
Rou

Pointe du Cheval Blanc

La Plateforme

Baie-de-Henne

Pointe du
Petit Paradis

Golfe de

la Gonâve

Pointe des
Latainiers

La Sou

Pointe Ouest

Pointe
Pierrot

Île de la Gonâve

③⑦

Anse du
Clerc

Cap
Rose

②⑧ **Anse d'Azur**

②⑨ Bonbon

Jérémie

**Les
Cayemites**

**Grande
Cayemite**

②⑥

Canal du Sud

Abricots

②⑦

Petite
Cayemite

Pointe Sable

**Presqu'île des
*Baradères***

Cap de
Dame Marie

V. Brg. de
Jérémie

Corail

Petit-Trou-
de-Nippes

Dame
Marie

220

Grande Anse

Chambellan

La
Bastille

Pestel

218

*Baie des
Baradères*

Anse-à-
Veau

Charlier

Anse
d'Hainault

Grande Anse

Sources Chaudes

Beaumont

2

Baradères

Nippes

Miragoâne

Cap
des Irois

Les Irois

Patate

**Parc National
Macaya**

L'Asile

St Michel
du Sud

Changieux

2

Tiburon

Massif de la Hotte

▲Pic Macaya
2347

Marceline

Kounoubois

Saut Mathurine

②④

Maniche

▲ Pic Tête Bœuf
1379

Virgile

Fond
des Blancs

Les Anglais

②③

Camp Perrin

Sud

Cavaillon

2

Aquin

Duverger

Grande
Pointe

*Baie des
Anglais*

Port-à-
Piment

213

Chantal

*Plaine
des
Cayes*

St Louis
du Sud

Laurent

Île
Grosse Caye

208

Laborieux

Les
Coteaux

②②

Les Cayes

Canal de l'Est

Port-Salut

*Baie des
Cayes*

Canal du Sud

Gelée

Saint Jean
de Sud

②⑤ **Île-à-Vache**

Pointe
l'Abacou

Port-au-Prince

PORT-AU-PRINCE

The crowded and chaotic capital of Haiti can be a daunting experience, but it also offers unforgettable human interest as well as artistic and architectural treasures

Maps:
Area 278
City 280

I t is difficult to fully come to terms with the capital and largest city in Haiti whose population, now close to 2 million, was only 150,000 a few decades ago. Port-au-Prince, like all of Haiti, is a unique place full of constantly confounding contrasts and enigmas, fascination and mysteries. The world press writes only of the negatives – crime, unrest and violence. But, in fact, Port-au-Prince is as safe as any large metropolis, especially if you follow simple guidelines. As in any populous city anywhere in the world, there are basic precautions that go a long way towards ensuring safety. Some of these are so obvious that they're often overlooked. It's always best to keep as low a profile as possible, given that any tourist stands out in Haiti. And it may not be just skin colour. It's clothing, shoes, spectacles, jewellery, your whole bearing will be like a flashing red light that says, "Look at me, I'm a tourist, a foreigner." The one essential: after dark, always take a taxi and don't walk, especially in the city centre. Don't drive on the long side roads in Delmas. Extra caution is needed at night because of the lack of street lights.

There is nothing to prepare the visitor, even after several trips, for the physical reaction to the searing heat that strikes almost like an assault on that first step through the door after the plane has stopped on the tarmac. It's a momentary halt, then a brief half-step backward as though you've been smacked in the face. That initial surprise passes and you continue down the steps and into the teeming airport terminal, but it will take some time to adjust to the sometimes stifling and oppressive heat in the city, the sheer number of people, the stares and occasional expressions of surprise.

BELOW: the markets of Port-au-Prince are always busy.

Skin colour in Haiti has always been a very complex issue, one that's undoubtedly difficult for a traveller to grasp. The term *blanc* (white) is used as a noun here, not an adjective, or as a title (instead of miss or sir, it's blanc). A *blanc* is anyone who is different, foreign, or who has achieved success, no matter how black the skin may be. And all *blancs* are believed to be rich with mounds of money and therefore should be separated from some of it. Your job is to spend only what you want. Think of it as a game. Just knowing this makes it much easier to keep things in perspective and retain a sense of humour. The truth is that visitors, by definition, will have more money in their pockets than many Haitians.

Armed with understanding, preparation is easy. Leave most jewellery and other valuables at home; dress conservatively; keep camera equipment out of sight until needed. Get as many of the smallest denomination bills as possible because vendors and taxi drivers rarely have change. (Don't panic if, when making a purchase, the recipient walks away with the

The detailed fretwork on the gingerbread architecture in Port-au-Prince and its suburbs such as Bois Verna and Pactot.

BELOW: the fading beauty of the Oloffson Hotel.

money; it is likely that he has only gone to look for change). Divide money into multiple small amounts in different pockets so as not to flash a big wad of notes for every purchase. Look out for clothing made specifically for travelling.

The layout of the city

Port-au-Prince ❶ crowns the middle of a large horseshoe-shaped bay at the top of La Gonâve Gulf. The very heart of Port-au-Prince for tourism is the Champs de Mars/Place des Héros de l'Indépendence area that includes: the National Palace, statues of heroes including the *Marron Inconnu*, the Maison de Tourisme, Musée du Panthéon National Haïtien (MUPANAH) and Musée d'Art Haitien (Museum of Haitian Art). The Marché de Fer (Iron Market), Sainte Trinité Episcopal Church and the Cathedral of Port-au-Prince are also nearby.

The original colonial core of the capital, dating from the 1740s, is bounded by Rue des Remparts to the north and Rue Pavée to the south. Through this central district, laid out in a grid system, runs Boulevard Jean-Jacques Dessalines, the chaotic main arterial road that leads northwards towards Cap Haïtien and south towards Jacmel. Permanently clogged with traffic and teeming with street vendors, this is where much of the city's business is conducted – from the fierce haggling of the Marché de Fer to the offices and warehouses of Haiti's import-export firms. Don't expect to see much in the way of colonial architecture, however, since a succession of fires and revolutionary upheavals have long since removed the earliest buildings. Instead, the city-centre commercial district is comprised of rickety century-old stores and town houses, interspersed with more modern concrete office blocks. While high sidewalks are often shaded by colonnades, the numbers of people occupying the pavement

GINGERBREAD ARCHITECTURE

Many of the residences built between the 1880s and the 1920s were embellished with intricate ornamentation, turrets, steeply angled roofs and "widow's walks" – narrow balconies running all around the house, high up near the top. Unlike other cities around the world where most gingerbread houses were pulled down to make room for new construction, in Port-au-Prince the buildings seem to have been left as they were. A good number of gingerbreads have been renovated and turned into art galleries, schools and offices, and some are still homes. The best examples are in the winding hills of Pacot, in Bois Verna, and all along the Rue Lamartinière.

The Oloffson Hotel is a Port-au-Prince landmark and one of the best examples of gingerbread mansions. The once stately green and white manse is close to the Champs de Mars yet a world away in Pacot. It has hosted the famous (and infamous) over the years and there is frequently an assortment of journalists and filmmakers, diplomats and politicians hanging about and trading stories. Authors Herb Gold and Graham Greene used it in their novels. Thursday night is usually a good night to go for dinner and enjoy the musical prowess of the owner, Richard Morse, and his band, RAM.

with small stalls or piles of goods make life difficult for the pedestrian. Still, it is worth visiting central Port-au-Prince, if only to experience the sheer vibrancy and survival skills of this vast sea of humanity.

Continual growth has spread the city further and further east across the **Plaine du Cul-de-Sac** (Cul-de-Sac Plain) and into the foothills of **Massif de la Selle**, the semi-circular wall of mountains that protects the city's back. Moving out from the city centre, the next demarcation includes the first suburbs built at the start of the 20th century. **Bois Verna** and **Pacot** are still mainly residential, displaying some of the elegance of those bygone times, with many streets brimful of mature trees and vibrant flowering plants in a riot of colours. The majority of the best remaining gingerbread buildings are peppered throughout, along with the Centre d'Art, art galleries, hotels such as the Oloffson and Prince Hotel and a few small restaurants. The sprawling suburb of **Delmas** is the next division: small shops line the main road and the offices of many non-governmental aid agencies are sprinkled among the woodsy side roads.

The Oloffson Hotel

Celebrated as the inspiration for the sinister Hotel Trianon in Graham Greene's *The Comedians*, this masterpiece of gingerbread architectural exuberance stands at the southern end of Rue Capois. White, with bell turrets, a twin staircase and a cool verandah, the **Oloffson Hotel ❷** *(see page 282)* is probably the best example of gingerbread style in Port-au-Prince. Set in spacious grounds, it was built at the end of the 19th century as a residence for the Sams, an élite Haitian family, before being turned into a military hospital during the US Occupation of 1915–34. Today, though faded, it remains Port-au-Prince's best-known hotel.

Maps:
Area 278
City 280

TIP

For tours contact the Republique d'Haiti Secrétairerie d'Etat au Tourisme, tel: 223 2143/223 5631. The tourism office can also direct you to Jacqualine Labrom, an Englishwoman living in Haiti who knows the country intimately and organises specialised tours.

BELOW: the streets are full of brightly coloured vehicles.

Every town and city has a cockfighting arena.

Centre of excellence

On the outskirts of the Champs de Mars, off Rue Capois on the corner of Ruelle Roy is the current home of the **Centre d'Art ⑧** (tel: 222 2018). The Pacot mansion, constructed in gingerbread style, is an elegant space for displaying art – ceramics, sculpture (including metal sculpture) and paintings hang along the original, wide, winding staircase and in a variety of rooms. The Centre is a popular venue for exhibitions of contemporary artists, just as the founders DeWitt Peters, an American teacher, and Selden Rodman, an art critic, had in mind when they first opened it in 1944 as a place for local painters to display their work. Peters worked as an English teacher in Haiti during the 1940s and became enamoured with the country in general and *art naïf* paintings in particular. He is credited with promoting the work of Hector Hyppolite *(see page 100)*, one of the talented group of artists whose work earned the Centre a reputation for excellence. Rodman, who supervised the artists painting the murals in the Church of Sainte Trinité, also wrote several books on Haiti.

Now almost extensions of the city, places like **Pétionville** and **Kenscoff** were towns up in the cooler hills, where only those with financial means built homes to escape the blistering heat of Port-au-Prince. Pétionville forms the next ring out from the city centre. Next, continuing out to the perimeter of the semicircle are the still higher locations of Montagne Noire, Kenscoff, Fermathe, Forts Jacques and Alexandre and Boutilliers.

Port-au-Prince is always a highly charged, dynamic beehive of activity during daylight hours. (The number of residents continues to swell exponentially in towns throughout Haiti. As the rural, agrarian economy shrinks, farmers who were previously self-sustaining go to the towns in the hope of finding

BELOW: the streets are crowded in Port-au-Prince.

employment, only to learn that they're competing for limited resources with so many others in the same situation.)

A result of this pattern is that where there were once beaches, the capital now has the world's largest shantytown. The area bordering the sea to the northern end of Port-au-Prince, La Saline, contains a vast, spreading expanse of slums, home to some 200,000 of Haiti's poorest people. The *bidonville* (shantytown) of Cité Soleil is particularly desperate, with no basic services, frequent flooding and a growing reputation for drug-fuelled violence. (This is the only place in all of Haiti that tourists should really avoid unless they have a resident as a guide.) The nearby port area, **Bicentenaire** (also called Cité de l'Exposition), was remodelled for the city's 1949 bicentennial. Almost everyone still calls the main road running through it by its old name, "Boulevard Harry Truman". This area is safe during the day, but should be avoided at night.

Colourfully painted *tap-taps,* buses and trucks serve as public transport throughout Port-au-Prince and its suburbs. They are usually so full of bodies that it's hard to imagine how those crammed inside will get out alive.

Touring the city centre

Champs de Mars , bounded by Rue Légitime, Rue Capois, Rue Mgr. Guilloux and Rue du Marron Inconnu/Rue Piquant, is described as a park, but it is easier to think of it as a group of park-like areas divided into sections by the roads that traverse them. Many of the main city-centre tourism sites fan out from Champs de Mars. The **Maison du Tourisme** (Mon–Sat 8am–noon and 2–6pm) is at the corner of Rue Capois and Rue Magny, making it an excellent central reference point.

Map on page 280

The Champs de Mars also acts as a practice area for local driving schools. Watch out for VW Beetles being driven by novices around the monuments.

BELOW: plastic sheets used as innovative sails, Cité Soleil.

Standing at the Maison de Tourisme the expansive area spread out directly in front is the Champs de Mars. Turn left, and walk to the end of the park along Rue Capois to Rue Légitime (most likely there won't be a street sign), a narrow street, only one block long. Take care crossing the road as it's quite difficult to figure out exactly where any car in the intersection is heading. Try to cross near someone who looks familiar with evasionary tactics.

The unobtrusive, white building on the corner is the **Musée d'Art Haïtien** **D** (Museum of Haitian Art; Mon–Sat 10am–4pm; entrance fee). It has one of Haiti's finest *art naïf* collections with work by Philomé Obin, Hector Hyppolite and Préfète Duffaut among others. Be aware that when the museum is showing one of its superb short-term exhibits, the *art naïf* paintings are put away. If that happens, the Centre d'Art and major galleries are quite accessible. The museum has an interesting gift/handicraft shop with a good assortment of paintings, books and crafts for sale at reasonable prices.

Beyond the museum on Rue Légitime, a tall fence with a door hides a very large parking area. Just drive across the grass to where other vehicles are parked. This is also the entrance to the café and gift shop for those not visiting the museum. Don't be surprised if a young man approaches as you near the entrance. He will more than likely be an artist and will want to show his work. If you stop for a glance, a few more artists with paintings for sale will also gather round. They do not usually go for the hard sell, so a pleasant smile and friendly refusal should be sufficient if they don't have the masterpiece that catches your eye.

Behind the museum, in its private garden, the **Café du Jardin du Musée** (Mon–Sat 10am–4pm) is a little hideaway, the museum's garden café and a

BELOW: *The Paradise* by Wilson Bigaud, Musée d'Art Haïtien.

good place to relax with lunch, a snack or a cold drink (try to sit at a table close to one of the fans). At lunchtime it's quite popular with French Embassy staff from across Rue Capois.

Continue on Légitime, pass the museum's fence to reach the **Maison Défly Ⓔ**, the pink house next door. Set back from the street, it has a little pink roundabout in the middle of a gravel parking area/entry in front, as if to allow a moment for visitors to make the transition from the frenetic pace outside the gate to the more tranquil atmosphere inside. Now a school, it was built by an army commander in 1896 in the Victorian "gingerbread" style. Someone will be pleased to show the building to anyone who expresses an interest.

The pompiers (firehouse) is just a bit further along Légitime, and next, behind a long wrought-iron fence, is the building housing the offices of the Secrétairerie d'Etat au Tourisme (Secretary of State for Tourism). Don't be intimidated if you are ignored – just enter and ask at the desk, and if no-one is there, go up the large staircase (the gate on the staircase will probably be unlocked before 4pm) and ask the receptionist on the first floor. Try the Maison du Tourisme *(see page 285)* for leaflets and maps.

The end of Rue Légitime is just a few steps further; on the corner on the left is a small hotel catering mainly for Haitians who come to the capital to conduct business in that neighbourhood. Turn right on Avenue Magloire Ambroise. The sections of the park are on the right. All along the Champs de Mars, the fences are lined with second-hand books, interspersed with a wide variety of small items for sale, and vendors also sell candy, food and drinks. You can go in to the park at the next entrance and wander around. There may be people filling huge plastic jugs with water from a pipe flowing into

Map on page 280

TIP

When visiting the Secrétairerie d'Etat au Tourisme it is best to make an appointment in advance, if you want to speak to someone at length.

BELOW: fresh produce on sale at a street market.

a big cement basin, or a group of young men playing football on an impromptu playing field – the long cement promenade.

At the second street look left, to see a long, mustard-coloured building, the former army barracks, **Casernes Dessalines** (no longer in use, and closed to the public). Enter the park and continue in the same direction to the **Musée du Panthéon National Haïtien** (MUPANAH) **F**. There are often groups engaged in lively discussions in this area of the park, reminiscent of "Speakers' Corner" in London's Hyde Park. The whole museum is underground except for a few architectural elements – a large fountain (that may never have water in it) and some fanciful, futuristic skylights, reminiscent of high-tech US architect Buckminster Fuller, which give the impression of a sculpture garden.

The Musée du Panthéon National has some informative historical exhibits about early Haitian leaders including diorama displays of clothing, Toussaint L'Ouverture's pocket watch, documents and an oil painting of King Henri Christophe by Welsh artist Richard Evans, who directed the monarch's Art Academy at Sans Souci Palace *(see page 310)*. The original anchor from Christopher Columbus's flagship, *Santa María*, which sank after hitting the reef near Cap Haïtien on Christmas Eve 1492, is also on display.

Place des Héros de l'Indépendence

Turning left at the museum exit, walk two blocks to the gleaming white **Palais National G**. It dominates the large, open square and its tree-lined grounds include an incongruously green lawn. The palace resembles a gigantic spun sugar wedding cake, which belies some of the egregious events that have taken place within its walls. Most recently, President Aristide made a stand

If you're curious to see a 'Vaudou show', ask at the Oloffson, but expect to pay a hefty fee to the officiating 'houngan'. Alternatively you can wait until you go to Jacmel and make an appointment to see Mme Yclide La Guerre (see page 324)

BELOW: *Le Marron Inconnu with the Palais National in the background.*

there during the 1991 coup and was barely saved from losing his life only by the timely arrival of the French ambassador. The present edifice was constructed in 1918 on the site of the previous one, which was blown up in 1912, with the then president still inside. The palace is not open to the public, but passers by are no longer made to walk on the other side of the square – as they were in the days of "Papa Doc" Duvalier.

Across the square, *Le Marron Inconnu* (The Unknown Slave) , the striking statue by Albert Mangonès, depicts a man blowing the call to revolution on a conch shell. Other statues of Haiti's independence heroes – Dessalines, Pétion and Toussaint L'Ouverture – and an eternal flame dedicated to those who died for Haiti's independence complete the square.

Mobile art

If one could just find a place to sit with a cool drink and watch the *tap-taps* passing, it would be like a moving psychedelic art gallery with messages in Kreyòl, English, and French incorporated into themes from religion, sport, Vaudou and even purely geometric designs. Some of the designs could easily be displayed in any of the city's galleries. There are images of women, the Virgin and Child and motifs from nature, and humorous adages that manifest the Haitian wry sense of satire and religious proverbs.

Just as in other parts of the Caribbean, vans used for public transport are given colourful names by their drivers, but Haitians have taken this form of indentification to a higher level. Don't be surprised to see a *tap-tap* approach you bearing the label: "*paix, amour*" (peace, love) or "*sans Jesus tout est nul*" (all is nothing without Jesus).

Try the Iron Market for wood sculptures and other crafts. Be sure to haggle to get the best price.

LEFT: onions for sale on a city street.
BELOW: the People's Statue.

Marché de Fer

It seems impossible in a dry, dusty, often dirty city that *tap-taps* always look so gleamingly clean and shiny, yet they do. *Taps-taps* constantly congregate in front of the **Marché de Fer** (Iron Market) ❶, crossing and re-crossing paths as they ply Port-au-Prince with their passengers.

The Marché building, on the frenzied Boulevard Jean-Jacques Dessalines, is an iron structure topped by two minarets, painted a pleasing ochre. Legend has it that the structure was manufactured in France for the Turkish government, but that in the late 1880s, Haiti's President, Hyppolite, bought it when the pre-fabricated pieces of the building were shipped to the Caribbean by mistake.

The several blocks surrounding the Iron Market throb with vitality as only a market can. Hawkers of all ages pass with baskets of varying sizes on their heads, heaped with a phenomenal assortment of items – giant steel wool pads, bolts of fabric, piles of plastic plates and washing-up bowls. *Tap-taps* and private vehicles drop passengers here and there, start and stop in unpredictable places, or try to speed by, so great care and attention are vital in this area.

This is one place where it's good to have a Kreyòl speaker with you. It's also one of the main places to be particularly protective of bags, wallets and cameras. Photographers will find a host of colourful and often bizarre subjects in the market, but remember that Haitians are not keen on having their pictures taken, so it is always best to ask permission before lining someone up in your viewfinder. Alternatively bring a telephoto lens for your camera, or find an unobtrusive spot (next to impossible in the sea of curious humanity here), be discreet and choose your moment.

BELOW: vendors at the Marché de Fer.

The entrances to the actual Iron Market building are obscured by the merchandise stands packed together outside, but just pass through them at any small opening then find one of the open doorways. To get your bearings before plunging into the warren of narrow aisles inside, stand facing the building. The left half contains mostly household items – kitchen goods and an amazing assortment of food – and it is basically a big open space with stands crowded everywhere. The right half is jammed with individual booths of 1 sq metre (9 sq ft) and separated from each other by high, dark, thin wooden walls. This is the section for paintings, sculptures, handicrafts and souvenirs.

Once inside, there is little light and even less air circulation. The smell of sweat, salted fish, spices and overripe fruit can be truly overpowering. The whole milieu feels very congested and the aisles are usually packed. Although a few stalls have a fan, it's really not the place for anyone who suffers from claustrophobia. Also be prepared for a crush of sellers trying to solicit business. They endeavour to take everyone to their stalls and failing that, tag along, resisting all attempts to shake them. Eventually only one is left and he sticks like glue, so that he'll get a commission on anything you buy because he tells the vendor that he brought you to them.

Among the profusion of art and artefacts, treasures and trash, it is possible to find some top notch handicrafts, but it's good to have prior knowledge of comparative quality and prices elsewhere. If shopping for paintings, make sure they're original oils, not acrylics or copies. This is the place to buy soapstone sculptures, mahogany carvings, decorative wrought-iron items, and Vaudou prayer flags and accoutrements. While the prices here can be very reasonable, they will certainly be inflated by 50–100 percent for any tourist and it's imperative to bargain. Vendors think less of you, not more, if you don't haggle.

Map on page 280

Paintings produced by Adam Léontus and Jasmine Joseph in the 1960s decorate the panels around the choir gallery and the organ in the Sainte Trinité Episcopal Cathedral.

BELOW: the high altar in Sainte Trinité Episcopal Church.

Map on page 280

Hector Hyppolite was a Vaudou priest and house painter when he was plucked from obscurity and his artistic work exhibited at the Centre d'Art.

BELOW: Port-au-Prince is colourful at carnival time. **RIGHT:** buildings on the city streets are unmissable.

Eglise Sainte Trinité

The **Eglise Sainte Trinité Episcopal ❿**, about four blocks from the Champs de Mars, at the corner of Rue Courte and Rue Pavée, is a great place to watch the busy world go by and take photographs of *tap-taps*, without being as conspicuous as at the Iron Market. The church contains very impressive murals painted by some of Haiti's greatest *naïf* artists, including Philomé Obin, Castera Bazile and Rigaud Benoît. Traditional biblical scenes are peopled with Haitian faces the artists knew, and are set in Haitian backgrounds that they could recognise and identify with. These unique murals demonstrate that spirituality itself, no matter how it is expressed, is the most important factor in religious practice. The paintings should have gone a long way to resolving the debates about whether co-mingling Christian and Vaudou symbols diminishes one or the other.

Ambrose Thompson is a wonderful gentleman who enjoys sharing his intimate knowledge of the details of the murals and artists with interested visitors. Usually in the church at some time during the day, his stories are fascinating and he would appreciate a few gourdes for the telling of them.

High Art in Sainte Trinité

Works of art by famous Haitian artists line the walls of the Church and stand proudly behind the altar. Most were painted between 1949 and 1951 and illustrate stories from the Bible. Displayed in the apse are *The Crucifixion* by Philomé Obin, *The Nativity* by Rigaud Benoît (left panel in the apse), *The Ascension* by Castera Bazile (right panel) and *The Angels* by Gabriel Lévêque (above the three apse panels).

On the south side of the building in the Lady Chapel are *The Miracle at Cana* painted by Wilson Bigaud when he was just 22 years old, *The Flight Into Egypt* by Toussaint Auguste (above the east window), *The Visitation* by Fernand Pierre (above the west columns) and *The Anunciation* by Adam Léontus (on the outside of the Lady Chapel).

The South Transcept of the church houses *The Temptation of Adam and Eve* by Toussaint Auguste (above the transcept door), *The Temptation of Christ in the Wilderness* by Préfète Duffaut (above on the left) and the *Native Street Procession* also by Duffaut (above on the right). In the North Transcept you will find *The Casting out of the Money Changers* and *The Baptism of Christ* both by Castera Bazile.

A small school is attached to the Eglise Sainte Trinité Episcopal, and there are occasional concerts of choral and classical music (for details call: 222 5638). There is also a little gift shop in an adjoining building, selling a good range of books and postcards which you can send to the folks back home.

Three blocks down Rue Courte stands the larger, but less aesthetically appealing pink-and-white Catholic **Notre Dame Cathedral**. It was completed in 1915, and some say the twin-spired structure bears a passing resemblance to the Sacré Coeur in Paris. The cathedral contains a vast shrine to the Virgin Mary. On Sunday, there are huge crowds of fervent worshippers as well as a great many beggars, hoping to benefit from some Christian charity. ❏

HISPANIOLA'S TROPICAL FLORA AND FAUNA

The Dominican Republic offers a more spectacular variety of plants and wildlife than its neighbour. But there are still areas of natural beauty in Haiti

Much of Hispaniola has been devastated by deforestation, especially in Haiti where trees are felled to make charcoal or for firewood. The removal of the forests has reached danger level in some areas, laying waste to the land and exposing it to the harsh elements. In spite of this both the Dominican Republic and Haiti remain gems of the Caribbean with bright, rare and exotic flowers. Samaná in the east of the Dominican Republic and the fertile central valley of Cibao – the nation's bread basket – sustain important agricultural crops such as sugar cane, tobacco, coffee and cocoa, while the Artibonite Valley in Haiti is that country's rice basket. Fruit trees laden with coconut, mango and orange grow everywhere, but cashew *(above)* and cacti thrive only in the dry regions.

FLORAL TRIBUTES

In Santo Domingo pink bougainvillaea adorns the walls of colonial homes. Tall palm trees line the Malecón and shade the city's parks, and the botanical gardens are brimming with fragrant flora.

Elsewhere, tropical flora flourish in the cool mountains and national parks such as southwestern Parque Nacional Sierra de Baoruco. In alpinesque Jarabacoa and Constanza there are mountainside meadows of wild flowers and pine forests at the foot of Pico Duarte. Hato Mayor, in the east, has a horticultural centre with a variety of exotic plants from anthuriums and bromeliads and an aviary and butterfly house. Beautiful orchids grow in abundance; 300 species have been identified so far.

▽ **BEAUTIFUL BUTTERFLIES**
Colourful butterflies can be seen flitting among the pretty mountain flora in the east near San Pedro de Macorís and in the botanical gardens in Santo Domingo.

△ **IGUANAS LOVE DRY HEAT**
The iguana, a protected reptile, inhabits hot, dry bush areas of Hispaniola including southern Haiti's Parc National Macaya.

◁ **A GREEN EMBLEM**
The *cotica* (also called the green parrot) is the Dominican Republic's national bird. Spot it in the native palm forests.

▷ **LOUNGE LIZARD**
Crocodiles lounge around the salt water of Lago Enriquillo on the hot, arid Isla Cabritos and Etang Saumâtre, east of Port-Au-Prince.

⊲ ON THE RÍO CHAVÓN

The picturesque views over the Río Chavón are a feast for the eyes. Flowing through a ravine below Altos de Chavón, the river is bordered by forest land and vibrant wild flowers.

△ BANANA BOUNTY

The banana is believed to have been introduced to Hispaniola from the Canary Islands, but its name is thought to derive from West African Bantu.

△ THE RARE HUTIA

A rare endemic mammal, the hutia (*Capromys Pilorides*) lives in forests such as the Massif de la Selle, Haiti.

▷ FEARSOME CREATURE

The rhinoceros iguana (*Cyclura Cornuta*) appears fearsome but in fact tends to be timid.

THE ANIMAL KINGDOM

Nature lovers are drawn to Hispaniola because of its national parks, salt water lakes and virgin cloud forest which support rare wildlife. In the Dominican Republic the vast Parque Nacional del Este and Isla Saona in the southeast are home to great turtles and they are ideal for spotting some of the rarest birds in the Caribbean such as the Hispaniolan lizard cuckoo. Deciduous forest and mangroves are the natural habitat of the endangered hutia, solenodon and the rhinoceros iguana. The hot dry conditions on Isla Cabritos make it ideal for crocodiles, iguanas and flamingos. The area around Etang Saumâtre, east of Haiti's capital, has similar wildlife to Isla Cabritos, and more than 100 species of waterfowl. Patient visitors may glimpse the shy manatee at Manatí Park Bávaro in the east, also a preserve for reptiles, birds and dolphins. A variety of marine life call the warm Antillean waters home, including the banded coral shrimp *(above)*. And the humpback whale mates on the Banco de la Plata *(see page 156)*. There are no poisonous snakes on the island.

EXCURSIONS FROM PORT-AU-PRINCE

Map on page 278

To escape the heat and crowds of the capital take a hike over a mountain range, visit the cool hill top retreats of the well heeled, or explore the workshops of Haiti's famed metalwork artists

Port-au-Prince

Outside the capital, a hilly land unfolds which offers relief from the hustle and bustle and oppressive heat of the city. To the south are Pétionville and Kenscoff, which have fabulous views of the city landscape below. East of Port-au-Prince is Croix-des-Bouquets and the beach resorts of the Côte des Arcadins lie to the north. At the present time there are few destinations recommended for tourism northeast of the city. Route Nationale 3 (RN3) to **Hinche** is actually 128 km (80 miles) of dirt track that requires a four-wheel-drive vehicle and takes at least five hours on a good day. The area around Hinche has been the axis for peasant unrest for a long time. Until the situation changes, it's preferable to visit the other parts of Haiti that are beautiful and easier to reach.

Less than an hour's drive east of Port-au-Prince and still on the Plaine du Cul-de-Sac, **Croix-des-Bouquets ❷** is one of the country's little-known jewels. This small, neat town provides most of the wonderful metal sculptures sold in Haiti. The material looks like wrought iron, but is actually metal from recycled oil drums. Wander along the main street and down a few of the lanes to discover many interesting workshops and their artisan inhabitants who are happy to show off their designs. Some of the larger pieces with intricate cutouts and Vaudou symbols are truly exceptional. One caveat – almost everyone in the village speaks only kreyòl, so be sure to travel with a phrase book or an interpreter.

On the approach to Croix-des-Bouquets, just at the beginning of the main part of town, the large, fenced-in area on the right is a livestock market and *abattoir* (slaughterhouse) where people bring their animals to be sold and slaughtered. There's a very lively market every Friday lining the streets in the vicinity.

Ville-Bonheur ❸, a small village on the Central Plateau, in the hills near **Mirebalais ❹**, attracts thousands of people for an annual pilgrimage every 15 July. Visitors include practising Catholics, Vaudou practitioners, and some who believe in both faiths. The 35-km (22-mile) trip from Port-au-Prince takes about three hours. The origins of the pilgrimage lie in events which occurred in 1884, when locals reported seeing an image of the Virgin Mary in a palm tree. They built a church to commemorate the spot.

The stunning waterfall, **Saut d'Eau ❺**, about 4 km (2½ miles) away, is a very sacred Vaudou site where believers bathe to purify themselves, before lighting candles to enlist the help of the ancient spirits believed to live there. The ceremony is one of many examples of overlapping Christian and Vaudou traditions and sites in Haiti.

LEFT: carrying baskets on the road from Port-au-Prince to Kenscoff. **BELOW:** pilgrims at Saut d'Eau.

This pretty door detail is characteristic of Haitian architectural style.

There is considerable potential for the future development of environmentally friendly ecotourism at the inland salt-waterlake, **Etang Saumâtre ⑥**, but currently there is no real infrastructure. For the more adventurous and hardy who will go anyway, the north shore offers better opportunities for viewing birds and wildlife, including flamingos and rare American crocodiles. The habitats on the south shore have been affected by the highway to the border.

PÉTIONVILLE AND HILL EXCURSIONS

Some travel guides refer to **Pétionville ⑦** and the hill towns above it as "excursions" from Port-au-Prince. While these are separate and distinct destinations, their proximity to and short travel time from the capital make them more like suburbs. So Pétionville makes a satisfactory base when choosing a hotel for your sojourn.

Pétionville

BELOW: the hubbub of Place St Pierre.
RIGHT: a colourful *tap-tap* is an everyday sight.

At 450 metres (1,500 ft) above sea level and several degrees cooler than downtown, Pétionville was once a refuge for the capital's élite. That hasn't changed, but now that it is more accessible, it is also a middle- to upper-class suburb. International aid organisations and embassies call it home, too. Named for the mulatto general, Alexandre Pétion, who unified Haiti's south during the early 19th-century revolution, Pétionville has many of Haiti's finest hotels and restaurants. There is also a casino, a 9-hole golf course and a few tennis clubs.

The town is teeming with trendy, often-changing restaurants, and has numerous night spots, art galleries, and boutiques. Most of them are within or close to a six block area bordered by Rue Lamarre and Rue Grégoire, Rue Panaméricaine

Map on page 278

(Avenue John Brown) and the Place St Pierre. Except for those few established places in Port-au-Prince that will always draw patrons and devotees, Pétionville is the place for anyone considering an evening out.

Three parallel roads lead up to Pétionville from Port-au-Prince. Route de Delmas (called Delmas), the northernmost, probably has the most traffic and minivan-type public transport. All streets that cross it are numbered (eg. Delmas 31, Delmas 60), making destinations in this populous district relatively easy to find. Street numbers are included in addresses and when giving directions. These numbered roads can be quite long. Some of them stretch between Delmas and the next main artery, Avenue John Brown, so it's important to determine exactly which main road is nearer your destination or it could be a long, hot walk.

Avenue John Brown is fun. First, everyone calls it **Lalue**. Second, it changes names part way up, at about Delmas 60, and becomes Rue Panaméricaine, (or just Panaméricaine). Of the three, it has the most *tap-taps* and *publiques* (the shared taxis with a red ribbon on the rear view mirror). In the middle of Pétionville, Rue Panaméricaine meets the end of Delmas, as well as Delmas 105 (right at the fork). Delmas 105 (also called Route de Frères) becomes Boulevard du 15 Octobre (the date Aristide returned to Haiti in 1994). It is a little longer leaving Pétionville this way, but it might bypass much of the city-centre traffic. It passes the airport, then intersects with RN1.

The southernmost road is Route du Canapé Vert (called Canapé Vert, literally meaning Green Canopy). This is the prettiest way to go from Port-au-Prince up to Pétionville, and it has the best views and the least traffic. Each bend in the road opens up a new vista as you make the scenic ascent.

From **Champs de Mars** to Pétionville, depending on the traffic and driver, it

Route Noailles in Croix-des-Bouquets contains some of the best metalwork workshops.

BELOW: Canapé Vert in the hills.

is a fascinating 15-minute, animated drive with the opportunity to observe the tumultuous hubbub of day-to-day life along the way. There's also the chance of the ultimate Port-au-Prince commuter experience – the hair-raising half second of pure panic when a fast-approaching vehicle threatens a head-on collision.

Head for the hills

Refreshing excursions into the cooler, serene hills above Pétionville merit one or two days of leisurely exploration. You will be rewarded with outstanding views of Port-au-Prince harbour, the city and the Plaine du Cul-de-Sac from both the destinations and the winding roads between them. However, if time is short, the visit could be condensed into a half day. If you are planning to use public transport, *tap-taps* and *camionettes* leave from near the Pétionville market.

Kenscoff is still a small hill station with many beautiful summer homes and a weekly market. Fermathe hosts the Baptist Mission. Boutilliers has the best views. And Forts Jacques and Alexandre have cool pine groves along with excellent views. A recent addition to these bucolic panoramas is the proliferation of construction up in the hills and the profusion of spectacular multi-million dollar homes throughout the area. In a land of such stark poverty, the ostentatious wealth of the fortunate few seems particularly conspicuous in the heights overlooking steamy Port-au-Prince.

Starting from Place St Pierre in Pétionville, drive past the police station and the surrounding swarms of people. Continue on Route de Kenscoff for about 10 minutes and turn right at **United Sculptors of Haiti,** which is worth a stop to look at woodcarvings. The road passes a large quarry and an enormous, ersatz castle. Built as a tasting room by the **Barbancourt Rum Company**, it has been

BELOW: an ersatz castle built for Barbancourt rum tasting.

mostly closed for years due to a dispute within the family. It was a disco for a brief period and a new project for a restaurant has been proposed.

Barbancourt still produces Haiti's fine rums at its distillery on RN1. The rums are made from sugar cane juice rather than the molasses often used elsewhere. A visit to one of the cane juice distilleries on the Plaine du Cul-de-Sac is an excellent excursion that could be combined with a tour of former plantation sites on **La Route des Esclaves** (The Slave Route) and a trip to Croix-des-Bouquets *(see page 297)*.

The road to **Kenscoff** ❽ provides great views of Port-au-Prince as it twists and winds its way up to the cool hill resort at 1,500 metres (4,900 ft) above sea level. There are some beautiful country homes whose owners spend July and August here to escape the heat in the city. **Hotel Florville** has live music on weekends, and is a nice spot for refreshments or a meal. **L'Infini** restaurant also has live music at weekends. At the end of the road, **Le Pistacchio**, a modest, family-run restaurant with excellent food may be open at weekends, too. Kenscoff has a small weekly market that is interesting because of the way it is spaced along the streets. The market is much less crowded and frenetic than most others, but you will still be expected to haggle for a bargain. Ask in Pétionville to find out on which day the market is held.

Kenscoff is difficult to surpass, yet for hikers **Furcy** is the next plateau. Because the road after Kenscoff is in poor condition, it may take considerable effort to reach the summit, which is distinguished by its radio mast. The panorama south over the pine and montane cloud forests that cover the **Massif de la Selle** ❾ makes the effort well worthwhile. Furcy is the jumping-off spot for the 5–6-hour hike down to the Arcadian **Auberge de la Visite** at secluded

Map
on page
278

ABOVE: bars
and restaurants
have live music
at the weekend.
BELOW:
riding through
the rolling hills.

Map on page 278

Independent Haiti had no navy, so in the event of an invasion the plan was to set the plains on fire and retreat into the mountain fortresses. There was never any need to test the plan, but the Caco guerrillas used some of the forts during the battle against the 1918–20 US occupation.

BELOW: all smiles.
RIGHT:
an impression
of country life.

Seguin (50 km/30 miles) in **Parc National La Visite.** Furcy is scheduled to undergo development as a tourist destination in the future.

Back on the main road, continue up winding switchbacks that present another verdant vista around each turn, as the air becomes noticeably cooler. About 20 minutes later, just after a rather sharp turn, the **Mountain Maid Mission** appears on the right. If the car goes hurtling past a wall on the left covered with brightly coloured paintings, that's the spot, so slow down, turn around and go back to the mission. Some folks visit the Baptist-run mission in **Fermathe** just for lunch in the cafeteria because it serves American-style hamburgers, french fries and ice cream. A school in the complex teaches useful skills to underprivileged children, such as classes in crafts, farming and irrigation. The resulting orderly terraced hills, often shrouded in mist, can be admired from large, open windows in the cafeteria. It's mesmerising to sit and watch the changing tableau, from a bright, golden sun burnishing the green hills, to soft, hushed, grey-blue mist concealing the sky and mountain tops.

Much of the mission's production is sold in its two shops. One sells potted plants, seeds, some produce and excellent bakery goods. The other is a handicraft and souvenir shop with very good prices. Just outside the mission grounds, other handicrafts not available in the mission shop are for sale, and, of course, there are those paintings on the wall across the road.

The Forts

Fort Jacques and **Fort Alexandre** ⑩ were built by Haitians after they won independence from France, to guard against future invasion attempts. A turn-off near the mission leads to Fort Jacques 10 minutes away. The walls of the 1804 fortress are intact after restoration in the early 1990s. For a small sum, a young boy will unlock the entry gate, but there really isn't much to see inside. The main reason to visit is for the breathtaking views – west to Port-au-Prince and north over the Plaine du Cul-de-Sac. Fort Alexandre was never finished and very little remains of the original structure.

The other reason to visit the remains of the two forts (built on adjoining summits and said to connect underground) is to enjoy a cool, refreshing respite from the heat. The scent of pine trees is a rare pleasure and it is possible to picnic at either place.

On the way back to Pétionville, stop at another pleasantly cool spot 1,000 metres (3,300 ft) above Port-au-Prince. When the sky is clear, **Boutilliers** ⑪ has the best views of the city and its entire basin. And it is the most spectacular place to watch the sunset.

About an hour's drive north of Port-au-Prince is the **Côte des Arcadins** *(see page 342),* best known for its luxury resorts and beaches. The towns which line the coast offer a variety of diversions including scuba diving, snorkelling and horse riding. North of Cabaret is Montrouis and nearby the resort of Moulin sur la Mer, which is home to the **Musée d'Ogier-Fombrun.** The museum is especially significant to visitors following La Route des Esclaves because the display boards (in French) give a full history of Haiti from the Taínos and the slave trade to postwar times. ❏

THE NORTH COAST

Haunted by the legacy of its turbulent past, the area around Cap-Haïtien, the country's second city, is rich in history and dramatic scenery, combined in its spectacular palace and fortress

Maps:
Area 278
Town 309

Today the north coast is economically, politically and geographically remote from the capital, Port-au-Prince, but in the past it scooped most of Haiti's major historical events. In 1492 Columbus arrived on these shores and built the first European fort in the New World. The fertile Plaine du Nord, which surrounds Cap-Haïtien, was not so much the "bread basket" as the "sugar bowl" of the island during the colonial period, and the great northern plantations flourished by exporting their sugar to Europe. But the success of the plantations was directly proportional to the suffering of the slaves and consequently the north was the crucible of the slaves' revolt which led to Haiti's independence. The only discernible remnants of the grand plantations are isolated gate posts dotted around the northern landscape. There are many coastal forts in the area, constructed both before and after independence. The flamboyant kingdom of former slave King Henri Christophe has endowed the area with more spectacular edifices, including the Citadelle and the Sans Souci palace. The coastline, especially to the west of Cap-Haïtien, is some of the most beautiful in Haiti and has many shipwrecks to explore. And Île de la Tortue, the island off the coast of Port-de-Paix, has a rich and colourful history due to the filibusters and buccaneers who used it as a hideaway during the 15th century.

PRECEDING PAGES: a view from the Citadelle La Ferrière. **LEFT:** the ruins of Sans Souci palace. **BELOW:** colourful Cap-Haïtien.

Cap-Haïtien ⓬ has a casual and relaxed atmosphere which acts as a counterpoint to the frantic pace of Port-au-Prince. The atmosphere is particularly enjoyable in the early evening as Cap-Haïtiens rest on their balconies, chatting, joking and fanning themselves. Cap-Haïtien is luckily bereft of the usual sharp hustlers and would-be guides, which makes strolling around town a pleasant experience.

The city has a homogenised architectural style owing more to Spanish than French influence. The streets are narrow, which always gives shade on one side whatever the time of day. The centre of town is laid out in a simple grid system and uses numbers and letters for identification. All the east–west running streets are numbered Rue 1 to 24, beginning at the southern end of the city. The north–south streets, parallel with the coastline, have been designated letters, from Rue A to Q. These start from the street closest to the Boulevard, the wide avenue which runs alongside the sea front.

Historically, the roots of Cap-Haïtien can be traced to a small settlement called Bas-du-Cap, established by buccaneers in the 17th century. The small town was renamed Cap-François by the French authorities and that was modernised to Cap-Français in the mid-18th century. Thanks to the extremely fertile Plaine-du-Nord that surrounded the city, Cap-Français became France's wealthiest colonial capital. It was soon celebrated for its opulent neoclassical architecture and referred to as the "Paris of the Antilles". After independence in 1804, the city was renamed, with good reason, Cap-Haïtien. The city has been devastated by two great fires in the 18th century, razed to ground by Henri Christophe at the beginning of the 19th century and flattened by an earthquake later that century, so very little of its former grandeur remains today.

One of the finest vestiges of colonial architecture is the **Roi Christophe Ⓐ**, a hotel on Rue 24B that was originally built for the French governor in 1724. The style is more reminiscent of Spanish colonial than French, housing a shady central courtyard surrounded by pillared archways. Its marble-floored terraces look out onto a verdant walled garden, beyond which are the busy town streets. Continuing north from the Roi Christophe, across a small canal into the area called Carenage, the street eventually joins the coastal road which winds its way to **Plage Rival**, the dirty, litter-strewn city beach. The city's three old French fort sites are along this route. A couple of piles of rusty, hollow cannon-balls on the left is all that remains of Fort Magny. **Fort Joseph** is perched on the edge of the cliff on the right, but access is prohibited. The most impressive site is **Fort Picolet**, where some of the staircases and walls are still standing and where a considerable arsenal of antique cannons can be seen.

The **Place d'Armes Ⓑ**, enclosed by Rues F and H and Rues 20 and 18, is a sleepy, spacious square in the centre of town. In the past it was the scene of a number of bloody showcase executions by the French. Many of the martyrs of the Haitian revolution died here. François Makandal, the maroon chief turned poisoner, was burnt at the stake here in front of an audience of thousands of slaves. Chavannes and Ogé, leaders of a mulatto uprising, were publicly tortured in the square and Boukman, the Vaudou priest who inspired the slaves to rebellion during a clandestine ceremony in Bois Caïman, was beheaded. Now young students read books and eat ice creams in the shadow of the domed **Cathédrale de Notre Dame** , built in 1774, and the Université du Roi Christophe, which was built on the ruins of a post-independence royal palace.

There is an iron market to the southwest of the Place d'Armes, bordered by Rues I and K and Rues 9 and 11 where women hawk a cornucopia of fruits, spices and vegetables. Further south, between Rues I and K and Rues 2 and 4, there is a more domestic market, selling pots, pans and everything imaginable that can possibly be moulded from plastic. At the point where Rue 17 hits the Boulevard there is a small craft market where paintings, embroidery and wooden carvings are on sale.

Philomé Obin, the north's most eminent painter, was born and lived in Cap-Haïtien, from 1891. His house still stands on the corner of Rue L, also known as Espanole, and is worth a visit. Further along Route Nationale 1, about 5 km (3 miles) south past the gaudy yellow city gates called **Barrière Bouteille**, is the district of **Vertières**. This is the historic site of Dessalines' victorious battle on 18 November 18 1803, which led to the capture of Cap-Français, the defeat of the French and liberty for the black slaves. There is a roadside monument dedicated to the heroes of the liberation, built in 1953 to commemorate 150 years of freedom.

During the colonial period there were more than a thousand vast plantations located on the **Plaine du Nord** to the south of Cap-Haïtien. Although most of the ruins are lost there are some reminders, such as the monument to Toussaint L'Ouverture on the site of the Bréda plantation. A society dedicated to the

Makandal was a maroon chief originally from Guinea. Expert in the skill of poisoning, he hatched a plan to eliminate the cruel colonists. Arsenic was his chosen toxin because it was a common insecticide, but he also used roots, berries, polluted earth and ground glass. His campaign of terror lasted for six years.

BELOW: in the historic quarter.

Some of the statues and monuments in the grounds of the Sans Souci palace have survived the 1842 earthquake and neglect.

BELOW: riding from Milot, overlooking Sans Souci.

protection of Haiti's historical sites, ISPAN, is on Rue 15B. It can supply information about the various locations in the country.

Sans Souci Palace

Three years after independence, Henri Christophe, a former slave, crowned himself king of the northern province. Christophe attempted to imitate the royal dynasties of Europe, building nine palaces, eight châteaux and the most marvellous of his creations, the awesome Citadelle. Henri built palaces at Jean Rabel, Cap-Haïtien, and Petite-Rivière but the jewel in his crown was his elegant **Sans Souci** palace ⓭ (daily; entrance fee) from which he held court to a newly created nobility. Even though Sans Souci was partially destroyed by the earthquake of 1842, which also flattened Cap-Haïtien, the skeleton remains and still conveys a sense of its original beauty. It is a startling apparition in the prosaic Haitian countryside, especially through the early morning mist. Sans Souci can be seen on a day trip from Cap-Haïtien by taking the Rue de l'Aéroport to Milot, 20 km (12 miles) outside the city.

Sans Souci was commissioned in 1810, during the height of Henri Christophe's regal pretensions, and completed by 1813. With a burning desire to rival the grandeur of Versailles, he created the most ostentatious palace in the West Indies. It contained state chambers, banquet halls, ballrooms and even surreptitious spy holes through to the kitchens to check on the poisoning habits of his cooks. Cabinet makers, painters and stone masons were brought from Italy, France and England to contribute to the sumptuous decorations. There was even a basic under-floor cooling system, fuelled by nearby mountain springs. The palace itself was modelled on the Prussian palace at Potsdam, but

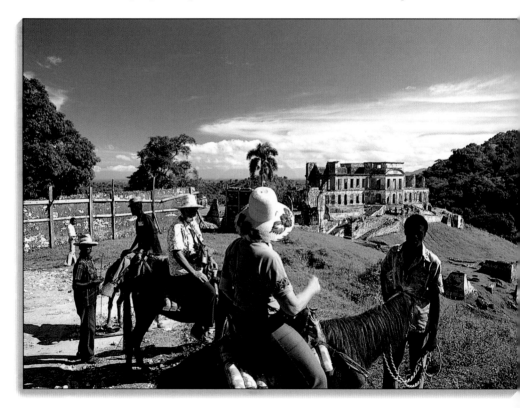

the ornamental gardens were designed to resemble those in Versailles. The palace grounds covered 8 hectares (20 acres) and the outbuildings included a printing press, library, hospital, mint and barracks. This was the hub of Henri Christophe's northern administration, situated inland as protection against a sea-borne attack.

Map on page 278

The Citadelle

Milot is the starting point for the trek, be it on foot or horseback, up to the **Citadelle La Ferrière** ⑭ (daily; entrance fee). The formidable Citadelle is a potent symbol of the severe paranoia within Haitian society during the early 19th century. The fear of re-invasion and further enslavement was deep-rooted and the Citadelle was built to combat any attack. The grim colossus sits on the peak of the 900-metre (2,950 ft) **Pic La Ferrière**, dominating the landscape. There is a car park near to Sans Souci where you can buy tickets for both the sites, costing around 25 gourdes, and another car park closer to the base of the Citadelle where horses can be hired for about 50 gourdes. The 1.5 km (1 mile) hike to the summit of the Citadelle is quite arduous, so take a sun hat and plenty of water.

Work on the mighty Citadelle began in 1804 but it wasn't until 1817 that the last stone was dragged up the vertiginous Pic La Ferrière. An army of more than 20,000 conscripted former slaves hauled thousands of tons of stone, bronze cannons and cannon balls up to the site. The design was the work of Henry Beese and Henri Barre, an English and French architectural collaboration hired by Christophe. At first sight, the Citadelle resembles the prow of a gigantic, modernist ship thrusting its way through the mountains. The shape is stunning and almost futuristic for its time. The fortress, with walls 4 metres (13 ft) thick

Designed by the mulatto engineer Henri Besse, La Citadelle was Henri Christophe's final grand gesture and resting place. Partially paralysed by a stroke he shot himself in the head as Republicans converged on Sans Souci in 1820.

BELOW: the cannons still stand guard.

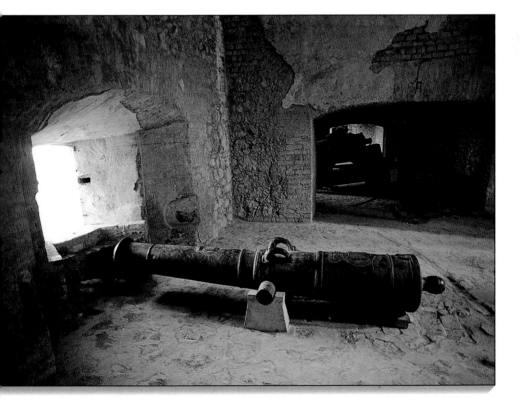

BELOW: the ruins of Fort Dauphin.

and reaching a height of 40 metres (130 ft) in places, was impenetrable and held enough supplies to feed a garrison for over a year. From the apex the army could overlook Cap-Haïtien, the coast, the northern plains and the southern routes. The view of the **Chaîne du Bonnet** including the **Mount Bonnet à l'Evêque** is spectacular. It was within the royal suite of Sans Souci that Henri Christophe shot himself – some say in the head, others say in the heart – with a silver bullet in 1820 as his rebellious subjects rose up against his autocratic rule, but it was high within the confines of the Citadelle that his body was finally laid to rest encased in a vat of quicklime.

The road to **Fort Liberté** ⓯ is a left turn off the Route de l'Aéroport, a few kilometres out of Cap-Haïtien. It's hard to believe that this dusty one-horse and one-telephone town was once a historically strategic city. The only reminders are the remains of the old forts dotted around the wide bay. **Fort Dauphin**, built in 1732, is in the best condition and can be found by following the main road through the town gates and straight to the sea front. The red stone structure snakes around the bay and houses a powder room, arched vaults and the remnants of an old chapel. The town was called Fort Dauphin by the French but renamed Fort Liberté by Toussaint L'Ouverture when he captured it in 1796. More recently, in the 20th century, Fort Liberté was the site of the world's largest sisal plantation until the production of nylon killed the market.

The route between Cap-Haïtien and Fort Liberté passes through a small town called **Limonade** and close by the small coastal village, **Bord de Mer** ⓰. This is generally believed to be the site of **La Navidad**, the first European fort built in the New World, though the only evidence which points to this conclusion is a wooden stake found on the site and carbon dated as originating from the 15th century. Columbus dropped anchor in the **Baie d'Acul**, which is west of Cap-Haï-tien, on 21 December 1492. On Christmas Eve his flagship, the *Santa Maria*, was sunk by coral further along the coast. The wreckage was used to build a fort, La Navidad, where Columbus left a garrison of 40 men. A year later, the fort had been destroyed and the troops killed by the indigenous Amerindians.

West of Cap-Haïtien, on the northern coast of the cape, are some of the most beautiful beaches, bays and cliffs to be found in Haiti. The western continuation of Rue 21 from Cap-Haïtien forms the rough route into this area and takes about 20 minutes by car. The first accessible beach is **Cormier Plage** which has a small hotel complex with diving and sailing facilities.

Further along is **Labadie Nord** ⓱, a walled peninsula, owned by the Royal Caribbean Cruise Lines, which is somewhat of an anomaly in this otherwise remote area. Three times a week, on Monday, Tuesday and Thursday, the cruise line deposits about 1,000 passengers to jet-ski, swim, sunbathe and consume food and drinks. The headland is stunningly beautiful but probably best enjoyed on one of the quiet days when the entrance charge is around US$2, as opposed to US$20 on the cruise ship day. The road continues for another 2 km (1 mile) past Labadie Nord to **Belli Beach** and water taxi access to Labadie Village, a simple fishing village, and many other hidden coves and bays.

The only other major town on the northern coast is **Port-de-Paix** ⓲, a smug-glers paradise where the honest men deal in second-hand mattresses from Miami. It's an oft-forgotten but very lively and interesting port. The wharf is the ideal place to absorb the character of the town and get a sense of the crazy world of Haitian commerce. The quay side can be piled high with second-hand fridges, bicycles, generators or T-shirts depending on the boat in dock. The

Map on page 278

BELOW:
a cruise ship dwarfs a tourist at Labadie Nord.

Map on page 278

The name filibusters originates from a 17th century French translation of fly boats, which describes the small makeshift craft that they used for pirating. And their habit of curing their meat over large low fires, called boucans *by the Amerindians, gave the pirates the name buccaneers.*

BELOW: the beach and landscape around Labadie.

whole area around the wharf transforms into a raucous street market when the ramshackle boats arrive. Historically, Port-de-Paix was the first capital of the French colony of Saint-Domingue in 1665. In an attempt to settle the buccaneers the French authorities released 100 female prisoners, mainly prostitutes and pickpockets, and shipped them to Port-de Paix. "I take thee without knowing, or caring to know, who thou art…" are recorded as the marriage vows in Port-de-Paix during this period. There are a couple of interesting churches, the attractive blue and white stucco **cathedral** on Avenue Notre Dame and the dome-roofed **Église Montfort** just off Rue du Quai. There is a typical Haitian iron market primarily selling food off Rue Sténio Vincent and Rue La Forêt.

From Port-de-Paix a rough road runs westwards towards the remote townships of **Jean Rabel** and **Môle St Nicolas**. Once a fertile agricultural area, the northwest is now the desolate site of Haiti's worst deforestation. Poverty and isolation have encouraged the development of a charcoal industry, with the result that almost all trees have been felled and turned into charcoal, which is then shipped to Port-au-Prince. A succession of droughts and near-famine conditions have turned the arid area into the country's poorest region, a situation made worse by occasional violent disputes between big landowners and landless peasants.

Heading back along the coast, boats leave for **Île de la Tortue ⑲** from **Saint-Louis du Nord**, 15 km (9 miles) east of Port-de-Paix. Passengers and their baggage are carried on to the boats on the shoulders of sailors as the wharf is almost a ruin, but the 10 km (6 miles) across the channel is exciting and invigorating.

Within 30 years of the arrival of the Spanish in Saint-Domingue, French and English pirates or filibusters were setting up covert bases in the region from which they could attack passing ships. La Tortue (or Tortuga in Spanish) was soon recognised as the perfect spot from which to wreak havoc on the merchant ships and silver fleets. The island served as a haven for the buccaneers to divide the spoils, fix their boats and drink and be merry. When sharing the plunder, the wounded were always paid off first, the amount according to the number of limbs missing.

There are no relics of La Tortue's filibustering past, but the foundations of its biggest fortress, **Fort de la Roche**, can be found at a spring above **Basse-Terre**. The boats from Saint-Louis du Nord anchor off the small wharf at **Cayonne**, which although merely a coastal hamlet, sells soft drinks and food. There is a narrow concrete road ascending steeply to **Palmiste**, the main village on the island. Skilful negotiations are needed in order to secure a place in one of the very few cars on the island that run up and down the road. During this ride the views of the **channel** and mainland Haiti are beautiful. Once in Palmiste rudimentary lodgings can be secured through the local Catholic priest, Bruno Blondeau. There is only one main road running east–west along the island and a couple of pickup trucks run back and forth all day long. The best beach is at **Pointe Ouest**, recently singled out as one of the top 10 beaches in the Caribbean. There are some caves containing pre-Columbian relics on the island that can be reached from Palmiste with the aid of a local guide. ❏

Empire Builders

La Citadelle with 4-metre (13-ft) thick walls rising to almost 40 metres (130ft) above the crest of the 914 metres (3,000 ft) high Pic La Ferrière, is a colossal monument to both the Haitian revolution and the two black generals who, after leading the country to independence, became its first two monarchs.

By the time Jean-Jacques Dessalines read the declaration of independence in Gonaïves on 1 January 1804, he had long established a reputation for great courage and cruelty. Born circa 1760, "The Tiger", who came from a plantation near Grande Rivière du Nord, distinguished himself during the Night of Fire which marked the beginning of the rebellion, by sawing people in half.

The massively built illiterate ex-slave who fought bare chested, rapidly rose to become Toussaint L'Ouverture's "most ferocious lieutenant". Although he lacked his beloved leader's intellect and gift for strategy, after Toussaint's capture it was The Black Fury's ruthlessness which brought swift victory.

Having symbolically torn the white from the French tricolor to make the Haitian flag, Dessalines emulated Napoleon, when he had himself crowned Emperor in 1805. Using the bayonet "for morale", he set about restoring the economy, seizing French- and mulatto-owned plantations for the state. He had a series of forts built in the mountains behind the major ports, to guard against invasion. Construction on La Citadelle, commanding the coast high above Cap-Haïtien, was begun in 1805. But the Emperor, with his taste for women and protracted banquets, did not have long to savour the imperial lifestyle. He was assassinated by the mulatto faction at Pont Rouge on 17 October 1806.

He was succeeded as provisional head of state by Henri Christophe, son of a black father and mûlatresse mother born either in St Kitts or Grenada circa 1767. Angered by the new constitution which limited his powers, Christophe marched on Port-au-Prince. After reaching stalemate with the mulatto leader Pétion, Christophe withdrew to set up the northern state which became the Kingdom of Hayti in 1811, when he was crowned Henri I.

Although an illiterate autocrat like Dessalines, Christophe had a high regard for culture and education. A confirmed anglophile, he invited English teachers to set up schools in the kingdom and created an aristocracy, complete with a Duke of Marmelade and a Count of Limonade.

His policy of enforced labour and the trade he developed with America and England gave him the wealth for a grandiose construction programme, aimed at establishing the new black state in the eyes of the world.

Work on the Sans Souci palace, in the foothills below La Citadelle, began in August 1811 and was completed by September 1813. The four-storey palace was made of brick plastered with yellow stucco, and red tile roofs. Among rooms of marble floors and hardwood panelling were banqueting halls, an audience chamber, an arsenal and chapel. It was here that the king shot himself, and the palace was stripped of its contents. ❑

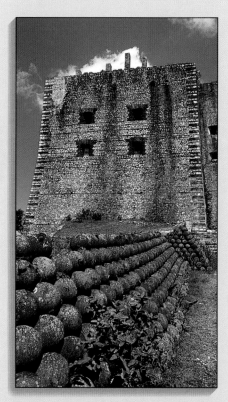

RIGHT: rusty cannon balls lead the way to La Citadelle.

THE SOUTH

*Remote, undeveloped and often difficult to reach,
the wild southern peninsula has some of Haiti's finest beaches,
most extensive forests and friendliest towns.*

Map
on page
278

South of Port-au-Prince, splendid and sleepy, southern Haiti is along mountainous, sparsely populated peninsula of about 14,400 sq km (5,000 sq miles). A long coastline alternates between sheer, steep, rocky cliffs and isolated, white or black sand beaches that stretch for miles. It is the only place in Haiti where significant expanses of evergreen forest remain intact.

The mountain chain running from east to west along the middle of the peninsula divides it roughly in half. Here nature-lovers and hikers looking for ecotourism adventures will find one of the last uncrowded sanctuaries. The **Massif de la Selle** anchors the eastern end together with the highest peak in Haiti – **Pic La Selle** at 2,674 metres (8,770 ft). **Parc National La Visite** *(see page 302)*, with its majestic pine forest, montane cloud forest, steep waterfalls and immense limestone caves ready to be explored, also shelters some endangered bird species, including the beautiful Hispaniolan trogon *(Temnotrogon roseigaster)* and the White-winged warbler *(Xenoligea montana)*, as well as wintering migrants.

At the western end of the mountains is **Massif de la Hotte**. There are few roads, so it is quite difficult reaching **Parc National Macaya**, but definitely worth the effort to enjoy the evergreen-forests, and Haiti's other cloud forest atop **Pic de Macaya** at 2,347 metres (7,700 ft) it is the national park's highest peak. Scaling the mountain is a challenging two-day climb to reach the summit and two days back. Macaya, is home to 50 endemic varieties of orchids, and two mammals found nowhere else. The Hispaniolan Hutia *(Plagiodontia aedium)* and the Solenodon *(Solenodon paradoxus)* called *"nez long"* (long nose) which is about the size of a small rat, both inhabit this wilderness *(see page 319)*. It is also home to the rare Grey-crowned Palm Tanager *(Phaenicophilus poliocephalus)*, the Peregrine falcon *(Falco pergrinus)* and the black-capped petrel.

Relatively undiscovered, the South today lives like a colonial gem on the verge of a tourism explosion. It is known mostly for its charming towns sprinkled with once-lovely Victorian architecture, death-defying but magnificent mountains and difficult travelling conditions. The tropical climate at sea level sustains beautiful bougainvillaea, orchids and a plethora of rainbow-coloured vines.

Haiti's transport plans for the south include constructing a paved road around the coastline. It will connect perpetually isolated towns such as **Tiburon** with **Les Irois** on the furthest tip of the southwest coast, and **Dame Marie** with **Abricots**, a mirror image on the north and west extremity. The completion date isn't definite, but it will certainly make an enormous impact on every aspect of southwestern life.

PRECEDING PAGES:
boats off
Île de la Gonâve.
LEFT: carnival time.
BELOW:
statue and street
sign in Jacmel.

Papier mâché *animal masks are a speciality of Jacmel's artisans. People parade through the streets wearing these and other types of mask and colourful costumes at carnival time in the run up to Lent.*

Below: a beautiful balcony in Jacmel.

There is also talk of a highway from Port-au-Prince to Jérémie that will reduce driving time from 12 hours to about three. If and when that happens, it will cause an instantaneous transformation. Jérémie has already begun preparations.

Travel by road

To reach the south from Port-au-Prince take Boulevard Harry Truman (also called Bicentenaire), to Route Nationale 2 (RN2) west toward Les Cayes. It parallels the coastline, traversing the populous, busy, slow-going Carrefour district of Port-au-Prince. The bypass road – which is under construction – will shorten the trip by an hour, but a completion date is still uncertain. In the meantime, enjoy the scenery which includes a variety of unusual business names such as: Pharmacie Christ Vivant (Pharmacy of the Living Christ); L'éternel c'est mon berger (the Eternal is my Shepherd) and Shalom Auto Parts.

After driving for 45 minutes, the lush, densely-populated **Léogâne Plain** comes into view, allowing glimpses of rural life. Small villages dot the plain and bumpy byways intersect RN2. After crossing the stone-studded Momance River, turn onto any side road to take a brief detour and explore.

At the Carrefour Dufort intersection (km 40/mile 25) a short distance after Léogâne, the road ahead leads to Miragoâne and Les Cayes. Instead, turn south (left) onto a scenic road that snakes its tortuous way up and down the crests. As it passes through mountain-top market villages, there are glorious views of country life – cottages clinging precariously to the steep sides of cultivated hills and people walking along the road with all manner of items skillfully balanced on their heads.

Route Nationale 204, sometimes called **Route de l'Amitié** (Friendship

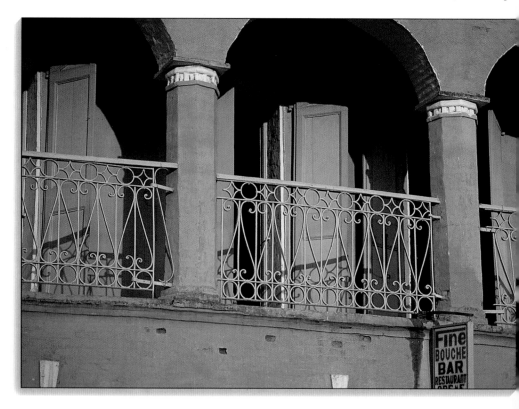

Route), was built by the French (some say to shorten the trip of their compatriots who often make the journey to their favourite beaches on the lush south coast). Rounding the final, dramatic curve, the bucolic river basin is spread out below with the first view of Jacmel harbour. Diminutive streets wind down small hills to a palm-fringed, dark-sand beach. Adjacent piers provide docks for both cruise and commercial ships. The piers were constructed in time to welcome the 21st century, together with a convenient space for artisans whose workshops were previously hidden away in their homes.

An enchanting town

The road entering **Jacmel ⑳** presents the most inviting approach to any town in Haiti. Immediately, everything looks cleaner, neater and less crowded than elsewhere. Turn right onto Avenue de la Liberté. After a few short blocks, it empties into the gated parking area of the white-washed **La Jacmelienne Hotel**. There's a striking view through the open, arched entry out past the sky-blue swimming pool, to a line of white, wooden lounging chairs, and, finally, to the sparkling harbour beyond.

Jacmel is an enchanting town, defined by a large, horseshoe-shaped bay. When the town was built in the late 19th century, wealthy coffee merchants imported cast-iron pillars and balconies from France or the United States to adorn their charming Victorian homes and New Orleans-style mansions. In the late 1990s, Jacmel was selected as one of three prime places for future tourism expansion. In addition to improved infrastructure, much of the Tourism Development Plan centres around restoration of the harbour and original architecture.

Jacmel's small size encourages exploration on foot. An easy stroll will reveal

Map on page 278

With a limited telephone service in Jacmel, the Jacmelienne Hotel is an unofficial message centre. Almost everyone passes there when looking for someone, sometimes leaving messages. Delivery isn't guaranteed, however.

BELOW: a view over the market and cathedral in Jacmel.

TIP

If you are looking for a guide ask for Michel Jean, who speaks English and French. His detailed knowledge brings Jacmel alive and his bargaining skills will more than offset any tip for his services. He can also arrange a car and driver or horses and a guide for a trip to Bassin Bleu.

BELOW AND RIGHT: bright murals and house painting reveal a creative community.

little hidden lanes, the beautifully restored area around Rue du Commerce and the lively commercial centre around the **Marché de Fer** (Iron Market). This, too, was built in Europe and imported in 1895. The hubbub, once reserved for Saturday's market day, now only stops on Sunday.

So many of Jacmel's sights are uncelebrated that it's well worth hiring a local guide to point them out. Traditionally, payment has been negotiable and guides work for tips as they are confident the visitor will be well pleased with their services. In general, it simplifies matters to ask in advance if there is a fee and to agree on payment before setting off.

Guides usually wait just outside the entrance gate at the Jacmelienne Hotel and that's often the only way to contact them. It is also a bit difficult to tell who is a guide and who is not, since they wear the same tee-shirt and jeans ensemble as all the other young men in town. But there have been discussions about organizing the guides with official name tags and this system may be implemented at any time.

Visitors accompanied by a guide are usually protected from unwelcome solicitations. Tour guides from the capital employ a local guide, Michel Jean, when they organise a trip to Jacmel *(see Tip in margin)*. Please bear in mind that, while multiple offers of guide services may be vexing, the work provides a legitimate source of income in a country with high unemployment, so try to remain unruffled.

While exploring Jacmel, be on the lookout for murals – various signs and admonitions handpainted on walls – that are artistic or whimsical, or discover a variety of striking Victorian buildings. Turning a corner, you may suddenly hear a band in full flight as it practices. In the middle of the square, the market women stand guard at their stalls and tables spread with shoes, blankets or trinkets, seemingly oblivious to the joyful sounds of the town. And there, in the centre of a small park, a costumed dance troupe may be practicing their routines for the next festival parade.

Jacmel's main carnival remains one of the best and most popular in Haiti. It takes place a week before the one in Port-au-Prince (in the run-up to Lent) but it is more orderly and less overwhelming. As in Port-au-Prince, there are weeks of practice before the actual event, so it is possible to enjoy the flavour of the pre-celebrations even if your visit doesn't exactly coincide with the carnival. Creatively elaborate *papier mâché* masks, fanciful animal costumes and playful music distinguish the Jacmel carnival.

Rara (or Rah Rah) is another music-oriented celebration. Called the rural carnival, it takes place from Ash Wednesday to Easter and is anchored in ancient Vaudou traditions where revellers "raise the roof". At this time of the year, Rara bands can be seen on roads all over Haiti, playfully parading along to their hypnotic music, gathering followers like the Pied Piper of Hamelin.

Papier mâché masks and carved-wood animal figures are only two of the many handicrafts in the repertoire of Jacmel's artisans. Brightly painted objects – boxes, trays, toys and furniture – are another speciality. A typical shiny black lacquer-like base covered with parrots and/or, flowers in vibrant colours may well make an ideal souvenir or gift to take home. Like Préfète Duffaut *(see page 100)*, some of Haiti's best-known painters were born and raised in Jacmel, where Selden Rodman made his home and was one of the first people, along with DeWitt Peters, to promote Haitian *Art Naïf*. Invariably there are less known, albeit superb, artists with small studios sprinkled throughout the town, waiting to be discovered.

Map on page 278

Fragrant Caribbean bougainvillaea.

BELOW: dressed up as devils at Jacmel's Carnival.

Because many colonial buildings are still in use, it's easy to visit them. A former residence on Rue Seymour Pradel has been transformed into an American-owned art gallery named **Salubria**. On leaving the gallery, turn left and walk up a small hill to the **Manoir Alexandre** (tel: 288 2711). This century-old patrician home is now a guest house with one of the best views in Jacmel and reasonable rates.

The Marché de Fer was erected two blocks east at Rue Veuve, Rue de l'Église, and Rue Vallières. Smaller, and much more manageable than its Port-au-Prince cousin, it has no walls. Vendors sell mainly produce, meat and food stuffs – no souvenirs in sight. The **Cathédrale de St Phillippe et St Jacques** stands in the middle of the block, directly across Rue de l'Église from the market.

Hidden behind the vendors at the corner with Rue Vallières sits the unprepossessing building where Simón Bolívar lived in exile and where the flag of Venezuela was created. Bolívar trained troops in Haiti and left from Jacmel on his voyage to liberate South America from Spanish rule. Later he was seemingly ambivalent about Haiti's independence because, it is said, he had agreed with Alexandre Pétion not to publicly acknowledge Haiti's support, since Pétion was fearful of renewed European aggression and reprisals.

The first part of Jacmel to be renovated was Rue du Commerce, a wide, pleasant, partly brick-paved street. Many of its 19th-century homes and warehouses are well preserved and have been turned into galleries or *artisanat* (handicraft) shops. The Boucard family home at the corner with Grande Rue is especially noteworthy, and the Vital family warehouse dates from 1865. In the middle of the block between Grande Rue and Avenue de la Liberté the former residence of Selden Rodman stands out – truly a showplace with much of the original wrought-iron work still intact on stairways, balconies and bridges across the substantial, flower-filled courtyard. It was converted into a peerless haven for guests in 1999. Although there is no sign or number on the outside, it's easily found, right next to **Créations Moro**, the comprehensive lacquerware shop at number 40.

Back to nature and onto the beaches

To get back to nature after exploring the city for a while, take Rue Roosevelt, passing some lovely old houses as well as new construction. After a short, easy walk to the top of a hill, there's a gently rolling meadow with several large shade trees and a wonderful, expansive view over all of Jacmel, the harbour and beyond. It has a remarkably rural feel, for a place that is so close to town.

Continue along the path for a grand circle tour of an area that will probably be filled with houses and shops in a few short years. Companions on the path might be either going to market or returning home, the women carrying large baskets on their heads brimming over with produce or charcoal, prodding their fully laden donkeys to get them to move. Men carry machetes or push wheel barrows full of unwieldy items such as long tree branches and sugar cane stalks.

Heading east, Jacmel's famous fine sandy beaches are close by. They'll be even more accessible upon

Map
on page
278

completion of work to pave the road as far as Marigot. From Jacmel centre take Avenue Barranquilla east toward the airport, where **Le Rendez-Vous** restaurant stays open for snacks all day, seven days a week. Nearby **Fort Ogé** rates a brief stop. An obscure, virtually unknown relic of colonial days, is the **Habitation Price**, where the ruins of a former plantation contain a unique steam engine (nonworking). Built by the English scientist James Watt (1736–1819), there is only one other engine like it in the world. They were used commercially in the sugar cane industry when most other steam engines were busy pulling railway carriages. This might make an interesting stop for someone with plenty of time to spare and who enjoys a treasure hunt. Since there are no signposts, just turn left after the airport onto a bad road requiring a four-wheel-drive vehicle, especially during or after rain. Even if you find the place, there won't be a lot to see because the engine is in a poor state of repair.

Back on the road toward Marigot, *artisanat* shops in small houses beckon all along the route. After 7 km (4 miles) turn right down a side-road to reach the beach, **Plage Cyvadier**, which is actually a little cove with a strip of sand and small rocks. An eponymous small hotel is situated high above the cove, with several buildings, housing the guest rooms, delightfully placed among the verdant gardens and lawns. A freshwater swimming pool graces one end of the grounds, and there is a pleasant outdoor terrace (where the restaurant can serve your fresh lobster) under the bougainvillaea, near the steps leading to the pebble and sand beach. The hotel's owner donates part of the establishment's profits to a local school, so a stay at Cyvadier Plage can also help a good cause.

Continuing east, the next beach sits right alongside the road 15 km (9 miles) from Jacmel. **Plage Raymond-les-Bains** has fine white sand and gentle waves

BELOW: on the way to market.

TIP

When arranging a trip to Bassin Bleu:

● Try to secure a guide, driver and four-wheel-drive vehicle in Jacmel before setting off.

● Agree on a price in advance.

● Be sure to rent horses in Jacmel – hiring them near the falls may prove more expensive.

BELOW:
St Louis du Sud
on the south coast.

that lap the beach, making swimming easy and keeping it a popular choice with local people, especially at the weekend. A bit further along, the small town of **Cayes Jacmel** is home to a unique craftsman. Worth a visit, Joseph Franck Pierre builds precise scale models of old sailing ships like the *Santa María*, *Cutty Sark*, and many others. There is also a little park commemorating Toussaint L'Ouverture's sojourn in town.

Plage Ti Mouillage, the next beach on the route, is a favourite with French expatriates. There are actually two beaches, the first of which has a basic restaurant and the second offers small beach homes for rent. The expatriates often stay in **Marigot**, a little coastal village 10 km (6 miles) further east. From here, a steep, rough trail requires a good four-wheel-drive vehicle to complete the climb up to **Seguin** and on to Parc National La Visite. The area north of Marigot has a well known hiking trail usually approached from Furcy *(see Excursions from Port-au-Prince, page 302)*.

Excursion to Bassin Bleu

Back in Jacmel there isn't much to see west of the town. So head north for a detour to the falls nearby, passing La Vallée on the way. **Bassin Bleu** ㉑ is actually a series of big, natural, deep, blue-green pools and three spectacular waterfalls, which descend in tiers through a fern-covered limestone gorge. An excursion from Jacmel takes most of a day so don't be fooled if locals say it isn't far, or that it doesn't take much time to get there. And don't even think about going if it has rained. In fact, visitors whose itineraries include hiking or driving in remote areas would be best advised to plan to travel during the cooler, dryer season from October to May.

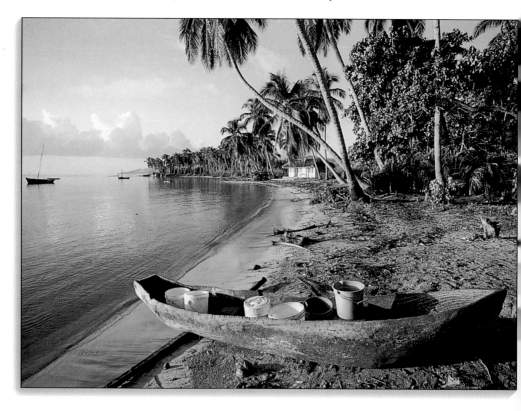

The 12-km (7-mile) journey to Bassin Bleu is a memorable one. It starts with an adrenaline-pumping drive across the **Jacmel River**, swerving around other vehicles traversing the same path. Avoiding the multitude of people washing themselves, their clothes, their animals and their vehicles also takes skill. Next, it's bumping up, down and around the hills, competing with herds of passing animals for the right-of-way. When it is impossible for the vehicle to go another inch, everyone gets out and transfers to horseback for the last kilometre to the first waterfall. The horses may be smaller than expected and look suspiciously like donkeys.

The expedition to Bassin Bleu is best tackled with a local guide. When making arrangements some prerequisites for an incident-free trip should include the following suggestions. Make arrangements in Jacmel rather than Port-au-Prince because the intricacies of a trip to the falls are better known locally. Be sure to hire a guide who really knows how to get there and agree on a price in advance.

Horses are necessary for the final part of the trip to Bassin Bleu as no vehicle can drive all the way. Rent them in Jacmel to avoid having to negotiate on site. A local guide always takes over from the Jacmel guide at this point. Naturally, there's a small additional fee.

Finally, be aware that the last kilometre is very steep. Arrival at the last waterfall requires the aid of a rope (and perhaps a little push from the guide). After the hike up to the edge of the last pool, you are lowered down with the rope to reach the water and then, of course, it's back up the rope to get out. The startling blue of the pool can sometimes be a murky green from runoff if there has been recent rain.

Alternatively, the whole Bassin Bleu excursion can be made on foot or horse-

Map on page 278

Hundreds of different animal and plant species thrive in Parc National Macaya, including: 102 different kinds of fern; 99 mosses; 11 butterfly species; 57 types of snail; 28 kinds of amphibian; 34 reptiles, 65 bird species and 19 bats.

BELOW: washing clothes in the river next to the market at Cavaillon.

back, starting out from Jacmel. It takes two to three arduous hours each way. Intrepid hikers will be rewarded with some wonderful views on the trail.

The far south and southwestern peninsula

John James Audubon, famous ornithologist and painter was born in Les Cayes in 1785. Christened Jean-Jacques, he was the illegitimate son of a French naval officer and a Creole woman. Audubon went on to illustrate the monumental Birds of America.

All the way to Les Cayes from Port-au-Prince, RN2 provides a sufficiently smooth asphalt road in excellent condition and the scenic 200-km (120-mile) drive takes about 2½ hours. The road runs parallel to the north coast of the peninsula for the first hour. After Léogâne, the siren's call of the broad, beautiful beaches will be tempting, but keep going for another 20 km (12 miles) to a compact little town named **Grand-Goâve** (Big Goâve). Bathing beaches between Grand-Goâve and its inaccurately named, much larger neighbour, **Petit-Goâve**, (Little Goâve) are worth the wait. Petit Goave, is a charming colonial town which sits at the head of a lovely harbour where small boats offer rides to **Cocoyer Beach**, the small sand island out in the bay.

Miragoâne overlooks the next cove, 26 km (16 miles) further on. Still a smugglers' port, it mirrors its larger siblings, Jacmel and Jérémie, with pretty, narrow streets winding down the hill to a bustling harbour. Rather than gold from looted sailing ships, the booty today is contraband from Miami – clothing, shoes and household supplies.

From Miragoâne, the main road turns south to **Les Cayes ㉒**, the site of an annual three-day music festival, the **Fête de Notre Dame**, held on the second weekend in August. The beachfront venue imparts a unique flavour and competition is stiff because Petit-Goâve also hosts a festival on the same weekend. Entertainment includes top expatriate Haitian bands that have achieved stardom and notoriety in Europe, Canada and the US, including Tambo Combo,

BELOW:
preparing the land for planting in La Vallée.

Map on page 278

RAM and Ti Vice *(see page 111)*. Many young Haitians living abroad return home for the festival weekend, driving back and forth between the two towns.

Les Cayes has beautiful beaches – calm water and sand like icing sugar – with a couple of basic hotels providing overnight shelter. The town has two other claims to fame – it is the closest town to **Parc National Macaya**, and it is the place where the best road and the worst road in Haiti meet. The best is RN2; the worst is RN7 or RD214.

An extremely difficult road from Les Cayes to Jérémie in the north of the peninsula, RN7 allows access to the national park, the peak at Macaya, the **Kounoubois Caves** ㉓ and **Saut Mathurine** ㉔, all near **Camp Perrin**. Camp Perrin still exhibits a few traces of its French colonial origins, such as **le canal de Davezac de Castera**, a canal built in 1749. The Kounoubois caves nearby are sacred Vaudou sites.

It takes half a day to reach the University of Florida base at Plaine Durand on the edge of Parc National Macaya. This very basic camping facility remains the only place to stay in the park. It takes another two days each way to make the difficult trek up to the summit of the **Pic de Macaya** (2,347 metres /7,700 ft). Plan well in advance if you intend to make the hike, because you will need to employ an experienced local guide and take along sufficient supplies for the trip.

West of Les Cayes, road conditions are relentlessly bad and will remain so until completion of the coast highway project. Driving is definitely not recommended after rain because the rivers are swollen and can be treacherous. From Les Cayes it takes about two hours (and possibly a flat tyre) to reach **Port Salut** which is a great place to enjoy fresh seafood and lobster on the beach. A small island just off Macaya Beach, **Coq Anglade**, is little more than a coconut palm-

There was once a waterfall at Saut Mathurine but it was diverted in a hydro-electric scheme to provide power for the southern region.

BELOW: view over Corail to the ocean.

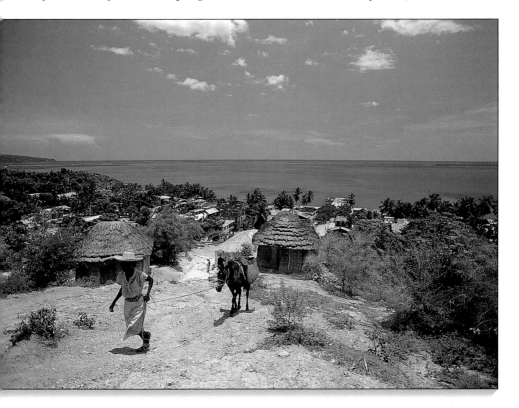

studded expanse of sand. It is possible to walk (or wade) out to reach it. Two other often deserted, undeveloped, palm-lined beaches nearby are **Gelée Beach** and **Pointe Sable**.

The Islands

Like Île de la Tortue (Turtle Island) up north, **Île-à-Vache** (Cow Island) ㉕ made a perfect pirate's refuge, thanks to numerous hiding places among indentations in the coastline's sheer rock cliffs. Pure white sand beaches bless the rest of the shoreline of this idyllic island near Les Cayes.

Henry Morgan, the infamous English buccaneer who later became governor of Jamaica, used Île-à-Vache as a safe harbour. Here, too, he prepared for his siege of Panama, and in 1668 his ship exploded just off the island's coast.

Although Île-à-Vache is only a short boat ride from the mainland, the ferry schedule benefits workers in Les Cayes who live on the island. It leaves the island at 10am, returning from Les Cayes at 4.30pm, thereby precluding a day trip without organizing transfers from a local fishing boat. A local fisherman will probably be happy to take you across for a small fee, but luckily, there is now an alternative solution.

The **Port Morgan** resort solves the lodging problem on Île-à-Vache. Guests can stay overnight and soak up the calm, peaceful atmosphere of the island. A planned PADI scuba diving facility will open up exploration of the underwater habitat around the island. If arranged in advance Port Morgan will pick up guests in its own boat.

Les Îles Cayemites ㉖ lie off the north coast of the southern peninsula just north of **Pestel**, a pretty fishing village of pastel-shaded houses with a French fort. Thanks to its prime location midway between Miragoâne and Jérémie, Pestel is ideal for watersports and beach activities. **Grande Cayemite**, a large, inhabited and cultivated island, has two towns, an extensive necklace of myriad tiny reef outcroppings and a lighthouse that flashes continually. **Petite Cayemite** is a small beach island. Distinctive from the air, a large stretch of land, the **Presqu'île des Baradères** (meaning almost an island), appears to be an island, but is actually attached to the coast at the western end.

The City of Poets

Travelling to Jérémie by road is a long and arduous journey, with a none too safe 12-hour ferry ride as an alternative. If the budget allows, it would be wise to travel by air. Flights from Port-au-Prince to Jérémie feel almost like a tailor-made tour. All that's missing is the commentary. Some of Tropical Airways' aircraft have a window that bows out like a big bubble, just behind the cockpit on either side of the plane. If the flight isn't full and conditions are calm, some pilots may allow a passenger up front to stand at the window and shoot a few memorable photographs. The panoramic view of the land below is spectacular.

After take-off, the flight passes over a shantytown Cité-Soleil and a boat-speckled Port-au-Prince harbour. The shimmering water below changes colour from muddy brown, due to the run-off at the shore, to dark blue, then quickly to successively lighter, cleaner tones of turquoise as the shallow shoals and reefs surrounding **Île de la Gonâve** pass beneath the silver wings.

Flying slowly across the island, there is time to examine the aerial perspective of the reef system extending a good way out from land. Infinite colour variations of the water are apparent throughout the flight. Hues turn from almost white with just the slightest tinge of blue in shallows where the bottom is obviously sand, to sapphire blue where an edge of the reef suddenly drops away.

On the other side of Île de la Gonâve, flying almost parallel to the Îles Cayemites gives passengers a good look at crops in the fields, two small villages, and surrounding (known as fringing) reefs.

Jérémie ㉗ is in the midst of a renaissance, partly due to a re-awakening of civic pride after the scourge of the Duvalier years and their aftermath. Thanks in part also, to the increased number of flights since Tropical Airways started service in 1999. A new airport building is planned to accommodate the growing number of visitors who are bringing new life to this long deserted town.

In 1964, Papa Doc Duvalier ordered the closure of Jérémie's port, in retaliation for local opposition to his dictatorial methods. With its coffee and cacao exports almost cut off overnight, the town fell into a protracted decline, and the road from Les Cayes literally crumbled away. For many years the town stagnated, living on its memories. Today, however, a measure of optimism is returning, and the population is growing once more, as Haitians who have lived and worked abroad build retirement homes and local farmers invest a lifetime's savings in houses in the town.

By the beginning of the 21st century Jérémie, the once-booming coffee- and

Map on page 278

Jérémie was once a thriving coffee producing centre but exports were sharply reduced during the 1960s when the town was isolated from the rest of the country by the dictator, Papa Doc Duvalier.

BELOW: at home in Grande Cayemite.

*Haitian cacao
produces chocolate
using traditional
methods.*

BELOW:
coffee workers
preparing beans.

cacao-exporting centre known as the "City of Poets" (because of the town's notable poets such as Émile Roumer), remained undiscovered by most tourists. The neglected cast-iron-adorned Victorian buildings are beginning to be painted and renovated. Coffee growing and exporting are increasing, though they had continued through the years, but on a smaller scale because much of the land was given over to food crops during the hard times.

On the wharf and in large cement yards behind the warehouses, visitors can watch the start of the chocolate production process, virtually unchanged today. One man heaves a heavy sack on his shoulders; a second slits a corner of the sack. The first worker walks back and forth distributing the falling cacao beans in even rows, while the second rakes the beans to spread them for drying in the sun. Luckily for sweet-tooths, the September to February growing season for cacao makes chocolate available for Christmas and Easter. Even more fortuitous for Jérémie is the fact that a world shortage of chocolate has led companies like the US candy giant Hershey, with its cooperative in Dame Marie, to look to Haiti to fill the gap.

From the centre of Jérémie, Rue Roumer (named for the celebrated Haitian poet) becomes Rue Borges on the way up to the guest houses which sit above the central area, also called Borges. Driving up the pock-marked, rain-ravaged streets requires a sturdy four-wheel-drive vehicle and even those can barely make the climb.

Almost everyone in Jérémie seems more friendly and open, less guarded than in other places in Haiti. Perhaps because Jérémie has been isolated for so long and has had precious few visitors, residents have not yet had experiences to make them wary of strangers. It's certainly a completely different experience to

Map on page 278

see one stranger standing on the wharf with a guidebook in hand, as opposed to a throng of 500 excited, loud passengers just disgorged from a cruise ship.

Another reason is that most strangers in the region recently have been there as part of international aid programmes. They continue to make tremendous strides in tackling health problems, particularly for women and children isolated in the mountains. The small clinic run by the Haitian Health Foundation is staffed by a team which includes multilingual doctors and American nurses. The modern equipment is some of the best in Haiti.

Born in Jérémie, General Alexandre Dumas, the father of Alexandre Dumas *père* and grandfather of Alexandre Dumas *fils* would be proud of his native town. He rose to be a general in Napoleon's revolutionary French army, while his son wrote the famous novel *The Count of Monte Cristo*. The Dumas family typified the old light-skinned élite, educated in France who dominated Jérémie and incurred Papa Doc Duvalier's wrath.

The use of generators, in the face of constant power cuts, has re-invigorated nightlife in Jérémie. Two of the many places to party are **Le Vertigo Beach**, a lively disco, and **Ma Folie**, a large spot with a restaurant on one level and dancing to bright flashing lights on the floor above.

As in other places, such as Cap Haïtien and Jacmel, the **Alliance Française** offers a multitude of activities and classes. It has a restaurant and tennis courts, and is an excellent place to find out what's happening in town. The **Castillo Restaurant and Bar** has it all, it opens at 7am for breakfast and continues until 3am the next morning when the disco closes.

Jérémie's most famous delicacy is undoubtedly *Comparette*, a type of not-too-sweet, cake-like bread (also rolls) made from flour, cinnamon and ginger. Bring

Some Peace Corps volunteers work way up in the mountains. There are no telephones, no electricity and no running water. It is a six hour walk, each way, to town.

BELOW: a country cottage.

Map
on page
278

some as a gift to a Haitian anywhere else in the country and it is likely to be greatly appreciated.

Much of Jérémie reveals spectacular views of the coastline. High regions provide uninterrupted vistas of steep cliffs that seem to run out to infinity. Empty white sand beaches sparkle in the sunlight and the startling, brilliant blue sea merges into frothy white clouds at the horizon. Colours are constantly changing. An early morning, pale pink tint as the sky awakens from slumber deepens to darker rose, melts into a golden glow that suddenly bursts into bright sunlight. Throughout the day the greens and greys, the muted or electric blues run through the rainbow's hues at the whim of the clouds. Sunsets are breathtaking. Night skies seem to reach down to enfold the observer, perhaps because the air is clear and there are no other lights to rob the stars of their brilliance.

Excursions from Jérémie

Anse d'Azur ㉘ is picture postcard perfect. This scenic, sand beach lies halfway between Jérémie and the airport. Look for a small opening in the vegetation, then walk past the foundations of a building and down steep cement steps to the long, half moon-shaped cove. The calm, shallow waters, sheltered by the curve of the lush green, hilly coast, are ideal for snorkelling. Just a short swim from the beach, the rusted metal frame of a sunken boat (with part of its engine intact) sticks up from the water. A variety of small fish dart in and out. There's also a good-sized cave at the end of the beach, which you can enter by swimming or wading a short distance.

BELOW: people from Jérémie are friendly.
RIGHT: the hills dwarf a sailboat in St Louis du Sud.

Further west around the coast is **Anse du Clerc**. The drive here is a bone-jarring, bouncing trip along the rock- and pothole-strewn dirt tracks and requires rocky river crossings.

Along the way take a slight detour to **Bonbon** ㉙, a picturesque fishing village. It is not a place to buy souvenirs, but it provides a window in to the lives of rural Haitians, without having to hike for hours to an isolated mountain village.

Bonbon consists of a group of about twenty quite small and neat little mud houses painted in the blues, pinks and greens that are not uncommon in the Caribbean. It must take great skill to perfect the colours so that they survive the punishing tropical sun. There is a police commissary and a small school-house with open sides and a line of benches where the children sit during lessons. In an area set a little apart, local women sit on the ground to sell their wares – a few small fish, some fruit or vegetables and a few household items spread out before them. Care-free children run around happily in various states of undress. It's heart-wrenching to notice that some exhibit signs of malnutrition. However, they are unsurprisingly curious to look over any strangers who appear so far off the beaten tourist track.

A scenic 7-km (4-mile) ride from Bonbon over low mountains and around a scenic bay leads to **Abricots**, the centre of *artisanat* for the district. Literally the end of the road, only dirt tracks continue from here to the town of **Dame Marie** located at the western tip of the peninsula. ❑

CENTRAL HAITI, THE WEST AND THE ARTIBONITE VALLEY

Map
on page
278

The centre of the country consists of vast grasslands, a fertile valley and a resort coastline, all divided by inhospitable mountain ranges, making travel by four-wheel drive imperative

Grass covered savannah dotted with grazing cattle stretches as far as the eye can see over the Plateau Central, for this vast, flat, sparsely populated region, bordered by the Massif des Montagnes Noires to the south and the Chaine de la Grande Rivière du Nord to the north, is mainly an agricultural area. In the centre of it all lies the little town of Hinche, where the cows, goats, chickens and other livestock are brought to market twice a week. It is not an easy ride to Hinche, 171 km (80 miles) away from Port au Prince, the RN 3 crosses the Plaine du Cul-de-Sac simply enough before climbing over the Montagnes du Trou d'Eau, then winding down to Mirebalais on the upper reaches of the Rivière de l'Artibonite. From here the road becomes rough and difficult, especially after rain and since Hurricane Georges caused the Barrage de Peligré (dam) to overflow in 1998, destroying much of the road system. It is advisable to travel in a four-wheel drive or expect a long seven-hour bus ride.

The Rivière de l'Artibonite flows west through a giant chequer board of paddy fields, known as the country's rice basket, which are home to a wide variety of egrets and many species of heron. Just over the mountain range to the south – "Behind the mountain there are more mountains" so the Creole saying goes – runs the Côte des Arcadins where Haiti's best beach resorts lie, washed by clear blue water, perfect for swimming and snorkelling. Opposite, three small sandy islands or cays, called the Arcadins, provide good diving around their coral reefs.

PRECEDING PAGES: paddy fields in Haiti's rice basket. **LEFT:** rice drying in the sun. **BELOW:** Bassin Zim.

Hinche – a central market town

A quintessentially rural town, **Hinche** ⓷⓪ (pop. 53,000) comes alive on market days. Peasants pour in over the bridge across the broad River Guayamoue, hoping to sell their cattle, pigs, goats and large basins full of turkeys balanced on their heads. The market is on Rue Stenio Vincent, east of the *tap-tap* depot, and it spills out into the surrounding streets, transforming the town. Here many small restaurants offer typical Haitian dishes of rice, beans and meat.

Rue J.J. Dessalines leads south from the bus station to **Place Charlemagne Péralte**. This dusty square is dedicated to the heroic son of Hinche, Charlemagne Péralte, who was the leader of the Cacos Resistance against the US military occupation in 1915. The Cacos were a band of black partisan irregulars from the Plateau Central originally formed in 1867 in opposition to the Government. They survived, on and off, as a resistance force until their prodigious struggle against the US military and its practice of *corvée*, enforced labour gangs for road building. After nearly two years of guerrilla warfare, Péralte was captured and executed by the US army which soon crushed the rebellion. The square is overlooked by Hinche's 16th-century cathedral whose interior easily rivals that of the modern one on Rue C. Heureuse.

About 15 km (9 miles) northeast of Hinche is **Bassin Zim** ㉛, a stunning waterfall which flows rather than cascades over a massive smooth rock into a 50-meter (164-ft) wide milky blue pool. It is a wonderful pool for swimming, although there are no changing facilities, just the odd rock to hide behind. From there a local guide (for a small fee) can show you the way, chopping away at the undergrowth with his machete as he goes, to the **Grottes du Bassin Zim** about a 20-minute walk along a small path that requires some scrambling and climbing. The caves, hidden among rich green ferns and trees, are cold and dark and contain some ancient wall drawings, thought to be relics of the indigenous Taíno Indians. Bassin Zime is at the end of a 5-km (3-mile) track past Papaye, off the road to Cap-Haïtien; a four-wheel-drive vehicle is a necessity as there are no buses. However, a *tap-tap* can take you to the hot springs at **Cerca-la-Source** ㉜, 30 km (19 miles) east of Hinche near the border – an experience in itself.

The fertile Vallée de l'Artibonite

The source of the Rivière de l'Artibonite lies across the border in the Dominican Republic. When it finally reaches the west coast of Haiti it has broadened into a grand and powerful navigable river, irrigating the fertile rice-producing region of the **Vallée de l'Artibonite**. The landscape around **Pont Sondé**, on RN1, 110 km (68 miles) is a patchwork of many small, intensely green, rice paddies delineated by a network of irrigation canals. Turning east you reach the

BELOW:
bagging the rice
can be tiring work.

Map on page 278

small unassuming market town of **Petite Rivière de l'Artibonite** ㉝, where two blocks behind the restored church stands the **Palais des 365 Portes** built by Henri Christophe as his provincial headquarters. There are actually only about 60 exterior doors and windows on this fascinating building which has since been used as both a school and a town hall.

Continuing east, the road leads uphill to the remains of **Fort Crète-à-Pierrot** where, in 1802, Dessalines' army of slaves bravely withstood General Leclerc's French forces in a key battle in the blacks' struggle for independence. The view of the river is splendid from here. After rejoining RN1 at L'Estère, the road continues north to Gonaïves passing the dusty, desert-like region of **Savane Désolée**, strewn with brushwood and dotted with large cacti.

West coast blues

Although historically important as the spot where Haiti's independence was declared by Dessalines in 1804, **Gonaïves** ㉞ is notorious as the most charmless city in the country. Sprawling, flat and dusty, it lies beside slovenly, brackish beaches and much of the municipal architecture is modern and soulless. **Place de l'Independence** contains a monument to Dessalines, depicting him at the helm of a ship representing Haiti. An ugly, modernist cathedral dominates the square which doubles as an expansive bicycle repair yard, lined with stalls fixing and selling wheels, tyres and frames: the bicycle is king in Gonaïves. The **Memorial de l'Independence** stands on Rue Liberté to the west, leading down to the ramshackle, but busy, docks. Avoid the beaches just to the north of town, as they are believed to have been used as a dump for US toxic ash in 1988.

South of Gonaïves, 75 km (46 miles) away, you come to the lively port of

Dessalines, about 20 km (12 miles) to the north of Petite Rivière along a rough road, was made Haiti's capital by the rebel leader after declaring independence in 1804. A hike into the surrounding hills with a guide will reveal the remains of the seven forts that Dessalines built to protect his stronghold.

BELOW: market day in Hinche.

Map on page 278

TIP

The spacious dockside Venus Restaurant, on the western edge of Saint-Marc's central park, is a perfect place for watching the cargo ships laboriously unload by rowing boat.

BELOW: a peaceful moment by the sea, Arcahaie.
RIGHT: mother and daughter returning home from market.

Saint-Marc ㉟, an idiosyncratic, tumbledown town crowded with wooden, two-storey houses held together by corrugated iron, cardboard and hope. Saint-Marc was an important port during the colonial era and still handles and exports the sugar, bananas and rice produced in the Vallée de l'Artibonite. On the edge of town, small lard and soap factories provide more employment.

Smart resorts on the Côte des Arcadins

The **Côte des Arcadins** ㊱ runs from Delugé, 16 km (10 miles) south of Saint-Marc to Cabaret 45 km (28 miles) away and has long, white beaches with safe, shallow waters for bathing. The coastline is backed by the denuded **Chaine des Matheux** mountain range and to the southwest, 5 km (3 miles) out to sea, lie **Les Arcadins**. These three sand cays are encircled by a clearly visible coral reef which provides endless entertainment for scuba divers. At the northern end, the small town of **Montrouis** has developed a good reputation for its tasty, cheap roadside food. The main road is lined with covered stalls serving a range of dishes from rice and beans, *mayi moulen* and fried *lambi (see page 138)* to fresh avocados and pineapples.

Most of Haiti's luxury beach resorts are located along the Côte des Arcadins and offer all-inclusive deals as well as day tickets for non-residents, which usually include a meal and the use of sports facilities. The resort of **Moulin sur la Mer** (tel: 223-5700), 3 km (2 miles) north of Montrouis, is built around a restored 17th-century colonial building, housing a museum dedicated to the colonial period. An intact sugar press stands outside. The privately owned **Ouanga Bay Beach Hotel** (tel: 257-7889), 8 km (5 miles) south of Montrouis, has a warm and friendly atmosphere and has a nightclub with live music at weekends. Further south, the **Plage Publique** lies awkwardly, but promisingly, between the more upmarket, expensive all-inclusives of **Kaliko Beach Resort** (tel: 298-4609) and **Wahoo Bay Beach** (tel: 223-2950) which organises horse-riding trips into the mountains. The public beach was opened in 1997 by President Preval as a free beach for Haitians and has a lively atmosphere with impromptu bands dotted about, wild soccer games and people selling drinks and cheap food. The **Kyona Beach Club** (tel: 257-6863) is the most accessible resort from Port-au-Prince and therefore the busiest.

Ile de la Gonâve ㊲, 20 km (12 miles) out in the Golfe de la Gonâve, is the largest of Haiti's coastal islands and is overpopulated by families trying to scrape a living fishing in the depleted waters, and farming in mostly arid and inhospitable conditions. Boats leave daily from a small wharf at **Carries**, north of Wahoo Bay Beach, which was once Baby Doc Duvalier's beach house.

The last major town before Port-au-Prince, 30 km (18 miles) away, **Cabaret** ㊳ is a strange anomaly of Haitian architecture standing as a sad and desperate relic of Papa Doc's fragile ego. The town was conceived and partially built in 1961 as Haiti's answer to Brasilia, and named Duvalierville. Recently renamed, all that remains of its Duvalierist legacy is an enormous, modernist cockfighting stadium. ❏

INSIGHT GUIDES
TRAVEL TIPS

New Insight Maps

Maps in Insight Guides are tailored to complement the text. But when you're on the road you sometimes need the big picture that only a large-scale map can provide. This new range of durable Insight Fleximaps has been designed to meet just that need.

Detailed, clear cartography
makes the comprehensive route and city maps easy to follow, highlights all the major tourist sites and provides valuable motoring information plus a full index.

Informative and easy to use
with additional text and photographs covering a destination's top 10 essential sites, plus useful addresses, facts about the destination and handy tips on getting around.

Laminated finish
allows you to mark your route on the map using a non-permanent marker pen, and wipe it off. It makes the maps more durable and easier to fold than traditional maps.

The first titles
cover many popular destinations. They include Algarve, Amsterdam, Bangkok, California, Cyprus, Dominican Republic, Florence, Hong Kong, Ireland, London, Mallorca, Paris, Prague, Rome, San Francisco, Sydney, Thailand, Tuscany, USA Southwest, Venice, and Vienna.

☀ INSIGHT GUIDES
The world's largest collection of visual travel guides

CONTENTS

Getting Acquainted

Area: 48,442 sq. km (18,704 sq. miles)
Population: 8 million. Seventy percent is mulatto – of mixed European and African descent – and the remaining 30 percent is composed of blacks, Caucasians and Asians.
Language: Spanish
Religion: Apostolic and Roman Catholic
Time Zone: Eastern Standard Time (Daylight Saving applies during summer). At noon in Santo Domingo it is 5pm in London, 6pm in Madrid and Rome, 2pm in Buenos Aires and 11am in Mexico City.
Currency: the national currency is the peso but US dollars are widely accepted
Electricity: 110–120 volts, 60 cycles, as in the United States is the most common. All hotels have emergency power generators.
International Dialling Code: 809

Geography

The Dominican Republic has three main mountain systems: the Central Range, the Northern Range and the Eastern Range. The Central Range is the largest in area. Features of this range are Pico Duarte, the highest peak in the Antilles at 3,087 metres (10,128 ft), waterfalls such as Baiguate and Jimenoa, and several national parks and scientific reserves. The Central Range also gives rise to some of the country's most important rivers, including its longest river, Yaque del Norte, which is ideal for river rafting.

The Northern Range runs parallel to the Central Range, separating the Cibao Valley from the Atlantic Coastal Plain. The highest elevation of this range is Pico Diego de Ocampo, which is also a scientific reserve. El Morro in Monte Cristi is also noteworthy as are the Siete Hermanos (Seven Brothers) keys – ideal for scuba diving and fishing. The amber mines near Puerto Plata are also in this mountain range. The Eastern Range is the shortest of the three ranges.

There are also five *sierras* or minor mountain ranges: Sierra de Samana, Sierra de Yamasa, Sierra de Martin Garcia, Sierra de Neiba and Sierra de Bahoruco.

Several rivers irrigate the Dominican Republic, some of which are used to generate electric power via hydroelectric dams.

Climate

The average temperature in the Dominican Republic is 25°C (77°F) year-round. The climate on the coasts is more tropical than in the central part of the country, where temperatures are cooler.

The average amount of rainfall varies depending on where you are in the country. On the northern coast the rainy season falls in Oct–April/May and in the south it is from May–Oct/Nov.

The northern and eastern towns have the most rain. Average annual rainfall:

Puerto Plata	176 cm
Monte Cristi	167 cm
Santo Domingo	138 cm

Economy

Four major industries sustain the Dominican Republic's economy: agriculture, mining, tourism and duty-free zones. In recent years tourism and duty free zones have been the most dynamic money-earners. Presently, tourism provides the greatest economic gain to the country, followed by duty-free zones in which textiles, electronic equipment, cigars etc are produced for export.

According to Dominican law, the decimal metric system should be used. However, pounds and ounces are used in weighing solids and cooking oil, fabrics are measured in yards, and petrol (gasoline) and motor oils are measured by the imperial gallon (128 oz). On the other hand, rum, beer and other liquids are sold in bottles of 0.756 litre. Land surfaces in urban areas are measured by square metres and in rural areas they are generally measured by "tarea" (1 tarea = 624 sq. metres).

The main exports in the agricultural sector are coffee, cacao, sugar, pineapples, oranges, plantains, bananas, vegetables and flowers. The Cibao Valley region is not only rich in agricultural products but is also home to large deposits of ferronickel and the largest open-air gold mine on the continent, La Rosario Dominicana. Other mined exports are gypsum, marble and rock salt.

Government

Like other parts of Latin America, in the 20th century the Dominican Republic went through periods of political unrest, violent changes in its government and civil war. However, in the last four decades it has been able to develop into a representative democracy.

The Dominican Republic's democratic government is divided into three branches: Executive, Legislative and Judicial. Free elections take place every four years. The capital city and seat of government is Santo Domingo. The president names the provincial governors, who are his representatives in those provinces. The Senate elects the judiciary.

Planning the Trip

Visas & Passports

A visa is not required to enter the Dominican Republic for citizens of the United States, Canada, Spain, France, UK, Germany, Switzerland, Italy, Venezuela, Scandinavian countries, Panama, Uruguay, Costa Rica, Japan, Dominica, Brazil, Argentina, Antigua, Bermuda, the Netherlands Antilles, Guadeloupe, Martinique, Jamaica, Mexico or Trinidad and Tobago. Citizens of these countries only require a US$10.00 tourist card, and proof of citizenship (passport, original birth certificate, etc.) are required. Visitors from all other countries need an entry visa.

Customs

Articles classified as personal luggage will not be a problem for clearing customs. You are permitted to bring into the country 1 litre of alcohol, 200 cigarettes and gift articles with a value of no more that US$100. Your reception may depend on where your flight is coming from and the attitude of the inspector greeting you, but usually he or she will let you through with a friendly smile. Your luggage may be inspected.

Money Matters

The Dominican monetary unit is the peso (RD$). Coins are 1, 5, 10, 25 and 50 cents and 1 peso, and bills are in denominations of 5, 10, 20, 50. 100, 500, 1000 pesos. You will receive more for your dollars or pounds if you exchange them at a commercial bank upon your arrival in the country. By law, banks are

Health Precautions

The Dominican Republic is a safe destination provided you take the proper precautions. It is advisable to visit your family physician prior to travelling to the island. Make sure you review your immunization records with your doctor in order to verify what you need. The vaccinations recommended to all visitors to the tropical Caribbean islands are Hepatitis A and Hepatitis B.

Tap water is not safe to drink on the island. Visitors should drink bottled water or purified water which is available everywhere. For people travelling to major hotels and resorts, there are clinics available on the premises. Otherwise, local hospitals and clinics will treat independent travellers. In any case, make sure you have adequate health insurance.

required to place a slate in public view stating the exchange rate for the day.

Most hotels, restaurants and commercial establishments accept major credit cards and they are legally bound to use the correct exchange rate on them. US dollars are also widely accepted.

What to Bring

A simple wardrobe of light-weight clothes made of natural fibres (cotton, linen, etc) will be most comfortable while touring during the day. Be sure to pack bathing suits, sunscreen, sunglasses and comfortable shoes.

When visiting churches, men should uncover their heads as a sign of respect. Women do not need to cover their heads these days, though it is customary to wear a long sleeved dress and veils when attending a religious service. Entering a church wearing shorts may be interpreted as offensive.

Men attending a conference or on a business trip will occasionally need to wear a jacket and tie, and

may need a tuxedo. On formal occasions a white suit is worn here and ladies wear evening gowns. On cool nights, from November to February, ladies may wish to carry a light shawl.

Getting There

Direct scheduled or charter flights from Europe depart from airports in London, Madrid, Rome, Lisbon, Amsterdam, Bonn, Dusseldorf, Stuttgart, Brussels, Frankfurt, Helsinki and Paris, among others.

North American routes link the Dominican Republic with Toronto, Montreal, Ottawa, Quebec City, Halifax, Dallas, Minneapolis, Boston, Newark, New York and Detroit. There are also direct flights from Latin American cities including Caracas, Panama City, La Paz, Santiago de Chile, Buenos Aires, Bogata and Cancun.

Over 60 charter airlines fly to the international airports of Puerto Plata, Punta Cana and Santo Domingo.

AIRLINES

From Europe: British Airways, British Caledonian, Air France, Alitalia, Air Europa, Hapaz, Air Portugal, AOM Minerve, Condor, Lloyd, Martinair Holland, LTU.
From North America: American Airlines, TWA, Northwest, Air Atlantic.
Inter-Caribbean: Air France, Air Santo Domingo, Air Guadeloupe, Aeroportal, ALM, American Eagle, Cubana de Aviacion, Dominair, Lynx Air, Copa, Sky King, Iberia.
From Central America: Copa, Lacsa.
From South America: Aeroperu, Aeropostal, Aces, Aserca, Iberia, Aerolineas Argentinas, Lanchile.

Tour Operators

Tour companies with offices in the Dominican Republic.

SANTO DOMINGO

Caribbean Connections
Siervas de María 2
Naco., Santo Domingo
Tel: 549-4010; fax: 566-8393
Email: James.garcia@codetel.net.do
Omni Tours
Roberto Pastoriza 204
Santo Domingo
Tel: 565-6591; fax: 567-4710
Email: Omni.tours@codetel.net.do
Premiere Tours
Dr. Jacinto Mañón
Edif. D'Roca Plaza 201
Santo Domingo
Tel: 563-0790; fax: 566-9243
Email: Premiere@codetel.net.do
Also has offices in Puerto Plata,
Punta Cana and Juan Dolio.
Prieto Tours
Ave. Francia 125
Santo Domingo
Tel: 685-0102; fax: 682-8929
Email:Prieto.tours@codetel.net.do
Offices also in Puerto Plata, Punta
Cana, Samaná and Juan Dolio.
Temptation Tour and Travel
Plaza Francesca
Abraham Lincoln, Suite 229

Santo Domingo
Tel: 227-6688; fax: 227-6696
Email: Temptation@codetel.net.do
Touridea
Leonor de Ovando 57
Santo Domingo
Tel. 685-7525 FAX 682-0302
Email: Touridea@codetel.net.do
Also has an office in Punta Cana.
Turinter
Leopoldo Navarro 4
Santo Domingo
Tel: 686-4020; fax: 688-3890
Email: Turinter@aacr.net
Also has offices in Puerto Plata and
Punta Cana.

THE NORTH

Cafemba Tours
Centro Convenciones Playa Dorada
Puerto Plata
Tel: 586-2177; fax: 586-6313
Email: m.jiminian@codetel.net.do
Coco Tours
Puerto Plata
Tel: 586-1311; fax: 586-1237
Email: Steve@cocotours.com
Go Dominican Tours
Puerto Plata
Tel: 586-5969; fax: 586-8641
Email:
Go.dominican.tours@codetel.net.do

Getting Hitched in the Dominican Republic

Tropical weddings in the Dominican Republic are increasingly popular with couples who want to combine the ceremony and honeymoon and bring friends and family along too. Whether you want to tie the knot on a picture-postcard beach or in a pretty Caribbean chapel, most tour operators, hotels and resorts offer all-in packages. Some hotels have dedicated wedding planners who can organise packages that include an indoor or outdoor ceremony, the services of a civil judge, wedding cake, champagne and flowers. Other services include music, photography and video.

Reservations should be made at least one month in advance.

Popular places to get hitched are Samaná, Punta Cana and Playa Grande, or lively Santo Domingo, Puerto Plata, Boca Chica and Playa Dorada.

Before the ceremony the couple must fulfil a three-day residential requirement and provide the following official documents translated into Spanish:
● a notarised statement of their country of origin, legalised in the Dominican Consulate, indicating their current marital status.
● legalised copies of any divorce papers.
● valid passports (also required for any foreign witness).
● an original birth certificate.

Practical Tips

Postal Services

The Dominican postal service (Inposdom) has offices in every city as well as in airports and resorts.

Telecommunications

The international dialling code for the Dominican Republic is **809**. The country has a modern telecommunications network via telephone, telex, cable, internet and fax, available 24 hours a day, every day. Public payphones are commonplace in towns and cities. Most hotels have a public phone.

Two main telephone companies serve the entire country:
Cotedel, 8am–10pm daily. Services include internet access and fax.
Tricom, 9am–5pm Mon–Sat.

There are also several other smaller companies which provide a telephone service including Turitel and All America.

Embassies & Consulates

The following countries have diplomatic representation in Santo Domingo:
Canada: C.Eugenio de Marchena 39, tel: 685 1136, fax: 682 2691, email: e.canada@codetel.net.do
Haiti: Juan Sanchez Ramirez 33, tel: 686 5778, fax: 686 6096, email: Amb.haiti@codetel.net.do
Malta: Agustin Lara 45, tel: 549 5576, fax: 549 5974
UK: 27 de febrero 233, tel: 472 7111, fax: 472 7574
USA: Cesar Nicolas Penson, tel: 221 2171, fax: 686 7437

International Organisations

Apostolic Nunciature
Maximo Gomez 27
Tel: 682 3773; fax 687 0287
Email: nuncap.rd@codetel.net.do
UNESCO-PNUD
Anacaona 9 Mirador Sur
Tel: 531 3403; fax: 531 3507
Email: salhailu@codetel.net.do
UNICEF
Aybar Castellanos 165
Tel: 540 2868, fax: 540 3905
Email: Unicef@codetel.net.do

Disabled Travellers

The Dominican Republic is not yet fully equipped to accommodate disabled travellers, but it is possible to find hotels that meet your needs. Consult your travel agent, or one of the following organisations that specialise in advising disabled travellers:
Access to Travel Magazine Inc.
PO Box 43, Delmar,
NY 12054 1105, USA
Tel: 518 439 4146
Fax: 518 439 9004
Accent on Living
P.O. Box 700, Bloomington,
IL 61702, USA
Tel: 800 787 8444 or 309 378 2961
Fax: 309 378 4420
Email: acntlvng@aol.com
Partners of The Americas
1424 K Street, NW, Suite 700,
Washington, DC 20005, USA
Tel: 800 322 7844 or 202 628 3300
Fax: 202 628 3306
Email: info@partners.poa.com
Royal Association For Disability and Rehabilitation (RADAR)
12 City Forum, 250 City Road,
London EC1V 8AF, UK
Tel: 020 7250 3222
Fax: 020 7250 0212
Minicom: 020 7250 4119
Email: radar@radar.org.uk
Society for the Advancement of Travel for the Handicapped (SATH)
347 5TH Ave, Suite 610, New York,
NY 10016, USA
Tel: 212 447 7284
Fax: 212 725 8253
Email: sathtravel@aol.com

Women Travellers

Women travelling alone can move around relatively safely in the Dominican Republic. Stick to populated areas by day and night. And don't be surprised if local men blatantly attempt to charm you.

Travelling with Children

Most larger hotels and resort complexes offer facilities and a range of entertainment activities for children, as well as the services of trained child minders.

Medical Services

There are clinics and hospitals in most large towns and cities. Ask at your hotel to recommend a doctor or the nearest pharmacy.

Hospitals

Centro Cardiovascular
Josefa Perdomo 152
Santo Domingo
Tel: 682 6071

Hospital Jose Maria Cabral
Ave. Central
Santiago
Tel: 583 4311

Centro Médico Oriental
Sta. Rosa
Puerto Plata
Tel: 586 2210

Security and Crime

In an emergency, dial **911**. This 24-hour number will connect you with the police, Red Cross, fire service, civil defence and emergency centres.

Due to the authorities' crackdown on drugs, the Dominican Republic is one of the safest destinations in the Caribbean. However, it is important to be cautious. Do not carry large amounts of money on your person; do not leave valuables unattended at any time and avoid walking along unlit streets after dark.

The Department of Tourism has a

Media

There are five morning newspapers and two afternoon papers with nationwide circulation, edited in Santo Domingo: *El Caribe, El Nuevo Diario, El Siglo, Hoy, Listin Diario, El Nacional* and *Ultima Hora*. The morning paper, *La Informacion*, is edited in Santiago de los Caballeros. There is also a weekly English newspaper, *Santo Domingo News,* with information oriented towards tourists, and a magazine, *Bohio Domincana*, with international coverage and specialising in tourist information, published in English and Spanish.

There are 179 AM-FM radio stations and 10 television stations. Most hotels also offer cable TV.

special security force called the *Politur* or *Policia Turistica* (Tourist Police). Officers provide information and guidance to visitors on security matters. For more information, contact:
Tel: 221 4660; fax: 682 3806 in Santo Domingo (main office) or Tel: 586 3676; fax 586 3806 in Puerto Plata.

Business Hours

In general shops and places of business are open at the following times:
Banks: Mon–Fri 8.30am–3.30pm
Government offices: Mon–Fri 7.30am–2.30pm
Commercial offices: Mon–Fri 8.30am–12.30pm and 2.30–6.30pm, or 9.am–5.30pm
Shops: Mon–Fri 9am–7pm. Large stores stay open Saturday, and sometimes on Sunday, until 2pm.
Note: some shops and businesses close for siesta or a long lunch break between 12.30 and 2.30pm.

Public Holidays

January 1	New Year's Day
January 21	Day of Our Lady of Altagracia
February 27	Independence Day
March or April	Easter (variable)
	Good Friday (variable)
May or June	Corpus Christi (variable)
September 24	Day of Our Lady of Mercedes
December 25	Christmas Day

The following holidays are observed on the closest Monday to these fixed dates:

January 6	Epiphany
January 26	Juan Pablo Duarte's birthday
May 1	Labour Day
August 16	Dominican Restoration Day
November 6	Constitution Day

Tipping

In addition to an 8 percent tax restaurants add a 10 percent service charge to all bills, which is passed on to employees. If you receive exceptional service it is appropriate to give an extra tip.

Religious Services

Ninety percent of Dominicans are Roman Catholic, but other denominations include Anglican, Baptist, Evangelical, Seventh day Adventist and Mormon. Services in English are held in some city churches. The synagogue in Santo Domingo has a service on Friday evening.

Getting Around

From the Airport

The Dominican Republic has 8 international airports including Las Américas International, 20km (12 miles) east of Santo Domingo; Herrerra International (to be replaced by the new La Isabela airport) in the capital city; General Gregorio Luperon 18km (11 miles) from Puerto Plata; Punta Cana; La Romana; Cibao International in Santiago. The María Montez International in Barahona and the Arroyo Barril International in Samaná do not have a regular air service yet.

Most hotels and tour operators can organise transportation for ferry clients to and from the airport. But if you are travelling independently then your best bet would be to take a taxi. Always agree on a fee for the journey before entering the taxi.

Driving

Driving in the Dominican Republic can be hairy, so you are advised to drive defensively and with extreme caution. If you are involved in an accident, as a visitor, you will be expected to foot the bill for any repairs, even if the prang is not your fault. Ensure that any motor vehicle insurance you buy is fully comprehensive.

Remember to drive on the right.

CAR RENTAL

Car rental can be very expensive and involve bureaucratic form filling. To hire a vehicle drivers need to be at least 25 years old with a valid driver's licence from their country of origin (or an international licence) and have a major credit card. Hiring a motorbike (*motoconcho*) is an inexpensive and convenient alternative to a car for getting around town.

If you plan to tour the island it would be wise to rent a 4-wheel-drive vehicle which can handle the sometimes rough, hilly country roads. While many roads are well-maintained others, especially in remote areas, appear to be little more than two-vehicle dirt tracks.

All the major car rental agencies, including Hertz, Avis, Thrifty, Budget and Dollar have a booth at the airports and in larger cities. Alternatively, book before you leave home.

Avis
Ave. Abraham Lincoln
Esq Sarasota
Santo Domingo
Tel: 535 7191

Antigua Autopista Duarte km2
Santiago
Tel: 582 7007

Carretera Luperon km 4½
Puerto Plata
Tel: 586 4436

Casa de Campo Resort
La Romana
Tel: 221 0972

Marquez 35
La Romana
Tel: 550 0600

Budget
Ave. JFK Esq-Lope de Vega
Santo Domingo
Tel: 562 6812

Hertz
Mercantile Santo Domingo
Ave. Independencia 454
Santo Domingo
Tel: 221 5333
Fax: 221 8927

Hotel Flamenco
Proyecto Playa Dorada
Puerto Plata
Tel: 320 1025

Fax: 221 8927
Casa de Campo Resort
La Romana
Tel: 523 8988
Fax: 221 8927

Hotel Carabela
Bávaro
Tel: 221 2728
Fax: 221 8927

Nelly Rent a car
José Contreras 139
Santo Domingo
Tel: 508 0088; 535 8800

Las Américas Airport
Santo Domingo
Tel: 549 0505/09
Fax: 549 0693

Calle Estrella Sadhalá No. 204,
esq. Proyecto
Santiago
Tel: 233 0034
Fax: 563 6695

Gregorio Luperon 32
La Romana
Tel: 556 2156
Fax: 556 2861

Punta Cana Beach Resort
Punta Cana, Higuey
Tel: 221 2662 (ext. 7119)
Fax: 687 8745

Centro Comercial Playa Dorada
Puerto Plata
Tel: 320 4888
Fax: 320 2239

La Union International Airport
Puerto Plata
Tel: 586 0505

Thrifty
Hotel Santo Domingo
Avenida Independencia
Santo Domingo
Tel: 685 9191

Calle Jose Maria Heredia 1
Gazcue
Santo Domingo
Tel: 685 9191
Las Américas Airport
Santo Domingo
Tel: 685 9191

By Air

Air Santo Domingo is a local airline that offers daily scheduled flights between the airports in or near the country's tourist and business centres.

By Taxi

Private taxis are available 24 hours a day in Santo Domingo, Santiago and Puerto Plata and can be found outside the major hotels.
    Not all taxis are metered so it is recommended that visitors always agree on a fare before getting into the vehicle so there will be no misunderstanding when you reach your destination.
    As long as the weather is fine jumping on the back of a *motoconcho* (motorbike) taxi is a quick and inexpensive way to get around.

Public Transport

Public buses, *carros publicos* (public taxis) and minibuses offer an inexpensive and efficient way to get around Santo Domingo and other cities and towns. Fares are usually preset at the resorts, but if you are travelling independently you should agree on the fare before you get on board.

Where to Stay

Accommodation

The Dominican Republic has earned a reputation for its large, modern all-inclusive beach front resorts. There are, of course, smaller, simple hotels, charming guest houses and villas if that is your preference.
    Children are usually welcome and some of the resorts have special programmes to keep them amused.
    Below is a selection of the accommodation on offer. Rates and facilities are subject to change.

Santo Domingo

Expensive
Hispaniola Hotel
Ave Independencia, corner of Abraham Lincoln
Tel: 221 1511 or (800) 877 3643
Fax: 535 4050
Email: res@pwmonline.com
Newer sister of the Santo Domingo Hotel which is directly across the street. The two hotels share a casino.

Hotel Price Guide

Room rates for two persons sharing:
● **Expensive:** more than US$60
● **Moderate:** US$30–60
● **Budget:** under US$30

Hotel El Napolitano
George Washington 101
Tel: 687 1131
Fax: 687 6814
This 72-room hotel has views on to the Malécon, a dance club and casino. At the lower end of this price bracket.

Hotel Lina
Ave. Maximo Gomez, corner of 27 de Febrero
Tel: 563 5000
Fax: 686 5521
Email: h.lina@codetel.net.do
This 202-room hotel is a member of the Spanish Barcelo hotel chain. Best known for its restaurant **Lina**, which is among the best in the country.

Melia Santo Domingo Hotel
George Washington 365
Tel: 221 6666 or (800) 336 3542
Fax: 687 8150
Email: Meliasdb@codetel.net.do
This 260-room hotel has views onto the Malécon, a tennis court, casino and a dance club that is popular on Friday and Saturday nights.

Renaissance Jaragua Hotel
George Washington 367
Tel: 221 2222
Fax: 686 0582
Email: h.jaragua@codetel.net.do
Modern and glitzy hotel with lots of amenities including a gym and an indoor lagoon with geese. Complimentary champagne on arrival. Luxury penthouse available.

Moderate

Betty's Guest Quarters
163 Isabel La Catolica, Plaza Maria de Toledo
Tel: 688 7649
Rooms in an Art Nouveau-style building with a roof garden; on a quiet street in the Zona Colonial.

Hostal Duque de Wellington
Ave. Independencia 304
Tel: 682 4525
Fax: 688 2844
Email: hotelduque@codatel.net.do
Tasteful decor, rooms with air conditioning, telephone and bath.

Hotel El Señorial
Presidente Vicini Burgos 58
Tel: 687 4367
Fax: 687 0600
Biggish, two-storey hotel. All rooms have air conditioning, private bathroom, telephone and cable TV.

Hotel Kara
Presidente Vicini Burgos
Tel: 685 3837
Fax: 221 1706
Quality hotel that is popular with American and German visitors. Air

conditioned rooms with ensuite bathroom. Breakfast included.

Hotel Villa Italia
Ave. Independencia,
near Ave. Alma Mater
Tel: 682 3373
Fax: 221 7461
Email: hotel.villai@codatel.net.do
A selection of rooms, suites and an apartment. All with air conditioning, private bathrooms and telephone.

La Cazona Dorada
Ave. Independencia 255
Tel: 221 3535
Fax: 221 3622
Email: cazonadorada@codatel.net.do
Rooms with air conditioning, fridge, cable TV, ensuite bathrooms and telephones. There is also a pool, jacuzzi and restaurant.

Budget

Apart-hotel Sea View
Calle el Numero 2
Tel: 221 4420
Near the city's casinos and clubs and within walking distance of the Zona Colonial and the Mercado Modelo. The apartments have small, clean rooms with air conditioning and private bathrooms.

Hotel Rafael
Ave. Independencia 19
Tel: 685 0084
Rooms with air conditioning, TV and private bathrooms. No hot water or electric generator. Also a few cheap, tiny rooms that share a bathroom.

The Southeast

BÁVARO

Expensive

Bávaro Beach Resort
Bávaro
Punta Cana
Tel: 686 5797
Fax: 688 7808
Email: bavaro@codetel.net.do
This resort is the largest and most popular complex on the Costa del Coco. Five hotels on the same property with 18-hole golf course and lively nightlife and restaurants.

LA ROMANA

Expensive

Casa de Campo
East of La Romana centre
Tel: 523 3333 or (800) 877 3643
Fax: 523 8548
Email: res@pwmonline.com
Two Pete Dye-designed golf courses and sporting Clay Centre. All-inclusive resort with hotel rooms and 150 villas. Several swimming pools, nine restaurants, a dance club, and a private airport. Reservations required six months in advance.

La Reina Cumayasa
Near Soco
Tel: 555 7506
Fax: 550 8105
Above Río Cumayasa; reminiscent of a Mediterranean castle.

Budget

Apart-hotel Libra
Hector Rene Gil 11
Tel: 556 8820
Fax: 556 4833
Most rooms with air conditioning, kitchen, fridge and private bath.

Hotel Condado
Calle Altagracia 55
Tel: 556 3010
Twenty-four rooms. Negotiable rates depend on the number of beds in a room and whether there is air conditioning or fan.

Hotel Frano
Padre Abreu, a few doors down from the Olimpo
Tel: 550 4744
Rooms with air conditioning and private bathroom.

Hotel Olimpo
Padre Abreu, corner of Pedro A. Lluberes
Tel: 550 7646
Fax: 550 7647
Air conditioned rooms with private bathroom. Swimming pool and restaurant.

PUNTA CANA

Expensive

Club Mediterranée
Apartado Postal 106, Higuey La Altagracia, Punta Cana
Tel: 687 2606

Fax: 687 2896 or 685 5287
Features four multi-level U-shaped
blocks, three restaurants and a
huge swimming pool. All-inclusive
rates available. Optional excursions.
Punta Cana Beach Resort
5 km (3 miles) south of Club Med
Tel: 972 2139 or 221 2262
Fax: 541 2286
Email: reservas@puntacana.com
Villas and spacious rooms in
3-storey buildings on the beach.
Water sports and other activities
included in rate.

The Northeast

SAMANA

Expensive
Hotel Cayacoa
Loma de Puerto Escondido, on a
bluff overlooking central Samaná
and the bay
Tel: 538 3131
Fax: 538 2985
Email: ohrd.h.cayacoa@codetel.net.do
All-inclusive resort with 82 air
conditioned rooms and cabins,
swimming pool and restaurant.
Private beach. Peak season is
whale-watching time (winter).

Hotel Price Guide

Room rates for two persons
sharing:
● **Expensive:** more than US$60
● **Moderate:** US$30–60
● **Budget:** under US$30

Cayo Levantado Beach Resort
Cayo Levantado
Tel: 538 2988/3141
Fax: 223 8705
Email:ohrd.h.cayacoa@codetel.net.do
All-inclusive resort with 44 rooms
and a great restaurant.
Hotel Gran Bahia
Los Cacaos
Tel: 538 3111
Fax: 538 2764
Email:ohrd.h.gbahia@codetel.net.do
All-inclusive, with 106 rooms,
pool, tennis court. The hotel
offers excursions to Cayo
Levantado and seasonal whale-
watching tours.

The North & West

PUERTO PLATA

Expensive
**Puerto Plata Beach Resort and
Casino**
East end of the *malécon*
Tel: 586 4243 or (800) 348 5395
Fax: 586 4377
All-inclusive resort; 216 rooms in
Victorian-style village buildings,
casino, two restaurants, pool and
babysitting service. Activities
include scuba diving lessons,
windsurfing and sailing.

Budget
Apart-hotel Lomar
East end of the *malécon*
Tel: 320 8555
Fax: 586 5050
Spacious rooms with air
conditioning, telephone, cable TV,
private bathroom. Some with ceiling
fan and balcony with sea view.
Hotel Ilra
Calle Villa Nueva 25
Tel: 586 2337
Nine cheap, basic rooms, each with
a fan and a mosquito net over the
bed. Shared bathroom.
Hotel Jimesson
Calle J F Kennedy 41
Tel: 586 5131
Fax: 217 7586
Twenty-two rooms, all with air
conditioning but no hot water.
Portofino Guest House
Ave. Hermanas Mirabal 12
Tel: 586 2858
Fax: 586 5050
Thirteen rooms in a one-storey
building with swimming pool. With
air conditioning, private bathroom,
parking and inexpensive
restaurant.
Hotel Victoriano
Calle San Felipe, corner of Calle
Restauracion
Tel: 586 9752
Twenty-five rooms with cable TV and
private bathroom. Ceiling fan or air
conditioning. Friendly management
and own generator.

SANTIAGO DE LOS CABALLEROS (CIBAO VALLEY REGION)

Expensive
Hotel Aloha Sol
Calle del Sol 50
Tel: 583 0090
Fax: 583 0950
The hotel's restaurant has local and
international dishes.

Moderate
Hotel Ambar
North on Ave. Estrella Sadhala
Tel: 575 1957
Fax: 576 2572
Thirty-six air conditioned rooms with
TV. Bar and restaurant.
Hotel Don Diego
Across from the Hotel Ambar
Tel: 575 4186
Fax: 582 8830
Forty rooms, a pool, tennis court,
disco and a Chinese and
international restaurant.
Hotel Gran Almirante
Ave. Estrella Sadhala
Tel: 580 1992
Fax: 241 1492
Comfortable rooms. At top end of
this price bracket.
Hotel Matum
Ave. Las Carreras
Tel: 581 3107
Fax: 581 8415
Fifty well-kept rooms, cable TV,
pool, disco and casino.
Hotel Santiago Camino Real
Calle del Sol, corner of Calle Mella
Tel: 581 7000
Fax: 582 4566
Comfortable rooms with air
conditioning. Good restaurant with a
beautiful view.

Budget
Hostal del Cibao
Calle Benito Moncion 40
Tel: 581 7775
Fax: 582 3593
Fourteen cheap, second floor rooms
with private bath, fans and TV.
Hotel Colonial
Salvador Cucurullo 115
Tel: 247 3122
Fax: 582 0811
Rooms with TV and balcony.

Where to Eat

The Dominican Diet

An integral part of the basic Dominican diet is rice, which is prepared in several different ways. For instance, *locrio* is a combination of rice with different types of meat; *moro* is rice with various vegetables (beans, peas, etc.), and *la bandera dominicana* (the flag) is the name given to the national dish – a simple plate of white rice, red beans, meat and *tostones* (fried green plantains).

In addition, each region has its own popular dish, such as goat with Creole sauce in the northwest, fish with coconut in Samaná and *Janiqueques* (pancakes, literally "Johnny cakes") in the eastern part of the country. The favourite food of the native Indians is *cazabe* or cassava bread.

Restaurants & Cafés

As well as plenty of places serving native Dominican dishes, there are restaurants specialising in Spanish, French, Italian, Mexican, Oriental, German, Arabian and Argentine cuisine.

SANTO DOMINGO

Hotel Melia Santo Domingo
George Washington 365
Tel: 221 6666
Three restaurants:
La Terraza
Open daily, 6.30am–midnight. Buffet breakfast until 11.30am. Sandwiches and full meals. **$$–$$$**
The Antoine
Open for buffet lunch Monday to Friday 11am–3pm. Buffet changes daily. **$$**

La Canasta
Open daily 8pm–6am. Chef's salads, Cuban sandwiches, Dominican stew, fish sticks, filet mignon. **$–$$**
Hotel Santo Domingo
Ave. Independencia and Ave. Abraham Lincoln (opposite Hotel Hispaniola)
Tel: 221 1511
Two restaurants:
The Alcazar
Popular buffet Monday to Saturday noon–3pm. Includes two or three meat dishes, two seafood dishes and a pasta dish. Good selection of salads. **$$**
El Cafetal
Open 6am–1am daily. Breakfast buffet 6–11.30am, lunch menu noon–5pm (soups and typical Dominican dishes) and Italian cuisine after 5pm. **$$**

Meal Deals

Average price per person for a main course or buffet meal:
● **$$$**   More than US$15
● **$$**   US$8–15
● **$**   Under US$8

Renaissance Jaragua Hotel
George Washington 367
Tel: 221 2222
Three restaurants:
The Manhattan Grill
Sirloin steak, filet mignon, grilled fish and lobster on the menu. **$$$**
Latino Restaurant
The menu features *paella valenciana* (seafood mixed with rice), *chivo guisado* (goat stew), grilled pork chops, *churrasco* (Argentine-style beef steak) and grilled mixed platter. **$$**
Café Jaragua
Cafeteria open 24 hours. Specialities are Dominican *sancocho* with rice and fried chicken with honey mustard sauce. **$$**
Restaurant Bucanero
Ave. España Puerto Sans Souci
Tel: 592 2202
Selection of seafood such as king crab and seabass stuffed with lobster. Daily 11am–midnight. **$$**

Restaurant El Fran'Boyan
Ave. George Washington
Creole cuisine. Specialities include shrimp salad, soup and oven baked chicken. Daily 8am–2am. **$**
Restaurant Lina
Grand Hotel Lina
Ave. Máximo Gómez
Tel: 563 3500
Very elegant yet affordable. A pianist plays romantic songs every night. Varied cuisine: pasta, seafood dishes, red meat and poultry. Reservations are recommended. **$$**
Restaurant Vesuvio
Ave. George Washington 521
Tel: 221 1954
Italian restaurant serving hot and cold antipasti, pasta, seafood, beef and veal dishes. **$$–$$$**

The Southeast

JUAN DOLIO

El Sueño
Carretera Vieja
Pizzeria which serves authentic home-cooked style Italian cuisine. **$**

LA ROMANA

Cafeteria Restaurant La Candela
Hector Rene Gil 42
Tel: 556 3138
Serves great hamburgers and chicken sandwiches, typical Dominican food and tropical drinks. **$**
D'Alondra Pizzeria
Castillo Marquez 88
Tel: 550 4115
This outdoor place serves decent pizzas with various toppings. **$$**
De America Restaurant
Calle Reales
Semi-formal setting, quality food at reasonable prices and good service. Appetizers, salads, and main dishes. Delicious tropical drinks. **$$**
Don Quijote
Diego Avila 42 (opposite Parque Central)
Tel: 556 2827.
Higher prices than at De America, but it has the best chef in town. **$$**

Café Culture in Playa Dorada Plaza

The café culture of Latin America can be enjoyed just a few kilometres east of Puerto Plata.

Caribbean Coffee and Tea
Inside Harrison's Jewellers
This coffee shop offers a long list of liqueur specials, hot and cold chocolate drinks as well as tasty pastries and cookies. Daily 9.30am–10pm.

Hemingways Café
Tel: 320 2230

Shish Kabab Restaurant
Castillo Marquez 32 and Calle Reales
Middle Eastern specialities; traditional Dominican drinks. Open for breakfast. **$$**

SAMANÁ

Café de Paris
Ave. Malécon
The menu includes pancakes, pizzas, salads, ice creams and crêpes. Great selection of drinks such as piña colada, rum punch, and margaritas. **$**

La Gina Restaurant
Ave. Malécon
Great seafood is the house speciality. Breakfast, sandwiches and spaghetti as well. **$–$$**

Piazza del Plebiscito
Ave. Malécon
Sandwiches, cheeseburgers and French fries. **$**

Restaurant Camilo
Ave. Malecon 3
Tel: 538 2495
Casual but classy place overlooking the bay. Serves a variety of salads, pasta, meat, chicken and seafood. **$**

PUERTO PLATA

El Provocon
Calle Separacion, corner of Salome Ureña
Tel: 970 1200
Indoor and al fresco dining. Open 24 hours. Specialises in barbecued grilled chicken. **$**

Excellent American and Mexican food accompanied by driving rock and reggae music (live bands), and a great atmosphere. Open noon–late.

Rum Runners Bar
Tel: 586 8388
A lively bar opposite the Playa Dorada resort complex main gate, on the road to Puerto Plata. Jeep safaris are also organised from this place.

Hansi's Wienerwald
Ave. Malecon (no phone)
Oceanside café. Breakfasts, *Wiener schnitzel*, cheeseburgers. **$**

Porto Fino Guest House
Ave. Hermanas Mirabal 12
Tel: 586 2858
Nice setting and well-presented, yet inexpensive food. Pasta and meat dishes and pizzas. **$**

Restaurant Roma II
Calle Beller 45
Tel: 586 8358
The best Italian in town. Serves a variety of pastas and 17 different pizzas. Reservations are recommended. **$$–$$$**

Sam's Bar and Grill
Calle José del Carmen Ariza
Opens from breakfast till late every day. Music is strictly American. **$**

Aguaceros Bar and Grill
Ave. Malecon 32
Tel: 586 2796
Mexican specialities, international cuisine, seafood and pasta. Live music once a week. **$$**

Fast Food

Fast food in the Dominican Republic is usually served by street vendors or local shaded shack-style establishments. Some of the tasty morsels on offer include:

Chicharrones – strips of pork, fried to a frazzle (the chicken version is known as *chicharrones de pollo*).

Pollo picante – chicken coated in various spices and deep fried.

Janiqueques – pancakes fried in oil.

Drinking Notes

The national drink is rum and it is so popular that some brands of the nectar are distilled for the domestic market and only a small percentage is exported. Look out for Brugal, Barcelo and Bermudez rum which can be found all over the Dominican Republic.

The best quality rums bear the inscription *ron onejo* or *extra viejo* – both meaning aged rum – or *gran reserva*. Whether you try this lubrication straight or in a cocktail be careful, it will definitely have a kick – most Dominican rum is 40 percent proof.

Rum Cocktails

Almost every bar and club offers a staggering number of rum cocktails. And don't forget you can usually opt for a non-alcoholic version of any drink.

Cuba Libre is rum and coke with ice and a slice of lemon.

Daiquiri is rum with crushed ice and fruit.

Pina Colada is crushed pineapple, coconut cream and a dose of rum.

Coco Loco is fresh coconut mixed with rum and coconut cream.

Mamajuana is a delicious blend of rum, wine and honey infused with wood bark and herbs.

Culture

Museums & Galleries

SANTO DOMINGO

Faro a Colón (Columbus's Lighthouse Monument)
Ave. Boulevard Alfaro
Tel: 592 1492
Controversial and phenomenally expensive museum which was built as a monument to, and mausoleum of, Christopher Columbus. Exhibits include reproductions of historical documents and other artefacts. Open Tues–Sun 10am–5pm.

Plaza de la Cultura

Santo Domingo's Plaza de la Cultura is the city's cultural hub. On the plaza are several important museums, as well as the **Biblioteca Nacional** (National Library), the **Cinemateca Nacional** (National Film Library) and the **Teatro Nacional** (National Theatre).

Museo de Arte Moderno (Museum of Modern Art)
Pedro Henriquez Ureña
Plaza de la Cultura
Tel: 685 2153
An excellent display of contemporary Dominican art, well worth a visit. Open Tues–Sun 9am–5pm.
Museo de Historia Natural (Natural History Museum)
Plaza de la Cultura
Tel: 689 0106
Disappointing exhibition of the natural world. The display boards are only in Spanish. Open Tues–Sun 10am–5pm.

Museo de Juan Pablo Duarte (Pablo Duarte Museum)
Calle Isabel La Católica 308
Tel: 687 1436
Museum in the house where Pablo Duarte was born. Open Tues–Sun 10am–5pm.
Museo de las Atarazanas (Atarazanas Museum)
Calle Colon 4
Las Atarazana
Tel: 682 5834
A small maritime museum which contains some interesting booty recovered from conquistadors' ships. Open Thurs–Tues 9am–5pm and Sun morning.
Museo de las Casas Reales (Royal Houses Museum)
Calle las Damas and las Mercedes
Tel: 682 4202
Once the home of the Royal Court. Exhibits include colonial artefacts, coats of armour, antique coins and treasure from shipwrecks. Open Tues–Sat and Sun morning.
Museo del Hombre Dominicano (Museum of the Dominican Man)
Pedro Henriquez Ureña
Plaza de la Cultura
Tel: 687 3622
The museum has many interesting artefacts and exhibits which examine the Taíno, African and Hispanic influence of present day Dominican Republic. Open Tues–Sun 10am–5pm.
Museo Mundo de Ambar (Amber Museum)
Arzobispo Meriño 452
Tel: 682 3309
Displays of Dominican mined amber and gems from around the world. There is also a gift shop which sells amber jewellery. Open daily 9am–5pm.
Museo Nacional de Historia y Geographia (National History and Geography Museum)
Cesar Nicolas Penson
Plaza de la Cultura
Tel: 689 0106
A museum which takes visitors on a short journey through history from the 19th century onwards. A lot of attention paid to Trujillo's dictatorship. Open Tues–Sun 10am–5pm.

Museo Numismatico (Numismatic and Philatelic Museum)
Pedro Henriquez Ureña and Leopoldo Navarro
Tel: 688 6512
Collection of coins and stamps. Open Tues–Sat 9am–5pm

SOSÚA

Museo de la Comunidad Judía de Sosúa (Museum of the Jewish Community)
Calle Dr Alejo
Tel: 571 1386
Small museum displays the history of the Jews in the town. Open Mon–Thurs 9am–1pm.

PUERTO PLATA

Museo del Ambar Dominicano (Amber Museum)
Calle Duarte 61
Tel: 586 2848
Exhibits some good examples of ancient amber with fossilized inclusions. Open Mon–Sat 9am–5pm.
Museo de Arte Taíno (Taíno Indian Art Museum)
Calle Beler 22
Tel: 586 7601
The museum plots the pre-Columbian history of the Taínos. Exhibits include an excavated tomb. Open daily 10am–5pm.

SANTIAGO DE LOS CABALLEROS

Museo des Artes Folklórico Tomás Morel (Tomas Morel Folklore Museum)
Calle Restauracion 174
Tel: 582 6787
Brightly-coloured traditional carnival masks and costumes. Call ahead, opening hours are variable.
Museo del Tabaco (Tobacco Museum)
Calle 30 de Marzo
An insight into the history of one of the Republic's important industry's. English-speaking guides available. Open Mon–Fri 9am–5pm.

HIGUEY

Sanctuario de los Taínos (Taino Sanctuary)
Carretera Otra Banda 4
Otra Banda
Tel: 551 1094
A small preserve of Taíno memorabilia. Open Tues–Sun 9am–12.30pm and 2.30pm–5pm.

Theatres

SANTO DOMINGO

Teatro Nacional
Plaza de la Cultura
Tel: 687 3191
Offers great performances of drama, contemporary dance, ballet and opera. There is a good view of the modern stage from anywhere in the theatre which can accommodate 1,700 people.
Palacio de Bellas Artes
Avenidas Máximo Gómez and Independencia
Tel: 682 1325
A beautiful building but only occasional drama and festival performances and art exhibitions.
Casa de Teatro
Tel: 689 3430
Experimental theatre. Call for details and locations of performances.

Carnival & Festivals

February is **Mardi Gras** time, one of the oldest traditions of the island. Each region has its own carnival and the season concludes with a colourful parade down Avenida George Washington (known as the *Malécon*) in Santo Domingo. Festivities in La Vega are considered to be the best but there are also carnivals in Santiago and Monte Cristi.

The famous two-week **Merengue Festival** which takes place in July in Santo Domingo, along the Malécon, is a lively fun event which attracts crowds of Dominicans from all over the country and foreign visitors too. In October Puerto Plata is the venue for the north's own Merengue Festival and cultural event.

Excursions

Guided Tours

In the Dominican Republic all of the all-inclusive resorts are affiliated with tour operators who offer their specialist tours to visitors. However, if you are travelling independently, you can book the tour of your choice with one of the following agencies:
Colonial City Tours
Tel: 687 5245
Fax: 685 1332
Tours around the Zona Colonial, Santo Domingo. Available in English, Spanish or French.
Mon–Fri 8.30am–5.30pm, Sat 8.30am–noon.
Maxima Aventura
Rancho Baiguate, Jarabacoa
Tel: 574 6890
Fax: 572 4940.
Excursions to Pico Duarte, rafting, canyon trips, horse riding, trekking and quad rides; trips to Salto de Baiguate and Salto de Jimenoa.
Get Wet
Puerto Plata
Tel/fax: 586 1170
River rafts trips, canyoning, caving and cascading down waterfalls.
Franz's Aventuras del Caribe
Hato Viejo 21, Jarabacoa
Tel/fax: 574 2669
Rafting, jeep safaris and hikes to Pico Duarte.
Rum Runners Jeep Adventures
Puerto Plata
Tel: 586 8388
Fax 586 2729
Jeep safaris.
Iguana Mama
Cabarete
Tel: 571 0908
Fax: 571 0734
Excursions to Pico Duarte, horse riding, mountain bike tours, scuba diving and specialist family trips.

Top Trips

Samaná–Cayo Levantado
In the northeast, you can drive through the countryside to the white sanded bay of Samaná. The waters around Samaná Bay are a whale sanctuary and every winter (Dec–Mar) humpback whales mate close to shore. Once in Samaná, head to the Fisherman's Marina for a motorboat trip to Cayo Levantado (Barcardi Island). Contact **Victoria Marine** on the Malécon, tel: 538 2588.

Santiago–Jarabacoa
A driving tour through the mountains of Jamao Al Norte. From the top of the mountains you have an impressive view of the lush Cibao Valley. Visit a coffee plantation near Moca/La Vega. Then drive on to Jarabacoa for a horse ride or take a jeep safari to the waterfalls. Don't forget your bathing suit and walking shoes.

Water Rafting
Raft through the rapids and canyons of the Río Yaque del Norte and see some mountain scenery in the Cordillera Central that's only accessible from the river.

Playa Grande and Laguna Gri-Gri
A trip to the Costa Verde, Río San Juan, where you can take a ride in a motor launch through the crystal clear waters of Laguna Gri-Gri, featuring mangroves and bird life.

Las Cascades
Adventure trips by jeep through the sugar cane fields of Imbert to Las Cascades with its caves and eight level waterfall. You can explore, dive, climb or just swim in the refreshing clear waters.

Santo Domingo City Tour
Cultural highlights of the capital city, founded in 1496 by Bartolomé Columbus (brother of Christopher Columbus), are the Palacio Nacional, Faro a Colón and the Zona Colonial (old Santo Domingo) including the Panteón Nacional.

Nightlife

There is plenty of nightlife in the Dominican Republic, including discos, bars with music, nightclubs and hotel floor shows. The following is a selection of popular night spots – nightclubs, café-bars and discos:

Santo Domingo

Bachata Rosa
Arazana 9
Tel: 688 0969
Live music.
Bar Marrakeh
Hotel Santo Domingo
corner of Ave. Independencia and Abraham Lincoln
Tel: 221 1511
Live music.
Fiesta.
Hotel Jaragua
George Washington 367
Tel: 221 2222
Guacara Taina
Ave. Mirador Sur
Tel: 530 2666
Live music.
Il Capuccino
Máximo Gómez 60
Tel: 689 8600
Jubilee Discoteque
Hotel Jaragua
George Washington 367
Tel: 221 2222
Las Palmas
Hotel Santo Domingo
corner of Ave. Independencia and Abraham Lincoln
Tel: 221 1511
Live music.
Merengue Bar
Hotel Jaragua
George Washington 367
Tel: 221 2222
Live music.
Nightclub
Hotel Napolitano
Ave. George Washington 101

Tel: 687 1131
Live music.
Omni
Hotel Melia Santo Domingo
Ave. George Washington 365
Tel: 221 6666.
Punto y Corcho
corner of Ave. A. Lincoln and Gustavo Mejia Ricard
Tel: 683 0583
Steak House Café
Gustavo Mejia Ricard 52
Tel: 565 7137

Puerto Plata

Andromeda Playa Dorada
Heaven's Hotel
Tel: 320 5250, extension 851
Calígula
Jack Tar Village Hotel
Tel: 320 3800, extension 2248
Crazy Moon
Paradise Beach Club
Playa Dorada
Tel: 320 3663
Hemingways Café
Playa Dorada Plaza
Tel: 320 2230
Live music.
La Barrica
Manolo Tavares Justo
Tel: 586 6660
A 24-hour disco.
Orion
30 de Marzo, corner of 12 de Julio
Tel: 320 8956
Disco.

Shopping

What to Buy

Jewellery
Amber and larimar make authentic souvenirs and both gems can be bought all over the island. For guaranteed high quality, visitors are advised to try one of the Amber Museum's shops or Harrison's in Santo Domingo.

Haitian Art
Beautiful traditional Haitian art is sold in shops and galleries in the Republic. Groups of women in headscarves at the market or in the fields are common subjects.

Crafts
A wide variety of crafts made by local artists can be found throughout the island, including pottery, ceramics, and items made of amber, larimar, horn, wood, leather or snail shells. Look out also for embroidered and locally manufactured cotton fabrics.

Sport

Outdoor Activities

SPECTATOR & PARTICIPANT

The Dominican climate is ideal for surfing, while the hilly terrain is great for hiking or horse riding. And then there is baseball, the national sport. Catch a game if you can.

Fishing

For information on sport fishing, contact **Club Nautico de Santo Domingo**, Andres, Boca Chica, tel: 685 4940. For information on deep-sea fishing excursions with professional instructors contact **Actividades Acuaticas**, Boca Chica, tel: 523 4511; in Puerto Plata, tel: 320 2567.

Athletics

Practised at the Olympic Centre, Juan Pablo Duarte, tel: 540 4010.

Baseball

Professional and amateur baseball is played from October to January. For information call **Liga de Baseball**, tel: 567 6371.

Basketball

Practised in the Olympic Centre and in private clubs year round.

Billiards & Bowling

Practised at Sebelen Bowling Centre, tel: 540 0101.

Boxing, Fencing, Judo, Karate

Contact the Carlos Teo Cruz Coliseum and hotels and sports clubs. Table tennis is also available at the Coliseum.

Golf

Most of the larger resorts have their own golf courses or access to established clubs. Some of the more spectacular courses on the Amber Coast overlook the sea. For information contact the **Asuciacion Dominicana de Golf** (Dominican Golf Association), tel: 689 7737.

Motor Racing

For information about motor racing contact: **Autopista de Las Americas**, Km 16.5, tel: 687 6863; **V Centenario Race Track**, Autopista de las Americas, Km 14.5, tel: 687 6060.

Polo

Polo is played at the Casa de Campo resort near La Romana and elsewhere on the island. For information call: 523 3333.

Tennis

Amateur and professional tennis is played in the Olympic Centre, Juan Pablo Duarte, tel: 540 4010. There are also courts on the grounds of luxury resorts and at private clubs.

Language Schools

The country's two main language schools are in Santo Domingo.

AmeriSpan is an American programme. The course costs around US$1,250 for four weeks which covers 20 hours of one-to-one instruction per week, a private room with a host family, three meals a day and airport pick-up. For more information write to AmeriSpan at P.O. Box 4000, Philadelphia, PA 19106, USA; fax: (215) 751 1986; on the web: http://www.amerispan.com

Entrena also specialises in one-to-one tuition. Classes are for six hours per day, five days a week, and the course costs about US$375 for four weeks. Instruction is also offered on an hourly basis at US$10 per hour. Write to Entrena at Calle Rafael Bonnelly 26, Santo Domingo, Dominican Republic, tel: 567 8990; fax: 566 3492, email: entrena@codetel.net.do.

Language

The official language in the Dominican Republic is Spanish, and although most people at the tourist resorts speak some English it is useful to know a few key words and phrases.

Useful Phrases

Yes *si* (see)
No *no*
Please *por favor* (por fa-vor)
Thank you *gracias* (grass-ee-ass)
Excuse me/sorry *perdone* (pair-don-ay)
Please speak slowly *por favor hable despacio* (por fa-vor a-blay des-pasio)
Do you speak English? *habla usted inglés?* (a-bla oo-sted ing-lays)
I don't understand *no entiendo* (no en-t-en-do)
Hello/hi! *hola* (oh-la)
Good day/morning *buenos días* (b-wen-os dee-os)
Good night/evening *buenos noches* (b-wen-os noch-es)
Goodbye *adios* (a-dee-os)
See you *hasta luego* (as-ta lu-way-go)
How are you? (singular) *cómo está?* (com-o es-ta)
How are you? (plural) *cómo están?* (com-o es-tan)
Okay/fine *muy bien* (m-wee-bee-en)
Bill (check), please *La cuenta por favor*
How much? *Cuanto cuesta?*
You're welcome *De nada*
Can I see a room? *Puedo (Podemos) ver un cuarto?*
What is the rate? *Cual es el precio?*
A single room *Un cuarto sencillo*
A double room *Un cuarto doble*
Key *llave*
Bathroom *Reterete, lavabo*

Further Reading

Background Reading

James Ferguson, author of the excellent *Traveller's History of the Caribbean* (Windrush Press/Interlink Books, 1998) and *Traveller's Literary Companion to the Caribbean* (In Print, 1997) and contributor to this guide, recommends the following books on the Dominican Republic and Haiti.

Dominican Republic

NON-FICTION

Emelio Betances, *State and Society in the Dominican Republic* (Westview Press, Boulder CO, 1995). An academic but readable analysis of the relationship between political and economic power.

Harry Hoetink, *The Dominican People* (Johns Hopkins University Press, Baltimore, 1982). Fascinating detail on where the country's culturally mixed population comes from and how its immigrants arrived.

David Howard, *Colouring the Nation: Race and Ethnicity in the Dominican Republic* (Signal Books/Lynne Rienner, Oxford/Boulder CO, 2000). Looks at troubled relations between the Dominican Republic and Haiti and analyses the Dominican obsession with race.

David Howard, *Dominican Republic in Focus* (Latin America Bureau/Interlink Books, London/New York, 1998). Very useful short introduction, covering everything from Columbus to bachata.

Frank Moya Pons, *The Dominican Republic: A National History* (Hispaniola Books, New York, 1994). An accessible history of the country by its foremost contemporary historian.

FICTION

Julia Alvarez, *How the Garcia Girls Lost Their Accent* (Plume-Penguin, New York, 1991). A perceptive story of a Dominican family caught between the US and La Isla.

Julia Alvarez, *In the Time of the Butterflies* (Algonquin Books, Chapel Hill NC, 1994). The horrors of the Trujillo period skillfully brought to life in a (real-life) tale of murder and heroism.

Junot Díaz, *Drown* (Faber & Faber, London, 1996). Tough and gritty short stories from the barrios of New Jersey and the Dominican villages left behind by the emigrants.

Manuel de Jesús Galván, *Enriquillo (1889)* (The Cross and the Sword, Victor Gollancz, London, 1956). The classic story of the Taino cacique and his impossible revolt against Spanish colonial rule.

Pamela Maria Smorkaloff, *If I Could Write This in Fire: An Anthology of Writing from the Caribbean* (New Press, New York, 1994). Excellent anthology, including work by the Dominican Republic's "national poet", Pedro Mir.

Haiti

NON-FICTION

Charles Arthur and Michael Dash (eds), *Libetè: A Haiti Anthology* (Latin America Bureau/Markus Wiener, London/Princeton). A comprehensive collection from and about Haiti, covering every imaginable topic.

CLR James, *The Black Jacobins: Toussaint L'Ouverture and the San Domingo Revolution* (Allison & Busby, London, 1991). Classic 1930s account of the slave revolution and the birth of independent Haiti by the Caribbean's greatest historian,

David Nicholls, *From Dessalines to Duvalier: Race, Colour and National Independence in Haiti* (Macmillan, Basingstoke, 1995). The essential analysis of Haiti's trajectory from independence to dictatorship.

Ian Thomson, *"Bonjour Blanc": A Journey Through Haiti* (Penguin, London, 1992). A hair-raising and often hilarious account of travelling off the beaten track.

Amy Wilentz, *The Rainy Season* (Jonathan Cape, London, 1989). Atmospheric account of Haiti's troubled times in the aftermath of the Duvaliers.

FICTION

Alejo Carpentier, *The Kingdom of This World* (Penguin, London, 1980). The Cuban master of magical realism recreates the Haitian revolution and the bizarre building of the Citadelle.

Pierre Clitandre, *Cathedral of the August Heat* (Readers International, London, 1987). A surreal novel of poverty, political violence and spiritual redemption.

Edwidge Danticat, Breath, Eyes, Memory (Soho Press, New York, 1994). Sombre tale of alienation and political repression as experienced by a Haitian-American woman. Also author of *Krik? Krak!* (Soho Press Inc. 1995) and *The Farming of Bones* (Soho Press Inc. 1998).

Graham Greene, *The Comedians* (Penguin, London, 1984). The British novelist's unforgettable evocation of the evil and fear of the 'Papa Doc' Duvalier period.

Jacques Roumain, *Masters of the Dew* (Heinemann, London, 1978). Socialist-realist depiction of Haitian peasant life and the importance of collective action.

Getting Acquainted

Haiti

The République d'Haiti occupies the western third of the second largest island in the Caribbean (Hispaniola) which it shares with the Dominican Republic. The north coast is bathed by the Atlantic Ocean while the Caribbean Sea enfolds the south. The Windward Passage traverses the west coast, where Haiti is a mere 120 km (75 miles) away from Môle St. Nicolás.

Area: 17,142 sq. km (10,714 sq. miles) – the second largest Caribbean nation.

Landscape: Two-thirds of Haiti is mountainous, much of the rest is semi-arid, and the coastal areas are mild and humid.

Capital: Port-au-Prince

Population: 7 million.

Language: Kréyol and French.

Time Zone: Eastern Standard Time; GMT –5. Daylight Saving is not observed during summer.

Currency: Gourde (gd) and Haitian dollar.

Electricity: 110 volts, 60 cycles AC, as in the USA.

Literacy: 48 percent of males, 42.2 percent of females (1995 est).

International dialling code: 509

The Place

Anyone planning a visit to Haiti should understand that it is not a destination for everyone. It is a country of extreme contrasts where million-dollar (US$) homes are being built while the general economy is in shambles. Extreme poverty is pervasive, leading to poignant malnutrition in children everywhere, and crime. Democratic traditions are weak – scheduled elections are continually postponed and there hasn't been an elected legislature in years.

Yet Haiti – as vibrant as the colours in its *Art Naïf*, as mysterious as its *vaudou* (voodoo) ceremonies, as exciting as its music, Carnival, and Rara festivities, as charming as its gingerbread architecture – can easily become addictive. It is a country for people who have travelled extensively and are therefore familiar with the complexities of the Third World. Visitors also need not be easily deterred by the exigencies of getting around when there are frequent delays, a barely functioning telephone service and a small (but increasing) tourism infrastructure.

Government

Haiti, the first Black Republic, and only the second Republic in the world (after the USA,) was formed in 1804 after a war of independence with France. The constitution was approved March 1987, suspended June 1988 and most articles were reinstated in March 1989. There was a coup in October 1991. And finally a return to constitutional rule in October 1994.

According to law, presidential and legislative (parliamentary) elections are to be held every five years, but elections were cancelled in 1997, 1998, and 1999, so the country has not had a prime minister since 1997. President René Préval was elected in 1995. Early in 1999 he declared the terms of most members of parliament "expired", in order to force an election that year, but it, too, had to be cancelled.

The country has universal adult suffrage over 18 years old.

EXECUTIVE BRANCH

The chief of state is the president – currently René García Préval – who has been in office since 7 February, 1996. The president is elected by popular vote for a term of at least five years. The last election was held 17 December 1995, and then every five years after that in 2000, 2005, 2010 etc.

The head of government is the prime minister. The prime minister is appointed by the president, then ratified by the congress. Because there have been no official elections since 1995 and when the then prime minister, Rosny Smarth resigned in June 1997, ratification of a new prime minister has been in political gridlock ever since highly

Climate

Basically, there are two seasons – dry and rainy. The peak season, from November to March, sees temperatures ranging from 23–32°C (70–80°F) during the day and 15–27°C (60–70°F) at night. In July and August, searing temperatures hover around 32–36°C (80–95°F) with high humidity. The two rainy seasons are roughly from April to June and September to October. Haiti sits directly in the hurricane belt and has been hit with devastating results such as the death and destruction caused by Hurricane Georges in 1998. Hurricane season is from July to October.

The temperatures in Cap-Haïtien are slightly lower than in Port-au-Prince, around 31°C (88°F) in the summer and 27°C (81°F) during winter. West of Port-de-Paix, the far west, has very low rainfall which has left it barren, arid and increasingly unable to support its rural peasant population.

The Departéments

Haiti has nine regional administrative divisions known as departéments just as they are in France. They are: • Artibonite • Centre • Grand'Anse • Nord • Nord-Est • Nord-Ouest • Ouest • Sud • Sud-Est controversial elections in April 1997.

The cabinet is chosen by the prime minister, in consultation with the president.

The legislative branch is bicameral, consisting of the national assembly: the senate which has 27 seats has a six-year term, with one-third elected every two years; the chamber of deputies has 83 seats, elected by popular vote for a four-year term.

The judicial branch of the government is the superior court (*cour de cassation*).

Currency

One US dollar (US$1.00) = 16.5 Gourdes (16.5Gds) at the time of writing. There is another, unofficial, currency system in use – the Haitian Dollar. One Haitian dollar (H$1) = 5 Gds. Therefore US$1 = about H$3.

Please note that when a price is quoted in dollars, be sure to ask, if it is Haitian or US dollars, otherwise you could be in for a nasty shock.

Population

Haiti has a population of approximately 7 million. Ninety-five percent are direct descendants of black African slaves and 5 percent are mulatto and varying combinations other races. The following statistics are from 1999 estimates:
• 65 percent of the population is under 25 years old.
• 42 percent (1.5 million male, 1.4 million females) are under 14 years old.
• 54 percent (1.8 million males, 2 million females) are 15–64 years old.
• 4 percent (141,000 males, 142,000 females) are 65 or over 65 years old.
The infant mortality rate is 97.64 deaths per 1,000 live births. Life expectancy in Haiti at birth is 50 years old for men and 54 years old for women.

Business Hours

Banks are open 9am–1pm and 3–5pm Monday to Friday. Shops usually open 8am–4pm with an hour for lunch at noon. On Saturday, they are open 8am–noon.

Post offices open 8am–8pm Monday to Friday and 8.30am–noon on Saturday.

Government Offices officially open 7am–4pm Monday to Friday.

Language

Haitian *Kréyol* (Creole) and French are the two official languages of Haiti, but *Kréyol* is the main language of the country. Many people in larger towns, especially those involved in the tourism industry, speak some English, French, Spanish and/or French Creole. Still, the average person (around 85 percent of the population) speaks only *Kréyol*. While all Haitians understand and speak it some of the time, French (a necessity for professional career advancement) is limited to the "élite" and middle classes.

Since the 1990s there has been a major shift towards the increased official use of *Kréyol*. Radio stations increasingly broadcast in *Kréyol*, musicians use it in their songs, authors write in *Kréyol* and some politicians give speeches in the language.

Religion

Eighty percent of the population are practising Roman Catholics and around 16 percent are Protestants. Of that 16 percent Baptists make up 10 percent, Pentecostalists 4 percent, and Seventh Day Adventists 1 percent. One percent of the total population are atheist and a further 3 percent are of unknown religion.

The influence of *Vaudou* (Voodoo) is ubiquitous. Vaudou is a blend of religions from West Africa (mainly from Dahomey – present-day Benin and the Congo River basin), that permeates the everyday life of a large majority of the Haiti's citizens.

Public Holidays

January 1	New Year's Day and Independence Day (1804)
January 2	Heroes of Independence Day/ Ancestors Day
Good Friday	March/April
Easter	March/April
April 7	Toussaint L'Ouverture Memorial Day
May 1	Labour Day
May 18	Flag Day
May 22	National Sovereignty Day
August 15	Assumption Day
October 17	in memory of the death of Jean-Jacques Dessalines
November 1	All Saints' Day
November 2	All Souls' Day
November 18	Vertières Day
December 5	Pan-American Discovery Day (celebrates Columbus' landing near Cap-Haïtien)
December 25	Christmas Day

Vaudou acquired an overlay of Catholicism in colonial times when slaves disguised their *loas* (spirits) as saints. Today major vaudou ceremonies often coincide with Catholic celebrations and some religious sites are visited by both Catholic and Vaudou pilgrims at the same time.

Class Differences

The origins of class struggle are, sadly, based on colour. Lighter skinned mulattos evolved over time into an élite ruling class after independence in 1804. They lived in the south, which became the Republic of Haiti. Ruled by the liberal mulatto general, Alexandre Pétion, centred in Jérémie and the area that later became Pétionville, The élite spoke French, studied and travelled abroad and were more educated than their black fellow countrymen in the north who had been forced back to work on plantations and denied education by the dictator Dessalines and his successor, Henri Christophe. Although Haiti was re-unified in 1818, there were then two ruling classes. The rivalry continued between the mulattos and the increasingly wealthy black middle classes.

Economy

Unemployment is estimated at 60 percent. Haiti has the lowest per capita income in the Western Hemisphere. About 75 percent of its citizens live below the poverty level and 70 percent depend on subsistence farming to survive. The rural community is being depleted as people move to the towns and away from agriculture.

In spite of the high unemployment, workers are imported from the Dominican Republic, Cuba and the Philippines for construction projects.
• **Labour force:** 3.6 million (1995)
• **Main industries:** Sugar refining, flour milling, textiles, cement, tourism, light assembly based on imported parts.
• **Agricultural products:** coffee, mangoes, sugar cane, rice, corn, sorghum and wood.
• **Environmental issues:** extensive deforestation (much of the remaining forested land is being cleared for agriculture and used as fuel), soil erosion; inadequate supplies of potable water.

Transportation

There are 13 airports; three with paved runways and 10 unpaved. There are ports and harbours in Port-au-Prince, Jacmel, Cap-Haïtien, Saint-Marc, Gonaïves, Jeremie, Les Cayes, Miragoâne, Port-de-Paix.

Essentially, there are no railways in Haiti.

Planning the Trip

Visas and Passports

Citizens of Australia, Canada, the UK, and the USA require only a valid passport and a return or onward ticket. No visa is necessary for a stay of up to 90 days.

Customs

Visitors are allowed to enter the country with 250g (9 oz) of tobacco, and one litre (2 pints) of alcohol.

Health Precautions

Vaccinations against malaria, typhoid and polio are advisable. Rabies is also a potential hazard. Medical insurance is highly recommended as medical facilities are not often as well equipped as Western ones, and emergency airlift is very costly.
• Be careful what and where you eat, food poisoning occurs frequently among tourists.
• All water should be boiled, otherwise stick to bottled water.
• If you are on any medication be sure to bring it with you, chemists, though plentiful, are not always convenient.

Bring an insect repellent with the highest percentage of "deet" you can find. One brand found in the USA (available through REI stores, catalogues and website) is called *Jungle Juice*. It contains 99 percent deet. Be aware that this is a strong chemical and some people may be sensitive to it. An excellent alternative is called *Skin So Soft* made by Avon. It is actually a bath oil but when applied directly to the skin it is a good deterrent and doesn't have an offensive smell.

A suggested personal medical kit would contain: sterile bandages, gauze, plasters, scissors, tweezers, cottonbuds, antiseptic, a suture kit; disposable syringes, antibiotic cream, antihistamines – internal and topical for allergic reactions or bites, insect repellent, sun screen, remedies for common headaches, muscle aches, diarrhoea.

One of the nicest things a visitor can do is to take (and leave) medical supplies that might be in short supply in Haiti. Contact an international aid agency for advice on what to bring.

Insurance

MEDICAL

Local doctors and hospitals often expect immediate cash payment for health services, so travellers are strongly recommended to take out a comprehensive travel insurance policy which includes medical repatriation by air in the event of serious illness. See your travel agent for advice. US citizens can find useful information about medical emergencies abroad, including overseas insurance programmes, in the brochure, *Medical Information for Americans Traveling Abroad*, available from the US Department of State's Bureau of Consular Affairs, auto fax: (202) 647 3000.

Scuba divers can join DAN (Divers Alert Network). Besides being a non-profit organisation that funds research, DAN has one of the best travel accident insurance policies.

THEFT

Theft outside the home is often covered under residential household insurance policies, check with your before you leave. A copy of the police report is usually required for any claim. If travelling with valuable equipment such as cameras and scuba gear, consider additional baggage insurance and/or a rider on just the most expensive items.

Money Matters

For several reasons, Haiti is one country where the preferred place to change money is a bank. Banks give the best exchange rate, they are more secure, and the notes are less likely to be counterfeit. A hotel is also good, but the rate will be lower than the bank's. Banks exchange only US dollars and US dollar traveller's cheques

The three banks with the best bureaux de change are Sogebank, Unibank, BNC (Banque Nationale de Credit), all have branches in the larger cities. Other principal banks in the country include the National Bank of Haiti (BNRH), Central Bank, Bank of Nova Scotia, Banque Populaire, Banque Nationale, Banque Nationale de Paris, Banque de L'Union Haitienne, Citibank, Promobank and Union Bank.

Always take along the receipt that came with the purchase of the traveller's cheques each time you go to the bank. This receipt, with the cheque numbers on it, is required in addition to a passport or photo ID, in order to exchange traveller's cheques at the bank. Without it, the traveller's cheques won't be cashed. Be prepared for long queues in most banks for any kind of service. Bank locations:
Promobank in Port-au-Prince, corner of Lamarre and Ave John Brown; Blvd du Quai; and Rue Eden.
Scotiabank in Port-au-Prince, Route de Delmas (beneath the Canadian Embassy); and Rue des Miracles near the corner of Blvd Dessalines.
Citibank in Port-au-Prince, Route de Delmas.
Sogebank, **Banque de L'Union Haïtienne** in Cap-Haïtien: all 3 are on Rue A between Rue 10th and Rue 11th.
In Jacmel there is a bank on Ave. Baranquilla Jérémie.

What to Wear

Clothing in Haiti is casual but discreet. Swimsuits and beachwear should not be worn in town. Only a few of the high class restaurants require formal dress for dinner.

Leave expensive jewellery at home and keep cameras out of sight until needed.

Tourist Information

Haiti has no Tourist information offices outside the country, but it does have some diplomatic representation.

HAITIAN EMBASSIES ABROAD

In the Bahamas: PO Box 666, East Street, Nassau, tel: (809) 326 0325; fax: (809) 322 7712.
In Canada: 112 Rue Kent, suite 1308, Ottawa K1P 5P2, tel: (613) 238 1628.
In the Dominican Republic: 33 Ave. Juan Sánchez Ramírez, Santo Domingo, tel: (809) 686 5778; (809) 686 6096.
In Jamaica: 2 Munroe Road, Kingston 6, tel: (876) 927 7595; fax: (876) 978 7638.
In the US: 2311 Massachusetts Avenue NW, Washington, DC 20008, tel: (202) 332 4090 ex. 4092; fax: (202) 745 7215.
There are also Haitian consulates in: Miami, Florida; Boston, Massachusetts; New York; Chicago, Illinois and San Juan, Puerto Rico.

ON THE WEB

There are various websites online where you can glean additional information regarding Haiti. It is important to note, though, that travel information on many of the sites is not kept upto date. Below is a randomly selected list:
www.i-port.net/sd-hgv-port
www.haitionline.com/index.html
www.haitiglobalvillage.com/sd-sod-textfader/default.htm
www.medalia.net/Artists.htmlhttp:/
www.travelfacts.com/tfacts/htm/ha
i/haidest.htm
www.belimage.com/radio/haitinews
.htm
www.info.usaid.gov/countries/ht.html
www.igc.apc.org/wohaiti/index.html
www.sightseeing.com/HAITI.htm

www.caribtourism.com
www.caribbeantravel.com (the Caribbean Hotel Association).
www.washingtonpost.com/wp-srv/inatl/longterm/worldref/countr
y/haiti.htm
www.ahad-kreyol.org

Photography

Bring extras of anything that is difficult to replace, spare batteries and film.

The current crop of strong airport x-ray machines can destroy or seriously damage film. Do not put any film – exposed or otherwise – into checked luggage. The machines at the security check points are not quite as bad, but the effects of multiple trips through these machine are cumulative. Carry all rolls of film in a zipped plastic bag and ask the security person to check it by hand. Sometimes they'll insist that it go through the machine, but each time it is hand-checked is a help.

Getting There

BY AIR

Airline schedules and routes in and to Haiti are constantly changing. New airlines start up and more airlines are adding or increasing service to Haiti.

Airlines servicing Haiti include: Aero Caribbean, Air Canada, Air d'Ayiti, Air France, Air Guadeloupe, ALM Antillean Airlines, American Airlines, Canada 3000, Caribint Air, Copa, Lynx Air, Tropical Airways and United Airlines.

For information in the Port-au-Prince area contact one of the offices listed below, which are at the airport unless otherwise stated:
Aero Caribbean, tel: 222 1792.
Air D'Ayiti, tel: 246 2300/5755/ 2692.
Air Canada, tel: 246 0441/0442.
Air France, Champs de Mars, B.P. 1161, tel: 222 4262; fax: 223 0172.
Air Guadeloupe, tel: 246 1215.
ALM Antillean Airlines, 69 Rue Pavée, tel: 222 0900.

What to Bring Checklist

- Insect repellent.
- An electronic mosquito repeller and mosquito coils to light at night.
- Sun block or tanning lotion (can be combined with "deet" for double action).
- Plastic "Ziplock" bags in various sizes.
- Photocopies of all documents – passport, credit cards, driver's licence, etc. Carry these and leave originals in the hotel safe.
- An international adaptor and a transformer if visiting from outside the US.
- Anti-itch remedies – Calamine lotion, antihistamines
- Decongestant, diarrhoea and

motion sickness relievers.
- Ear plugs.
- Nasal spray.
- Anti-jet lag remedies.
- Liquid hand sanitizer
- Moist babywipes.
- Calculator.
- Small torch.
- Glasses/sunglasses.
- Small backpack.
- Lighter/matches.
- Paperclips.
- Small notebook.
- Sewing kit.
- Stain remover.
- Sellotape.
- Credit cards.
- Prescription medication and vitamins or supplements.

American Airlines, 29/31 Delmas, tel: 246 0100/0159/0205; 249 0311; Ave Marie-Jeanne, Bicentenaire, Canada 3000, tel: 257 2740.

Caribintair, Copa Panama, tel: 246 0737/0778; Rue du Quai, 249 0203; tel: 249 1575.

Lynx Air. Tel: 262 1386.

Tropical Airways D'Haiti, Domestic and International, Rue Panaméricaine, PV, tel: 256 3626/7/8; fax: 256 3629/298 3445; Cap Haitien; tel: 262 1226; Jérémie, tel: 284 6989; Port-de-Paix, tel: 268-5770.

Routes include: American Airlines flights to Port-au-Prince from New York, Miami and San Juan. There are also direct services to Port-au-Prince from Paris, Santo Domingo, Martinique and Guadeloupe.

Flights from Canada are available on Air Canada and the charter carrier Canada 3000. Lynx Air flies between Fort Lauderdale, Florida and Cap-Haïtien. Tropical Airways flies between Port-au-Prince or Cap-Haïtien and Miami, Santo Domingo, Providenciales, Nassau, Kingston, Santiago in Cuba, and an increasing number of places. ALM flies from Curaçao. Haiti Transair and Turks and Caicos Airways fly to Port-au-Prince from Miami, New York and

Montreal. Turks and Caicos Airways also flies between Cap-Haïtien and Providenciales. Air D'Ayiti has regular flights to Miami.

Lynx Air run a regular commercial

Flying Times

New York to Haiti – 3 hours 20 mins
Miami to Haiti – 1 hour
San Juan to Haiti – 1 hour 10 mins
Santo Domingo to Haiti – 40 mins
Montreal to Haiti – 4 hours.

air service from Fort Lauderdale International Airport, Florida to Cap-Haïtien. For further information call (954) 772 9808 in the USA or 262 1386 at Cap-Haïtien airport.

There are domestic flights from Port-au-Prince. Caribintair run two flights a day between Port-au-Prince and Cap-Haïtien. The company has offices in Port-au-Prince, tel: 246 0737/0778; fax: 249 1575 and at Cap-Haïtien airport on 262 2300.

Departure Tax

There is a US$25 departure tax and a 10Gd security tax, both payable in cash only.

BY LAND

There are exit and entry fees to be paid in both the Dominican Republic and Haiti, travelling in either direction. Haiti requires a *laissez-passer* when leaving by road, in addition to the departure tax of US$10 plus 25Gds in cash.

The official border crossings with the Dominican Republic are at Jimaní in the south (the Santo Domingo–Port-au-Prince route) and Ouanaminthe in the north (the Santiago de los Caballeros–Cap-Haïtien route).

The Route Nationale 1 leaves the north of Port-au-Prince, passing through Saint Marc and Gonaïves before arriving at Cap-Haïtien. The journey takes about seven hours by car. In order to reach Port-de-Paix take Route 105 which leaves the Route Nationale 1 about 5 km north of Gonaïves. The drive takes about five hours and requires a 4-wheel-drive vehicle.

By Car

Rental cars cannot be taken over the border and the nuisance of police checks at roadblocks in Haiti makes driving yourself ill-advised anyway.

By Bus/Coach

In addition to the hot, overcrowded public buses that run daily between Port-au-Prince and Santo Domingo, and between Cap-Haïtien and Santiago de los Caballeros, you can sometimes find an air conditioned tour bus (*terra bus*) through a travel agency with advance planning.

Buses for Cap-Haïtien leave Port-au-Prince at the Estation O'Cap on Blvd La Saline and drop off near the city gates in Cap-Haïtien on Rue L. The trip costs around 100 gourdes (US$6) for a one-way trip. Tap-taps for Cormier and Labadie Plage leave from Rue 21 Q and cost about 5 gourdes each way. Buses and tap-taps for Milot and Fort Liberté leave from Rue Lapont south of the city and cost 15–30 gourdes (US$1 to US$2) per trip.

BY SEA

Other than the cruise ships that disgorge their passengers at a private beach at Labadie on the North Coast for about 8 hours, regular cruise ships ceased calling in Haiti after the 1991 coup. With new piers in Jacmel, new roads, and other improvements in infrastructure, this is expected to change when Haiti is ready to receive passengers by sea.

Royal Caribbean Lines has three ships that stop for a day at Labadie Beach, near the Cap-Haïtien suburb, Cormier Plage. It is an isolated beach laden with amenities including watersports and shopping. Nearby Amiga (previously Rat) Island has wonderful snorkelling and offers an educational tour which looks at the making of artificial reefs. Scuba diving can be arranged through Jean Claude at Cormier Plage Hotel.

The three ships whose itineraries include this stop are *Enchantment of the Seas*, *Grandeur of the Seas*, and *Majesty of the Seas*. The cruise ship pier was completed in the south coast town of Jacmel at the end of 1999, so more cruise itineraries are sure to include this jewel of a town.

Specialist Tour Operator

Trips Worldwide in the UK organise tailor-made holidays to the not so well-known Caribbean islands, Central and South America. For more information and a brochure contact them at: 9 Byron Place, Clifton, Bristol BS8 1JT, United Kingdom, tel: 0117 987 2626; fax: 0117 987 2627. Email: info@tripsworldwide.co.uk

Embassies and Consulates in Haiti

The **Secrétairie d'État au Tourisme** is at 8 Rue Légitime, Port-au-Prince, Haiti, tel: 223 5631/0723, 221 5960; fax: 223 -5359/5388; email: set@haititourisme.com; website: www.haititourisme.com
British Consulate, Hotel Montana, Rue F. Cardoza, Port-au-Prince, tel: 257 3969; fax: 257 4048.
Canadian Embassy, 1st floor, Scotiabank, Delmas 18, tel: 223 2358/8882; fax: 223 8720.
US Embassy, 5 Blvd Harry Truman, Bicentenaire, Port-au-Prince. For mailing purposes contact P. O. Box 1761, Port-au-Prince, tel: 222 0354/0368/0200/0612; fax: 223 1641.
US Consulate, 104 Rue Oswald Durand, Port-au-Prince, tel: 223 0989/8853/9324/7011; fax: 223 9965.

TRAVEL ADVISORIES

For travel advisories on vaccinations, visas and security before you leave home, contact:
US Department of State Overseas Citizens Services, tel: (202) 647 5225; **Canadian Travel Advisory Line**, tel: 800 267 6788; **British Travel Advice Unit**, tel: 020 7238 4503/4504; **Australian Travel Advisory Line**, tel: (06) 261 2093.

Practical Tips

It is worthwhile repeating, Haiti is a mutable country where everything is subject to change, almost from moment to moment. As such, prices, addresses and telephone numbers could change – possibly in the time between lunch and dinner on any day. It's part of what makes Haiti so frustrating... and so fascinating.

Etiquette

As you travel through the country treat the people with warmth and consideration and they will usually respond accordingly.

Eye contact is important, as is a smile and a sense of humour. Haitians survive by laughing at themselves and their situation. In a social encounter, it is essential to acknowledge the presence of each person with a word, a handshake or a nod.

People generally greet each other with *bo'ju* (bonjour) before noon, or *bo'swa* (bonsoir) later in the day. This is especially true outside the larger towns, where visitors should follow the local lead and say hello to anyone they meet. *Salud* (pronounced "saloo") may be easier and it's acceptable at any time of day. Be sure to greet someone before asking for help or directions.

Based on the ubiquitous assumption that all *blancs* (any foreigner) wealthy enough to travel can afford to spend their "limitless" funds. Any legitimate attempts to separate you from your cash can be treated with humour, consideration or indignation as appropriate to the individual situation.

Telephone and Fax

Haiti's country code is **509**. Local services and facilities are not particularly reliable, often making telephone contact difficult.

When trying to make a telephone call, be aware that a busy signal doesn't necessarily mean the recipient is on the phone, and a ringing tone doesn't necessarily mean that no one is there, or that the phone is even ringing at the other end, or that there's a working phone in service at that number. Be patient, it has been known to take hours to make a connection.

The entire country, including government offices, can be affected by an unannounced service disruption. A cellular telephone is the best way to avoid such problems, check the system used in Haiti before leaving home.

Phonecards are an option for making calls from public telephones and can be purchased at the post office and from hotels. Cards include the MCI prepaid international telephone card which can be purchased in the US or Haiti. There is also an AT&T calling card account which must be activated before leaving the US. Sometimes it seems that the MCI international operator is the easiest person to reach in the country.

There is a Teleco office on Rue 17 in Cap-Haïtien, close to the Boulevard, tel 262 0000 which is open 24 hours a day. Another office is in Port-de-Paix on Rue Estimé.

Postal Services

Post offices in the main towns are generally open 8am–4pm. All mail must be sent from a post office, although some hotels will organise a mail service for postcards. For larger items use an international courier, most have offices in the larger towns and the cities.

In Cap-Haïtien the post office on Rue 16–17 A is open Mon–Fri 8.30am–4pm, Sat 8.30am–noon.

In Port-de-Paix the post office on Rue Dessalines is open Mon–Fri 8.30am–4pm and Sat 8.30am–noon.

Media

Radio is by far the most popular medium and the country has a healthy mix of music and talk radio programming. Among the most listened to is *Radio Haiti Inter* which plays music and has news in French. Both the *BBC World Service* and *Voice of America* broadcast to Haiti.

Most newspapers and magazines are in French. Popular dailies include *Le Nouvelliste* and *Le Matin*; weeklies *Haiti en Marche* and *Haiti Progrés*. *Libète* is a weekly paper produced in *Kréyol*. The US-published *Haiti Observateur* has some news stories in English.

Weights and Measures

Lengths
metric to imperial
1 millimetre (mm) = 0.04 inches
1 centimetre (cm) = 0.39 inches
1 metre (m) = 3.28 feet (ft)
1 kilometre (km) = 0.62 miles

imperial units to metric units
1 inch = 2.54 cm
1 foot = 30.48 cm
1 yard = 0.91 metres
1 mile = 1.61 km
1 int nautical mile = 1.85 km

Area
metric to imperial
1 sq cm (cm²) = 0.16 in²
1 sq m (m²) = 1.2 yd²
1 hectare (ha) = 2.47 acres
1 sq km (km²) = 0.39 mile²

imperial to metric
1 sq inch (in²) = 6.45 cm²
1 sq foot (ft²) = 0.09 m²
1 sq yd (yd²) = 0.84 m²
1 acre = 4046.9 m²
1 sq mile (miles²) = 2.59 km²

Volume/Capacity
metric to imperial
1 cubic cm (cm³) = 0.06 inches³
1 cubic decimeter (dm³) = 0.04 ft³
1 cubic meter (m³) = 1.31 yd³
1 litre (lt) = 1.76 UK pints/2.11 US pints
1 hectolitre (hl) = 22 UK gallons/26.4 US gallons

imperial to metric
1 cu inch (in³) = 16.39 cm³
1 cu foot (ft³) = 0.03 m³
1 fluid ounce (fl oz) = 28.41 ml
1 UK pint = 0.57 l
1 US pint = 47 l
1 UK gallon = 4.55 lt
1 US gallon = 3.78 lt

Mass
metric to imperial
1 milligram (mg) = 0.02 grain (gr)
1 gram (g) = 0.04 oz
1 kilogram (kg) = 2.20 lb
1 tonne = 0.98 UK tons
1 tonne = 1.1 US tons

imperial to metric
1 ounce (oz) = 28.35 g
1 pound (lb) = 0.45 kg
1 UK stone = 6.35 kg
1 ton = 20 cwt = 1.02 tonnes
1 US ton = 2000 lbs = 907 kg

Temperature
Centigrade to Fahrenheit
Multiply by 1.8 and add 32

Fahrenheit to Centigrade
Subtract 32 and multiply by 55

Tourism Offices in Haiti

There are three Maison du Tourisme offices (tourist information). Situated in the heart of the tourist areas, they are open 9am–4pm to provide information such as maps, details about tours and staff will answer questions.
In Port-au-Prince: corner of Rues Capois and Magny, tel: 221 5496.
In Jacmel: Avenue Barranquilla No. 165, tel: 288 3305.
In Cap-Haïtien: Rue 24 Boulevard, Cap Haitien: tel: 262 1061. Call ahead, opening times are erratic.

Travellers with Disabilities

Haiti is preparing to modernise itself for tourism. The country still needs time to develop facilities which will make it accessible to disabled visitors. As the infrastructure improves the current situation is likely to change. For the present, it would be extremely difficult and uncomfortable for anyone with a physical disability to travel in Haiti.

Access to public transport and tourist attractions is severely limited. It seems as though there are construction sites everywhere in cities and towns.

In the countryside, a paved road is rare and it takes some effort, even for the able-bodied, to reach notable landmarks.

Most hotels have steps to negotiate in order to pass from one area to another. Only hotels with more than three or four floors have lifts but power cuts make these unreliable.

Tipping, Taxes

Hotels and restaurants usually add a 10 percent service charge to the bill. Some hotels also charge a daily energy tax.

For exceptional service in restaurants you can give waiters a small additional tip (in gourdes). Taxi drivers do not expect a tip.

Religious Services

Many churches hold wonderful services with beautiful music. Ask at your hotel for suggestions.

Medical Treatment

Medical care, facilities, and supplies are limited and the level of sanitation is generally lower than in a developed country. One of the best x-ray facilities in Haiti is in a small clinic in Jérémie, which could be too far away in an emergency.

Medical Facilities

In Port-au-Prince: Hôpital du Canapé Vert, 83 Route du Canapé Vert, tel: 245 0281. 24-hour service.
In Cap-Haïtien: Hospital Justinien, Rue 17 Q, tel 262 0512. Situated high above the town; Clinic Antoni Constant, Rue 16 L No.46, tel 262 1577. Recommended by many of the hotels.

The Red Cross

The Red Cross in Cap-Haïtien can be contacted at Rue 17 P, tel: 262 0634. In Port-de-Paix contact: tel: 268 4141 and the general hospital on tel: 268 6264.

Security and Crime

The media publicises the car-jackings, armed robberies, and break-ins in Haiti but these offences are not directed exclusively at foreigners.

Use the same common sense you would use at home and try to be aware of your surroundings. Keep valuables out of sight (preferably in the hotel safe) and divide currency into small portions in different pockets. Be alert, especially on public transport and in crowded places. Keep car doors locked at all times, especially when sitting inside. Don't walk around Port-au-Prince after dark, and monitor potential danger areas by checking with the hotel and the embassy at home. Avoid travelling at night.

Emergency Numbers

Police	Tel: 114
Fire	Tel: 115
Red Cross	Tel: 118

Visitors should exercise extreme caution when driving along Route Nationale 1, the airport road, in the port area and in Cité Soleil, as crimes involving vehicles occur regularly. While a lot of crime occurs in these areas, neighbourhoods in Port-au-Prince, such as the Delmas road area and Pétionville, formerly considered safe, have witnessed an increasing incidence of crime.

Holiday periods, Christmas and Carnival, especially, see a significant increase in violent crime.

The Police

The police station in Cap-Haïtien is at Rue 25-26 A, Carenage tel 262 0951; in Port-de-Paix call 268 5383.

Getting Around

Orientation

Getting around Haiti can be difficult for a number of reasons, the main ones being language – non-*Kréyol* speakers may find it hard to make themselves understood – and a lack of tourist infrastructure. There are no scheduled sightseeing tours. Road conditions, especially in the mountainous interior, are poor. The fastest, safest, and most comfortable, albeit most expensive, way to travel between Haiti's main cities is by air.

From the Airport

Taxis are usually available at the airports. There are three basic types of taxi: local **regular** taxis take individual passengers directly to their destinations, local **shared** taxis (the least expensive) stop briefly to drop off other passengers on the way to the furthest destination, and the **ACGH** (Association des Chauffeur-Guides d'Haiti – Haiti Association of Chauffeur-Guides) taxis. The latter are the same as regular taxis in terms of the type and condition of vehicles, but the drivers are accredited by the ACGH. They are supposed to have some training in tourism, wear the same type of white shirt-cum-uniform with an ACGH pin. Therefore these taxis are more expensive.

The government sets a scale of fares but this is not necessarily set in stone.

A good transport choice for groups is **Agence Citadelle** which runs a door-to-door air conditioned minibus shuttle which includes a "meet and greet" service at the airports in Port-au-Prince and Cap-Haïtien for around US$10 per person. Call the Port-au-Prince office well in advance of the trip to make arrangements, tel: 222 5900; 223 5900).

One of the regular tap-tap services can take visitors into the city centre usually dropping off at Rue 10 A.

By Air

It takes less than one hour to fly anywhere in Haiti from Port-au-Prince. Unless you have booked a private charter, flying between any two cities requires a transfer in Port-au-Prince.

Domestic Carriers

Air D'Ayiti has 5 flights per day to Cap-Haïtien and Port-de-Paix, as well as to Jérémie. Tel: 246 2300/5755.
Tropical Airways D'Haiti fly from Port-au-Prince to Cap-Haïtien, Jérémie, Port-de-Paix and Pétionville. The service is excellent, planes are comfortable and staff are friendly. Tel: 256 3626; fax: 256 3629, 298 3445; Cap-Haïtien, tel: 262 1226; Jérémie, tel: 284 6989; Port-de-Paix, tel: 268 5770.
Caribintair is a long-time carrier between Port-au-Prince and Cap-Haïtien, Jérémie, and Santo Domingo in the Dominican Republic. Tel: 510 8040; 298 3040/3041

By Car

TAXIS

Taxi fares will inevitably be inflated for visitors, except when there is a meter in the vehicle. And even if there's a meter in the taxi, don't assume that it's working, ask the driver before starting the trip. It's also wise to agree the fare for the journey in advance. Ask someone at the hotel what the typical fare is and then try to negotiate as close as possible to that.

Other than the *publiques*, taxis can't be flagged down, they must be called. A hotel is the easiest place to find a regular taxi, the

hotel receptionist will usually telephone a reliable taxi service for anyone who asks, not just guests. Contact:
Nick's Taxi Service, Tel: 257 7777
Sunny Taxi, Tel: 257 7716.
Both are based in Pétionville and have metered radio taxis.
Akenssa Taxi, Rue 14B No. 178, tel 262-2210. An upmarket taxi hire firm in Cap-Haïtien.

Publiques

In Port-au-Prince *publiques*, with a red ribbon hanging from the rear-view mirror, are shared taxis that can be flagged down on the street. These taxis travel along a set route and the drivers speak only *Kréyol*. Be sure to ask if the *publique* is passing the desired stop. The destination of the first passenger in the taxi determines the route and the driver will stop to pick up and drop off others along the way. It is one of the best, fastest and least expensive ways to get around the city. The fare is usually 5 gourdes unless the destination is somewhere far out. *Publiques* stop working around 7.30pm.

In Cap-Haïtien local communal taxis charge about 10 gourdes for all destinations in town.

Chauffeurs-Guides

Chauffeurs-Guides are taxi drivers who cater to foreign visitors. They often wait outside the bigger hotels and at the airport. They can be used like regular taxis, hired by the hour or, for a half-day or day tour. Many of these drivers speak some French and/or a little English, and have some training to prepare them to work with tourists.

Book through the Association des Chauffeurs-Guides. Tel: 222 0330. The dispatch office is in Port-au-Prince city centre on Blvd Harry Truman, near the US Embassy.

Driver-owned Taxis

Driver-owned taxis can be spotted easily, look for the double '0' painted on their doors, and a registration number painted on the bonnet.

City Street Names

Several major Port-au-Prince thoroughfares have two names, the official one used for maps and in the telephone book, and the unofficial one commonly used in conversation. Taxi drivers are often only familiar with the unofficial name. For example, Blvd Jean-Jacques Dessalines is called Grand Rue; Ave Lamartinière is known as Bois Verna (pronounced Bwa Vèna); Ave Jean Paul II is referred to as Turgeau (pronounced Too-joe or Tee-joe); Ave John Brown is called Lalue and as Pan Américaine in Pétionville; Ave Paul VI is referred to locally as Rue des Casernes; and Ave Martin Luther King is called Nazon.

Chauffeur-driven Rental

Secom, Pétionville, tel: 257 1913/2847. The auto rental company in will hire out a driver with their cars. The price for the service is very reasonable if it is only needed for a normal 8 hour day, but it can be expensive if a driver is required in the evening.

CAR RENTALS

If you're determined to drive, despite the warnings, then it's best to call ahead and reserve a vehicle in plenty of time as there are rarely enough rental cars to meet demand. A wide variety of vehicles can be rented from various agencies in Port-au-Prince and Pétionville. Daily rates are around US$60 to US$165 (for four-wheel-drive).

Don't hesitate to ask for any special deals and discounts on offer. There are often special rates for rentals of a week or longer. Please note that cars rented in Haiti cannot be taken over the border to the Dominican Republic.

Drivers with US, Canadian and European licences generally do not need to obtain a special licence for travelling around Haiti. Driving is on the right-hand side of the road.

Rental Agencies

Avis, tel: 246 4161/2696; fax:246 2640.
Budget, tel: 246 2324.
Hertz, tel: 246 0700. Also has an office close to the airport at the Centre Multidynamic tel 262 0369.
Secom, tel: 246 2799/257 1913.

By Bus & Tap-tap

Camionettes (minibuses) and **tap-taps** (open-backed pickups with brightly painted wooden chassis) have fixed routes and fares. They are usually packed to capacity and therefore difficult to board with luggage. They generally stop running by 8.30pm.

To reach Pétionville from Port-au-Prince catch any of the tap-taps which run along Ave John Brown.

Tap-taps regularly run along two main routes in Cap-Haïtien on Rue L, from Rue 15 L to the city gates and along Rue A, from Rue 10 A to the airport. Each trip costs 2 gourdes.

Tap-tap Art

Tap-taps are mini-vans, buses and trucks covered in brightly coloured geometric designs and delicately wrought art, inscribed with humourous mottos and religious messages in *Kréyol*, French and English. The pictures usually tell a story and some use images to make a social or political comment. Below are a few examples of tap-tap art:
• *Recherchez Le Bien de la Ville*
Look for the good in the city
• *Welcome to Don de Jesus*
Welcome to God's gift
• *Merci Manman*
Thank You Mother
• *Sans Jesus Tout est Nul*
All Is Nothing Without Jesus
• *Souv de mon Pere et ma Mere*
Remembrance of my Father and my Mother
• *Paix, Amour*
Peace, Love
• *Peuple D'Egypte. Oh! La Femme*
People of Egypt Oh! The Woman

Driving

Road conditions in Haiti are very poor and paved roads in Port-au-Prince and the major provincial capitals are littered with potholes. Most roads in the countryside are unpaved and unlit. Traffic laws are similar to those in the US but are not generally enforced.

Port-au-Prince traffic is congested most of the day as a result of the poor roads, undisciplined driving, badly maintained vehicles, a plethora of street merchants, itinerant mechanics and so many pedestrians.

The utter chaos and poor road conditions are an unnerving, white-knuckle, hair-greying experience. It isn't easy to determine who has the right of way in any traffic situation. Drivers will make a third lane on narrow streets where there's barely room for two. Vehicles have been known to pass stationary traffic by mounting the pavement. And when there are roadworks, there is rarely any warning or detour signage.

Excursions

Most organised tours are pre-planned for groups only, so try to make arrangements well in advance of arrival.

TOUR OPERATORS & TRAVEL AGENCIES

Agence Martine
17 Rue de Miracles, Port-au-Prince; 18, Rue Oge at Geffrard, Pétionville, tel: 257 2740; fax: 257 2824.
Voyage Chatelain 76, Rue Geffrard, tel: 223 2400/2961/7882; fax: 223 5065.
Operates the Terra Bus to Santo Domingo.
Horizon Tours
192-B, Ave. John Brown, tel: 245 8208/5671; fax: 245 8208.
Tours from Haiti to Cuba.
Sans Souci
Ave. John Brown, tel: 245 6395/6980/6407.

Cap Travel
Rue des Miracles and Bicentennaire, tel: 222 3150/9774; fax: 223 9452.
Napolitano
24, Ave. John Brown, tel: 223 8426/9796/9826; fax: 223 8498.
Omni Tours
34, Rue des Casernes, tel: 223 8870/8981; fax: 222 8351.

SPECIALIST TOURS

Some unique cultural, historical, environmental and adventure tourism is developing in Haiti.
Agence Citadelle S.A. and **American Sightseeing Haiti**
35 Place du Marron Inconnu, Port-au-Prince
Mailing address: PO Box 41, Port-au-Prince, Haiti, tel: 222 5900/223 5900; fax: 222 1792;
email: citagen@haitiworld.com.
The largest travel and tour company in Haiti. Services include: a "meet greet" and transfer; Airport Express; sightseeing charter tours around Port-au-Prince and to Cap-Haïtien; Intercity tours to the Dominican Republic. All tours are on air conditioned buses and minibuses or rental vehicles.
Voyages Lumiere
BP 15010
Pétionville
tel: 257 4004/5; fax: 257 3973/4;
email: ljacqui@haitiworld.com.
Jacqualine Labrom, an Englishwoman living in Haiti, specialises in Gingerbread House tours for small groups and knows Jacmel and Port-au-Prince like the back of her hand. She can also suggest tours elsewhere in Haiti, for any size group.
Residence Pauline
Mme LaRoche owns Residence Pauline which belonged to Napoleon's sister, Pauline. There are usually two group tours per week, on Tues and Thurs and perhaps another on Sat with a full lunch or tea. Individuals can sometimes join a pre-booked tour depending on the type of group. Contact: PO Box 30, Cap-Haïtien, Haiti, tel: 262 2098.

Where to Stay

Hotels

A 10 percent room tax is added to all hotel bills. An energy surcharge of about US$5 per day and a service charge may also be added.

Port-au-Prince & The West

PORT-AU-PRINCE

Expensive

Hôtel Oloffson
60 Avenue Christophe
Tel: 223 4000/4102; fax: 223 0919.
A city landmark – preserved old gingerbread mansion in a quiet residential area, yet close to the centre. Most rooms have air conditioning and ceiling fan, restaurant, bar, pool and a small souvenir shop. Unique ambiance created by Haitian-American musician-owner, Richard Morse, utilising Haitian art and antique furniture. His band, RAM, usually perform at the hotel on Thursday. A favourite haunt of journalists, photographers and politicians. **$$$**

Hotel Price Guide

Room rates for two people sharing:
● **$ = Budget** under US$15
● **$$ = Moderate** US$15–50
● **$$$ = Expensive** over US$50

Prince Hotel
30 Rue 3, corner Ave. N, Pacot
Tel: 245 2764/5; fax: 245 2756, 222 2765, 221 8604
A hotel in a quiet residential neighbourhood three blocks from the Oloffson. Rooms with air conditioning, restaurant, bar, pool. The original building is filled with eclectic art and antique furniture while the newer wing has modern motel-type furnishings. **$$$**

Moderate

Le Plaza
10 Rue Capois, Champ de Mars
Tel: 223 9800/9783/8697;
fax: 223 7232;
email: hiplaza@ acn2.net
Sometimes referred to as the Holiday Inn. A large hotel built around a lush tropical garden, convenient for the city centre. With 80 air conditioned, rustic rooms, pool, restaurant and bar. Has its own generator. **$$**

PÉTIONVILLE

Expensive

Hotel El Rancho
Ave. Panaméricaine
Impasse José de St. Martin
Tel: 257 2080/81/84, 257 9623;
fax: 257 4134
Hotel in a Spanish-style building set on a large lush property with mature trees and flowering plants. Large air conditioned rooms and 5 suites, pool, tennis courts, gym, casino, disco, restaurant and bar. The Presidential Suite has its own dining room and beautiful antique furniture, another suite features a red Victorian bath. **$$$**

Hotel Kinam
Place St Pierre, at corner of Rue Lambert
Tel: 257 6525/0462; fax: 257 4410;
email: kinam@haltiworld.com
Gingerbread-style hotel in an excellent location on the main square with friendly staff. The restaurant overlooks the pool and there is an intimate bar. Comfortable, charmingly decorated rooms in tropical style. Rooms at the back are quieter than those at the front. **$$$**

Hotel Montana
Rue Cardozo
Tel: 257 4030, 257 1920/21; fax: 257 6137;
email: htmontana@aol.com
Uninspiring architecture but spectacular view of Port-au-Prince and the bay from the poolside restaurant. Spacious, well appointed, air conditioned rooms are decorated in bright tropical colours. Two restaurants, a bar and a souvenir shop. **$$$**

Villa Creole
Ave. Panaméricaine
Impasse José de St Martin
Tel: 257 1570/71, 257 1609, 257 8106, 257 7228; fax: 257 4935;
email: villacreol@aol.com
Large welcoming family-run hotel in attractive Spanish architectural style, spread among courtyards and gardens with good views. Antique mahogany furniture, original paintings and a beautiful pool. Indoor and al fresco dining. All 72 air conditioned rooms have cable TV and telephone with voice mail. Internet access to guests. **$$$**

Moderate

Caraïbes Hotel
13 Rue Léon Nau
Tel: 257 2524
Charming, good value, quiet and simple hotel built in the 1920s. Rooms with air conditioning, large baths, bar, restaurant, TV lounge and pool. **$$**

Budget

Hotel Ibo Lélé
Rue Borno, on the way to Montagne Noir above Pétionville
Tel: 257 5668/1695; fax: 257 8012
Built in the 1950's the hotel has a spectacular view over Port-au-Prince. The rooms are reminiscent of typical American motel room, all have private bath, telephone, and terrace. Restaurant, pool, games room and jacuzzi. Has its own generator. Dancing on weekends. **$**

Ife Hotel
30 Rue Gregoire
Tel: 257 2168/0737
Modest, charming little refuge in the busiest part of Pétionville. No food service but it's close to excellent restaurants and nightlife. **$**

Sunset Suites
15 Route Ibo Lélé
Tel: 257 0553
Small, quiet hotel about a 15-

Hotel Price Guide

Room rates for two people sharing:
- **$ = Budget** under US$15
- **$$ = Moderate** US$15–50
- **$$$ = Expensive** over US$50

minute walk uphill from Place St Pierre. Six rooms with bath and hot water, TV in the lobby, and a pool in the garden. Meals can be ordered from Café des Arts (same owner). On the weekend during summer and holidays loud music comes from the nearby Ibo Lélé nightclub. **$**

GUEST HOUSES
Moderate
Doux Séjour
32 Rue Magny
Tel: 257 1560
Simple accommodation on quiet street five blocks from Place St Pierre. Weekly rates for rooms with fan and bathroom. **$$**
Hotel Tamarin
17 Route de Kenscoff
Tel: 275 7022; fax: 257 7022
Simple rooms in a hotel which is within walking distance of Place St Pierre. **$$**
Villa Kalewes
99 Rue Grégoire
Tel: 257 0817
Rooms in a villa, with a pool, near Place St Pierre and at the upper, quiet end of the street. **$$**

Budget
Marabou
72 Rue Stephen Archer
Tel: 257 1934
Just behind St Pierre church. The owner, Mme. Odette Weiner, puts on folkloric shows. **$–$$**

CÔTES DES ARCADINS

The beach resorts on the north side of the Gulf of La Gonâve are open to non-guests for day use and for meals. The biggest choice of food will be available on the weekend when it is busier.

Expensive
Kaliko
Km 61, Route Nationale 1
Côte des Arcadins
Tel: 298 4640; 222 8040 (Port-au-Prince); fax: 298 4610
Medium-sized hotel with 40 air conditioned rooms, restaurant, bar, tennis courts, pool. The beach is part sand, part pebbles. Pegasus scuba diving run by José Roy; boats too. **$$$**
Moulin sur la Mer
Km 77, Route Nationale 1
Tel: 222 1918, 245 1013 (Port-au-Prince); 278 6700/05; fax: 278 6720;
email: Moulinsm@haitiworld.com
Large resort set in a restored 18th century plantation house with a large pond and pretty gardens. A modern extension has large air conditioned rooms and filtered water. Guests use golf carts to get around the 20-hectare (50-acre) property. Dine in **Le Boucanier** restaurant at the beach. Lots of outdoor activites including pedal-boats, snorkelling and scuba diving. Busy on the weekends with day visitors from Port-au-Prince. The Oratory is used for weddings and a small building on the property houses the **Ogier-Fombrun Colonial Museum**, one of the best museums detailing the history of the colonial period in Haiti. **$$$**
Ouanga Bay Beach Hotel
Km 66, Route Nationale 1
Tel: 234 0430
Delightful beachfront hotel with friendly staff, balconied rooms and watersports. Live music at the weekend. **$$$**
Wahoo Beach
Km 64, Route Nationale 1
Tel: 223 2950; fax: 222 5332
Beach resort with garden, restaurant, pool and watersports. **$$$**

Moderate
Kyona Hotel Beach
Km 60, Route Nationale 1
Tel: 222 6788 (Port-au-Prince); 257 8663/9137; fax: 257 6850
Beachfront hotel in lovely location the closest to Les Arcadins, small uninhabited islands surrounded by coral reefs protected in a marine preserve. Rooms have ceiling fans; restaurant and bar. Great for snorkelling. Near the fishing village of Luly. **$$**

The North

CAP-HAÏTIEN

Expensive
Roi Christophe
Rue 24 B
Tel: 262 0414
An elegant, colonial building set in a leafy, walled garden in the centre of town with a decent restaurant. air conditioning, private bathroom and breakfast included. Credit cards accepted. **$$$**
Hotel Mont Joli
Rue B, Carenage
Tel: 262 0300; 222 7764; fax: 262 0326
Elevated position to the north of town commands great views of the city and bay. All rooms have a sea view, air conditioning, TV and private bathroom. Lively pool side restaurant and friendly bar. Credit cards accepted. **$$$**

Moderate
Pension Brise de Mer
4 Carenage
Tel: 262 0821
Overlooking the sea at the north of the city, a family run idiosyncratic hotel furnished with period furniture. Veranda with rocking chairs and terrace restaurant. All rooms have private shower and price includes breakfast and evening meal. **$$**
Les Jardins de l'Océan
90 Blvd de Mer
Carénage
Tel/Fax: 262 1169/2277
A lovely white-washed house converted with 8 guest rooms of different sizes (all with private baths). Also two air conditioned rooms and 10 more planned. French restaurant, terrace bar and a beautiful view of the harbour. **$$**

Budget
La Sargesse Hotel
Rue 9 A
Tel: 262 2116
Rough and ready but central. All rooms have cold water. Small restaurant. **$**

Le Flambeau & Chou Chou Hotel
At the bus station at Barrière Bouteille on Rue L
Standing side by side both hotels are very cheap and very basic. Simple rooms with shared bathrooms. **$**

LABADIE

The road ends at Labadie and there a growing number of delightfully isolated properties which are only accessible by boat.

Expensive
Cormier Plage
Tel: 262 1000
Just outside Labadie Nord this attractive beach resort is located on a beautiful stretch of sand with a fine restaurant and sporting facilities. **$$$**

Moderate
Habitation Labadie
Tel: 222 2245 (La Société Cap-Labadie)
Built on Pointe Sauvage, a small island off the coast of Labadie only accessible by boat. Suite accommodation, excellent cuisine, a small beach, beautiful pool, a pool bar and friendly ambiance. **$$**

Norm's Place
Tel: 262 0400
Secluded and atmospheric beachfront hotel near Labadie village. Originally a 16th century French fortress. Good food in the restaurant. Accessible only by water taxi. **$$**

Budget
Belli Beach Bar
Plage Belli
Tel: 262 2338
A group of small rooms and restaurant overlooking a tiny cove, beach and fantastic view. **$**

PORT-DE-PAIX

Moderate
Hotel Le Plaza International
Rue B Sylvain
Tel: 268 5448
Tourist class hotel on the sea front about 5 minutes out of town by car. air conditioned chalets and a good restaurant. **$$**

Budget
Bienvenue Hotel
Rue Stenio Vincent 92
Tel: 268 5138
Central hotel with clean rooms with private bathrooms. **$**

GONAÏVES

Gonaïves is the closest town to Soukri and Souvenance ideal for visitors attending Vaudou celebrations and pilgrimages. There are a couple of hotels for people who prefer to stay in traditional accommodation rather than in the peasant houses at the sites.

Budget
Family Hotel
Route des Dattes
Carrefour Laborde
Tel: 274 0600
Large, simple hotel with pool and secure parking. Some rooms have air conditioning, triple rooms also available; request meals in advance. **$**

The South

JACMEL

Expensive
Hotel la Jacmelienne
Rue St-Anne, on the corner of Ave de la Liberté
Tel: 222 4899, 288 3451; fax: 288 3453.
Hotel in an excellent location on a broad beach near the cruise ship pier and close to the centre of town. Rooms with bath, fan and minimal furnishings; a few have air conditioning; restaurant, bar and pool. Outdoor patio dining is

popular but the service can be lackadaisical. **$$$**

Hôtel de la Place
3 Rue de l'Église
Tel: 288 2832
This hotel is popular with Haitian business people visiting Jacmel. Some of the rooms have air conditioning. **$$$**

Setting Standards

Association des Micro-Enterprises Touristiques du Sud-Est (AHMETS), 40, Rue d'Orléans
Tel: 288 2840
The association sets standards – which members must comply to in order to join – and follows up Jacmellians who rent rooms to tourists in their homes. It is an excellent programme and a good way to meet Haitian families. Single and double rooms are available from AHMETS. **$**

Moderate
Manoir Alexandra
Near Rue Seymour Pradel
Tel: 288 2711
Beautiful gingerbread-style mansion with an incomparable view over Jacmel and its bay. Reasonable rates (around 300 gourdes) are per person not for the room. All rooms share baths. **$$**

Joe's Place
Rue du Commerce, next to No. 40.
Tel: 288 2805; fax: 288 3182
An unusual American-owned hotel. The magnificent property has been a coffee exporting house in the late 1880's and the former home of the critic and *Art Naïf* promoter, Selden Rodman. It retains its original ironwork features such as circular stairs and charming balconies. Same owner as budget-priced **Guy's Guest House** on Ave de la Liberté. Next door to Baruk's artisan shop with the beautiful lacquered and painted wood items. **$$–$$$**

Budget
**La Coquille Restaurant
& Guest House**
Rue de la Mandou
Small place in an interesting part of town, off the beaten path, quiet and safe. Basic rooms with private bath in a separate building behind the restaurant. Screened windows but if you're susceptible bring mosquito repellent. **$**

JACMEL ENVIRONS

Moderate
Hôtel Cyvadier Plage
Ave Barranquilla
Tel: 288 2834
Small hotel in lush gardens which overlook the cove. Restaurant with a terrace. **$$**

LES CAYES

Budget
Hotel Le Meridien
Carpentier
Tel: 286 0331
A small place with air conditioned rooms just 5 minutes from town. The hotel has a generator. **$**

PETIT-GOÂVE

Moderate
Le Relais de l'Empereur
In the centre of town by the main square.
Managed by a local family, the impressive house has witnessed a few showbiz parties in the past. It still has some original furniture from the mid-1800's when it was home to then Emperor Faustin 1. The bedrooms have large four-poster beds and big baths with gold plated taps. The hotel can

arrange a day out to Cocoyer Beach nearby, with a boat provided by a local fisherman and a barbecue lunch. **$$**

JÉRÉMIE

Budget
Auberge Inn
Rue Roumer
Refurbished and painted yellow the inn has an open porch and beautiful, original mahogany detailing and is furnished with some lovely antiques. A few of the rooms have a shared bath. The property which is the former district health building, stretches back to the next street, Rue Brouet. **$**
Hôtel La Cabanne
A pink building with flowers. The rooms, with fans, are rather neglected. Has a conference room-cum-dining room/bar. Well maintained exterior. **$**

JÉRÉMIE ENVIRONS

Budget
Anse du Clerc
Small, basic bungalows with a bed and table, no fans or toilets. Fresh water comes from the property's own spring. In a beautiful, bucolic setting on remote, expansive bay. Hammocks to relax in and solar electricity for about 12 hours a day. **$**

Where to Eat

What to Eat

Creole food is a combination of French, tropical, and African flavours using local spices. Most meat dishes are fried, such as: *taso* (fried beef), *kabri* (goat) *griyo* or *grillot* (fried pork), *poule* (fried chicken – pronounced pull-lay) and *lambi* (conch) – often served with *Kréyol sòs* (tomato sauce). *Langouste* (local lobster) is a speciality at the beach.

Hot sauces are common – *piment oiseau*, *ti malice* – and *banan peze* (fried plantain) are a frequent side dish or snack. *Djon djon* is a small, dried Haitian mushroom that adds flavour to many dishes. When served with rice the dish is also called *Djon djon*. Haiti grows some of the most delicious tropical fruit. It can usually be purchased in the countryside where it grows or in the city at markets and from vendors along the roads. There are plantains – from the banana family – which cannot be eaten raw and should be fried or boiled. Then there are small, very sweet bananas that melt in the mouth (bananes). Other fruits include: mangoes, watermelon, kumquats, Corosol (soursop), sweetsop and custard apples. Sugar cane can be peeled and the juice sucked directly from the stalk, try it it's refreshing.

Where to Eat

It is very difficult to standardize a restaurant rating system in Haiti because there is so much variation between restaurants which would otherwise be in the same category. There can even be a noticeable difference from one day to the next within the same restaurant. Price does not necessarily reflect quality of food, service or ambiance. Some of the eateries mentioned below are simple places with good food, but no phone so turn up and tuck in.

PORT-AU-PRINCE

Port-au-Prince currently has no real top-of-the-line restaurants. Except for Chez Rose, the distinctly limited dinner choices are in hotels, in Pacot.

Aux Artistes
Institut Français d'Haiti
Blvd Harry Truman at Rue des Casernes
Tel: 222 3720
Good for a snack after attending an event or visiting the library at the institute. 10am–4pm Tues–Fri, 9am–5pm Sat. **$–$$**

Café Jardin du Musée
2 Rue Légitime
(behind the Musée d'Art)
Tel: 222 8738
French and Haitian cuisine which is a favourite lunch spot of French Embassy staff. **$–$$**

Café Terrasse
11 Rue Capois at Rue Ducoste
Tel: 222 5648/5025, 221 2956
Lots of staff from international aid agencies lunch here. **$**

Chez Rose
Corner of Rue Quatre and Bellevue Pacot (near the Prince Hotel)
Tel: 245 5268
Very good Haitian/Créole food. The restaurant is open Mon–Sat noon–9/10pm. **$$**

Chez Yanne
19 Blvd Harry Truman
Tel: 222 0188/7676
Créole food in an air conditioned restaurant. **$**

Jerry's Subs
Rue Capois
Great sandwiches next to the Rex Theatre. **$**

Le Bec Fin
Rue des Miracles, below Grande Rue (Blvd. Jean Jacques Dessalines)
Good, simple Haitian-style food at very reasonable prices. **$**

Le Plaza (at the Holiday Inn)
Rue Capois
Restaurant with an inexpensive and expansive buffet lunch. **$–$$**

Rotisserie Lifran
Ave Delmar (near Imperial Cinema and Citibank)
Excellent barbecued chicken. **$**

Tiffany
12 Blvd. Harry Truman
Bicentenaire
Tel: 222 0993/3506
French, Haitian, American and Créole food. **$**

Restaurants in Hotels

Hotel Oloffson
60 Avenue Christophe
The hotel restaurant is open for lunch and dinner and serves Haitian and international food. There is an Al fresco dining area on the verandah. **$$–$$$**

Le Plaza Restaurant
(in Le Plaza Hotel)
10 Rue Capois, Champs de Mars
Tel: 222 0766
Good restaurant with a lunchtime buffet during the week. **$$–$$$**

Snacks and Ice Cream Parlours

Crème Maison
Ruelle No.4
Turgeau
Tel: 245 5592
Ice cream parlour.

Red Rose Ice Cream
Ave John Brown 261
Tel: 245 6062
Ice cream parlour.

PÉTIONVILLE

Cassagne
8 Rue Borno
Tel: 257 1223; fax: 246 0410
Haitian menu in a large old manor house with beautiful decor in a lovely setting. Excellent ambiance and service. Bar and music. **$$$**

Chez Gérard
17 Rue Pinchinat (near Place St Pierre)
Tel: 257 1949
Can be one of the best, but the French and Haitian food is inconsistent. Beautiful setting in a nicely landscaped courtyard. Bar for pre-dinner drinks and is also where dinner orders are taken from the blackboard *carte du jour*. Some vegetarian dishes available. **$$$**

Guess Who
49 Rue Gregoire (at Rue Louverture)
Tel: 256 3256
Nice setting for a casual lunch on a rooftop patio in the heart of Petionville. Creative dishes – anything from grilled brochettes to ravioli with cheese and basil. Service can be slow. A local hot spot during the evening when the bar is open and the menu is limited. Music on Thursday. **$$$**

La Plantation
Impasse Fouchard, off Rue Borno
Tel: 257 0979
A bit difficult to find, but definitely worth the search. The French chef prepares French and Haitian food. Relax with a drink in the bar-reception before moving on to beautifully landscaped indoor or outdoor dining area. Extensive menu but choices may not always be available. The Grand Marnier "pouch" is one of the best desserts. Excellent service. **$$$**

La Souvenance
8 Rue Gabart at Aubran
Tel: 257 7688
Gourmet French cuisine prepared with local and imported ingredients. One of the best and most expensive restaurants in Haiti. Consistent quality food. Friendly hospitable owners and excellent service. Drinks in the small lobby bar. **$$$**

Les Cascades
73 Rue Clerveaux at Ogé
Tel: 257 7589/7597/6704
Relaxing ambiance; paintings by local artists hang on the walls. The Haitian and French food can be excellent, especially if the proprietor is in the kitchen. Lobster bisque,

veal chop (imported) and bananas flambé or crepes suzette prepared at the table. Very good service. **$$$**

Café des Arts
19 Rue Lamarre
Tel: 257 1131/7979
French restaurant located below and owned by the Galerie Monnin. The atmosphere is reminiscent of eating places on the Left Bank in Paris. Open daily for lunch and dinner. regular live music.**$$–$$$**

Nature et Delices
49 Rue Grégoire
Tel: 257 4613
Deli and Health food store with freshly made sandwiches using the best ingredients. Wide variety of imported health foods and snack items. Good place for food to take on a picnic. **$$–$$$**

Beyrouth
31 Rue Villatte
Tel: 257 2658
Lebanese restaurant with a garden and reported to be very nice. Call in advance. **$$**

La Voile
32 Rue Rigaud (between Lamarre and Faubert)
Tel: 257 4561
Relaxed atmosphere and usually good quality French food. Friendly staff and good service. Regular menu with extensive list of daily specials. Good wine list. **$$**

Les Coin des Artistes
59 Rue Panaméricaine (beneath the Festival Arts Gallery)
Tel: 257 2400
Simple, often crowded place with a casual atmosphere. Fresh seafood from the neighbouring fish market and the grilled fish can be excellent. **$$**

Le P'tit (Pétit) Bistrot
40 Rue Grégoire
Tel: 257 3042
A tiny, semi-outdoor bistro tucked between two buildings on a main street serving good pizza plus French and Haitian fare. Cozy with friendly service. **$$**

Parasol Cafe
Choucoune Plaza
Tel: 257 4007/4008.
In the **Promenade complex** which is a small group of shops in the Choucoune Plaza above the Post Office on Rue Grégoire at Lamarre and Chavannes. The Promenade includes a bookshop, boutiques and a branch of Agence Citadelle travel agency. The cafe is one of two eating establishments. **$$**

1950
18 Rue Louverture (between Grégoire and Lamarre)
Tel: 257 1929
Lively bar popular with ex-pats (formerly the Bolero Bar). Specializes in pizzas, but uses American cheese. Al fresco dining area. Service can be inattentive. **$**

China Garden
Chinese mainly take-out mediocre, but very reasonably priced, food. Café-style with no chinese staff in sight. Serves large portions. **$**

Fabrizio
26 Rue de Louverture
Tel: 257 8433
Good Italian food, admirable quality pizzas and pastas plus huge portions. Regular tables in front section and a less formal, large family-style back room with big-screen TV. Casual, friendly and great value. When ordering red wine, ask in advance if you prefer it room temperature, or it will be served chilled. **$**

Fior di Latte
Choucoune Plaza
Tel: 256 4575
The second eating place in the Promenade complex. Serves sandwiches, salads, carpaccio and outstanding Italian-style gelatos on a nicely landscaped patio below the shops. Very fresh ingredients. Good for lunch. **$**

Muncheez
Ave Panaméricaine
Very popular place with some of the best pizza in Haiti. Take out or eat on the patio overlooking the hubbub of this busy street. **$**

St Pierre
Place St Pierre
Bustling bar and restaurant that is a favourite hangout of the French-Canadian expat crowd. Extensive menu ranges from pizza and steak to Greek dishes. **$**

Restaurants in Hotels

La Ville Belle
(at Villa Creole)
Ave Panaméricaine
Impasse José de St Martin
Tel: 257 1570/1571/1609
Excellent continental food in a relaxing covered, open-air setting overlooking the beautifully landscaped grounds and pool. Friendly bar and private seating areas which often attract the business and diplomatic crowds. One or two innovative dishes daily compliment the interesting if limited regular menu. On Sunday Prime Rib nights and Monday BBQ's, the regular menu is not available. Breakfast and lunch alongside the pool under a huge almond tree. **$$$**

Price Guide

Approximate cost of a meal per person:
- **$ = Inexpensive** US$5
- **$$ = Moderate** US$5–10
- **$$$ = Expensive** over US$10

Continental/Gourmet
(at El Rancho)
Route El Rancho
Tel: 257 2080/2082.
The El Rancho hotel has three different places to eat but the food all comes from the same, uninspired kitchen. There are tables around the pool which make a pleasant setting. Inside there is a dark dining room or a more atmospheric and pricier restaurant next door. Service is slow and inattentive. **$$$**

Hotel Kinam
Place St Pierre
Tel: 257 0462/6525
Haitian and Continental food served in an attractive setting overlooking the pool. Food and service in the restaurant are inconsistent. This is unfortunate because otherwise the hotel staff are friendly and very helpful. Go for drinks or a snack and enjoy the atmosphere. **$$**

Café Marabou
72 Rue Stephen Archer
(behind Place St Pierre)
Tel: 257 1934

Food currently reported to be in the "Tex-Mex" style rather than Creole. Good, friendly service and an outdoor courtyard. Occasional Haitian folkloric dance performances but call to find out. **$**

Le Tamarin
17 Route Kenscoff
Tel: 257 6900/6980
Open Sunday only. A cool respite. **$**

Fast Food

Hit Pizza, 21 Rue Lamarre, tel: 257 6433.
Fabrizio Pizza, Delmas, next to Radio Shack, tel: 246 3558. Three locations.
Dominos Pizza, Rue Panaméricaine near the turn for Villa Creole and El Rancho.

OUTSIDE PÉTIONVILLE

Altitude
1300 Route Kenscoff
Open weekends for excellent creole cuisine in refreshing Kenscoff environment. **$**

La Florville
Kenscoff
Very good Haitian and international food with live music. **$**

Mountain Maid Inn
Baptist Mission, Fermathe
Tel: 255 9807
Cafeteria-style American lunch and snacks of burgers, fries, and ice cream. **$$$**

CAP-HAÏTIEN

The restaurant and nightlife scene in Cap-Haïtien has shifted to the increasingly popular Carenage area (the northern end of Boulevard). Most restaurants serve the usual Creole and French melange, the only exception being a couple of pizza bars.

Éclipse
Rue du Boulevard
Carenage
Tel: 262 3523
Excellent bar and restaurant specializing in high-end traditional Haitian food, run by a lovely French couple. Relaxed, romantic atmosphere. Live music several times a week.Open Mon–Sat noon–midnight.

Mont Joli
Rue B, Carenage
Tel 262 0300
Classical Haitian/French fare at poolside restaurant with live music in the evenings. Attentive and friendly staff and a good selection of cocktails. **$$$**

Roi Christophe
Rue 24 B
Tel 262 0414
Excellent French/Creole menu in a sombre setting. The horseshoe shaped bar is excellent for meeting people. **$$$**

Cap 2000
Rue 5 Boulevard
Popular sea front restaurant serving Haitian food, sandwiches and ice-creams. Open 7am–11pm. **$$**

Les Jardins de l'Ocean
90 Carenage
Classical French cuisine served in the ground floor restaurant. Freshly-made pizzas on the roof terrace bar. **$$**

Marina Anacoana
Rue 13–14 Boulevard
Traditional food and drinks served at the jetty side cultural centre. **$$**

Advantage Bar Restaurant
Rue 18 K
Haitian fare in sweet local restaurant close to Place d'Armes with bright murals. Open 6am–10pm Mon–Fri. **$**

La Caille
Rue du Boulevard
Carenage
Bustling open-air locale two doors away from Éclipse. The patio dance floor is always crowded as are the tables teeming with patrons enjoying the serve-yourself snacks purchased from the frenzied small kitchen. **$**

Ozan Nan Na
46 Rue 18 A
Great cheap bar and restaurant overlooking craft market, serving sandwiches and Haitian plat complet. Open 9am–2am daily. **$**

PORT-DE-PAIX

Most the hotels in town have restaurants which are worth investigating.

Capitol Restaurant
Rue Estimé
Typical Haitian food. **$**

Chez Ketia Bar Restaurant
Rue Stenio Vincent
Small cheap restaurant. **$**

JÉRÉMIE:

Alliance Français
In addition to a restaurant, it has tennis courts and is the best place to find out what's happening in town. It's also a staple of the Expat social life.

Chez Patou
Rue Monseignor Beaugé
A restaurant in a red and white, two-storey building with a picture of an ice cream cone on it. It's also a snack bar and a good place to get a cold beer and ice cream.

Castillo Restaurant and Bar
28 Rue H Merlet
Tel: 284 5658/5659
Elaborate wrought iron decorates the outside while inside a beautiful wrought iron spiral staircase leads to the second floor restaurant. Open daily from 7am until the last person leaves. Serves breakfast, lunch, dinner and snacks. A balcony over the entryway is a nice place for an afternoon or evening drink. The menu is varied.

JACMEL

La Crevette Resto Club
Rue St Anne
Tel: 288 2834
Excellent location near wharf. Good seafood. Live music on the weekend.

La Jacmelienne
Rue St Anne
Tel: 222 4899
Al fresco dining is popular but the service is inconsistent.

Hôtel de la Place
3 Rue de l'Église on Place d'Armes
Tel: 288 2832

Haitian and American fast food served in a busy lively atmosphere. The terrace is a great place to simply enjoy a drink.

Drinking Notes

Most international liquors and liqueurs are available in night clubs, and the top end restaurants offer French wine. Distillers in Haiti make fine Barbancourt rum and the local "fire water" Clairin, made from sugar cane, flows liberally at Vaudou ceremonies. "Culligan" is the name used generically for filtered, sterilized and bottled water.

Bars & Nightclubs

Below is a listing of only a small selection of Haiti's nightlife. Most is dotted around the main towns with concentrations in the Port-au-Prince environs and Jacmel.

Pétionville

Cheers on Rue Villatte in Pétionville has a good bar and good food. It's popular with locals and visitors with money to spend.
Mango's at El Rancho, Route El Rancho, Pétionville.

Jacmel

Chez Dimicaté Bar
Ave. Baranquilla, facing Teleco
Congo Plage on Rue St Anne in Jacmel is a small inexpensive restaurant and bar in front of the Jacmelienne Hotel. It is usually lively on weekends.
Platinum Resto Bar on Rue du Commerce.
Samba in Jacmel is a very large indoor and outdoor space which has live music for dancing every night.The performers include local group Les Invincibles and international bands. Open 9pm–3am Mon–Fri, 7pm–3am Sat.
Yaquimo Plage in Jacmel is an open-air disco/club and restaurant.
Distraction Bar on Rue B H Jeune in Cayes Jacmel is actually a small basic guest house which serves food and drink accompanied by Haitian music in the evening.

Culture

Haitian Art

An original Haitian *art naïf* painting in bright, vivid colours makes a wonderful, but not inexpensive, gift for someone back home (*see Haitian Art page 99*).

In addition to the well-established artists whose work commands prices commensurate with their fame, there are many top-quality artists yet to be discovered.

In general, the well-known galleries are the best places to purchase art. However, there are excellent, undiscovered artists who display their work elsewhere because they are not represented by the galleries.

It is always a good idea to have an idea of prices before making a purchase. This can be complex in because many of the better-known galleries show only the handful of artists.

If you want to buy an original artwork then it would be wise to take a good look around before making a purchase. It will soon become obvious which pieces are mass-produced imitations. You can also visit artists in their studios and check out the Musée d'Art Haïtien in Port-au-Prince, as well as the smaller shops.

Check that the painting is done in oil, not acrylic and that it is on canvas. Also be sure to ask if the picture you are buying is actually a painting and not a print.

Remember that haggling (negotiating) to secure a good price is not only tolerated, it is expected. If you want to buy several things then negotiate for everything together as a group and you may get a good deal.

Art Galleries

PORT-AU-PRINCE & ENVIRONS

Pacot is the lovely neighbourhood in the outskirts of the capital. It is filled with flowering old trees and Victorian homes that surround the Prince and Oloffson hotels as well as some excellent art galleries.
Le Centre d'Art
58 Ruelle Roy, Pacot
Tel: 222 2018
An elegant space in a former mansion that supports artists by exhibiting their works in keeping with the intent of founders, DeWitt Peters and Selden Rodman.
Galerie Issa
17 Ave du Chili, Pacot
Tel: 222 3287
Issa was the model for "the Syrian Connection" in Graham Greene's novel, *The Comedians*.
It probably has more paintings than a warehouse and at good prices too. A good place to visit after narrowing down your preferences.
Galerie Carlos Jara
28 Rue Armand Holly, Debussy
Tel: 245 7164
This gallery has a fine art collection. Located ten minutes drive from Pacot.
Georges Nader Gallery
18 Rue Bouvreuil, Croix Desprez
Tel: 245 0565; and also at 50 Rue Grégoire, Pétionville
Tel: 257 5602/0855
Email: gnader@haitiworld.com
Gallery open Mon–Sat, 10am–7pm.
Damballa Art Gallery
Rue Magasin de l'État 243
A wonderful hole-in-the-wall gallery.
Dantor
77 Rue Fonts-Forts, across the little park from the main Post Office

PÉTIONVILLE & ENVIRONS

Expressions Galerie d'Art
55 Rue Metellus
Tel: 257 0112
Exhibits handicrafts as well as art and sculpture.

Galerie Mapou
8 Ave Panaméricaine
Tel: 257 6430
Galerie Marassa
17 Rue Lamarre
Tel: 257 1967/5424; fax: 257 8981
Has the work of modern artists and different media. Moro's lacquer ware from Jacmel exhibited here.
Galerie Monnin
19 Rue Lamarre
Tel: 257 4430
A family-owned gallery displaying painting and sculpture. Open Mon–Fri 10am–6pm, Sat 10am–2pm.
Galerie Bourbon-Lally
23 Rue Lamarre
Tel: 257 6321
Galerie Caribe
56 Rue Geffrard
Tel: 257 7048
Rainbow Art Gallery
9 Rue Pierre Wiener, Bourdon
Tel: 245 6655/6039
Displays and sells handicrafts as well as paintings.

JACMEL

Domond Artist Studio
76 Portail Léogane
Parizot Domond is an artist and a Vaudou *oungan* (priest). One theme of his art is the particular use of *Vaudou* symbols and colours that draw the viewer into the dreamworld he unveils. Domond comes from a rom a family of artists, all three walls of his one-room, open-front gallery are covered from floor to ceiling with their works. He speaks only Kréyol, so bring along a translator.

CAP-HAÏTIEN

Philomé Obin, Cap-Haïtien's most famous *art naïf* painter established the **École du Cap-Haïtien** (Cap-Haïtien School). Much of the art from Cap-Haïtien is inspired by the artist's neighbours going about their daily lives among the town's distinctive pastel-coloured buildings.
Galerie Toussaint L'Ouverture
Rue 16–17 B
Small gallery with good selection of local art and crafts.

Museums

Musée d'Art Haïtien
Rue Légitime
Port-au-Prince
Tel: 222 2510
One of the finest *art naïf* collections on the island. The museum makes space for travelling exhibitions by shelving some of the permanent displays, so call if you are visiting only to see the *art naïf*. Mon–Sat 10am–4pm.
Musée du Panthéon National
Port-au-Prince
Tel: 222 3167
An underground museum with interesting historical exhibits and artefacts.
Musée d'Ogier-Fombrun
Moulin sur la Mer, Montrouis
A compact but worthwhile museum, which plots Haitian history from Taíno times.

Tour the Forts

Haiti's ruined forts on the coast were built by the French or English in the 17th and 18th centuries, while inland fortresses were built by the Haitians after independence in 1804.

In the north, Cap-Haïtien shelters the ruins of three French forts: **Magny, Joseph**, and **Picolet**. They overlook the harbour entrance and the Atlantic Coast for as far as the eye can see in all directions. The remains include cannons, cannonballs, and parts of the foundations and walls.

Fort Dauphin in the town of Fort Liberté, east of Cap-Haïtien, dates from the 1730's. It is in fairly good condition and would make an interesting visit. There is no other reason to be in Fort Liberté.

The incomparable **Citadelle** (*see page 307*) is a massive mountaintop fortress that took 20,000 men 13 years to build. It is 19 km (12 miles) from Cap-Haïtien and can be seen from almost anywhere within a 32-km (20-mile) radius. It is an effort to reach the spectacular monument. The impressive building offers unparalleled 360° views.

Fort Jacques built by Pétion in the 19th century and **Fort Alexandre** are located in the beautiful hills above Port-au-Prince.

Festivals

CARNIVAL

Throughout Haiti, the finale of Carnival month are the three days before Ash Wednesday. **Jacmel's** festivities are the most popular because of the tradition of elaborate, imaginative masked costumes and lively fun. However the music is considered better in **Port-au-Prince**. There are free open-air concerts all over the city during the three or four weekends prior to carnival when bands are preparing for the final event. Few people wear costumes in the capital any more and the floats have less decoration than they formerly had. Still, nothing can compare with the experience of the explosion of music blaring from the stands and floats, together with the exuberant dancing and chanting crowds. There's a good view from the stands and it's safer too.

RARA

Rara, the "peasant carnival", runs from Ash Wednesday to Easter. Rara bands tour the countryside in brightly coloured attire, playing homemade wind instruments, beating drums, dancing and singing. Their antics can attract a following of a thousand or more people, and considerable drinking adds to the merriment. Léogane is one of the best places to experience Rara.

SAUT D'EAU

During July and August, local festivals – both traditional and religious – are held in many towns, including Petit Goâve, Souvenance, Soukri, Limonade, Plaine du Nord, and Ouanaminthe. The ceremonies at Soukri (near Gonaïve) are unique in that they honour the Congo loas (spirits) only.

Sport

Outdoor Activities

Though Haiti is no sporting mecca there are things to do for the more energetic visitors and sport to watch for the rest.

COCKFIGHTING

Cockfighting is a an activity that trancends race and class. Virtually every Haitian town has a cockfighting arena patronised by the poor and wealthy alike.

FOOTBALL

Football is a popular sport in Haiti, take in a game at the Sylvio Cator Stadium in Port-au-Prince or Parc St Victor in Cap-Haïtien.

WATERSPORTS

Cormier Plage
Labadie Nord
tel 262 1000
The luxury beach resort can organise a variety of watersports including scuba diving, snorkelling and sailing for guests and non-guests.
Pegasus Diving Services
B.P. 15785
Pétionville
Tel: 298 4621 (dive shop); 238 2471/3140 (workshop).
José Roy can organise dives in the waters along the Côte des Arcadins, which he knows like the back of his hand.

Shopping

Artisania

Haiti is famous for its high quality and unique arts and crafts. Papier mâché carnival masks and animals, brightly painted black lacquerware, unusual carvings and exceptional ironwork – from small *bibelots* to large decorative doors. Wall hangings of exquisite faces fashioned from leather, soapstone carvings, and items associated with Vaudou ceremonies are just a few of the possibilities.

All of the excellent outlets are too numerous to mention, so the main streets in which to meander are listed below, in addition to a sampling of the shops.

PORT-AU-PRINCE CENTRE

Marché de Fer (Iron Market)
Blvd Jean-Jacques Dessalines
Port-au-Prince
Mon–Fri 8am–4pm, Sat 8am–noon.
Haggling (bargaining) is expected and highly recommended even if a quoted price seems reasonable, the visitor can be sure that it is at least twice what the seller expects to be paid in the end.

The hot, crowded, covered market is crammed with a huge variety of items of varying quality. Soapstone and wood carvings, paintings, leatherwork, ironwork, printed fabrics, straw hats, *Vaudou* flags and small souvenirs all vie for attention. As well as shoes, clothing and foodstuffs. Note that salesmen and middlemen may almost come to blows as they compete to escort the shopper to their own or other stalls where they will be paid a commission for the introduction and subsequent sale.

PORT-AU-PRINCE ENVIRONS

Pacot has a wealth of handicraft shops and a visit to the area can make a delightful day out to feast the eyes and enjoy the architecture, painting, sculpture and crafts.
Comité Artisanal Haïtien
29 Rue 3
Pacot
Tel: 222 8440
Open Mon–Fri 9am–4pm, Sat 10am–noon. This excellent cooperative fills a large space with reasonably priced handicrafts from all over Haiti. Another shop sits right across the street. Go to the corner, turn left and walk three blocks, (passing the Hotel Oloffson) to Rue Capois for more shops.
Ambiance
17 Rue M
Pacot
A gingerbread home with fine examples of Haitian and international handicrafts.
Gingerbread
52 Ave Lamartinière
Bois Verna
Tel: 245 3698
Open Mon–Fri 10am–4pm, Sat 10am–1pm. Sells ironwork, papier-mâché, *Vaudou* flags, horn carvings and other artisania.

PÉTIONVILLE AND ENVIRONS

Pétionville is too full of artisan shops to list. Some shops won't let the visitor pass without stepping in for a look. **Rue Clerveaux** and around **Bourdon** are good places to explore, and the listing below shows a few places to start. Almost anyone in the smaller towns outside the capital will be able to point out studios, workshops and galleries.
Ceramic Art
Thomassin 35, Laboule
Tel: 255 7799
Fleur de Canne
34bis, Rue Gabart, Pétionville
Tel: 257 4266
Specialises in objects for the table. Everything is either made by them or for them. Items made to order.

Le Grenier
74 Ave Panaméricaine
A small antique shop with an
eclectic assortment of items.
Pierre Pierre
85 Bis
Route de Delmas
Tel: 246 5277
Sunny Home
393 Route de Delmas
Tel: 257 3230

CROIX DES BOUQUETS

Officially part of Port-au-Prince, this
small town about an hour from the
capital, is worth a visit. See where
most of the artisans who produce
the wonderful ironwork in the city
have their workshops.

JACMEL

Moro's on Rue du Commerce has
an extensive selection of beautiful
lacquerware and the friendly
proprietors will ship the goods
anywhere.
    Look around in the small shops
in **Rue St Anne**, and at **Zoo Art** in
Rue Triscotte.

CAP-HAÏTIEN

On Rue 17 near Boulevard there is
a small group of sheds where
artisans sell their crafts.

JÉRÉMIE

Abricots is a small town, about 7
km (4 miles) from Jérémie, which is
the artisan centre for the district.
    Comperettes is a delicious bread
which is found only in Jérémie.

Rum

Taking some local rum home is a
great idea. Try **Barbancourt** which
is considered the best for export.
Clarin is made from sugar cane and
is used in *Vaudou* ceremonies. A
good gift for friends who enjoy the
unusual.

Language

Kréyol

Kréyol (Creole) is pronounced
phonetically. E's are pronounced as
an acute unless they have a grave
accent. So *pase* becomes pas-ay in
speech. Another point to note is
that me is written simply as *M* but
is pronounced um

USEFUL PHRASES

Greetings
Hello *Bonjou*
Good-bye *Orevwa*
How are you? *Ki jan ou ye?*
What's up?/
What's happening? *Sak pase?*
What's new? *Ban m nouvèl ou!*
I'm okay *M la*
And you *E ou menm*

In conversation
What is your name? *Ki jan ou rele?*
Allow me to introduce myself *Kite
m prezante m*
My name is Paul *M rele Pòl*
I'm very happy to meet you *M bien
kontan fè konesans ou*
Do you speak Kreyol? *Ou pale
kréyol?*
...English? *anglè?*
...French? *fransè?*
...Spanish? *pannyòl?*
Yes, I speak Kreyol *Wi, m pale
kréyol*
No, I don't speak Kreyol *Non, m
pa pale kréyol*
Speak slowly, please *Pale pi
dousman, soivouple*
Do you understand? *Ou konpran?*
I understand *Mwen konprann*
I don't understand *M pa konprann*
Please *Sivouple!*
Thank you *Mèsi*
Thank you very much *Mèsi anpil*

Don't mention it *De ryen*
I'm sorry *M regrèt*
Be careful! *Pinga!*
What would you like? *Sa ou ta vle?*
I'd like... *Mwen ta vle...*
I'd like to learn Kréyol *Mwen ta vle
aprann kréyol*
I'd like orange juice *Mwen ta vle ji
zoranj*
What do you need? *Sa ou bezwan?*
I need... *Mwen bezwan...*
I'd rather... *M pito...*
How much is...? *Konben pou...?*
How much is the book? *Konben
pou liv la?*
It is $5.00 *Senk dola pou liv la*
What time is it? *Kilè li ye?*
It is 1pm *Li inè*
It is 2pm *Li dezè*
I'm hungry *Mwen grangou*
I'm thirsty *Mwen swèf*
It's hot *Li fè chò*
It's cold *Li fè frèt*

About town
Where is Main Street? *Ki kote
Granri ye?*
You go straight ahead *Ou prale tou
dwat*
You go straight along this street
Ou pran ri sila a tou dwat
You turn right *Ou vire a derwat*
You turn left *Ou vire a goch*
I am lost *M pèdi*

ART & PHOTO CREDITS

Tony Arruza 30, 66, 72, 90, 93, 95, 200, 284, 302
AKG London 23, 26L, 33, 42, 45, 46, 47, 48, 49
Steve Bly 12/13, 137, 143, 172L, 199
Bill Boyce 154, 272/273, 276, 282T, 287, 289L/R, 298R, 300, 316/317, 319, 322L, 325
Bridgeman Art Library 20, 29, 32, 36, 38, 40, 44, 50
Michele Burgess 310
Skip Brown 4, 144L, 152, 195, 203R
Thomas Conlin/Aquatic Adventures 150
Nancy Crampton 126
Editions d'e Art Daniel Derveaux 18/19
Gregory Drezdzon 140
Jean-Leo Dugast/Panos Pictures 125, 288, 289T, 308, 309, 310T
Sarah Errington/Hutchison Library 70, 292
Yves Fonck spine top, back cover center left, back cover center, 2, 2/3, 5, 6/7, 17, 21, 51, 71L, 73, 74, 76/77, 87L/R, 88, 92, 94, 99, 103, 107L, 131, 147, 270/271, 290, 297, 298T, 298L, 299, 304/305, 306, 311, 313, 314, 320T, 321, 322R, 326, 327, 329, 330, 331, 333, 334, 335
Marc French/Panos Pictures 67, 75, 104, 285, 338, 340
Eduardo Gil 28
Leah Gordon/Axiom 68, 106L, 123, 148/149, 323, 328, 341, 342
Leah Gordon 1, 100, 105, 108, 116, 127, 128, 130, 133, 283, 286T, 291, 307, 312, 315, 318, 320, 336/337, 343
Ronald Grant Archive 265T
Andreas M. Gross 35, 37R, 59, 69, 83, 119, 172R, 174, 178, 182, 188, 190, 208T, 211L, 212T, 213T, 215, 227, 323T, 331T
J. Hatt/Hutchison Library 109
J. Henderson/Hutchison Library back flap top left, 71R, 282
David Hoey back cover top right, 164, 201L
Jeremy Horner/Hutchison Library 180/181

Jamaica National Library 34, 28
Catherine Karnow back cover right, 4/5, 14, 23L, 52, 56/57, 58, 62, 63, 85, 86L, 91, 110, 122, 134, 138R, 139, 160/161, 162/163, 169, 186, 187T, 194, 202R, 204/205, 224/225, 226, 228, 229, 231T, 239, 240, 241, 242, 252T, 255, 263T
Monika Latzel 86R, 144R, 153, 168, 176, 210, 211T, 233, 242T, 245T, 245, 247, 248/249, 251, 344
M+W Fine Arts/New York/Jose Martin 31
Nancy Durrell McKenna/Hutchison Library 80, 82, 243, 263
Paul Murphy 39, 96/97, 171, 209T, 211R
Andre Pierre front flap top right, 274/275
P. Regent/Hutchison Library 135
Wolfgang Rossig/APA 5L, 24, 25R, 102, 114, 151, 173, 176, 177, 183, 184, 202L, 208, 209, 214, 218, 220, 221, 244, 258, 259, 260, 261, 266, 267, 171T, 172T, 174T, 210T, 220T, 253T, 260T, 303
Elizabeth Saft (courtesy of New York Public Library) 22
Kay Shaw Photography 339
Robert Smith 10/11, 111, 112, 113, 115, 117, 120, 121
Sean Sprague/Panos Pictures 132
M. Thomas front flap bottom left, back flap bottom right, back cover bottom center, 8/9, 60, 61, 81, 118, 124, 129, 136, 141, 142, 145, 146, 155, 158/159, 184T, 185, 189,

192/193, 196, 197, 201R, 206, 207, 216/217, 219, 222, 223, 230, 232R, 236/237, 238, 246, 250, 252, 254, 256/257, 264, 265L/R, 268, 269
Topham Picturepoint 232L, 332
Mireille Vautier 53, 64/65, 89, 98, 101, 106R, 107R, 138L, 281, 284T, 286, 293, 296, 301T, 301, 324
Ilona Weöres 191, 196T, 199T
Philip Wolmuth/Hutchison Library 78/79, 84, 175
Norbert Wu/NHPA 179

Picture Spreads

Pages 54/55 *Top row, left to right:* M. Thomas, Yves Fonck, Maurice Harvey/Hutchison Library. *Centre row, left to right:* Yves Fonck, Wolgand Rossig/APA, Yves Fonck. *Bottom row, left to right:* Catherine Karnow, Yves Fonck, Yves Fonck.
Pages 156/157 *Top row, all:* Mark Cowardine. *Centre row, all:* Mark Cowardine. *Bottom row, left to right:* Mark Cowardine, Monika Latzel, Bottom Time Adventures/Oceanic Society Expeditions.
Pages 234/235 *Top row, left to right:* Monika Latzel, Nancy Durrell McKenna/Hutchison Library, Nancy Durrell McKenna/Hutchison Library, Monika Latzel. *Centre row, left to right:* Monika Latzel, Nancy Durrell McKenna/Hutchison Library. *Bottom row, left to right:* Monika Latzel, Andreas M. Gross, Wolfgang Rossig/APA.
Pages 294/295 *Top row, left to right:* Andreas M. Gross, Steve Bly, Nancy Durrell McKenna/Hutchison Library, B. Jones & M. Shimlock/NHPA. *Centre row, left to right:* Wolfgang Rossig/APA, Daniel Heuclin/NHPA. *Bottom row, left to right:* David Hoey, Yves Fonck, Wolfgang Rossig/APA, Martin Harvey/NHPA.

Map Production: Phoenix Mapping
©2000 Apa Publications GmbH & Co
Verlag KG (Singapore Branch)

INSIGHT GUIDE
Dominican Republic & Haiti
Cartographic Editor **Zoë Goodwin**
Production **Linton Donaldson**
Design Consultants
Carlotta Junger, Graham Mitchener
Picture Research **Hilary Genin, Britta Jaschinski, Natasha Babaian**

Index

Numbers in italics refer to photographs

The two countries are included in the following index. To identify the location of each placename, follow the key:

(DR) = Dominican Republic
(H) = Haiti

☒ INSIGHT GUIDES

The world's largest collection of visual travel guides

Insight Guides – the Classic Series
that puts you in the picture

Alaska	China	Hong Kong	Morocco	Singapore
Alsace	Cologne	Hungary	Moscow	South Africa
Amazon Wildlife	Continental Europe		Munich	South America
American Southwest	Corsica	Iceland		South Tyrol
Amsterdam	Costa Rica	India	Namibia	Southeast Asia
Argentina	Crete	India's Western	Native America	Wildlife
Asia, East	Crossing America	Himalayas	Nepal	Spain
Asia, South	Cuba	India, South	Netherlands	Spain, Northern
Asia, Southeast	Cyprus	Indian Wildlife	New England	Spain, Southern
Athens	Czech & Slovak	Indonesia	New Orleans	Sri Lanka
Atlanta	Republic	Ireland	New York City	Sweden
Australia		Israel	New York State	Switzerland
Austria	Delhi, Jaipur & Agra	Istanbul	New Zealand	Sydney
	Denmark	Italy	Nile	Syria & Lebanon
Bahamas	Dominican Republic	Italy, Northern	Normandy	
Bali	Dresden		Norway	Taiwan
Baltic States	Dublin	Jamaica		Tenerife
Bangkok	Düsseldorf	Japan	Old South	Texas
Barbados		Java	Oman & The UAE	Thailand
Barcelona	East African Wildlife	Jerusalem	Oxford	Tokyo
Bay of Naples	Eastern Europe	Jordan		Trinidad & Tobago
Beijing	Ecuador		Pacific Northwest	Tunisia
Belgium	Edinburgh	Kathmandu	Pakistan	Turkey
Belize	Egypt	Kenya	Paris	Turkish Coast
Berlin	England	Korea	Peru	Tuscany
Bermuda			Philadelphia	
Boston	Finland	Laos & Cambodia	Philippines	Umbria
Brazil	Florence	Lisbon	Poland	USA: Eastern States
Brittany	Florida	Loire Valley	Portugal	USA: Western States
Brussels	France	London	Prague	US National Parks:
Budapest	Frankfurt	Los Angeles	Provence	East
Buenos Aires	French Riviera		Puerto Rico	US National Parks:
Burgundy		Madeira		West
Burma (Myanmar)	Gambia & Senegal	Madrid	Rajasthan	
	Germany	Malaysia	Rhine	Vancouver
Cairo	Glasgow	Mallorca & Ibiza	Rio de Janeiro	Venezuela
Calcutta	Gran Canaria	Malta	Rockies	Venice
California	Great Barrier Reef	Marine Life ot the	Rome	Vienna
California, Northern	Great Britain	South China Sea	Russia	Vietnam
California, Southern	Greece	Mauritius &		
Canada	Greek Islands	Seychelles	St. Petersburg	Wales
Caribbean	Guatemala, Belize &	Melbourne	San Francisco	Washington DC
Catalonia	Yucatán	Mexico City	Sardinia	Waterways of Europe
Channel Islands		Mexico	Scotland	Wild West
Chicago	Hamburg	Miami	Seattle	
Chile	Hawaii	Montreal	Sicily	Yemen

Complementing the above titles are 120 easy-to-carry Insight Compact Guides, 120 Insight Pocket Guides with full-size pull-out maps and more than 60 laminated easy-fold Insight Maps